YESTERDAY'S SCHOOLS

Public Elementary Education
in
Prince William County, Virginia

1869-1969

*A social and educational history
of a rural county in Virginia*

*To Johnna and Dave
Fondly —
Lucy Walsh Phinney*

❦ Lucy Walsh Phinney ❦

©1993 Lucy Walsh Phinney

All rights reserved, including the rights to translate or reproduce this work or parts thereof in any form or by any media.

Library of Congress Catalog Card Number 93-061701

ISBN:0-9612862-9-6

Table of Contents

Preface v
Introduction 1

Part I: Development and Growth, the First Hundred Years 5
    1. General Background 7
    2. Early School Boards 13
    3. Early School Administration 19
    4. Early School Districts 21
    5. Naming of the Schools 29
    6. The Early Schoolhouses 31
    7. Consolidation 35
    8. A Segregated System 39
    9. One Hundred Years Ago 43
    10. Mystery Schoolhouses 45
    11. Curriculum and Textbooks 49

Part II: The Schoolhouses 53
    Alphabetical Lists of Schools 55
    Chronological Lists of Schools 57
    Maps 59
    Known Locations of Schools 65
    Individual Schools 71

Appendix A: Superintendents of Schools 193
Appendix B: Those Interviewed for Book 195
Appendix C: Schools from 1970-1993 197
Appendix D: Specifications for 1906 Schoolhouse 199
Appendix E: Old Schoolhouses Still Standing 201
Appendix F: Sample Questionnaire 203

Primary Sources 205
Bibliography 207
General Index 211

*Dedicated to my husband
Stephen E. Phinney
without whose help this book
would not have happened*

PREFACE

The original intent of this book was not a book at all, but a booklet chronicling the rise and fall of the early schoolhouses of Prince William County, Virginia. However, as research progressed, it became clear that a booklet would not be adequate. It also became evident that some limitations would have to be put on the project. Thus, this study is concerned only with the County's public elementary schools from their beginnings in 1869 until they were fully integrated nearly a century later in 1966. Private institutions of learning which have flourished on occasion in Prince William County must be the subject of another paper as must the rise of secondary education which began in Virginia in 1906.

Over the nearly hundred years which are the subject of this book, there have been ninety-seven different schools occupying a total of 157 different buildings. The vast majority were of the one-room variety although two- and, occasionally, multi-room schools were built. These figures do not include another dozen or so schools which may be vaguely referred to once but whose existence could not be verified. To complicate matters further, several schools changed their name in midstream. Their individual stories became too fascinating and the overall picture too complex and interesting to condense into the originally planned booklet.

Research became both an obsession and a frustration. The obsession to gather every available scrap of information led me to school archives, museums, libraries, schoolhouses, maps, private homes and government records all over Prince William County as well as in Washington, D.C. and Richmond, Virginia. Bits and pieces came from unbound papers from the 1870s; School Board minutes of some of the districts dating from 1870 and for the next fifty years; old and faded photographs, receipts, daily attendance records of 100 years ago; thesis papers from two early Prince William County Superintendents of Schools; and memories of residents who attended or taught in those long ago schools. It was great fun doing, but it was also frustrating. Where were all the records? Why are there no School Board minutes at all from the districts on the eastern end of the county? When exactly did one County Board replace the six District Boards? When did a certain school open and when did another close? Many questions remain unanswered for now but it is hoped that missing links will be supplied by readers who would have been interviewed had their names been known by the author. Still, there is a lot of information gathered together here for the first time. It has been a very rewarding three years.

There are many individuals without whose help this book would not have come together. These are in addition to all those who so willingly shared their reminiscences with me and who are listed separately in Appendix B. My grateful thanks go to the Prince William County Historical Commission, which encouraged this study and to Historic Prince William, Inc., which had to share its president's energies and time while the research was being done. Invaluable help came from the Records Center of the Prince William County Public Schools and especially its director, Mrs. Nancy Sickle. There are many others who were of particular assistance: the directors of the Staff Library of the Prince William County schools, Fanchon Fischer and LaDonna Thompson; the staff of the Manassas Museum, especially Curator Scott Harris who shared every pertinent document in the Museum's collection with me; Mr. Don Wilson, Virginiana Librarian for the Prince William County Public Library system, who shared his knowledge and time with me in large amounts; Mr. Conley Edwards III, the head of the Public Services Section of the Archives of the Virginia State Library in Richmond, who cheerfully retrieved from the depths of the building all the relevant materials he could find; and

Mr. Stewart Layne of the Virginia Department of Transportation (VDOT) who generously sent to me copies of all the maps they had published since 1932 which had schools on them. A special thanks is also due to Mr. Charles McNoldy and the Prince William County Office of Mapping for help in preparing the map used in this book.

Additional, personal thanks go to Ms. Janet Townsend, former Prince William County archaeologist now with the National Park Service, without whose encouragement I would have quit before I really began. I owe a debt of gratitude to Maggie Rusciolelli who kept feeding me old newspaper articles about various activities of the schools, thus bringing them to life in a way no records or reports could. My great thanks go to Richard Fravel for his drawing of the Brentsville School used both on the cover and at the beginning of Part II; he says he does not work well under pressure, but I do not agree. To my daughters, Sara and Jennifer, I owe a great debt; they were critics, editors and cheerleaders and their support meant much. To my college son, Rob, who gave up letters from mom at home because mom was always writing The Book, thanks for not complaining. Lastly, without my husband, Steve, nothing at all would have been done. For the last three years, this has been as much his project as mine and for that reason, I dedicate the book to him.

INTRODUCTION

One of the first, and certainly the most common, questions asked about the early schools in Prince William County is, "How many were there?", following in quick succession with, "Were they all one-room schools?", "Were they all 'little red schoolhouses'?", and "Are any of them still around?" Only the answer to the last question is easy: there are twenty-three school buildings which opened before 1936 still standing and that number includes the four still in use as schoolhouses, all of which were fairly large buildings to begin with. Of those twenty-three, thirteen were one-room schools. Getting an exact count of the number of schools is not at all easy. Schools were often established in temporary locations and then moved into more permanent quarters, moved to larger buildings which may or may not have retained the original name, physically moved from one site to another, or given a new name when a new building replaced an old one even though the school body did not change. Taking all this into account, it is pretty safe to say that there were ninety-seven different elementary schools established in Prince William County in the one hundred years between 1869 and 1969. Over the lifetime of those ninety-seven schools, 157 different buildings were built, borrowed, rented, and moved. For example, the Antioch School occupied four different buildings during its lifetime; the elementary school in Nokesville also used four separate structures; the white school in Quantico met in three different schoolhouses. Of the 157 buildings, 102 were used as one-room schools, twenty-five were two-room schools and forty-one were schools with more than two classrooms. Several one-room schools actually occupied one room in a larger structure (a church or a Town Hall or a lodge or a home) before moving to a "real" one-room schoolhouse and, in cases like that, they were counted as one school, but two one-room schoolhouses. Schools which started out as one-room buildings but were later added onto were counted as both one-room schools and two- or multi-room schools because the "personality" of a school changes when its physical characteristics change. The reader can see the difficulties and pitfalls involved.

As to the question about the 'little red schoolhouses', an exact answer cannot be given because no records have been found for many of the earliest schools. With the exception of the later brick school buildings, only two of the early schools can definitely be counted as being red—the first Orlando School and the King's Crossroads School. There may have been others but it can't be proven. Most of the schools were built with wood siding painted white.

There is a certain romance involved with the idea of "the little red schoolhouse"[1]. Children of all ages, living in a small, closely knit, usually rural community, learning the basic lessons of an American education as well as the moral teachings of the day, create an appealing picture. Some may envy the simplicity of those days but life for a rural teacher in a one-room schoolhouse was anything but simple. She or he did not have the tools readily at hand which are taken for granted today. Maps, charts and books were scarce and in some schools did not exist at all. Certainly there were no films, videos, recordings or television shows to help portray the world outside the immediate vicinity. Imagination and resourcefulness were almost a prerequisite skill for a country school teacher. Heat did not happen at the turn of a thermostat nor did lights come on at the touch of a

---

[1] As noted above, most of the schoolhouses in Prince William County were not red; they were white frame buildings.

switch. Those conveniences came with hard, often dirty work, and it went on day after day after day.

Often both teacher and pupils had long distances to travel to their schoolhouse. Some rode horseback or drove a wagon, others had to walk in all kinds of weather on dirt roads or across farm fields. No copy machines made work sheets available to all the children, no telephone connected the remote schoolhouses with a central office or even a student's home and, in most cases, there was no principal's office to which miscreants could be sent. But there was individual attention so that both slow learners and faster students could master the material at their own speed. There was friendship, parental involvement, caring and challenge. The days of the small schoolhouses in Prince William County are over, but the legacy remains.

The earliest public schools in Prince William County, Virginia, were schools for the indigent or poor children. First appearing in the late 18th century, until 1869 they were the only public schools in the county. That they were only for the indigent means that they were not true public schools open to anyone desiring an education. They were public in that they were funded by public monies.

In the autumn of 1869 the first true public school in the County was established in Manassas. It met in a church room but it was open to any white child. This was the Ruffner School, or Public School #1. Shortly thereafter, a school for black[2] children was opened and this was School #2, or the Brown School. From then on, across the County in the six school districts, many one-room schoolhouses opened their doors over the next sixty years.

The last one-room school building to be erected in Prince William County was in the Dumfries District. This was the Thornton School, built in 1923 to serve the white children in an area now part of Prince William Forest Park. It closed in 1930 after just seven years of operation. The last one-room school to be established, as opposed to being built, in the county was Hickory Ridge, also in the Dumfries District. This little school began meeting in 1933 in a rented hall and continued there for the next ten years, never having a building of its own. The last one-room schoolhouse to close was the Brentsville School, which shut its doors at the end of the 1943-44 school year.

With these exceptions, schools built after the turn of the century were of two, three or four-room design. Often not all the rooms were used, but they were there if needed. In the western school districts (Gainesville and Brentsville) many of the original one-room structures were either added onto or rebuilt in the first twenty years of this century so they, too, became two or three or four-room schoolhouses. Sometimes, a second teacher was added to the school but a second room was not provided. The teachers shared a room and made the best use possible of cloakrooms and porches.

Then, in 1923, began the push to consolidate the one-room schoolhouses into larger, more centrally located schools where more equipment and supplies were available. Transportation became easier with the building of better roads and the development of automobiles and buses. Consequently, teachers and pupils were able to travel longer distances to attend school. During the decade of the 1920s, three larger schools, Occoquan, Nokesville and Brown, were constructed in Prince William County joining the earlier built Bennett, Greenwich and Aden consolidated schools. Dumfries and Haymarket also erected larger buildings in the ensuing ten years. As these six- and eight-room schools began to be used, the small buildings closed their doors. Nineteen schools, all one-room, were abandoned during the 1920s. Interestingly, when a new Bethel School was built in 1927 it had only two rooms although the school it was replacing had been a four-room structure. That, however, was the exception.

Over the years, the small schoolhouses gradually closed. At the start of the 1940s, there were only two one-room schools, Hickory Ridge and Brentsville. There were also three two-room schools still in existence at that time—Summitt, Macrae and Bethel. The Bethel School ceased being a public school in 1966, making it the last of the County's two-room schoolhouses. In addition, in the decade of the forties, there were two three-room schools and three four-room buildings; all the rest were larger.

While individual characteristics of the small schoolhouses were often determined by the community each served, such individuality became lost when centralization took over. Classrooms of twenty-five to thirty students all in the same grade learning the same material replaced classrooms of twenty to fifty children at all levels of instruction. The schools be-

---

[2]Schools in the South were divided into what were known then as White and Colored schools. To be historically accurate, those terms are used throughout this book when discussing the schoolhouses.

Introduction

gan to assume a certain sameness as they strove to conform to County standards. In these centralized schools, the school administration could provide more standardized instruction by teachers who had to meet qualifications set by the State Board of Education. It is interesting to note that School Based Management, hailed as an innovation of great importance by today's educators, is really an old concept, one which was used in this County for more than fifty years during the era of the one-room school.

Twenty-three of the County schoolhouses which opened between 1870 and 1950 still stand today and of those, four, enlarged and modernized, (Occoquan, Gainesville, Dumfries and Nokesville) are still used as schools. Nine of the buildings (Aden, Waterfall, the Dumfries District Cherry Hill schoolhouse, Bradley, the first Orlando school, the early Brown school, the English Church School, Hickory Grove and Groveton) serve as residences and are in good condition. The Haymarket Town Hall, which once was also a schoolhouse, is still in active community use as is the Quantico White school which today is the Lillian Carden Community Center. The Stone House on the Manassas Battlefield is known to millions of people for its role in the Civil War. The old Bennett School in Manassas is being used by the Prince William County Police Department for storage. Two of the old schoolhouses, Catharpin White and the first Occoquan school, are retail establishments. Four stand empty—Brentsville White, the first Purcell School, the Cherry Hill school in the Occoquan District, and Buckhall.

Today, Prince William County has thirty-nine elementary schools, all but four of which, as mentioned earlier, have been built since 1950. A new building, to be opened in 1994, is under construction in mid-county with another slated to be built in Gainesville in 1995. Four other schools of today carry the name of an earlier schoolhouse—Bennett, Neabsco, Coles and Woodbine—but they are in buildings which are relatively new. All the others are part of County history.

Part I:

Development and Growth, the First Hundred Years

Chapter 1.
GENERAL BACKGROUND

Although education has always been important to the citizens of Virginia, it has not always been readily available to everyone. In colonial Virginia, children were educated either at home by private tutors or governesses who came to live with the family or at parish schools like the one established for the poor of Prince William County in 1786 by the Reverend Thomas Harrison, rector of Dettingen Parish. Well-to-do citizens commonly sent their children abroad for their secondary education, often giving them into the care of family members who had not emigrated to the New World. Since many early settlers of Prince William County came from Scotland, they naturally sent their children back there for schooling. The children of the poor were sometimes schooled in a trade under the apprenticeship program. Slave children often were taught by the mistresses of the plantations and sometimes by the older children of the house.

As early as 1643, the House of Burgesses passed the first legislation affecting education. This law provided for the supervision of orphans' guardians by the county courts to ensure that the orphans' education was being properly provided. More often than not, this education took the form of an apprenticeship which lasted until the boys were twenty-four years old and the girls were either twenty-one years of age or married. It is recorded that a Mr. Samuel Jones, aware of the need to educate the poor and orphaned children of Prince William County, bequeathed 600 pounds in 1776 to Dettingen Parish[1] for that education, whatever form it took. Misunderstanding, mismanagement and legal battles, however, delayed the proper implementation of the Jones Legacy for nearly one hundred years. Finally in 1873, the funds were put to use as originally intended. They lasted until 1925 when they were divided up by the newly appointed Superintendent of Schools, Richard C. Haydon, among the districts which had once been a part of Dettingen Parish.

The establishment of a State public school system was a long held dream of Thomas Jefferson. Throughout his adult life, he worked to set up a means of providing an education for all the children of the Commonwealth.[2] Finally, in 1810, the first of several legislative acts which were to form the basis for the development of public education in the Commonwealth of Virginia, was passed. It established the Literary Fund, which became the cornerstone of public education funding by providing for the education of indigent children at state expense. The Literary Fund Act said that "all fines, escheats, and confiscations" that came to the State should be used for the purpose of education. This revenue, derived from interest on bonds and from fines, was the first money made available for schooling and it was decided that it would continue to be the primary source of funding upon which the School Boards should draw in their financial planning. It remains an important part of educational funding today.

Though awkward to administer and often low on capital, the Literary Fund was the reason for the establishment of the Primary School System in Virginia. It was the only State assistance for education

---

[1] In the 17th and 18th centuries, counties in the Commonwealth of Virginia were divided into parishes. These served both civil and ecclesiastical functions, one of which was to provide for the education of poor and orphaned children. Dettingen Parish covered much of what is now loosely called eastern Prince William County.

[2] "Historical Development of Virginia's Public School System, 1870-1970." *News Magazine of the State Department of Education Centennial Issue* Vol.5, Winter 1970, p.6.

prior to 1871. More importantly, "it established the principle of public money for public schools, provided a rudimentary public school system, and aided in developing the concept of education as a State responsibility."[3]

By 1827, the lack of funds had reduced the number of schools for indigent children in Prince William County to two, attended by only twenty of the 400 children who were eligible. Teachers could not be paid and bills were always overdue. Over the next twenty years, however, the situation would improve both in funding and numbers of students enrolled.

By a second act, passed in 1846, the District Free School System was established by the state legislature. Each county in the Commonwealth of Virginia was to be divided into school districts, each headed by a commissioner. The commissioners were to choose among themselves a county superintendent. The citizens of the county could then petition the court for a poll to determine if there was enough interest to set up a free public school system in the county, to be supported by local taxes with help from the Literary Fund. As before, it would be a system only for indigent children and Prince William County citizens were not sufficiently interested to take part. Only nine counties in Virginia adopted the District Free School System at that time.

The poor, by this time, were becoming reconciled to having their children educated at public expense and enrollment in 1846 at the free schools in the county rose to 362. Teachers were paid three or four cents a day per pupil so they searched hard for students. Recruitment of students went on at social events, church services and just about anywhere group of neighbors gathered together.

Attendance determined how long a school remained open; when the daily attendance fell, that school would be closed. In 1830, the average length of the school year for Prince William County was 107 days. During the early years of the 1840s decade, most of the free schools of the County were in session for nine months.[4] By contrast, in the 1850s, during the Civil War and the years just afterward, the school term lasted an average of only forty days.

Since, in 1850, it cost $1.35 a year to educate a child and a teacher was paid only three or four cents per child for the forty days school met, it is clear that virtually all the money available went to the teacher with little or nothing left over for supplies or buildings.

By 1866, Prince William County's budget for its free schools was $11,560, $7680 for 788 white students and $3880 for 388 black pupils. All twenty-nine teachers in the schools were white. Despite these efforts, illiteracy was common. One out of every seven white people and one out of every four in general (black and white) was not able to read and write. Two thousand County children aged five to twenty were illiterate yet only 316 attended the public schools.[5]

Following the Civil War, among the more well-to-do, rooms in private homes were sometimes opened up for classrooms and children from miles around came for lessons taught by governesses or young men in need of employment after the war. Other children learned trades by working for skilled laborers or tradesmen. The children of wealthy planters were occasionally sent away to private boarding schools but this was not common in Prince William County. A more usual type of school here was the "old field school", so called because it was usually built of rough wood or logs in an old abandoned field. Some of the teachers were only slightly more educated than their pupils, victims of the hard economic times after the Civil War. Tuition fees, agreed upon by the parents and teacher, financed these schools which were not really public schools at all. Poor children continued to be the responsibility of the Church and State and the Literary Fund provided for their education. With the advent of the Civil War, however, Literary Funds were diverted to the War effort and those early "public" schools were virtually closed.

In Prince William County, as in most of the South, the period after the war brought some renewed interest in public education. This was fostered, in large part, by northerners and Reconstructionists who hoped to re-educate the South. The machinery for the establishment of a county school system had been in place since the passage of the 1846 District Free School System legislation though Prince William had not taken advantage of it. In October of 1869, however, with the vigorous encouragement of George C. Round, a

---

[3]Ibid.,p.7.

[4]Work Projects Administration Writers Program. *Prince William: The Story of Its People and Its Places*. Manassas, VA: The Bethlehem Club, 1988, p.62.

---

[5]Ibid., p.64.

Union veteran who had settled in Manassas, the courts of Prince William County divided the County into six school districts: Brentsville, Coles, Dumfries, Gainesville, Manassas and Occoquan. Each district was headed by a commissioner and in December, those commissioners elected Mr. Round to serve as the county superintendent, which he did without salary.

The citizens of Manassas, aware that the Commonwealth was soon to enact a new constitution requiring statewide public education for all, decided to beat Richmond to the punch and open a true public school before being required. Because they did not have access to public funds, the people of Manassas raised, among themselves, subscription money totalling $150 to start the school. Twice that amount was secured from the Peabody Fund, established in 1867 by Northern merchant and philanthropist George Peabody to help education in the South. With these funds, a room in the Asbury Methodist Church on West Street in Manassas was rented and furnished for the school room. Miss Estelle Greene was hired to be the first teacher and in December of 1869 the first real public school in Prince William County was opened. Although the new State law governing public education would not go into effect for six months, the school, according to newspaper accounts of the time, was "carried on in conformity to the letter and spirit of the new constitution."[6]

That new constitution, known as the Underwood Constitution of Virginia, was ratified in 1869. It provided, in part, for the establishment of a State public school system for all children to be operational by 1876. It was the third major act in the establishment of Virginia's educational structure. As governed by the Underwood Constitution, the General Assembly quickly appointed Robert E. Lee's candidate, Dr. William H. Ruffner, to serve as the first State Superintendent of Public Instruction. He was required by the Constitution to submit a plan to organize the state's public school system within thirty days.

Public education for all, however, was not immediately popular. Free schools were looked on as charity schools by many.

Throughout the State there continued to be little progress in the public school system; many causes can be attached to this, but probably the greatest were bound up with the unpopularity of "schooling" and the fact that it was designed for "poor" children. Whatever the cause, few pupils were enrolled in these schools.[7]

Many people of the rural South viewed central government and its institutions with suspicion and even hostility. After the family, the local community occupied the most important place in a person's world. Putting the power over local education in the hands of the state was very unpopular with most of the general public. In addition, the idea of educating the black population did not sit well with much of the white citizenry. Indeed, it took almost thirty years for the idea of public education to firmly take hold in Prince William County. The majority of the children who went to school continued to attend the several private schools in the County.

It was in this atmosphere that Dr. Ruffner had to carry on his task. Although he had thirty days to complete his work, he presented the General Assembly with his plan in twenty-five days. The plan provided for a three-member State Board of Education made up of the Governor, the State Attorney General and a State Superintendent of Public Instruction. It outlined the duties of the State Superintendent of Schools and how he fit into the hierarchy of the public school system. The State Board of Education, rather than the county commissioners as had previously been the case, was given the responsibility of naming a Superintendent of Schools for every county in Virginia.

Dr. Ruffner's plan also provided for the division of all counties in the Commonwealth of Virginia into school districts with a Board of Trustees to preside over each district.[8] The duties of District Trustees as well as County Superintendents were enumerated. Teachers were to be employed and paid by the separate districts and certified by the county superintendent. In addition, a cost system was laid out whereby funds from the State and County treasuries, as well as local district taxes, would support

---

[6]Catherine T. Simmons. *Manassas, Virginia. 1873-1973.* Manassas City Museum, 1986, p.32.

[7]R. Worth Peters. "Secondary Education in Manassas, Va. 1890-1935." A Thesis Presented to the Academic Faculty of the University of Virginia, 1939, p.87.

[8]The six districts into which Prince William County had been divided in 1869 did not change under the new plan.

the schools. The plan further decreed that all children between the ages of five and twenty-one were entitled to free public education, though the system was to be segregated into white and colored schools.

Dr. Ruffner spent the next few months trying to build support for his blueprint for Virginia's new public education system. Despite a great deal of opposition, the legislature approved his plan on July 11, 1870 with the passage of the "Act to Establish and Maintain a Uniform System of Free Schools", known as the Public Education Act.

Dr. Ruffner was anxious to open at least a few schools in each county as soon as possible so the newly created State Board of Education immediately began to appoint local school officials to operate the system. In three months, 1,400 County Superintendents and District Trustees had been named. These officials then provided buildings, took the school census, selected teachers, and organized for work so that, by November, at least some public schools were open in all counties in Virginia. That Dr. Ruffner was eminently successful is clear; at the close of that school year, 130,000 pupils, under the tutelage of 3000 teachers, were attending 2,900 schools.[9]

One of the appointments made, on September 18, was that of Major William Willis Thornton as the first Superintendent of Prince William County Schools. He was, however, disqualified under the Fourteenth Amendment to the United States Constitution because of his "treasonous" participation in the Civil War against the U.S. Government. Mr. Thornton did serve as Acting Superintendent until April 6, 1871, when the State Board named William A. Bryant to the Superintendent's post. On July 16, 1872, Mr. Thornton, his disqualification abrogated by an Act of Congress, was reappointed and served until 1873.[10]

With the establishment of the 1870 Public Education Act, the citizens of Manassas turned their first public school over to the newly chosen Board of Trustees of the Manassas School District, Mr. George C. Round, Mr. J.T. Leachman and Mr. J.H. Butler. At the same time, the Brown School, a privately run school for the black children in Manassas, was turned over to the Manassas District Board. These two schools, known in those early days simply as the White School and the Colored School, formed the basis for the public school system of Prince William County.

Dr. Ruffner, realizing that, if public education in Virginia was to take root and grow, made compromises which narrowed the State's control over the system while broadening local authority. In 1873, he persuaded the General Assembly to transfer the selection of District Trustees from the State Board of Education to the local school districts. Textbook choice also reverted to the counties.[11] Localism became the foundation of the public schools, making them more acceptable to the communities whose characteristics and mores they reflected. Since children were not required to attend school, it was important to make their parents want them to attend.

On the local level, it is interesting to note that the six districts into which Prince William County was originally divided changed during the 1890s. The town of Manassas voted to become independent of the county in 1890 and take over the administration of the two schools within the town limits, Ruffner and Brown. This new school district became known as District #8 (the original Manassas School District retained its #5 designation) and it stayed that way for about six years. On February 17, 1896, the Manassas Town School District #8 was formally abolished and control of the Ruffner and Brown schools reverted to District #5.[12]

Additionally, there appears in the County School Board minutes of 1883, a reference to several small expenses incurred by a Potomac School District. A listing of disbursements and levies on the County school districts in 1881 makes no mention of a Potomac District so it evidently was not in existence then. The only additional allusion to it, other than in 1883, comes in the February 14, 1884 minutes of the County School Board. There it says that, after getting approval from the State, the Board agreed to the union of the Potomac and Dumfries

---

[9]"Historical Development of Virginia's Public School System, 1870-1970", p.8.

[10]Proceedings of the Board of Education of Virginia, 1870-73, Vol I.

[11]It is interesting to note that on July 1, 1993 the Prince William County Public Schools textbook office closed because under school based management, individual schools were responsible for their own textbook purchases.

[12]Prince William County School Board minutes of March 2, 1896.

School Districts, with all monies from the Potomac District being put into Dumfries' coffers.[13] When this short-lived district was created and what area of the county it covered are unknown. Presumably, it was the missing School District #7 but even that is conjecture.

In 1902, the Commonwealth of Virginia adopted a new State Constitution, which further refined the State public school system. To the State Board of Education were added three experienced educators elected by the Senate and two division superintendents selected by the Board. The State Superintendent of Public Instruction, previously chosen by the General Assembly, was now to be elected by the people. Lastly, the State was divided into school divisions with the magisterial districts within the counties keeping their separate school boards.

As interest in public education continued to grow, more and more improvements were made in the State public school system. The Virginia State legislature, in 1890, passed a law allowing the Trustees of the local school boards compensation for attendance at meetings of the District School Boards. This not only made it easier to attract qualified individuals to serve as Trustees, but it gave them a status which no volunteer position can hold. Statewide teacher certification had been provided for in 1891 but the exams were graded by the local superintendents. Beginning in 1904, a State Board of Education committee was assigned that task along with the inspection of schools throughout the State. Each committee member was assigned fifteen counties and they became very involved in all aspects of those counties' education. They helped plan school buildings and consolidate schools, they worked to train teachers, they devised ways to secure additional support for "their" schools.[14]

In 1906 the Mann High School Bill, also known as the "High School Act" extended the public school system to the secondary grades. The legislature authorized funds for high school programs if the local districts provided the buildings and paid the teacher salaries. The Strode Bill of 1908, among other things, appropriated $25,000 to encourage the replacement of one-room schools with graded elementary schools. This was to have a profound impact on the education of Prince William County. The Strode Bill also set construction requirements for school buildings to ensure that there was adequate space, light, ventilation and sanitary facilities for the children.

The first Course of Study for elementary schools was published by the State in 1907. Not all of Prince William County's teachers immediately agreed to use it, but some were willing to give it a try and eventually uniform lessons were taught throughout the county.

In the early years, County Superintendents of Schools were chosen more for their politics and personalities than for their educational expertise. Though they had very little professional training, were underpaid and often worked only part-time, they did serve as the leaders of the county school system as well as chief financial officer. They were respected members of the community, "fatherly figures...who stood above the fray and enjoyed...the entire confidence of the county".[15] Encouragement of the public school idea in Prince William County, as in the rest of Virginia, was one of the superintendent's most important functions. However, as time went on and the school system grew, it became clear to the State Board of Education that the superintendent's job was growing more and more crucial to the development of a successful educational system. Consequently, in 1916, qualifications for division superintendents were increased to include at least ten years of educational experience prior to their appointments. They also had to have a college degree with either some education courses or three years of teaching experience.

Teachers were scarce in the early years of the twentieth century. Trustees of the seven Districts had trouble supplying their schools with teachers. In 1917, Brentsville and Gainesville schools had to delay their openings due to lack of a principal.

Capital to run the schools was a problem in the early years just as it still is today. Just as teachers were scarce, so, too, were funds. In 1919, the citizens of Manassas had to pay taxes twice in order to have funds to keep the schools open for the nine months

---

[13]These two references to the Potomac District were found in Prince William County School Board minutes of 1883 and 1884, kept by the then Superintendent of Schools and Chairman of the County Board, Mr. H. W. Clarkson.

[14]"Historical Development of Virginia's Public School System, 1870-1970.", p.18.

[15]William A. Link. *A Hard Country and a Lonely Place. Schooling, Society and Reform in Rural Virginia, 1870-1920*. Chapel Hill: University of North Carolina Press, 1986, p.25.

required to qualify for credit for a school year. Even as late as 1926 Manassas students had to pay $5.00 for a month's tuition to keep the schools open for the nine months. During the Depression years, teacher salaries in the County showed a steady decrease. In 1930 the salary for a beginning teacher with a degree was $945 a year. By 1933 that salary had fallen to $810.

Localism continued to dominate the establishment and maintenance of the little schoolhouses in rural areas like Prince William County for almost fifty years. This situation was not unique to the county. As William Link says in *A Hard Country and a Lonely Place*, "Despite scattered and ineffectual efforts to establish a national educational policy, American schools developed from below and most commonly were established with only minimal involvement by state governments."[16] That is not to say that the schools were totally self-reliant. They depended on the county for tax money to help defray expenses and they sometimes had to go to a higher power to help in the settling of disputes. But by and large, the local District Trustees and the parents made the important decisions about school affairs: who was to teach, what was to be taught, how long the school term was to be, where the school was to be located, etc.. Education controlled from the most local level was a workable system for many years.

As time went by, the value placed on education continued to grow. Dr. Ruffner's acknowledgement of the importance of putting control over their schools in the hands of the local community ensured their survival and growth. By tripling the number of schools, teachers and pupils in the period between 1870 and 1900[17], schoolhouses had become a part of the landscape of the state as well as Prince William County. School terms were short and many children could not or did not attend, but clearly public education was here to stay. As Link says in *A Hard Country and a Lonely Place*:

> Whatever the reasons for its expansion, rural education in post-Reconstruction Virginia, far from being a static process, exhibited a dynamism in which growing numbers of schools.... School expansion depended on local enthusiasm and support, and rural education increasingly integrated itself into its environment, expressing community conditions and values and serving as clear windows on southern rural society. Housed in makeshift buildings—often barns, churches, and homes—nineteenth-century schoolhouses did not project the primacy of state power but blended into the topography. ...In an isolated, rural society, they were intensely local; in a culture that valued family above all, they were family-dominated; in a society based on strict racial and class rankings, they reflected widespread social inequality; an in an impoverished agricultural economy, they were poor and makeshift.[18]

In the years preceding and following the First World War, changes came rapidly to Prince William County schools. The school year lengthened to conform to national standards. Per capita expenditures for county pupils rose to nearly the national average. Compulsory education, school consolidation and the abolition of district control extensively changed the face of rural education. From make-do buildings to hastily erected one-room schoolhouses to four-room center schools to today's multi-million dollar structures, education in Prince William County has grown and changed over the more than one hundred years of its existence. The specific areas of change are the subjects of the next several chapters of the story.

---

[16] Link, p.4.
[17] Link, p.21.
[18] Link, p.23.

Chapter 2.
EARLY SCHOOL BOARDS

When Prince William County opened its first school in December of 1869, and for about six months after that, the six school districts into which the county had been divided were administered by Commissioners of Education. These District Commissioners chose the County Superintendent of Schools (Mr. George C. Round) and worked to establish a system of public education in each of their districts. With the enactment of the Virginia Public Education Act in the summer of 1870, the commissioners were replaced by District Trustees who had essentially the same responsibilities. The Trustees, as well as the County Superintendent of Schools, were named by the State Board of Education giving that entity more power than the local communities were comfortable. In April of 1872, ten Trustees representing the six Prince William County School Districts met at the County Courthouse at Brentsville to form the first County School Board. These representatives included William W. Thornton, who served as president based on his position as School Superintendent, John S. Powell, John S. Sinclair, George C. Round, A. F. Dunn and Charles G. Howison.[1]

The agenda of that first meeting of the County School Board was an ambitious one. Following the election of Mr. Powell as Vice-president and Mr. Sinclair as Secretary/Clerk, the Board ordered the Clerk to purchase record books required by the State law to keep an account of all proceedings. The Superintendent was ordered to inquire into the condition of the Jones Legacy[2] and hire counsel if necessary to recover whatever funds were due to the school system. A committee made up of George C. Round and Charles Howison was appointed to prepare By-Laws for the County Board. In addition, the busy Mr. Round was chosen, along with Mr. A.F. Dunn, to prepare a set of regulations to govern the Public Schools of Prince William County, a phrase always capitalized in the early School Board minutes. One final committee was formed (no members listed) to prepare an address to the citizens of the County explaining the new Free School System and how their tax money would be spent to support that system. This was a very important aspect of the County Board's duties; the general population viewed public education with suspicion and its merits had to be carefully explained.

A second meeting of the County School Board was held on April 23, 1872 and the main topic of discussion was, not surprisingly, school funding. The Board asked each of the six District Boards to levy a tax of three-fourths of a mill on every dollar's worth of Real and Personal property in their district to start a District School Fund. The Coles, Dumfries, Gainesville, Manassas and Occoquan Districts agreed to the motion made by the Occoquan Trustee, Mr. John S. Powell. Mr. John Sinclair of Brentsville requested a half mill on the dollar and that became the rate in his District. The County School Board also requested an additional three-fourths of a mill tax on every dollar's worth of property throughout the county to go into the County School fund. Thus the citizens had two school taxes levied on them: one for the School Fund in their district and another for the County School Board coffers.

The Board further asked the County Board of Supervisors to levy a tax of $1.00 on each dog and

---

[1] Minutes of the first Prince William County School Board meeting held on April 2, 1872.

[2] For an explanation of the Jones Legacy, see the chapter entitled "General Background".

earmark the money collected for the county Public Schools. This dog tax was agreed upon but the system was not without its troubles. In December of 1872, the School Board notified the Board of Supervisors that the tax assessors were not listing the dogs living in the county. This problem was apparently resolved, at least temporarily, because records show that the dog tax contributed to the school coffers from then until 1877 when the County Board passed a resolution against the dog tax which, they felt, being levied unequally in the County. Not every District was as vigilant as some in their collection of the dog tax and so the schools in those less diligent districts did not receive the funds to which they were entitled. At some later date, the dog tax was reinstated though apparently it was not earmarked solely for school funding. That the schools did continue to benefit from it is evident by County School Board minutes of August 9, 1897 which report that the Board of Supervisors agreed to give the surplus dog tax to the District School Boards.

The next year, at its February 4, 1873 meeting, the County School Board voted to raise the District School Tax to seven and a half cents on every $100 worth of Real and Personal Property in all districts except Brentsville, which asked for only five cents. The Board also decided to ask the Board of Supervisors for a seven and a half cent county-wide levy for the County School fund. Those rates lasted for less than one year. In November the Board raised the District levy to ten cents per $100 of property (with Brentsville again being the exception) and appointed a committee, made up of the six District Clerks, to ask the Board of Supervisors for more taxes. By September 1875, tax rates for the Manassas District were ten cents per $100 for the District and fifteen cents per $100 for the County. The Occoquan, Dumfries, Gainesville and Coles Districts paid ten cents to both the County and District. Brentsville's taxes remained the lowest: five cents per $100 for the District and ten cents for the County. There is no record of reactions by the citizens to these frequent tax raises but the system was young and everyone was feeling his way.

Raising monies for both the District and County School funds was not the only job of the County School Board. Minutes kept during the decade of the 1870s, the formative years, show that many issues occupied their time. For example, they awarded scholarships to deserving students to The College of William and Mary and to The Agricultural and Mechanical College at Blacksburg. They set up the rules and regulations governing the administration of the schools and decided that the average number of students necessary to keep the schools open was sixteen. The State Board of Education, in 1883, had set the minimum number at twenty if the teacher was to be paid the full salary. With fewer than twenty pupils, the teacher was to be paid per student. That rule was loosely enforced by the State which recognized that individual counties would have to be handled on a one-to-one basis. Prince William County had too many small rural schoolhouses to be able to abide by that number in every case and so the actual decision to close a school due to low enrollment figures rested with the District Board member appointed as the Trustee for that particular school. Similarly, when enrollment increased, the school Trustee was the one to make the decision about reopening the school. Every teacher was required to report to his or her Trustee any enrollment which fell to a monthly average of fifteen students or less. It was not unusual for a small schoolhouse to be closed for short periods of time during a difficult winter or one filled with illness. No difficulties seem to have arisen with the State over the matter though within the county, enrollment figures were a perennial problem.

Other areas of concern for the County School Board included, after 1873, the selection of the textbooks used by the schools. Funds for those books, particularly in the black schools, were always insufficient. Additionally, the Board commended the editor of *The Manassas Gazette* for his support of the Free School System in March of 1874 and checked the record books of all six District Clerks and Treasurers.

Another duty of the County School Board was to set the legal holidays for the schools. In 1893, for example, the following holidays were decided upon: Thanksgiving (at that time, the fourth Thursday of November had not been established as the national day of Thanksgiving), Christmas, Robert E. Lee's birthday of January 19, George Washington's birthday of February 22, Easter Monday and July 4 (although schools were not in session at that time of year, presumably the Superintendent and Trustees were entitled to a day off).

Occasionally, a unique problem presented itself to the County School Board for attention. For example, on January 1, 1894, Board minutes show that a major topic of the meeting was vaccinations and the need to enforce the laws requiring all pupils to have been vaccinated before entering public school. However, shortly afterward, the Board responded to public panic over the vaccine and the feeling that smallpox was almost gone and removed the requirement of a vaccine for school attendance.

The County School Board worked closely with the Superintendent of Schools who attended all its meetings as is still the case today. It was the County Board which set the salary of the Superintendent and suggested legislation to be sent to the State Education Department in Richmond. The Board often had to make decisions regarding county-wide personnel policies although individual cases were generally handled by the District Boards.

The most important duty of the County School Board was the administration of school funds. They not only collected the monies, but dispersed them. This power to administer funds came from an act passed by the General Assembly on March 3, 1879 as part of State Superintendent Ruffner's efforts to increase support for the public school system by returning control over important aspects of it to the local community.

Interestingly, at their March 2, 1874 meeting, the Prince William County School Board noted for the record its disagreement with George C. Round's bill introduced before the State legislature to provide for elected School Boards. In 1995, elected School Boards will become a reality in the Commonwealth of Virginia, 120 years after Mr. Round introduced his bill.

Improving the quality of teaching in the County was a matter of great importance to the County Board. They agreed to hold a Teachers' Institute in Manassas on the fourth Thursday in October 1874 with arrangements to be made by George C. Round and Mr. Thomas P. Hereford. All County teachers were to attend as mandated by the State Board of Education in 1871; failure to do so meant dismissal of the teacher and the closing of his or her school. Fortunately for the teachers, these strict rules were rescinded in September of 1877. In August of 1877, the Board set a requirement for an annual examination of present and would-be Prince William County teachers to be held a year hence in Manassas and, in December, the Board officially agreed with the Superintendent's policy of refusing to license teachers "who are habitually addicted to intemperance."[3] Another Teachers' Institute was held in 1881 at the County Courthouse in Brentsville. On February 4, 1901, the Board appropriated $250 to defray expenses of a Summer Normal School for white teachers. In 1910, it was decided to use County funds to pay the expenses of white teachers from each District to attend State education meetings in Richmond.

According to School Board minutes of 1890, the Board decided to require teachers to keep records of all students "in a neat and orderly manner" to ease the transition between teachers and grade levels. It was felt that too much time was being spent at the beginning of the school year for placement and classification of pupils. To ensure that such records would indeed be kept, the Board ruled that record books be turned in at the end of each school year by every teacher if he or she wanted to collect the salary due.

In 1895, the Prince William County Educational Association was organized. The School Board requested that all teachers and District School Board trustees "cooperate with the objects of said Association." Whether this association had any effect on the county educational system is unclear; no further mention of it is found in School Board minutes.

An interesting sidelight came into view when investigating the August 9, 1897 minutes of the County School Board. At that meeting, Mr. William H. Brown, the Gainesville District representative on the County Board, was commissioned to compile a map of Prince William County for a fee of $50.00. Four years later, on August 12, 1901, Mr. Brown presented his finished map to the Board along with a copy to be given to each of the schools in the County. Copies of that map, a useful tool for historians, are still available from the County Mapping Office.

Dealing with the County School Board was not always easy. On June 3, 1877 a committee of teachers asked the Board for funds amounting to $20 for medals and certificates to be awarded to the best spellers in the county. The Board decided that it was inappropriate to use County funds for that purpose but recommended that each school Trustee contribute as he was able from his funds.

Because the County School Board was concerned with informing citizens about their business,

---

[3]Prince William County School Board minutes of December 3, 1877.

they agreed, in 1909, to pay *The Manassas Journal* a yearly fee of $30 to publish the record of the Board's meetings. This practice continued for many years. Today, minutes of the School Board meetings are available on request to any County resident.

By 1910, the County School Board met semi-annually in either July or August and March. In addition, they were expected to be available for special meetings called either by the District Boards or the Superintendent. Contrast this with the biweekly meetings of the present School Board, but of course, today there are no District Boards to deal with the daily affairs of the schools. Those early Board members were paid (in 1903) $2.00 per meeting of the Board and special committee meetings, as well as expenses incurred with specific assignments for the schools under their jurisdiction.

While the County School Board set policies which were to govern the County school system, the real power behind the day to day running of the local schools remained, for many years, with the District School Boards. Having local control over the schools was the only way most rural communities would allow the school to exist. If no children were sent to attend classes and no taxes were paid to support education, then the system could not succeed. The State Board of Education was aware of this and wisely moved along a path of compromise with both County and local Districts Boards in setting up the machinery governing the running of the little schoolhouses. Those schools were the focal point for the rural communities and reflected the values of the citizenry. This dominance of localism continued until well into the 1920s when consolidation of the smaller schools into district schools forced busing of the children away from their local communities.

The District Boards, rather than the County School Board, really held power over Prince William County's educational system. Each District Board was made up of three citizens of the District, who were referred to as Trustees. One was chosen to be Chairman and another served as Clerk or Secretary. Because these were the people who kept the minutes of the meetings, their names are preserved in whatever School Board records survive. George C. Round served for many years as the Clerk of the Manassas District School Board and his handwritten minutes of the meetings are wonderful records of those early school years.

The District Boards met monthly and ran the daily operations of the schools in their districts. They decided what new schools needed to be opened, which ought to be closed and which should be consolidated. The District Boards set the opening day of school each year; hired the teachers and set their salaries; ordered supplies, including wood, textbooks, desks, etc.; sold the old buildings at public auction; bought new land when it was needed; and purchased insurance on the schoolhouses within the district.

The Superintendent of Schools attended occasional meetings of the District Boards but mostly the Boards acted on their own. They were accountable to the local Boards of Appeal which were made up of the heads of five families in each district. The job of the Boards of Appeal was to object to actions of the School Board when the community felt it necessary. Few records of such actions have been found.

Some aspects of education were shared by the State, the County and the separate Districts. Funding, for example, came from all three sources. In another example, the subject of outhouses or privies was a more mundane interest shared by the three jurisdictions. In 1899, the County School Board, in its minutes, decreed that,

> ...for the sake of propriety, health and comfort *two* convenient out-houses, as far apart as the nature of the grounds will permit, separated, when practicable, by a closely built fence, which shall be at least seven feet in height, shall be erected on the premises of every school-house in the county....

District Boards were required to have them built wherever needed but it had to be done according to specifications set by the State Board of Education: 4'x6' in size, built of tongue and groove lumber with galvanized roof, blinds on any windows and two coats of paint over all.

The State Board set other standards which the local school boards had to follow. For example, in 1923, a bulletin from the State said that "not less than two acres of ground" was required for a school yard. Several of the little schoolhouses in Prince William County would have to find additional adjacent land to purchase if they were to meet the state's standards. That same bulletin stated that each schoolhouse must contain at least forty lineal feet of blackboard space, one or two reference maps and "acceptable school furniture". Prince William County had to make sure that each of its schools met those standards.

As early as 1883, the State had set the salaries of teachers. Prince William County petitioned the State at that time to allow the county to set the salaries according to their own standards and apparently this request was granted. School records for the county show variations, based on District and race, in the salaries paid to teachers. This did not follow the pattern found throughout most of the United States, where the teacher's gender was the determining factor for the salary. In the country as a whole, men were paid more than women. In Prince William County, men and women were generally paid equal wages; the difference was that the white teachers were given more than the black teachers. For example, in 1892, a white teacher was paid $30 a month but a black teacher was given a salary of only $15-$20. Some Districts were able to pay their teachers a higher wage than other Districts, but the differences were small. By the early 1920s, the State decreed that teachers be paid a salary of not less than $85 a month for the mandatory nine months' school year. That this was a State regulation is interesting; how it was to be enforced is unclear. Black teachers' wages did not equal white teachers' wages until integration was effected and by that time, men were earning more than women.

In 1922, when Dr. Harris Hart became the State Superintendent of Schools, he persuaded the Virginia General Assembly to pass what was commonly called the County Unit Law, "[which] was the greatest single administrative improvement since the establishment of the public school system in 1870."[4] It was an enormous change for public school administration, centralizing it and increasing the bureaucracy needed to run the ever-growing system. The law put the County School Board, rather than the District Boards, in charge of all the county schools. Dr. Hart felt that the greater uniformity among the schools would be beneficial to the students and the petty differences about salaries, school terms, and the like would give way to greater administrative efficiency. The new law also encouraged school consolidation and larger enrollments in the centralized schools.

Teaching appointments were made by the District School Boards usually in June for the following school year, but when vacancies cropped up during the summer months or in the middle of a term, they were filled as they occurred. It was not always easy to find teachers but rarely was a school closed because none was available. The duty of hiring teachers passed to the County School Board in 1923. Like the District Boards before it, the County Board sometimes had difficulty filling a vacancy. The pool of qualified teachers became smaller in 1928 when a resolution passed by the County School Board forbade the hiring of any more newly married female teachers. Neither were women allowed to marry while teaching. This occasionally led to the situation where a school had no teacher assigned by opening day and so that school's opening had to be delayed until a suitable candidate was hired. It also sometimes happened that a School Board would need a teacher and either no applicants appeared or the Board was unable to agree on one candidate. This was most likely to happen during the school year when a teacher left his or her post unexpectedly. In such a situation, the District Board called a meeting of the school's patrons, or parents and friends, at the schoolhouse to discuss their next course of action. A good example of such a situation happened at the Waterfall School on October 24, 1891. Sixteen parents (a majority of those served by the school) representing fifty-eight children attended the called meeting. Three teachers had submitted applications to teach at the Waterfall School. Nine parents, representing thirty-three children, voted to hire Miss Susie E. Pattie; seven parents, with twenty-three children between them, voted for Mr. H.M. Owens. No one voted for Miss Fannie Melvin. The majority prevailed and Miss Pattie was hired by the District Board.

District School Boards are, of course, a thing of the past. A County School Board is responsible for administering the rules and regulations of the system. The "new" concept of school-based management is returning control of the schools back to their individual administrations. Again, the circle has come around: localism temporarily gave way to a State dominated system which quickly relinquished much of its power to the counties which now are giving it back to the local schools. It's an interesting phenomenon.

---

[4]"Historical Development of Virginia's Public School System, 1870-1970." p.20.

18 Yesterday's Schools

The contracts between the District Boards and the teachers hired tell a lot about the early schools. This summary dates back to 1916. (Courtesy of Prince William County Schools.)

School Trustees made up the District School Boards prior to 1923
(Courtesy of Prince William County Schools)

Posters like this one from 1929 were placed in public areas by the County School Board to advertise the sale of surplus school buildings.

Chapter 3.
EARLY ADMINISTRATION

As discussed in the chapter on the Early School Boards, the real power behind the running of the Prince William County public schools was held, in the first fifty years, by the District School Boards. The position of County Superintendent of Schools, established by the State Public Education Act of 1870, was largely one of politics, public relations and financial responsibility. It was a very necessary post, and a respected one, but the direct contact between the schools and the communities was through the District Boards.

After 1870, the State Board of Education, working from a list of eligible candidates, was responsible for the appointment of a Superintendent of Schools for every county in Virginia. The term of office was four years and the salary was paid from three sources: the State Board of Education, the Board of County Supervisors and the County School Board. In addition to their financial and political duties, the early Superintendents also served as the Executive Officer of the County Board. Their salary was commensurate with their position. In 1909, Prince William County's Superintendent of Schools George Tyler was paid $900.00 a year. By contrast, a white school teacher earned $25.00 a month for a seven or eight month school year.

As time went by and the public school system grew stronger and larger, it became clear that the job of School Superintendent was becoming very important to the development of the State's educational program. In 1916, the State passed a new law requiring that Division Superintendents have a college degree with some education courses and ten years' experience in education, at least three of which had to be in the classroom. Throughout the State the position became a full time one and it has remained thus ever since. Today, of course, the Superintendent is appointed by the County School Board to whom he is responsible. His salary is paid by the School Board which, in turn, receives its county funds from the Board of Supervisors.

During its first half century of existence, the office of the Superintendent of Schools was very unlike that office today. Actually, the superintendent had no office but kept all records in his home. He had no equipment and no secretarial help. He travelled to outlying schools and District Board meetings by horseback. In September 1906 the County School Board directed the Superintendent "to hire horse and buggy whenever necessary to visit the rural schools monthly." Finally, with the building of good roads and the coming of the automobile in the 1920s travel between schools became easier and certainly less time consuming.

The Superintendent worked alone until the 1920s when Prince William County became one of the first divisions in the State to employ a Supervisor of Elementary Instruction[1]. The county's first such supervisor was Miss Grace B. Moran, a graduate of a four-year college with twelve years of teaching experience, who was appointed in 1922 and served until 1927. By 1934, a supervisor for the black rural schools had been added to the staff. This position was held first by Jeanas Worker, also a graduate of a four-year college with twelve years experience at teaching. Her salary was $90 a month for an eight

---

[1] In 1906, secondary education had become part of the State's public school system, adding greatly to the work load already shouldered by the Superintendents. The addition of a supervisor for (white) elementary education meant that at least those responsibilities were shared.

months' term; her white counterpart was paid $180 a month for a ten months' school year.

The addition of these two positions to the school administration of the county greatly eased the burdens of the Superintendent. Although the number of schoolhouses decreased due to consolidation, and travel between them became easier with the advent of good roads and automobiles, the number of students grew larger each year and so did the numbers of faculty needed to teach them. Of even greater impact on the school administration in the early 1920s was the abolishment of the District School Boards.

In 1922, the Virginia General Assembly passed the "County Unit Law" which put the County School Boards, rather than the District Boards, in charge of all the schools in the county.[2] This move to create uniformity and centralization added inevitably to the responsibilities of the Superintendent of Schools, who, at that time, was Mr. Charles McDonald.

In 1925 came the appointment of Mr. Richard Challice Haydon as the county Superintendent of Schools. He had been a teacher in the county, as well as a principal and was well versed in the many areas of administration required in his new position. Changes were quickly made. The County School Board established a Superintendent's office in two rooms in the Manassas Court House. The Superintendent and the Supervisor of White Elementary Instruction shared one of the rooms; the other room housed the textbook department and business office. In 1934, the Supervisor of Colored Elementary Education also had an office in the School Administration's area. Clerical help came from students from the Manassas High School Commercial Department who worked two hours each day. When the County School Board took over the ordering and distributing of textbooks in 1932, that added to the workload, the School Board hired a professional clerical worker to oversee that area and also to lend a hand when needed in the main office. A telephone system, established in 1935, connected the central office with the four high schools and the three largest elementary schools. Buses also were used to maintain contact with the more remote buildings.

As control over the day-to-day operations of the schools passed from the District Boards to the County School Board and the Superintendent, changes had to be made. By the mid-thirties, school bus operations and maintenance, all general repair work to the schoolhouses and the distribution of equipment and supplies to the schools were all handled by a full time mechanic. This man, skilled in both automobile and general mechanics, was employed by the County School Board. The Superintendent, with the approval of the County Board, was responsible for purchasing all materials and supplies needed for the schools, for keeping all school records, for ordering all improvements to the buildings and for approving all bills prior to payment.

Despite the increased work load, Superintendent Haydon continued to work out of the two original rooms given to him in the County Courthouse. The business office and textbook department still shared one room while Mr. Haydon and the white Supervisor occupied the other. Both white and black Elementary Education supervisors reported to him daily and the three of them met every Saturday morning for discussion.

As the school system grew, so did the school administration. In 1952, the first Director of Instruction for the county was appointed. Ten years later, Dr. Sylvia Allen was appointed to the newly created post of Supervisor of Curriculum and Research. The Administrative Office has continued to expand and today hundreds of people are employed to run the county schools. Most of them, including the Superintendent of Schools, work in the central offices of the Prince William County schools in Independent Hill.

> **Gainesville School Board.**
>
> There will be a meeting of the Gainesville district school board at Haymarket, on Saturday, July 6, 10 a. m., at which time the appointment of teachers for the session of 1907-08 will be considered.
>
> Patrons of the schools are requested to be present.
>
> Teachers desiring schools are requested to send their applications to the clerk before that time. WM. H. BROWN, Clerk.
> td   Gainesville, Va.

The District School Boards hired their own teachers until 1923 as this advertisement from the Manassas Journal *of 1907 shows.*

---

[2]For a fuller discussion of this law, see the chapter on Early School Boards in this book.

Chapter 4.
THE EARLY SCHOOL DISTRICTS

Just before the first public school opened in the Asbury Methodist Church in Manassas in December of 1869, Prince William County was divided into six School Districts: Brentsville, Coles, Dumfries, Gainesville, Manassas and Occoquan.[1] This was in accordance with the 1846 state law, not previously taken advantage of by the County, which provided for a District Free School System. Each of the six districts was headed at first by a Board of Commissioners who were replaced in the summer of 1870 by a state appointed District School Board. These Trustees held the real power in the county schools although there was a County School Board to which they reported. Because each District obeyed laws of the Commonwealth of Virginia as prescribed by the State Board of Education, there were many similarities among them, but there were also differences reflecting the communities each served. It was the School Districts which ruled the County's educational system and it was the District Trustees to whom the people went for help. Thus the Districts—their beginnings, their power and influence, the changes they underwent—must be part of this study of Prince William County's early schools.

Though each District had distinguishing characteristics, they also had much in common. A study of the Gainesville District is also a study of all six early School Districts, though specific figures for each will vary, of course. The unique features of the other five Districts fill out the rest of this chapter.

---

[1]The six School Districts into which the County was divided should not be confused with today's Magisterial Districts of which there are seven. Schools today are County schools rather than District schools; students from one Magisterial District can, and do, attend school in another District. Separate School Districts existed until 1922.

GAINESVILLE DISTRICT

The Gainesville District, covering the northern section of Prince William County, was the second largest district in population. Only the Manassas District was more populous.

The first public school in the Gainesville District was the Buckland School which had actually operated as a private school as early as 1841. When the County instituted its public school system in 1870, Buckland became part of that system and was given the designation of District School #1. It was followed, over the next ten years, by Catharpin White, Antioch, Waterfall, Macrae, Gainesville, Hickory (Oak) Grove, Thornton and Thoroughfare White. They were numbered sequentially, in the order in which they were built, with Thoroughfare being given #9, and all began their lives as one-room schoolhouses. Antioch, Macrae and Thornton were schools for the District's black children; the rest served the white communities.

In the 1880s, four more schoolhouses were built in the District: #10 Mill Park, #11 Haymarket, #12 North Fork and #13 Piney Branch. All except the North Fork School were for white children and all but Haymarket were one-room buildings. These thirteen schools remained in use until the 1920's when consolidation of the small schools became a priority for the County School Board. The first to close were Buckland, Piney Branch, Mill Park, Thoroughfare and Waterfall. Several more shut their doors during the decade of the thirties so that by 1940 only Gainesville Elementary School, meeting in its new building erected in 1935, remained for the white students; both the Antioch and Macrae Schools continued to serve the black children. Gainesville was built as a four-classroom building; by 1940 both Antioch and Macrae had added a second room.

Those three schools served the district until 1953 when Antioch and Macrae were consolidated in a new building given the combined name of Antioch-Macrae. It served the community for thirty years, until 1982, as both a colored and, after 1965, an integrated school. From 1953 to 1973, the Gainesville and Antioch-Macrae Schools were the only two operating in the northern part of the county. In 1973, Tyler Elementary School was built on the John Marshall Highway less than one mile from the Gainesville School, which is still in use after fifty-eight years in the same building. The Antioch-Macrae School shut down in 1982. Of the early schoolhouses, only the Catharpin White, Gainesville, Antioch-Macrae and Waterfall buildings remain standing and only Gainesville is still a schoolhouse.

Like the other District schools of Prince William County and across the South as a whole, the Gainesville District schools were segregated until 1966. Four of the little early schoolhouses in the District served the black population: Antioch, Macrae (these two consolidated in 1953 as noted earlier), Thornton and North Fork. As in the other County school districts, the black schools operated for a term slightly shorter than the white schools or occasionally, when funds were short, they were closed altogether. The teachers were paid less, the equipment was in shorter supply and the classrooms were more crowded. The Gainesville School District Census Report of September 2, 1905 shows that of the 865 school age children[2] living in the District, 409 were black, 456 were white. The 409 black children had four schoolhouses available for them; the 456 white children had nine. Obviously, a much smaller percentage of the black school age children attended school. This was not an unusual situation in the County's School Districts.

Each School District had its own budget. In 1905, the total Gainesville School District budget amounted to $2,492.86, with the money coming from State, County and District funds. Teacher salaries took most of that amount - $2,446.00; other general expenses came to $313.20. Adding those two figures together, it is obvious that the District spent more than it took in; educational shortfalls are nothing new.

Maintaining adequate enrollment was a long standing problem in the Gainesville District in its early years. At its meeting on July 22, 1893 the District Board agreed to offer premiums of $5.00 to white teachers who achieved the highest enrollment in their schools for the coming school year. In addition, the teacher who showed the highest average daily attendance figures for that term would earn a $10.00 premium, which was equal to a third of a month's salary. This incentive represented a significant expenditure of District funds at that time. On the other hand, if enrollment fell below the State mandated daily average of twenty students, the teacher could petition the School Board to have that average lowered to fifteen. If this figure was still out of reach, the teacher would not be paid at all and would be obligated to notify the Board, through the Trustee in charge of that school, of the problem. The Trustee would then decide whether or not to close the school and, later, whether or not to re-open it. As a further added incentive to keep enrollment figures up, the Gainesville School Board agreed to pay for textbooks needed by indigent students who, without them, might not attend school at all. Funding for these programs came from State, County and District funds raised by a tax levy of seven and a half cents on every $100 worth of property and by the dog tax.

The value of books to learning was clearly known to all the District School Boards. At the June 2, 1905 meeting of the Gainesville Board, it was decided that any money raised by the individual schoolhouses for a library would be matched by the Board as long as the library was kept in the school building. Taking advantage of the new policy, the Haymarket School reported that it had raised $18.40 for a library, and the Board matched that sum as promised. Choosing the books for the library was an important enough matter to warrant the appointment of a committee consisting of a District Trustee, the teacher of the school and the County Superintendent of Schools to carry out the assignment.

The allocation of housekeeping chores was another area of education in which the District School Boards had a hand. In the summer of 1889 the Gainesville School Board approved the decision to suspend from school any boy who refused to cut wood or any girl who refused to sweep the schoolhouse floor and to report any such action to the Clerk of the Board.[3] Earlier that year, the Board had de-

---

[2] Public elementary schools, in 1905, were available for children aged seven to nineteen but attendance was not compulsory. There were no public high schools until the following year.

[3] Gainesville District School Board minutes of August 24, 1889.

cided that teachers would be held responsible for all damages done to the buildings. In addition, the Board would no longer furnish wood for heat. Patrons of each school (parents and friends) would have to take over that job.

There was one problem with which the Gainesville District School Board had to deal that was unique to that District. Students living in parts of neighboring Fauquier County sometimes attended school in Prince William County. In 1877, the District Board agreed to charge those students $1.00 per month to attend the schools in the District. This amount covered all expenses involved in educating a child whose parents did not pay a school tax in Prince William County. Though this situation did not occur often over the years, it is happening today when the County School Board must pay tuition to Fairfax County for Prince William County students who attend the Thomas Jefferson School for Science and Technology.

Because every School District had its own characteristics, a quick look at each proves valuable. Much of what concerned the Gainesville District Board also concerned the other District Boards, but there were interesting variations on the general theme.

BRENTSVILLE DISTRICT

The Brentsville School District is unique because of the intricacy of its school development plan, if indeed a formal plan ever existed. It appears more likely that the District Board handled each situation on an individual basis, making for a most complex story.

The first meeting of the Brentsville District School Board was held on December 3, 1870. At that meeting, Superintendent of Schools Thornton explained the duties of the local Board, which immediately moved to have a census taken of the District's children aged five to twenty-one. They paid Mr. John L. Sinclair to carry out this duty as well as "other services" for which he was paid a total of $20. At that meeting, the Board also contracted with Mr. P.G. Slaughter to take over the Brentsville schoolhouse (previously operated as a private school) for which he would be paid $50 a month, a large salary for that time.

In rapid order, the District Board took over the Nokesville schoolhouse, the Red Shoals school near Greenwich and the colored school near Fleetwood. A year later, the Sulphur Springs School was established and the Board began the search for a school site near Nokesville.

In the spring of 1872, the Board ordered that a school be established at Hershey's Shop near Aden and that the Rev. Mr. Hershey be appointed as the teacher at a salary of $25 a month. In October of that year, a new building for the Red Shoals school was erected as was one to replace the Brentsville Schoolhouse. Additionally, the Board rented a room for Mr. G. M. Goodwin to open a school for the children living in the Orlando Courthouse area of the County. Thus, two years after the advent of public education in the County, the Brentsville District already had schools in Brentsville, Nokesville, Greenwich (Red Shoals), Sulphur Springs, Orlando, Fleetwood and Aden. Then the story starts to become complicated as schools were built, moved, renamed, renumbered and closed.

In 1874, a second school for black children, called the Chapel Colored School, was opened and designed Colored Schoolhouse #2. Since no further mention is made of this school, it apparently did not exist for more than a year or two. The fourth schoolhouse actually built in the Brentsville District, and hence designated as #4, was the Chinn School for black children. It opened in 1875.

In 1876, the Holmes School was opened in a house rented from Mr. F. W. Holmes for $4.50 a month. Located across from the Belle Haven Church, this school eventually became part of the Dumfries District. The following year, the school at Sulphur Springs closed as soon as a new building at Towles' Gate, which was located five miles southwest of Brentsville near the Aden crossroads, was opened. It was called the Vancluse (Van Cluse) School and was given the #5 since it was the fifth building erected by the Board.

According to the Brentsville District School Board minutes of August 13, 1877, "The people of Bristoe Station and vicinity having given the Board of District School Trustees sufficient evidences of their ability to sustain a school with a legal average, it is ordered that a school be established at or near this point."

By 1878, the District had six schoolhouses: Brentsville (#1), Nokesville (#2), Red Shoals (#3), Chinn Colored (#4), Vancluse or Towles' Gate (#5), and Bristoe (#6). The Brentsville Schoolhouse was insured that year for $300; the rest were insured for $150 each. The other little schools which met in rented rooms apparently no longer were needed; they are not mentioned again.

For four years, no further schools were opened. The next one established was a Negro[4] school in the Greenwich neighborhood. It was held in a rented house and called the Baileysburg Colored School #7. It remained open for only two years when the County condemned the house in which the school was held.

During that year of 1882, the District Board ordered Mr. Dulin, one of the Trustees, to make arrangements to move the Nokesville Schoolhouse from its location near the railroad to another place "above and near the village of Nokesville."

The new log schoolhouse was completed in 1884 and kept its #2 designation in the District. At the same time, teachers in the District were having their salaries raised from $25 to $28 a month if they could keep an average daily attendance of twenty, up from fifteen. If their school fell below that average figure, the teachers would be paid $1.80 per student per month.

In 1884, the Allendale (Allen Dale) School was built and opened on October 28. On May 3, 1886, the Board authorized the sale of the Red Shoals schoolhouse as well as its benches for a total of $87 which was then used to purchase the English Church for use as a schoolhouse. The District had seven schools under its jurisdiction at this point: Brentsville (#1), Nokesville (#2), Greenwich (#3), Chinn (#4), Vancluse (#5), Bristoe (#6), and Allendale (#8).

The Brentsville School Board then began a period of moving schoolhouses around to new locations. On November 22, 1886, the Board ordered the Vancluse school moved on petition by the parents. In August of 1887 the Board ordered "that the Bristoe School be moved out on the County Road joining Church lot"[5] and placed on stone pillars. Then on September 5, 1887, it was ordered that the Chinn School be moved near Kettle Run and enlarged. This was not done. Instead a new and larger building was erected near the Kettle Run railroad bridge. It was still known as the Chinn School (#4). At the same time, the Board changed the number of the Allendale School from #8 to #7, filling the gap left when the short-lived Baileysburg school closed.

In 1890, the Board changed the name of the Vancluse School to the Hazelwood School keeping the #5 designation. It was some time, however, before the new name took hold. In May of the next year, the Board ordered that the Bristoe Schoolhouse be abandoned and a new building be erected near Chapel Springs. This decision was made following much discussion about moving the old school, but this time the Board decided against it.

The first seven months' school term (year) was approved by the Board in February 1893 which then made arrangements to notify teachers of the change. In June of that year, the Board ordered a new schoolhouse to be built in Bristoe.[6] Two years later another schoolhouse was added to the District with the building of the King's Crossroads School. In September of 1896, the name of the Chinn School was changed to the Kettle Run School, to reflect its geographic location. The last schoolhouse to be built in the nineteenth century in the Brentsville District was the Woodlawn School which opened on October 30, 1899.

For reasons not mentioned in the School Board minutes, the nine District schools were renumbered shortly after the turn of the century:

    #1 - Brentsville
    #2 - Bristow
    #3 - Allendale
    #4 - Hazelwood
    #5 - King's X Roads
    #6 - Nokesville
    #7 - Kettle Run
    #8 - Woodlawn
    #9 - Greenwich

Greenwich, which had held the #3 position for all the early years, was probably moved to the #9 slot in 1901 because in that year a new, graded school was built in the center of the village. The two-room, two-story building was shared with Fauquier County.

These nine schools served 513 white children in eight schoolhouses and 111 black children in one schoolhouse.

---

[4]This is one of the few instances where the term "Negro" is used. "Colored" was the preferred term for many, many years.

[5]Brentsville District School Board minutes of August 15, 1887, p.119.

[6]The spelling of "Bristoe" was changed, at least in the Brentsville District School Board minutes, to "Bristow" in the August 1, 1894 entry.

All the buildings were kept in good condition by "a special day of visitation and inspection" from the Trustee assigned to each building. They reported on the schools' needs and made sure that such repairs were made.

The Board had several other kinds of business to attend to regularly. In September of 1904, for example, patrons of several of the District schools petitioned the Board to allow the teachers to extend the school term if the patrons paid their salaries. The Board agreed to supplement such funds collected by up to $5 a month so that the teachers would stay on the job.[7] They had to arrange for wood for the schoolhouse stoves every year. Money to pay for salaries, repairs, new buildings, etc. was always on the agenda and not always in ready supply. The hiring and firing of all teachers was part of their job as was the furnishing of supplies to all white schools.

Beginning in 1904, a debate waged over building a schoolhouse in the village of Aden and closing the Hazelwood school. Several public meetings, very well attended, were held with the District Board as well as the Superintendent of Schools to decide whether or not to move the Hazelwood School or build a new, larger building. The debate continued over the next few years until 1908 when the Hazelwood and Allendale Schools were finally closed. The next year the four-room Aden Consolidated School opened to serve students who once attended those schools.

Most of the Board's energy during those four or five years was focussed on the establishment of a high school in the Brentsville District and the minutes reflect this. Routine matters were handled as they arose, but little new was done. The Board did agree to the establishment of a colored school at Brentsville in October of 1907 but the patrons had to furnish the building, all its furnishings, the wood for the stove, etc. The Board only agreed to pay the teacher's salary and that for only five months.

The last elementary school built in the Brentsville District was the Brentsville District High School—today's Nokesville Elementary School—to house grades one through twelve. That was in 1929; there has not been a new elementary school since that date.

By 1936, five white schools (Bristow, Aden, Greenwich, Nokesville and Brentsville) and one colored (Kettle Run) served the District. It was to be the last year for the Bristow School and Kettle Run had only two years left. By the mid-1940s, only Greenwich, Aden, Nokesville and Brentsville were still open. The last of the one-room schoolhouses in operation in Prince William County—Brentsville—shut its doors in 1944, as did the larger Greenwich School. Two years later, the Aden School closed, leaving Nokesville the only active schoolhouse in the District. Of the early schools, Nokesville, English Church, Aden, (first) Orlando and Brentsville Schools still stand.

COLES DISTRICT

The Coles School District was unique in two ways. First, it had the smallest number of schoolhouses and, secondly, all of its schools were for white children. There was not a large enough black population in the District to warrant the opening of a school for them. Because no early Coles District School Board records were found, all the information about the District schools had to be pieced together from tiny bits and scraps of materials found tucked away in boxes or memories. Nevertheless, a good picture of the District has emerged.

The first schoolhouse established in the Coles District seems to have been the Gold Ridge School, which opened its doors in 1874. Five others had been opened by the turn of the century—Hayfield, Purcell, Woodbine, Horton and Smithfield. All were one-room schools except Smithfield, which was a two-room building. Within ten years a seventh schoolhouse, Fayman, was in operation but by then, the Horton School had closed so, consequently, six schoolhouses was the maximum number ever found in the District at any one time.

By 1936, when consolidation of County schools was fairly complete, only the Woodbine School, recently enlarged to a three-room building, remained open to serve the children of the Coles District. The other schools were closed at the rate of one a year beginning in 1930. The students were bused either to Woodbine or to a nearer schoolhouse in a neighboring district. Despite the construction of another new and larger Woodbine school building in 1953, the area was growing fast enough that, in only two years, an even larger building was needed and so the Coles Elementary School was built. The 1953 Wood-

---

[7]Brentsville District School Board minutes of September, 1904, p.235.

up with the rapid growth of population. A total of sixteen elementary schools were built by the County. The first was the Jennie Dean School, built in 1960 in the Manassas District where Loch Lomond was built the following year and Parkside the next year. These three Manassas schools were followed in 1963 by Potomac View and Fred Lynn, both located in the Occoquan District. In 1964, the Manassas District opened Westgate Elementary and Featherstone was built in Woodbridge[8]. Two more schools were built the next year - Baldwin Elementary in Manassas and Elizabeth Vaughan in Woodbridge. The Occoquan District added two more schools in 1966, Rippon Combined Elementary and Middle Schools and Marumsco Hills Elementary. In 1967, the first school was built in the new Dale City and was named for the subdivision, Dale City Elementary. The Occoquan District acquired its seventh elementary school of the decade when Belmont was built in 1968. That was also the year when Tyler Elementary was built in the Gainesville District and Sinclair joined the ranks in Manassas. The last school built during the sixties was the second Dale City school, Bel Air, which opened in 1969.

The first hundred years of the Prince William County public school system began with a decade of growth as the movement got underway. The final decade of that first century was also a busy one as population growth created a constant need for more schools. That growth continues into the second century of public education with no sign of a let-up in the near future.

---

[8] Though located in Woodbridge, Featherstone was part of the Occoquan District when it was built. It was not until January 1, 1976 that the Woodbridge District was created from the Occoquan and Dumfries Districts.

An advertisement for the sale of Haymarket School appeared in the Manassas Journal *in October of 1947.*

Chapter 5.
NAMING OF THE SCHOOLS

Schools in Prince William County acquired their names in several ways. The majority of the early schools were simply known by the name of the community they served: Brentsville, Nokesville, Bristow, Greenwich, Lucasville, Occoquan, Haymarket, Antioch, Gainesville, Joplin, Manassas Park, Dumfries, Bethlehem, Wellington, Quantico, Aden, Fayman, Westgate, Groveton, Buckhall, Triangle, Buckland, etc.

When a schoolhouse was located near an important community landmark, it often took the name of that landmark. The Horton School, for example, was near Horton's Store and Post Office. The Mill Park School opened on land belonging to Mill Park Plantation. Similarly, the Hazelwood School was built on the Hazelwood Plantation. Belle Haven Church gave its name to the schoolhouse which the county built across the road from it. In later years, Rippon Elementary School was named for Rippon Lodge, the early 18th century plantation located nearby.

Geographical features found near a school site were also favorite sources of names for County schools. Often schoolhouses located along streams or creeks were named for them.[1] For example, Neabsco School was located near Neabsco Creek just as Catharpin School was built along Catharpin Creek; Cannon Branch School, Piney Branch School and Cabin Branch School were located along the stream branches of the same name. North Fork, Kettle Run, Sulphur Springs and Bacon Race schools were named in a corresponding manner. The Waterfall School in the northern part of the county was located, not surprisingly, near a waterfall; the Gold Ridge School was located near a gold mine in the Independent Hill area.

Names descriptive of the area in which they were built were not uncommon. The two Cherry Hill Schools (one in Dumfries and one in Woodbridge District), Hickory Ridge School and Hickory Grove School are examples of this. Parkside Elementary School, located on the Manassas Park side of Manassas, was given its name for obvious geographical reasons. Marumsco Hills School serves the Marumsco Hills area of Woodbridge.

Local families often had schools named after them. The Purcell School was named after a family prominent in that part of the Coles District in which the school was located. Minnieville School was named for the community nearby which, in turn, was named for Minnie Alexander, the local postmaster's daughter. The Bennett School in Manassas was named after the citizen who donated the land on which the school was built. Because the Bradley family gave some of their farmland for a school building, that schoolhouse was named in their honor. Similarly named was the Florence School, built on land belonging to the Florence family whose name was also given to the nearby store, post office and mill. The Washington-Reid School in Dumfries took the names of two well-known female community leaders who donated the land for the building. Baileysburg was the name of an area near Greenwich which grew out of a thousand acre plantation put together by Mr. Carr Baily and when a small school was established there, it was known as the Baileysburg School. The Macrae School was originally located on land owned by the Macrae family near Gainesville.

---

[1] The origin of all these names is the subject of another study. The information can be found in any of several books about Prince William County history.

McGregor, Manley and Smithfield Schools were probably named that way too, though no record has been found. The Allendale School was located on the Allen family's property near Aden. King's Crossroads School was named after the Al King family who lived nearby. The Chinn School was named for a prominent local family as was the Coles Elementary School.

Sometimes, schools were named for people of note outside the local area. For example, the Ruffner School was named after the first State Superintendent of Public Education in Virginia. The two Thornton Schools honored William W. Thornton, the first Prince William County Superintendent of Schools who served in that position from 1871-1883 and J. B. T. Thornton, Superintendent from 1887-1891. The Clarkson School was named for School Superintendent H. M. Clarkson who held that job from 1891 to 1905. Most interestingly, the Brown School, which served the black population of Manassas for many years and was in large measure supported by a group of Quakers from Philadelphia, was named to honor Mrs. Brown, one of the members of that generous Quaker group. The Jennie Dean School was named to honor the remarkable black educator who started the Manassas Industrial School for Colored Youth which was located on the same site. Sinclair Elementary was named for Mr. C. A. Sinclair, Sr., a prominent citizen of Manassas who served as treasurer of Prince William County for more than twenty-five years. R. Dean Kilby, first principal of the Marumsco School, was honored by having that school renamed for him when he left the principalship there. Mr. Fred M. Lynn was also honored for his years of service in education in the County by having a school named for him.

Mt. Pleasant, Greenwood, Woodlawn and Fairview are examples of school names chosen simply because they sounded pleasant. One school is even named for a flower found in the neighborhood —Woodbine. Romantically, Loch Lomond Elementary was named for the lake in Scotland, though it is appropriately located on the old Ben Lomond tract in Manassas.

Location on a road was sometimes used for the name of the school. The Summitt School, at the top of Tanyard Hill in Occoquan, got its name that way. The Thoroughfare School might fit into this category too, but it probably just assumed the name of the community it served.

Schools which were held in churches went by the name of that church although they were public, not parochial, schools. For example, the Mt. Zion School met in a room in the Mt. Zion Church on Joplin Road near Dumfries. Near Greenwich, a school was established in the old English Episcopal Church building and the school became known as the English Church school.

One old county school probably received its name by way of human error. The Red Shoals School in the Brentsville District was, very likely, known in its earliest years as the Red School because of its red color. With the difficulties inherent in reading old writing done in faded inks, someone could easily have seen the word "Shoal" instead of the word "School" and recorded it that way. Picking up an "s" somewhere along the years would have not been difficult and thus the Red Shoals School was born.

Over the course of time, the names of schools often changed. In the beginning, the colloquial names—those used by residents to simply indicate a school's location by its proximity to a public building, a large landholding, a small farm, a natural feature of the land—were used by almost everyone. As the school system became more sophisticated, "proper" names were assigned to the schoolhouses and if those names differed from the familiar designations, they did not catch on very quickly. Often a generation had to pass before the official name of a school gained widespread usage. Thus it is that several of the old schools were known by more than one name over their lifetime. Of course, in many cases, the School Boards continued to use the old names and their charm is a pleasant heritage today. At present, when schools are built in the county, the School Board invites citizens to suggest appropriate names, the only stipulation being that no living person can be so honored.

Chapter 6.
THE EARLY SCHOOLHOUSES

In 1870, following passage of the Public Education Act in Virginia, Prince William County set up local District Boards to coordinate and run the new schools which would soon be opening. The call went out from these Boards for citizens in the local communities to donate land and/or buildings which would be suitable for use as school property.

In the beginning, schools, both white and colored, were set up in existing buildings but, as funds became available, the District Boards were able to contract out for schoolhouses to be built. Specifications were set, bids were taken and contractors were hired. It usually took only a few months for a schoolhouse to be built and when it was completed, it was opened. With very few exceptions, these were all one-room schools and usually they provided all the space necessary. Larger buildings would have meant more wood for the stoves, another teacher to be hired, more supplies to be purchased, all with funds as limited then as they are today. As years passed, additions were sometimes built onto existing buildings or a new and larger schoolhouse would have to be built. The County's consolidation of white elementary schools in the 1930s, of course, meant that larger four- or six- or eight-room schools had to be built and gradually the one-room schoolhouses became a thing of the past.

Across the United States, schoolhouses were generally built out of materials available. In Prince William County, the abundance of trees supplied wood for the early school buildings with brick becoming the material of choice in the 1930s. There were plans available from the State Board of Education for the construction of one- or two-room buildings which resulted in a certain similarity of schoolhouses from a particular era. This was true not only in this County but across the State and Nation as well. There were always exceptions, of course. Some communities continued to make use of buildings already constructed and never built a new one; occasionally, a room in a local church was used as a classroom; one settlement, Purcell, built its second little schoolhouse out of metal. In general, though, the school buildings in Prince William County for at least the first fifty years of their existence, were small frame structures usually painted white.

During those early years, the County schoolhouses were heated by wood-burning stoves. Wood for the white schools was paid for by the District School Boards which contracted with a citizen who would supply a year's supply at a rate deemed fair by both sides. The colored schools generally relied on the parents or friends of the school to provide the supply of wood needed. In all cases, the teacher was responsible for starting the fire every morning (either she did it herself or she paid a student to go to school early and get it going) and keeping it going. School boys generally enjoyed the chore of bringing the wood from the wood pile into the schoolhouse to dry because it gave them a chance to leave the lessons behind and get out of doors. That this was not always the case is apparent from minutes of the Gainesville District School Board of August 24, 1889 which stated that any boy who refused to cut wood (and any girl who refused to sweep) could be suspended from school and the action would be reported to the Clerk of the School Board.

The wood-burning pot-bellied stoves were usually located in the center of the school room. Desks closest to the stove were the warmest and those in the more distant corners were cold. Older children and boys often had to give up the more comfortable seats to the youngest pupils or the girls who seemed less able to cope with the chilly weather. In addition to providing warmth to the classroom, in many of the schoolhouses the stove was used to prepare hot lunches for the students during the cold winter months. Girls would bring ingredients for soup in the morning and a pot would bubble away until the noon hour. Sometimes, mothers from the community would prepare the hot soup or hot chocolate for the pupils. How good it must have smelled in those little buildings on hot soup or chocolate days!

Drinking water was available at all the schoolhouses but it meant that someone, usually one or two of the bigger boys, would have to carry it in buckets from a pump in the schoolyard or, more often, from one on a neighboring property. The pail of water would be kept on a bench in the back of the room or in the vestibule and pupils dipped a scoop into the bucket to get water to drink. Some of the more progressive schools asked students to bring their own mugs from home but it was not until 1917 that the School Board passed a resolution requiring drinking fountains or individual cups for each student in each school.

The agricultural nature of Prince William County is apparent from the kinds of clubs available for school children during the early years of the 20th century. In 1912, Minnieville, Brentsville and Manassas schools established "Tomato Clubs" for girls. The next year, County School Board minutes report that the School Board appropriated $75 for prizes given by the Tomato Clubs; another $75 was approved the following year for demonstrations. The "Corn Clubs" were the equivalent groups for boys. In 1917, the Board approved $50 for two girls to attend a ten day course at Harrisonburg Normal School as part of their work in the "Canning Clubs". That same year, the Board approved money to be used as prizes in "Poultry Clubs" and in 1918, "Pig Clubs" were also mentioned.

With the advent of gas and electricity for heat in the 1920s and 1930s, the old wood and coal burning schools became a memory. The new consolidated school buildings had central heating; probably students in the large schools of the 1990s never even think about how their school is heated and yet it was a very important part of a student's daily life in the days of today's students grandparents and great-grandparents.

The spread of electricity across rural Prince William County changed the look of the schoolhouse. Kerosene and gas lamps gave way to electric switches which flooded the rooms with light on dark days or during evening programs. Most of the early schoolhouses depended solely upon natural light to illuminate the classroom and so the positioning of the building's windows was important. On dark days the teacher would often gather her pupils around her near a window and read to them since work at the desks would be difficult. Given the inherent dangers of kerosene or gas, it is surprising that fires seem to have destroyed only two of the county's schools — Bethel (and that was caused by a strike of lightning) and Kettle Run (and the blame for that was never established).

Janitorial service was non-existent for the little schoolhouses until the advent of the larger consolidated schools. It was the responsibility of the students, under the watchful eye of their teacher, to keep the school room clean. Both boys and girls swept the floors, cleaned the stoves and lamps if there were any, scrubbed the desks and tables, washed the blackboards and performed the many tasks required to keep up sanitary conditions. The District Board or Trustees might drop in any time and cleanliness was one of the things they looked for. From their reports, it was rare not to find things in good order.

Indeed, that very subject is the number one topic on the list of rules presented on August 4, 1883 to the District Boards by the County School Board which urged each Board to adopt them. The rules, which governed not only cleanliness but all aspects of school life were as follows:

1. "That the teacher shall see that the schoolhouse be kept in good order; that he shall prevent the pupils from defacing the schoolhouse and furniture; and shall, during the term, keep the key in his possession...."
2. Regular attendance was required unless "some good excuse" was given to the teacher.
3. "All pupils are required positively to obey their Teachers."
4. "On entering the school room every scholar should make a polite salutation to the Teacher."
5. No firearms or deadly weapons would be allowed on the school grounds. Expulsion would be the punishment for disobeying.
6. No tobacco was to be used during school hours by the pupils.
7. Teachers would set up staggered dismissal and recess times to prevent confusion.

These early rules of behavior became Prince William County's first Code of Conduct for its public school system.

The early schools were set up to serve the small community surrounding them. Children and teachers walked or rode a horse to the schoolhouse which was as centrally located in settled areas as possible. Each schoolhouse served the families who lived usually within a five mile radius of the building. When population shifts occurred, small schoolhouses were in danger of closing. A minimum of twenty children had to be met for a school to be kept open and that often meant that the teacher had to scramble to find pupils to fill the seats. Sometimes a teacher would bring her own children to the school in which she taught in order to bring the enrollment figures up to the minimum. It happened, of course, that schools had to be closed due to lack of pupils. In that case, another schoolhouse would be opened closer to the new center of population and then some children had to travel great distances to get an education.

For fifty years, schoolhouse locations were determined by the needs of the local communities. It was not until the 1920s and 1930s, when roads and transportation improvements made busing possible, that consolidation of the white schools, and later the colored schools, really began. Some parents were eager for their children to have what they considered the advantages of a larger school: more supplies and equipment, a variety of teachers, better and newer buildings, etc. Others worried that when the little schoolhouses were gone, the sense of community would also be lost and the children would no longer be satisfied with living on the farm. They worried that rural values would be replaced by a uniform standard not as well suited to their children. They were concerned with having to pay higher taxes to support the larger, more expensive schools. Nevertheless, pressures from both State and County educators to consolidate the schools prevailed and gradually across the County, as across the United States, the small schoolhouses were neglected, abandoned or converted into homes.

It is interesting to realize that what some educators and concerned parents today are demanding for the children goes directly back to the little rural schoolhouses. In Massachusetts there is a group called "The Small and Rural Schools Task Force," which is charged by the federal government to find ways to preserve and improve small and rural schools. Its recent chairman, Howard Colter, says, "There is more personalization in a small school. Parents have more control over programs and more accessibility. The community often pivots around the school."[1] In Prince William County, the Christa McAuliffe Elementary School, in the 1992-93 school year experimented with a program which educated students ages five through nine according to their ability rather than their age. This "experimental" program, of course, is the very method used to group students in the one-room schoolhouses of long ago. A quotation from Andrew Gulliford, in his study, *America's Country Schools,* is appropriate here:

> Out of necessity country schools have been practicing for more than a century what the most sophisticated education systems now encourage —smaller classrooms, programs that allow students to progress at their own rate and students who help each other learn. We seem to have come full circle in our appreciation of the community values inherent in the one-room school, where the teacher taught students of various ages and abilities in a familylike atmosphere....
>
> Country schools have always been important in the rural areas of this nation, as a symbol both of cultural continuity and of the opportunities to be gained from education. The role of country schools in America is not over.[2]

---

[1] Baldwin, Letitia. "New school superintendent settling in", *The Bar Harbor Times,* July 30, 1992, p.A5.

[2] Andrew Gulliford. *America's Country Schools.* Washington, DC: Preservation Press, 1991, p.45.

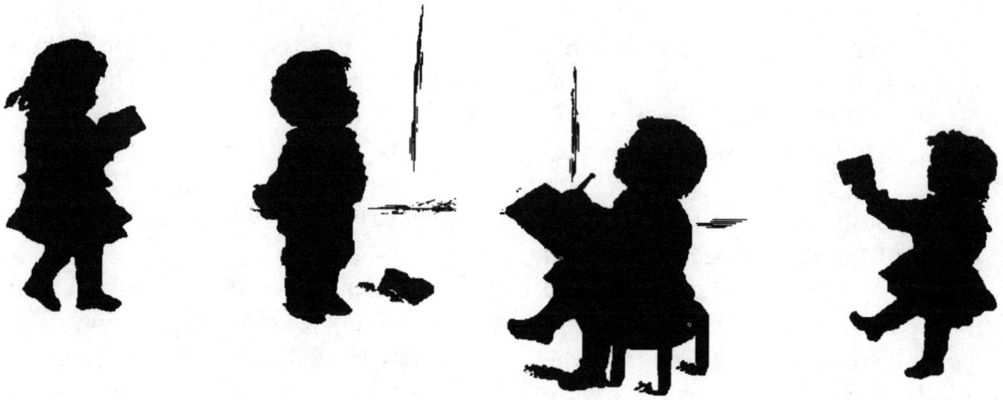

Chapter 7.
CONSOLIDATION

If the years between 1870 and 1920 can be called "The Early Years" of the Prince William County schools, then the period between 1920 and 1950 could be known as "The Consolidation Years". In the early 1920s, the State Board of Education decreed that "an enrollment of at least twenty pupils with reasonable assurance of an average daily attendance of that number is required to constitute a legal school, and no public funds shall be established or continued until this condition is complied with."[1] This ruling directly affected several of the small rural schools in the County. At the same time, improvements in travel made transportation of children to schools farther from home possible and this became an important consideration. Additionally, in 1922 the State Board of Education ordered that all one-room schoolhouses teach only grades 1-6. Seventh grade (high school preparation) was only to be offered at central schools where there was the most room. Consolidation became a necessity.

By 1933, Prince William County had further refined the system. One-room schoolhouses and their one teacher could only house grades 1-4; two-room schools with two teachers could teach grades 1-6 if they desired. The days of any remaining one-room schools were numbered. In those Depression years, it just did not make good economical sense to maintain two buildings when one would meets the needs of the children.

Consolidation was not always popular with the citizens. They knew that when the schoolhouse in their community was closed, the focal point of that community would be gone. Schools were used for more than daily education; they were community centers for meetings, shows and programs, sometimes even churches. Sending their children outside their community would take some of the control over what those children learned out of the hands of the parents and that was worrisome. Some parents would find it difficult to get to the schools for talks with the teacher or to attend programs in which their children took part. Such concerns are still voiced today when the School Board proposes busing children from the community in which they live to another area where their educational needs might be better met.

The first steps toward consolidation of schools in Prince William County came in 1923 when, in the Occoquan District, the Emory Chapel and Bacon Race Schools were closed and the children bused to Bethel. The following year Mill Park School in the Gainesville District and Groveton School in the Manassas District were both closed and the children bused to the Haymarket Elementary School. All told, between 1923 and 1934, the number of white elementary schoolhouses was reduced from forty-three to nineteen.

The County was not totally successful in its early consolidation efforts. A report from 1935 shows that among the nineteen existing white elementary schools, nine were one-teacher schools which were supposed to house first through fourth grades only. Actually, two still included grade seven, one went through the sixth grade and two more had grade five; only four had grades 1-4 as directed by the State. Of the five two-teacher schools, four included grades 1-6 as planned, but one still taught seventh grade. There were, however, five white elementary schools of more than three teachers which did have grades 1-7.[2]

---

[1] Proceedings of the State Board of Education, Vol. II, p.5.

[2] Richard C. Haydon. "An Administrative Survey of the Public School System in Prince William County, Virginia", A Thesis for Master of Science at University of Virginia, 1935, p.21.

In general, though, the plan worked and consolidation substantially lowered the number of white elementary schools in Prince William County as the following figures show:

1920:   22 one-room schools
        9 two-room schools

1925:   20 one-room schools
        5 two-room schools
        5 with three or more rooms

1933:   9 one-room schools
        5 two-room schools
        5 with 3 or more rooms

1940:   2 one-room schools
        4 two-room schools
        6 with 3 or more rooms

It is important to note that these consolidation efforts affected the white schools only. The fourteen colored schools remained as they were. In 1934, Superintendent of Schools Richard C. Haydon wrote on that subject:

The policy thus far has been to maintain a school in all the settlements with enough children to meet the minimum average and to leave it to those badly located to get to these schools. ...[This] leaves a good many outside of the compulsory attendance limits. It is probable that until financial conditions improve, no revolutionary plan in reference to negro schools will be possible.[3]

Consolidation of the colored schools was something to be aimed for in the future. Despite his gloomy prediction, Mr. Haydon nevertheless set forth a plan for combining the schools by busing the students to five centers. Writing in 1934, he recommended that consolidation of the colored schools be accomplished thusly:

North Fork would attend Antioch
Thornton would go to Macrae
Kettle Run and Manley would attend Brown
Quantico and Hickory Ridge would go to Cabin Branch
Neabsco would go to Summit

---
[3]Haydon, p.23.

Two years later, the Superintendent's plan began to be implemented. North Fork did combine with Antioch in 1936 and Manley students were sent to the Brown School. Two more years passed before the Thornton School joined Macrae and Kettle Run was combined with Brown. In 1939, the Quantico Colored School and Neabsco joined forces with Cabin Branch. The last to consolidate was Hickory Ridge which finally merged with Cabin Branch in 1943. By 1947, the Summitt School had closed leaving Antioch, Macrae, Cabin Branch and Brown open to serve the black children of Prince William County. Cabin Branch closed in 1950 when the Washington-Reid School was built; Antioch and Macrae merged in 1953; the Brown School was abandoned in 1954 and its students attended the Jennie Dean School. Desegregation was the final step in the consolidation of Prince William County's colored schools.

As consolidation proceeded, the School Board was left with unused and unneeded school buildings. These were usually offered for sale at public auction, the same way that the very old schoolhouses were sold when a newer structure had been built to take their place. Whereas, in the old days, proceeds from the sale of the land and/or building were deposited in the account of the local District in which they were located, the monies realized from the sale of property in the 1920s and later went into the coffers of the County School Board. For example, the Board decided at their November 7, 1928 meeting that they would sell the following schoolhouses in March of 1929:

Brentsville District: Nokesville, King's Crossroads

Dumfries District: old Cabin Branch School site

Gainesville District: Gainesville, Buckland, Waterfall

Manassas District: Groveton

Occoquan District: Occoquan, Woodbridge, Cherry Hill

The terms were to be cash or a time payment with 6% interest. Such sales were common in the county during the twenties, thirties and forties and the proceeds realized became an important part of the School Board's budget.

With consolidation, changes other than the loss of community schoolhouses and all that meant, were realized. One of these changes was the increase in size of the school libraries. As schools joined forces, their libraries were also combined though this did not significantly help the colored schools which had very few books to begin with. Larger buildings with more space meant that physically or mentally handicapped students could now be "trained" in special (and sometimes regular) classes. Probably the greatest change was in the system of busing.

During the first fifty years of Prince William County's public school system, children got to school either on foot or by horseback. Occasionally one hears about a private automobile carrying students to school, but these were rare. The roads were not comfortable for driving and in this rural county most people had little need for transportation beyond a horse and wagon. This began to change in the early 1920s.

In 1924 the first "school wagon" appeared. Mr. Wallace Partlow of Gainesville bought a Ford truck chassis which he outfitted with a handmade body, board seats and a canvas covering. He charged his neighbors a $2.00 yearly fee to transport their children to the Haymarket High School (also an elementary school). Mr. Partlow's daughter remembers,

> Pick-up began at the Cottage Farm two miles from Catharpin and proceeded along muddy roads with ruts, rocks, high water or choking dust to the intersection with the Gainesville road. If the "wagon" made it that far, the day at school was assured. The fee was not always forthcoming for a child's transportation, but teams were always on hand to pull the bus out of the mud if it got "hung up" in front of a man's property.[4]

By the beginning of the 1925-26 school year, there were five school buses operating in the county. They used the Model T Ford chassis with bodies built on but they offered little protection from the weather. Side curtains could be lowered in case of rain or snow or cold but they were not very effective. The school bus drivers owned their own vehicles and worked under contract with the County School Board for a small monthly salary. When roads became particularly bad, horses and wagons were substituted for the buses, but these offered even less protection from the elements. When the idea of consolidation of the little schoolhouses into larger district schools was first proposed, one of the worries of parents was the danger they felt they were subjecting their children to on the County's school bus fleet.

Nonetheless, as roads continued to be improved around Prince William County, consolidation moved ahead and by 1933 there were nineteen school buses operating. The "modern, glass enclosed bodies"[5] seated between thirty and seventy-five each, depending on the size of the vehicle. By 1935, the majority of the white students living beyond a mile and a half radius of their schools were bused. Only two of the one-room white schoolhouses were not served by buses. At the same time, none of the schools for black children provided buses. Those students had to walk no matter how far away they lived from the schools. The first buses for children at the colored schools started in 1938 when three of them were added to the fleet.

An early Prince William County School bus
(Gainesville School 50th Anniversary booklet)

Consolidation of the schools marked a very great change in the way of life in rural Prince William County. Communities no longer had a focal point to tie their citizenry together. This change affected the Nation as a whole as much as it did this County.

---

[4]Hattie Mae Partlow and Pauline Smith. *Now and Then With P.W.E.A.*, Prince William County Education Association, 1963, p.80.

[5]Haydon, p.21.

As Andrew Gulliford writes in *America's Country Schools*,

> The closing of one-room country schools forever changed the rural American landscape and diminished close community ties and a sense of social cohesion among rural Americans. Historian Wayne E. Fuller in *The Old Country School* (1982) acknowledges, "In all America there was, perhaps, no better symbol of the shared community life people remembered than the one-room schoolhouse standing in the center of an independent school district. ...The people of the district had voted for its construction, picked the place where it would stand and controlled its use when it was completed." He concludes: "At one stage or another of this process, they had, in most cases, even fought over it as families fight; yet it belonged to all the district's families, and because it was their own, most people in the community were interested in what took place there."[6]

The establishment of public education for all children in the Commonwealth of Virginia was the first building block in the State's educational system. Consolidation of the schools was the second block. Desegregation was the third.

---

[6] Gulliford, p.44.

"Snap the Whip" by Winslow Homer depicts a recess at an early one-room schoolhouse.

Chapter 8.
A SEGREGATED SYSTEM

Segregation was the way of education in the South since time immemorial. Black and white children were not educated together and, indeed, plantation owners who tried to teach their slaves were punished. Even following the Emancipation Proclamation, there was no equality in the education of the races. All the old school records refer to schools as either "white" or "colored". Although both were under the jurisdiction of the County and District School Boards as well as the Superintendent of Schools, this does not mean that they were treated equally.

From the beginning, the colored schools were more poorly equipped, were taught by teachers who usually did not have a college degree and who were paid less than their white counterparts. The colored schools were usually in session for terms shorter than those for the white children simply because there was not enough money to keep them open longer. When, in 1924, buses began to provide transportation for children going to school, it was only for white children. Young black students continued to walk often long distances along poor roads to get to their schoolhouse.

Taxes collected from the black community went more often for the white schools than for the colored schools, so the black communities in effect had to contribute twice (once in taxes and again in donations) to the county school funds. As James Anderson says in his book, *The Education of Blacks in the South,*

> In vital respects, the regionwide process of double taxation was an accommodation to the oppressive nature of southern society. It made the regular process of excluding black children from the benefits of tax-supported public education easier and more bearable for both whites and blacks. It said much about blacks' desire for education and their willingness to sacrifice for it, but it also said much about their powerlessness, their taxation without representation, and their oppression.[1]

The differences between the support given to the white schools and those for black children show up time and again in the lists of expenses incurred by the District School Boards in the county. For example, in 1892, the Brentsville District Board purchased maps, charts and dictionaries for six District schools: Brentsville, Nokesville, Greenwich, Vancluse/Hazelwood, Bristoe and Allendale—all white schools. Noticeably missing from the list is the Chinn Colored School. Similarly, in November of 1894 the Brentsville Board bought Kennedy Mathematical Blocks for all the District schools except #4, Chinn. Again, on January 27, 1896, the Board purchased seven sets of Primary Language study books although there were eight schools in the District, seven white and one colored. In April of 1899, seven Rand McNally maps of the United States in cases, seven maps of Virginia and seven maps of West Virginia were bought by the Board for a total of $161.91 (payable over two years). There were eight schools then, too.

Yet another example of the differences in the way white and colored schools were treated is found in minutes of the Brentsville District School Board

---

James D. Anderson. *The Education of Blacks in the South, 1860-1935,* Chapel Hill: University of North Carolina Press, 1988, pp.184-185.

from 1907. There it is recorded that the Board agreed to establish a colored school at Brentsville which was to be open for a five months' term with the teacher being paid $20 a month (white teachers at that time were paid $25 per month), providing the legal average daily attendance was maintained. "The patrons [were] to furnish building and furniture, wood and etc...."[2] No funds for the schoolhouse itself could be spared from the Board's budget. Yet at the same meeting, the Board approved the purchase of five new desks for the white Woodlawn School.

For more than half a century, funds to build and run the County schoolhouses were raised in large part from the citizens served by each school. It follows that in those communities where most citizens were poor, funds that could be spared for education amounted to less than in the more well-to-do and usually white areas. It does not ever appear that the desire for an education was less in the black communities; rather, their ability to raise funds was more limited. In report after report filed at the end of each school year by every teacher in the county, it was noted by the teachers of the colored schools that there were no books or, at best, very few books, in the libraries of their schools. They simply were beyond the means of the community which supported that school.

The inequities in the treatment of the schools continued well into the twentieth century. As late as 1959, when Mr. Russell Fincham, a black educator, was appointed to be principal of the Antioch-Macrae Elementary School, the discrimination persisted. Mr. Fincham, after teaching an entire school day, spent the rest of the day doing administrative business without the aid of either a secretary or a telephone. He even borrowed a truck from the County and drove, on his own free time, to Manhattan where a friend helped him secure textbooks which were more up to date than the ones supplied to his school by the County. "We definitely were way behind as far as other elementary schools, white schools, were concerned," Mr. Fincham later said.[3]

Figures from the 1906-07 school year show that it cost $303 per month to run a schoolhouse for white children. It cost $119 a month to run one for black children. This reflects the lower salaries paid to the teachers, the fewer months in which the schools were kept open and the scarcity of supplies purchased for those schools. There were, of course, some bright spots: special teachers whose worth was appreciated by the District Boards; groups of parents who worked particularly hard to provide for their children's needs in school; schoolhouses kept immaculate in spite of poor conditions. Hot lunches were being served in six of the colored schools by the 1930s, with the co-operation of the County welfare agency, to provide help for undernourished children. Also, by that time, every colored school[4] except for Thornton and Neabsco had a Community School League, a group of supporters who worked to improve the quality of education for their children in a number of ways. They purchased a library for each school and enlarged those buildings which were overcrowded (remember, consolidation did not include the colored schools at first). They raised funds to build a new schoolhouse when the County School Board would not agree to do so and to make salaries available to teachers so they could keep the schools open longer. Beautification of school grounds was traditionally the work of all the Community Leagues, both white and black. In addition, every colored school had a Junior League solely for activities for the students.

While white teachers almost always were high school graduates by the 1920s, it took a little longer before the same could be said for the black teachers. Even as late as 1920, few held high school diplomas. Many of those who did were graduates of the Manassas Industrial School for Colored Youth, founded by Miss Jennie Dean. There were exceptions, of course. Teacher training for those black students who wanted it and could afford it was available in Washington, DC at Minor College; at Virginia State College in Hampton; and at St. Paul Normal and Industrial School in Lawrenceville, Virginia. As the century moved on, most of the black teachers in Prince William County were graduates of one of these institutions. The holding of an ad-

---

[2]Brentsville District School Board minutes of October 4, 1907, p.274.

[3]Alexandra Stoddard. "Four teachers were in the vanguard of change in schools", *The Potomac News*, February 11, 1993, p.C3

[4]White schools had Community Leagues too but they did not have to use their funds in quite the same ways. Schoolhouses and their furnishings were provided for them by the District School Boards. This sometimes was the case for the black schools but not always.

vanced degree did not seem to change the salaries any, either of white or black teachers. Neither did years of experience seem to play any role in the salary scale. For example, during the 1925-26 school year, white female teachers were paid salaries ranging from $65 to $85 a month for the term of eight months. Black male and female teachers were paid $60, or rarely $65, a month for a seven months' term. If there were white male teachers, none filed a year end report. Interestingly, figures for 1933 show that white female teachers earned more per year than did white males ($693.50 vs. $675) and both earned more than black teachers ($400 for a male, $392.02 for a female). This flies in the face of most figures from other parts of the country where males earned more than females no matter what race.

A frequent complaint of the black teachers was the failure of school officials to visit their schoolhouses during the school year. School Superintendents, therefore, did not see the great needs of the children or the difficult conditions under which some teachers worked. This lack of visitation is not explained; it apparently was "the way things were". Because the black people were not allowed to vote, they had no say in who represented them either on the Board of Supervisors or the School Boards (both District and County).

Hopefully things began to improve after 1916 when the County School Board approved the expenditure of $60 a month for the salary of a Colored Supervisor of Rural Schools. This salary was raised to $100 a month the following year.

If sufficient help for the colored schools could not come from within the communities, and did not come from the District or County Boards, it did come from benefactors outside the State. Two particular sources of funds stand out. For many years, The Friends Society for the Aid and Education of the Freedman, a Quaker group from Philadelphia, had sent funds for the education of black children. When the schools became public in 1870, the Manassas District School Board wrote to the Friends and asked if they would continue to fund the colored school. They agreed and their gifts paid for teacher salaries, among other things, for many years. The section about the Brown School in Manassas has more information about this interesting relationship.

Secondly, beginning in 1914, some help came from Mr. Rosenwald, the multi-millionaire owner of Sears-Roebuck Company. When the members of the black community were able to buy land on which to build a school (land later donated to the County for that purpose) and raise some funds toward its building, additional money from the Rosenwald Fund was then donated and, along with public tax funds collected from black taxpayers of the community, was used to erect the building.

These schoolhouses were available only to the black communities and there were major conditions which had to be met. First, the rules said that "that the sites and buildings of all schools aided by the Fund shall be the property of the public school authorities," and, secondly, "that, in providing these buildings, it is a condition precedent to receiving the aid of the Fund that the people of the several communities shall secure, from other sources: to wit—from public school funds, private contributions, etc., an amount equal to or greater than that provided by the Fund."[5] Thus, the black communities had to donate money, land, time and labor in order for their children to receive "public" education. Between 1914 and 1927, Rosenwald money helped to build (by paying an average of 17% of the total cost) 306 schoolhouses in the Commonwealth of Virginia.

While many parts of the South failed to provide any schooling for the black children of the communities, this does not seem to be the case in Prince William County. Though the colored schools were physically inferior to their white counterparts, as noted above, there were schools available. By 1875, five years after the County began its public elementary school system, there were ten schools for white children and three for black children. By the turn of the century, there were forty-nine white schools and thirteen schools for the black population. Twenty years later, there were forty-five schools for whites, twelve for black children; by 1935, the numbers had reflected the effects of consolidation of the white schools which now numbered nineteen while there were still twelve schools for black children. In most cases, the colored schools had to serve a larger population of children than did those for white students. The following table, based on figures for 1900 as supplied by the then Superintendent of Schools Dr. H.M. Clarkson, illustrates this point:

---

[5]Anderson, p.159.

District	School Population			# of Schools		
	White	Colored	Total	White	Colored	Total
Brentsville	513	111	624	8	1	9
Coles	428	32	460	8	0	8
Dumfries	369	162	531	8	2	10
Gainesville	538	436	974	9	5	14
Manassas	812	369	1181	9	4	13

These figures remained much the same until consolidation in 1923 reduced the number of schools for white children. This did not reduce the number of teachers for those pupils; it merely increased the number of classrooms in the schools built as center or consolidated schoolhouses in the various districts of the county.

In 1954, the Supreme Court's decision in "Brown vs the Board of Education" that "separate but equal" education was unconstitutional was the beginning of the end for the County's segregated school system. The County School Board decided to comply with the order for integration by offering black students the option to attend the school of their choice. Not surprisingly, no black students chose to attend traditionally white schools. Indeed, it was five years before a black student entered a school she wanted to attend, rather than one she was assigned to attend.[6]

By 1964, seven county schools were integrated. That year, President Lyndon Johnson signed into law the Civil Rights Act which threatened to cut off all school funding unless desegregation was successfully implemented. To comply fully with the law, Superintendent of Schools Stuart Beville began to integrate the school faculties. In mid-1965 he assigned four women educators from traditionally black schools to teach at four white County schools (Featherstone, Loch Lomond and Dumfries Elementary Schools and Fred Lynn Middle School). With understandable trepidation, the women undertook their new assignments and the transfer was successful.

The student bodies, however, remained largely segregated. It was not until the 1966-67 school year, when students were assigned to schools on a regional basis, that the three remaining colored schools in the County (Antioch-Macrae, Washington-Reid and Jennie Dean) finally became desegregated. The following year, school population figures showed that there were 24,927 white students and 1,358 black students enrolled in Prince William County schools. The minority students were certainly at a disadvantage; for example, because of their small numbers they were not able to get elected to school or club offices.[7] Still, it is generally agreed that the transition was a peaceful one, although problems remained and are still unsolved today. In an interview in 1993, retired teacher and principal, Russell Fincham said, "You can desegregate, but it's hard to integrate. You can say we desegregated back in 1966 but we still have a ways to go....We aren't there yet."[8]

---

[6] That student was Joyce Russell, who chose to attend Gar-Field High School. At the same time, her younger brother enrolled in Occoquan Elementary School. The two were responsible for the official integration of Prince William County Schools. The year was 1961.

[7] For further information on the integration of Prince William County, see "Learning Together" in the Lifestyles section of *The Potomac News* of February 10 and 11, 1993, written by Alexandra Stoddard and Chris LeSonde.

[8] Stoddard, p.5.

Chapter 9.
ONE HUNDRED YEARS AGO

When all the available information about the early schools in Prince William County is put together, the differences between the schools of 1893 and those one hundred years later make an interesting study. No judgment is being made. The schools were run by concerned citizens and teachers then as they are now. It is simply the contrasts which are fascinating.

Much use has been made in this book of the "Administrative Survey of the Public School System in Prince William, Virginia", written in 1935 as a Master's thesis by the then Superintendent of Schools, Richard C. Haydon. His figures and evaluations of the schools in 1933 and 1934 have been invaluable in seeing an overall picture of the system as he viewed it. The annual report of the Prince William County Superintendent of Schools for the 1892-93 school year, Mr. H. M. Clarkson[1] makes equally interesting reading about the County schools one hundred years ago.

At that time, there were no public secondary schools but there were fifty-four public elementary schools, forty-one for white children and thirteen for black.[2] Fifty of these schools were one-room frame buildings; one was a one-room log cabin; three were graded schools. The three graded schools (Ruffner and Brown in Manassas and Occoquan in the Occoquan District) had two grades with one teacher for each grade. There were no schools built of either stone or brick at that time. Only thirty-seven of the schoolhouses had outhouses although none had indoor plumbing. Forty-seven had what the Superintendent called "suitable grounds"; forty-seven, but not the same forty-seven, had "good furniture". The total value of the buildings owned by all the Districts combined was $15,100. All schools were open, on average, almost six months during the year though generally the white schools were open longer and the colored schools had shorter school years.

In 1893 only 57% of the eligible white children attended school. Those 1,540 children were taught by fourteen white male and twenty-eight white female teachers with an average class size of thirty-five students.[3] On the other hand, 559 black children, 45% of those eligible, were taught by three black men and ten black women for an average of forty-three students per teacher. In 1993, with compulsory education a law, all children attend school but there are no figures available showing the percentage which attend public, as opposed to private or home, schools.

Teacher salaries, in 1893, were calculated on a monthly basis because the schools ran on a month to month schedule. Colored schools were open fewer months than were white schools but there was little uniformity in the length of the school year among any of the schools.[4] Community desires as well as enrollment figures determined when the term started and ended. At that time, white female teachers were paid the highest salary, $24.90 on a monthly average. White males earned a monthly salary of $24.12. Black teachers of both sexes were paid less than their white counterparts in all cases. Today, teachers' salaries are computed on a yearly basis; the average teacher salary in Prince William County in 1993 was $36,540 per year.

---

[1] Mr. Clarkson served as Superintendent of Prince William County schools from 1891-1905.

[2] In 1993 there are thirty-nine public elementary schools in Prince William County.

[3] Some children continued to be educated either at home or in privately run schools. Some did not attend any school at all.

[4] The average school year lasted six months for white schools, five for colored, but those figures reflect variations of up to two months.

On an average daily basis, only 72% of the white and 61% of the black children actually enrolled in school attended. This was fortunate because the total seating capacity in the white schools was 1,520 while that of the colored schools was 350. A serious overcrowding problem would have occurred, particularly in the colored schools, had all those enrolled attended. In 1993, of the children who were enrolled in Prince William County's elementary schools, better than 95% attended regularly.[5]

Students in 1893 ranged in age from three-and-a-half to eighteen years of age, all studying in the same classroom. Parents generally supplied their children with books but in the 1892-93 school year six white children were helped by the County School Board, at a total cost of $2.28. In contrast, the textbook rental fees for elementary school children in 1993 was $11.00 per child.

As noted earlier in the chapter on School Districts, in 1892 the school system was divided into seven Districts—Dumfries, Occoquan, Coles, Manassas, Gainesville, Potomac, and Brentsville—as well as the Manassas Town District. This District separated from Manassas District #5 because of struggles between the Manassas Town Council and the District Board of Education over control of the two schools within the city, Ruffner and Brown. The Manassas Town District existed from September of 1890 to July of 1894 and was referred to as District #8. The two districts then ran their schools cooperatively until February 1896 when the Virginia General Assembly abolished District #8 following several legal battles.

Funds to run the schools during the 1892-93 school year came from several sources, as is the case today. An accounting of funds available to the County schools one-hundred years ago follows:

State Funds = $5594.94
County Funds = $2434.01 (from taxes)
District Funds = $1730.18 (from District levies)[6]
Other Funds = $111.03 (investments, donations, etc.)

For the 1992-93 school year, comparable figures[7] read:

Federal Funds = $6,184,755
  (note that Federal Funds were not available in 1892-93)
State Funds = $102,672,878
County Funds = $136,045,472
From previous year's budget = $7,994,938
Other = $1,410,755

The total figure of $254,308,798 for 1992-93 reflects available revenue for both elementary and secondary schools as well as special education facilities. One hundred years ago, there were no public secondary or special education schools in the county so all monies went to elementary education alone.

The 1892-93 year was typical of most years of the county public education system during the twenty years or so surrounding the turn of the century. Numbers varied, of course, but at least until 1906 when secondary schools were added to the public school system, basically little changed. Funding was always difficult but so was transportation and communication between the administrative center and the outlying schoolhouses. Keeping enrollment figures high enough to warrant the maintaining of a school in some communities was a continual struggle. Lack of materials and books made teaching difficult. Both teachers and pupils often had to travel long distances to attend school and some found it necessary to board away from their families during the week because of that. Nevertheless, the system survived and grew. Problems were solved, at least temporarily, and children were educated.

The problems faced by the educators of today are not the same problems faced one hundred years ago, of course. Sheer numbers—21,709 elementary school students enrolled in 1992-93—account for many of the difficult situations encountered by teachers and administrators today, but problems are problems, and the schools have had to deal with them throughout the County's history. Despite them all, and despite the great changes in Prince William County's public school system during the 124 years of its existence, the basic goals of the public school system remain the same, even after one hundred years.

---

[5] Prince William County Public Schools Report No. SBCORD, "Cumulative ADA and ADM for the Year", June 23, 1993.

[6] Superintendent of Schools Clarkson noted in his 1892-93 report that Potomac District #7 was not represented at meetings of the County School Board although the other Districts regularly sent one their members. Potomac District did not respond to repeated written requests by the Superintendent for an Annual Report so no numbers from that District could be figured into his year-end report.

[7] Prince William County Public Schools. "Basic Information for FY 1993", Prince William County, Virginia, June 1993.

Chapter 10.
MYSTERY SCHOOLHOUSES

In almost every School District in Prince William County, there seem to have been "mystery schoolhouses", ones which survive as casual references but never appear in official lists of schools. Sometimes, they are one sentence entries in District School Board minutes which do not get mentioned again. Occasionally, a year end report of a school will show up, but nowhere is that school talked about in Board minutes or Superintendents' lists or anyone's memories. In several instances, a school is indicated on the 1901 Brown map of Prince William County but no other reference to it was ever found. Were it not for the briefest mention on a scrap of paper, these schools would be totally lost to history. What happened to them? Did they actually exist and function? Were these colloquial names for schools which later became known by another name? Were they, perhaps, one room set aside in a church or assembly hall or home which lasted one year before a "real" school could be built? Did a community simply establish its own school before the District Board could be persuaded of the necessity of a school in that area? Possibly they were private institutions which never became part of the public school system. Present resources do not give answers, but to make this account as complete as possible, those mysteries are included here along with what little information has been found. They are also included, in most cases, in the chapter about the District in which they were found but, in the hope of jogging the memory of a reader who can fill in some gaps, they are set apart in this special chapter. Maybe hearing their names will bring to mind a lost record book, or a personal recollection, or an old report card in a trunk in the attic. The author hopes so.

During the time period when these "mystery schoolhouses" existed, the county was divided into school districts which governed the educational system of Prince William County. The little known schools were found in four of those districts—all but Occoquan and Gainesville—and they are gathered together here under the district in which they were apparently located.

BRENTSVILLE DISTRICT

In the very first entry of the minutes of the Brentsville District School Board on December 3, 1870, mention is made of a **"Colored School near Fleetwood"**. No map shows such a school and there is no further talk of it in the Board minutes. Even in later years, no colored school was established in that area. Was this a privately run school for the black children of the area which the School Board did not take into the public system?

During that first meeting of the Brentsville Board, the trustees also talk of a school "in a house near Manuel's". More than one Manuel owned property in the Nokesville and Parkgate areas of the District but no schoolhouse is shown on any of them. Since there is no more talk of such a school in the minutes, it is impossible to definitively say if **Manuel's School** became another school when a suitable building was erected, but it is true that a Mr. Manuel owned a piece of land near the later site of the Allendale School.[1] Perhaps Manuel's School evolved into the Allendale School although no defi-

---

[1] William H. Brown's map of Prince William County, drawn in 1901 from U.S. Geological Survey "and other data and corrected with the assistance of reliable residents of the County", shows that P. Manuel and G. Manuel were landowners in the mid-county area where the school supposedly existed.

nite link appears in School Board minutes which usually follow the lineage fairly clearly.

In March of 1872, District Board minutes record that the school trustees ordered that a school be established at **Hershey's Shop** which would receive immediate repairs to make it suitable for a classroom. The Reverend Mr. Hershey was appointed as the teacher for a salary of $25 per month. The name Hershey appears on the 1901 county map at a site on Aden Road at the juncture with the old Law's Ford Road about a mile northwest of the community called Aden but whether this was the location of the Shop is unknown. Its name never is mentioned again. It is not even known whether or not such a schoolhouse was ever opened.

To add to the mystery, in January 1874, a **Chapel Colored School** is alluded to but it is never referred to again. Could this be the same school as Hershey's? In other words, could the Reverend Hershey's school been known as the Chapel School because he was a man of the cloth? There were several churches in the area; was this school held in the chapel of one of them? Was his school one for black children? His salary of $25 a month was the salary paid to white teachers but perhaps the Brentsville District Board paid him the same. Those questions remain unanswered.

Then, in June of 1874, the Board minutes say that "Colored School House #2" was built with District Funds. This apparently was the beginning of the Chinn School which became #4 in the District. The number two may have meant that there was already one colored school in the Brentsville District but which one was it? Hershey's? Chapel Colored? Another one altogether?

In August 1876, another mystery comes to light. On that date, the Brentsville Board opened a school in a house belonging to F. W. Holmes. They paid $4.50 a month for the use of the room and appropriated $2 for a cord of wood to heat the building. Miss Fannie E. Taylor was appointed as the teacher. The Board minutes go on to locate the school as being across from Belle Haven. That is the location of the **Holmes School** but a school by that name is only mentioned during the 1876 school term. Then it comes up again in the Dumfries District where it remained opened using the name of the Belle Haven School until 1927. Are these the same schools? Did the District boundaries change or become better defined? The Holmes area was quite a distance from the present limits of the Brentsville District.

The Prince William County School Board minutes of March 2, 1874 refer to **Snephen Springs School #5**. The teacher, Miss Wakeman, was having difficulty maintaining the necessary enrollment figure for those years of fifteen. Since no other mention is made of such a school, it seems likely that the writer meant the **Sulphur Springs School #5**. The Clerk of the County School Board at that time was a Manassas resident who probably had never seen the school and was not familiar with its name since it was not in his District.

COLES DISTRICT

The Coles District also had its "mystery school," **Horton**. Again, the only mention of it was found on the 1901 Brown map. There are no written records of the school, but there have been no School Board minutes found from the Coles District at all. Perhaps this mystery would be solved if those records ever come to light.

DUMFRIES DISTRICT

Another District which had "mystery schools" was Dumfries. The only reference to a **Mt. Pleasant School** is found on the 1901 map of Prince William County done by Brown. It was located about two miles south of Dumfries on the east side of what was then known as the King's Highway. The site of the schoolhouse, about one mile north of the settlement of Forestburg at the junction of the King's Highway and Forest (Joplin) Road, indicates that it probably served that community. The school does not appear on any listings of County schools nor are there records of any kind for it. Its opening date, its closing date, the makeup of its students are all unknown. Did it later become known by another, more common, name?

According to the County School Board minutes of October 4, 1883[2], a **Greenwood School** had opened for the school year. That is the only official reference to a school of that name. It does not appear on any map, or any listing of schoolhouses and it is not mentioned again in those School Board min-

---

[2]Minutes of the Prince William County School Board covering the years 1872-1921, p.101.

utes. Those same minutes of October 4, 1883 report that a special committee recommended that a new school in the Dumfries District be built "upon the Telegraph Road, on the farm known as Round Top, about four hundred yards from the ford of Powell's run, on laid road...."[3] No **Round Top School** appears on the 1901 map nor does the location match that of any known schoolhouse. It is possible that this could be the Greenwood School, but the wording indicates that the schoolhouse had not yet been built on October 4, 1883, when the Greenwood School opened. Whatever happened to it is another mystery.

The **Wakefield School** is yet another relatively unknown schoolhouse in the Dumfries District. It is not even known if it was a private or public school. The only mention made of the "old Wakefield school" is in a County Deed Book of 1885 which records the purchase of land for the Minnieville School near the site of the school. Minnieville was located where what is now Cardinal Drive forked to go either to Dumfries or Neabsco Mills, so apparently the Wakefield School was situated there too.

To round out the list for Dumfries, the list of "mystery schools" must include the **Nelson School**. As was often the case, only the 1901 map of the County mentions this schoolhouse, located within the present boundaries of Prince William Forest Park.

MANASSAS DISTRICT

Some mystery or uncertainty surrounds the existence of the **Stone House School**. Only two brief references to such a school were found in the minutes of Manassas District School Board[4] and the Manassas Battlefield Park has no information about it. Local residents do not recall it, yet it did exist. Why the mystery?

---

[3]Prince William County School Board minutes covering the years 1872-1921, p.101.

[4]August 10, 1916 and May 15, 1918.

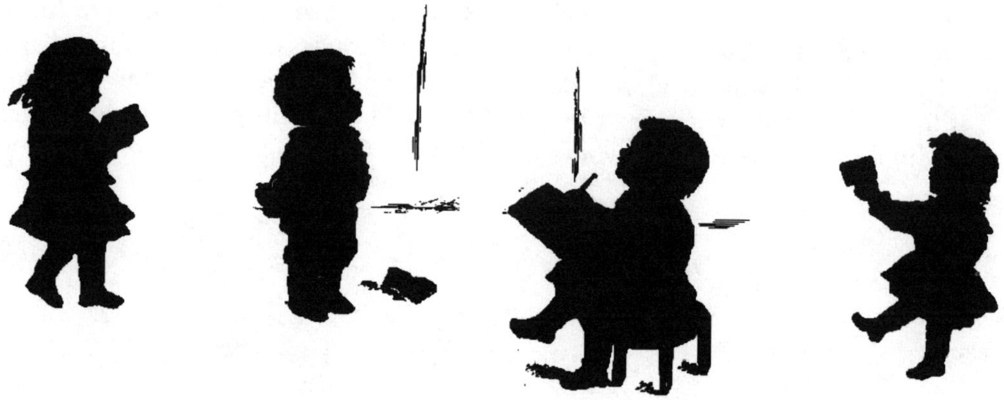

Chapter 11.
CURRICULUM AND TEXTBOOKS

Children in the small county schools were taught according to their abilities rather than by grade level. Sitting two at a desk, they shared what textbooks were available. The curriculum for each child was prepared to meet his or her individual needs and progression occurred when a child was ready. In a small classroom, it was inevitable that a child would hear each lesson several times. He would hear it when older students recited for the teacher in front of the room and he would get it, later, in his own lessons. It was not uncommon for some children to get to the fifth or sixth level already familiar with the material presented there. It was individualized instruction at its best, or at least at the teacher's best.

Reading, grammar and spelling, history and geography and arithmetic were the major components of the curriculum in Prince William County's early schools. Textbooks were chosen by the County School Board, not without discussion and disagreements as School Board minutes show, but purchased by the students. They were often passed down through families or sold to younger students. Because books were scarce, particularly in the earliest days of the public schools, rote memorization was a common learning technique. This was especially true in arithmetic where students were drilled daily in addition, subtraction and multiplication tables. Figuring in one's head was an admired skill; today's students must "show all work" in order to earn credit for it.

In the earliest years of the schools, several texts were commonly used in the schools. The youngest pupils learned from primers before they moved on to readers. The most famous readers of all were the McGuffey Eclectic Readers, first published in 1836 and used, not only in Prince William County schools but across the nation, for nearly a century. Besides a Primer, there were six levels of McGuffey Readers, the last of which would challenge a high school student today. A good description of the Readers comes from Stanley Lindberg in his 1976 book, *The Annotated McGuffey*:

> First of all, the Readers were not graded for what we conceive of as "first grade", "second grade", etc. They were simply arranged in order of increasing difficulty. Most classes were held in one-room schoolhouses (with children from six to the late teens under a single teacher), and every child used the First Reader until he or she qualified for the Second, which might have been at age seven or possibly as late as fourteen. The length of the school year was not the same for all pupils, since many children simply could not attend during harvesting season or spring planting.... Most nineteenth-century students finished at least the Second Reader, but many left school permanently before completing the Third. For many years anyone who had finished the Fourth Reader was considered very well educated indeed.[1]

McGuffey's Readers were not the only books used for language studies in the early Prince William County schools. Webster's blue spelling book and Murray's English grammar text were also employed for many years. In 1878, the County School Board added Ellsworth's *Writing Books* to the curriculum.

---

[1] As quoted by Elizabeth Harrover Johnson in *Sea-Change*, Princeton, NJ: Pennywitt Press, 1977, p.44.

While primers and readers were the basis for classroom learning, they were not the only textbooks used in the County schools. In 1877, the County School Board formally adopted Mary Tucker McGill's (Magill's) *A History of Virginia for the Use of Schools* as the approved text on that subject. Matthew Fontaine Maury's *Geography* was used in most schools as was Holmes' *U.S. History*, which was replaced in 1878 by Blackburn and McDonald's *U.S. History*.

In 1900, the County School Board, using a list of approved texts from the State Board of Education, voted on the books to be adopted by the County. While not every book suggested by the State was accepted, most were and they formed the nucleus of the curriculum for several years.[2] Pupils were to be provided with a list of those which they would be using during the school year so that the parents could purchase them. The books accepted into the County curriculum were at that time were:

Johnson's *Primer*
Merrill's *Speller*
Johnson's Series of Readers
Warren Colburn's *Intellectual Arithmetic*
Venable's *New Elementary Arithmetic*
Venable's *Practical Arithmetic*
Hyde's *Practical Lessons in the Use of English*
Hyde's *Practical English Grammar*
Whitney and Lockwood's *English Grammar*
Maury's *Elementary Geography*
Maury's *Manual of Geography*
Magill's *History of Virginia*
Lee's *Primary History of U.S.*
Jones's *School History of U.S.*
Natural System of Vertical Writing
Smithdeal's Slant Copy Books
Cutter's *Beginner's, Intermediate and Comprehensive Physiology*
Paul Bert's *First Steps in Scientific Knowledge*
Worcester's *Dictionaries*
Thompson's *New Short Course in Drawing*
Riverside Literature Series

McGuffey's Readers do not appear. For the first time in nearly one hundred years of private and public education, they were replaced by "more modern" texts. The list also shows the first appearance of science and physiology textbooks. According to Andrew Gulliford in *America's Country Schools*, "Physiology texts appear to have been a concession by public schools to the growing temperance movement, although many also stressed the evils of tobacco."[3] Hygiene also was an integral part of the early curriculum in the County schools, but apparently no book was used.

In 1907, the first Course of Study for elementary schools was prescribed by the Virginia State Board of Education. While not all teachers in the County used it, it became increasingly popular and was in general use by the 1920s. In 1932, that course of study was felt to be "too traditional" by the State, so all counties in Virginia which had school supervision, as did Prince William County, were asked to study new concepts being considered. Work on this new curriculum continued for another two years when what was called The New Course of Study was approved. Prince William County became part of the field testing group for this new curriculum. Five teachers were chosen to try it, send in reports and recommend innovations. In 1935, the number of teachers trying out the New Course increased but according to then Superintendent of Schools, Richard C. Haydon, immediate acceptance throughout the County was impossible. A large number of the small one- and two-room schools held back from using it because it was difficult for just one or two teachers to be qualified as an expert in all the fields—music, art and drama as well as the traditional subjects— required of them. A lack of the books needed for the New Course was another problem, especially for the small schoolhouses (and particularly the small colored schools) although the School Board and Community Leagues were assisting as much as possible, according to Haydon.

An account of an exhibit of elementary school work[4] which appeared on page one in *The Manassas Journal* of May 11, 1933 gives a good idea of what the schools were teaching then. The show was held in the Manassas High School gymnasium and

---

[2]It is interesting to note that, with the exception of a few books adopted by unanimous vote of the Board, every one of the books supported by Mr. George C. Round was rejected.

---

[3]Andrew Gulliford. *America's Country Schools*. Washington, DC: Preservation Press, 1991, p.56.

[4]At least it was an exhibit of the work of white elementary schools. No colored schools participated.

attracted visitors from every corner of the County. The bold type is the addition of this author.

CHILDREN SHOW SCHOOL WORK

Exhibit Large and Better Than Ever

The exhibits at the gymnasium last Saturday were the most complete that has yet been placed before the eyes of admiring friends and patrons.

The prevailing scheme was that of nature with considerable stress on the progress of transportation.

Purcell featured a Japanese scene, showing burden carriers, houses, bridges, etc.

Aden's exhibit was an Indian tepee and bird house.

Hickory Grove's exhibit was again splendid for a one-room school. The showing of progress of transportation was very complete and educational while a side project dealing with "Neighbors" was done equally well. The table carrying "carriers" was furnished with articles made mostly by the children, illustrating passage on both land and sea.

Woodbine had a farm scene and a circus.

Greenwich dealt with birds and the Spring. The sand table had scenes of settler days and also a bird scene.

Gold Ridge had something out [of] the usual with "Ye Old Quaint Shop," pretty in its setting and sure enough quaint in its presentation. The lower section of this was a cross section of a farm house. Their sand table was a complete exhibition of comforts for birds, fountains, rests, houses, etc.

Forest Hill majored on bird life, with a rural scene for the sand table.

Quantico stepped out [of] line with a railroad station and a real train on a track. It was quite realistic. The sand table carried a number of carved figures made from bar soap. No other school had anything like this exhibit.

Bethel also had a tepee and stressed wild life.

Buckhall fancied the Japanese idea and had a very pretty little exhibit very much like that of Purcell.

Occoquan took its place with the leaders for a most extensive array. This school with Dumfries, Bennett and Nokesville had the largest displays. Their main features were a Japanese village, and a rural scene, both of which were very complete in scope.

Brentsville went back to the days of Noah for a start and put an Ark in its exhibit.

The bird sanctuary of **Catharpin** was one to catch the eye, being about as pretty as anything on the floor.

Right next door was **Dumfries** with "Animal Park," an exhibit that showed much patient labor. This school had the only exhibit under glass, a Chinese scene showing agricultural work, with beautiful mountain scenery in the background.

Woodlawn showed a farm house (the Wee-wee house).

Bennett had probably the most extensive showing. First there was an old plantation scene, with darkies, mansion house, etc; next modern and colonial transportation; then a modern country home, with flagstone walk, trees, birds, etc., all exceedingly pretty; next a village, quite detailed; then a desert settlement, with cactus plant; then a table for a circus, and lastly, one for bird life.

Haymarket featured transportation and pets, the latter being shown in their cages. They also had a Dutch scene, with windmill, very well executed.

Bristow stressed composition work; **Cherry Hill**, bird life, and **Hayfield**, geography, accompanied by a quaint little merry-go-round.

In addition to the above, all the schools also had some sort of art exhibit. It must have been quite a show.

Textbooks are continually changing in today's schools. The use of television, calculators, computers, video cameras and the like brings the world to children quickly, globally, easily. The curriculum is "developed" to address problems faced by the modern child at the beginning of the twenty-first century. Yet, when all is said and done, it is the classroom teacher and a supportive community which determine the success of any educational system. It has always been that way.

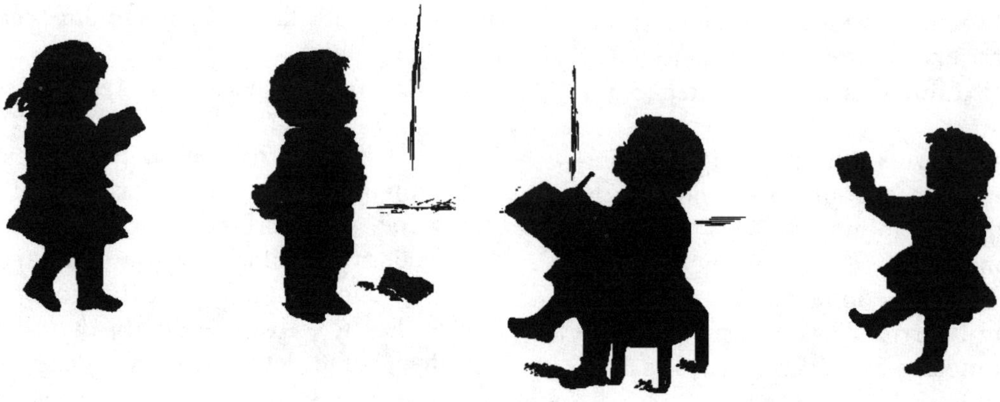

Part II:

The Schoolhouses

*Brentsville School, the last of Prince William County's one-room schools to close.
Drawn by Richard Fravel.*

ALPHABETICAL LIST OF THE SCHOOLS

Aden School
Allendale School
Antioch (Murray) School
Antioch-Macrae School
Antioch-North Fork School—
 see Antioch (Murray) School
Bacon Race School
Baileysburg School
Baldwin School
Bel Air Elementary School
Belle Haven School—see Holmes School
Belmont Elementary School
Bennett School
Bethel School
Bethlehem School
Bradley School
Brentsville Colored School
Brentsville White School
Brentsville District High School—
 see Nokesville School
Bristoe (Bristow) School
Brown School
Buckhall School—see Oak Hill (Hammett) School
Buckland School
Cabin Branch (old) School
Clarkson School—see Cabin Branch (old) School
Cabin Branch School—see Cabin Branch (old) School
Cannon Branch School
Catharpin School
Cherry Hill (Dumfries District) School
Cherry Hill (Occoquan District) School
Chinn (Marstellar) School/(Kettle Run)
Coles School
Dale City Elementary School
Dean (Jennie Dean) School
Dumfries School

Emory Chapel School
English Church (Red School, Sunnyside) School
Fairview (Hedges) School
Fayman School
Featherstone Elementary School
Florence School—see Thornton (Florence) School
Forest Hill School
Fred Lynn Elementary School
Gainesville School
Gold Ridge School
Greenwich School
Greenwood School
Groveton (Brownsville) School
Hayfield School
Haymarket School
Hazelwood School—see Sulphur Springs
Hickory Grove (Oak Grove) School
Hickory Ridge School
Holmes School
Joplin School—see Forest Hill
Kettle Run School
Kilby (R. Dean) School—see Marumsco School
King's Crossroads (Herring) School
Loch Lomond School
Lucasville School
Macrae (McCrae) School
Manassas Park Elementary School
Manassas Village School
Manley School
Marumsco Elementary School
Marumsco Hills Elementary School
McGregor (Roy's) School
Mill Park School
Minnieville Elementary School
Mt. Pleasant School
Mt. Zion School

55

Neabsco Elementary School
Nelson School
Nokesville School
North Fork School
Oak Hill (Hammett) School
Occoquan/Occoquan District (Occoquan) School
Orlando School
Parkside Elementary School
Piney Branch (Red Hill #2) School—
    see Red Hill School
Pittsylvannia School
Potomac View Elementary School
Purcell School
Quantico Colored School
Quantico White School
Red Hill School
Red Shoals School
Rippon Elementary School
Ruffner School—see Manassas Village School
Sinclair Elementary School
Smithfield School
Stone House School
Sulphur Springs (Towle's Gate) School
Summitt School
Thornton (Elliott, Catharpan Colored) School
Thornton (Florence) School
Thoroughfare Colored School
Thoroughfare White School
Triangle Elementary School
Tyler Elementary School
VanCluse School—see Sulphur Springs School
Vaughan Elementary School
Wakefield School
Washington-Reid School
Waterfall School
Wellington School
Westgate School
Woodbine School
Woodbridge School
Woodlawn School
Yorkshire School

CHRONOLOGICAL LIST OF SCHOOLS BY DISTRICTS

BRENTSVILLE DISTRICT SCHOOLS, 1869-1969

Brentsville School	1871-1944*
Nokesville/Brentsville District High/ Nokesville	1870-present*
Red Shoals School	1870-1886
English Church (Red School, Sunnyside) School	1886-1901*
Sulphur Springs(Towle's Gate)/ Vancluse/Hazelwood	1871-1908
Orlando School	1872-1932**
Baileysburg School	1882-1884
Chinn(Marstellar) School	1874-1896
Bristoe School	1877-1936
Allendale School	1884-1908
Kettle Run School	1888-1938
King's Crossroads(Herring) School	1895-1926
Woodlawn School	1899-1935
Greenwich School	1901-1944
Aden School	1897-1946*
Brentsville Colored School	1909-1918

*Still standing

**First building standing

COLES DISTRICT SCHOOLS, 1869-1969

Gold Ridge School	1874-1932
Hayfield School	1881-1935
Purcell School	188?-1933*
Smithfield School	189?-1930
Woodbine School	189?-present*
Horton School	189?-1906?
Fayman School	190?-1931
Coles Elementary	1955-present*

*Still standing

DUMFRIES DISTRICT SCHOOLS, 1869-1969

Dumfries School	1873?-present*
Wakefield School	1870s
Greenwood School	1883-1899?
Forest Hill/Joplin School	1885-1938
Minnieville School	1886-1931
Cabin Branch(Old)/Clarkson/ Cabin Branch School	1889-1950
Thornton(Florence) School	1890-1930
Holmes/Belle Haven School	1895?-1927
Mt. Pleasant School	Late 19th- early 20th c
Nelson School	c.1900
Cherry Hill School	1900's-1939*
Neabsco School	1901?-1939
Quantico Colored School	1910-1939
Quantico White School	1910?-1956*
Mt. Zion School	1925-1928
Hickory Ridge School	1933-1943?
Washington-Reid School	1950-present*
Triangle Elementary	1959-present*

GAINESVILLE DISTRICT SCHOOLS, 1869-1969

Buckland School	1870-1924
Antioch(Murray)/Antioch/ Antioch-Northfork	1871?-1953
Waterfall School	1871?-1927*
Macrae(McCrae) School	187?-1953
Red Hill/Piney Branch (Red Hill #2) School	1870s-1920s
Catharpin School	1874-1936*
Gainesville School	1875?-present*
Hickory Grove(Oak Grove) School	1877-1935*
Thornton (Elliott, Catharpin Colored)	1877-1938

57

Yesterday's Schools

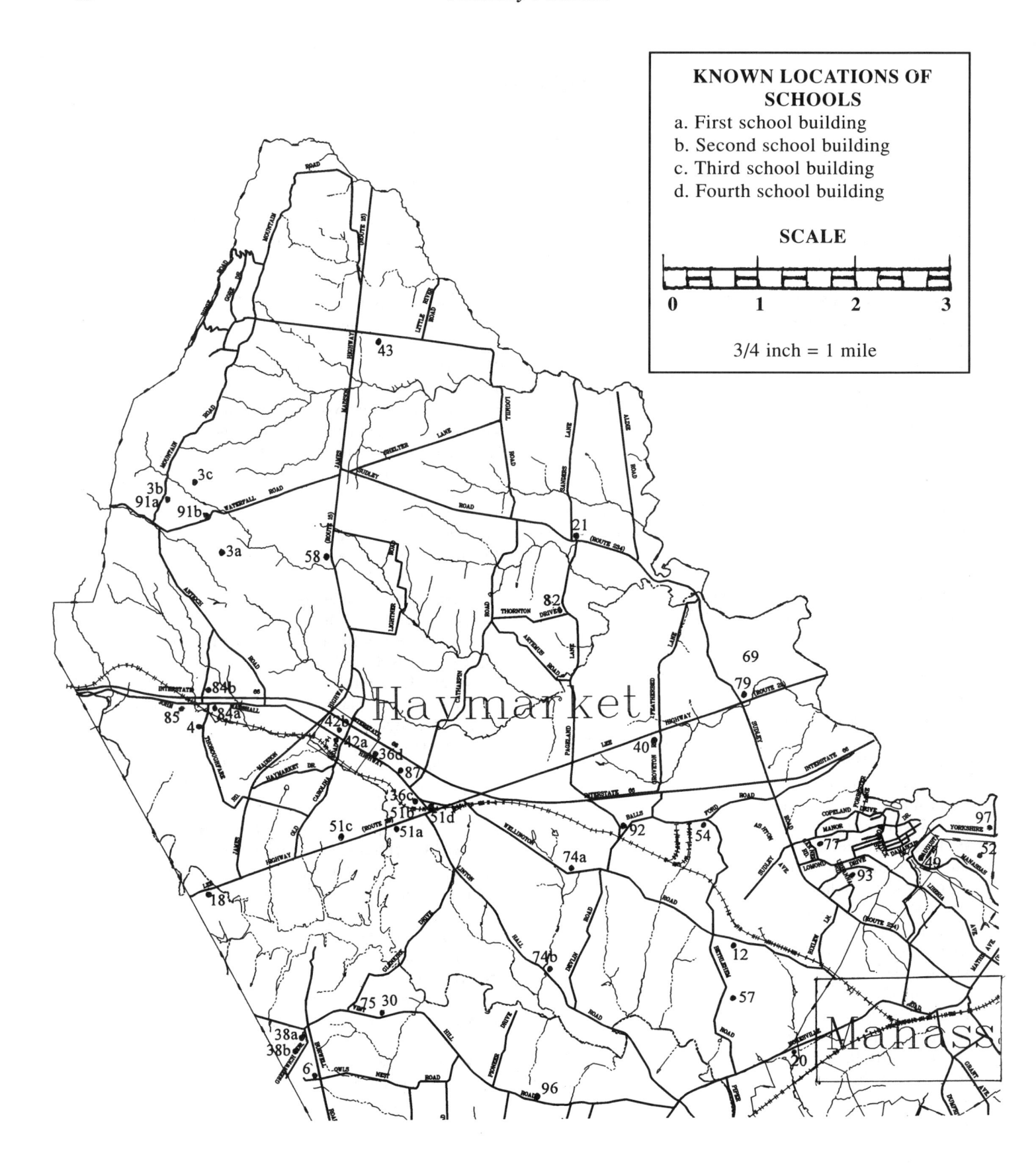

KNOWN LOCATIONS OF SCHOOLS
a. First school building
b. Second school building
c. Third school building
d. Fourth school building

SCALE

3/4 inch = 1 mile

PRINCE WILLIAM COUNTY

Map Section 61

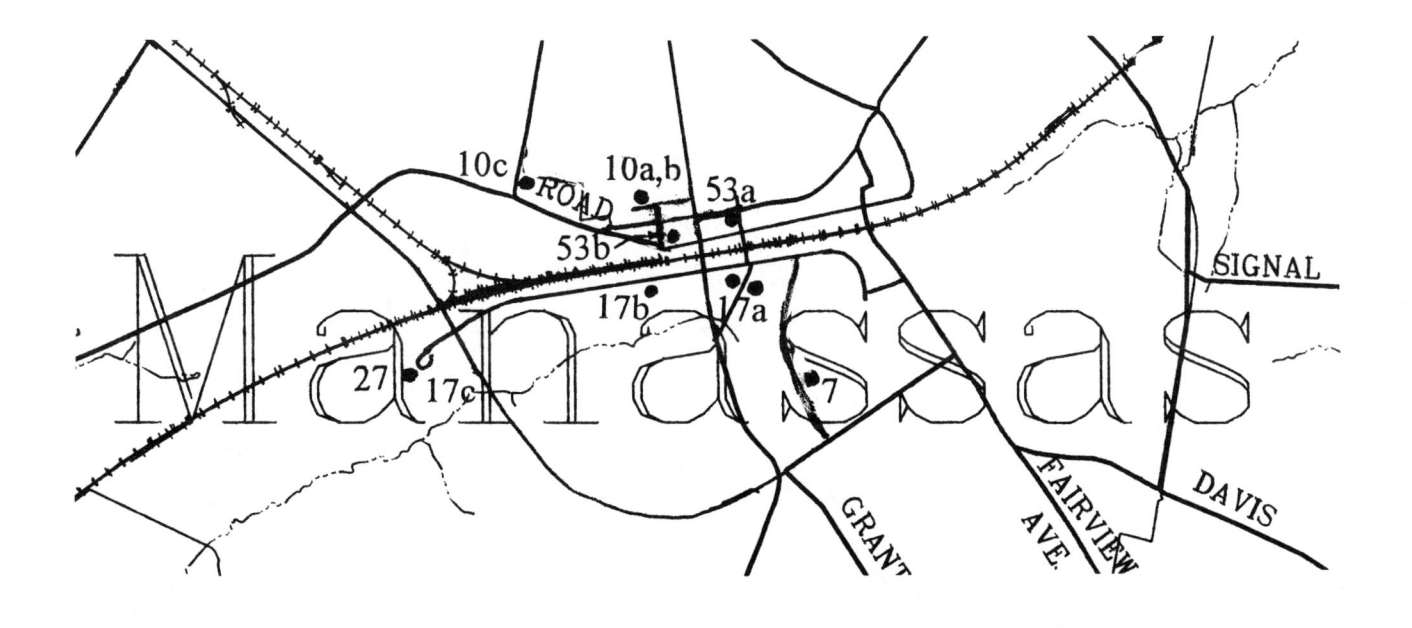

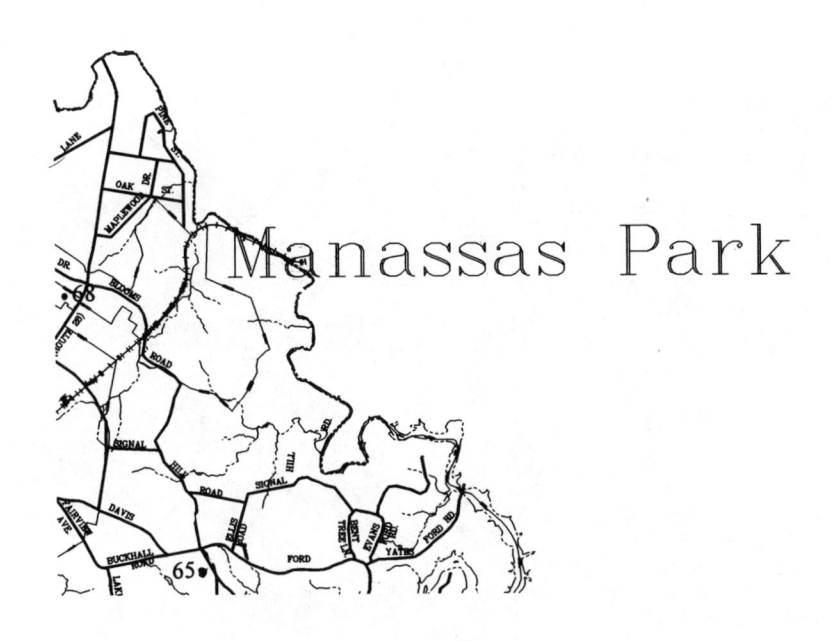

—**NORTHERN SECTION**

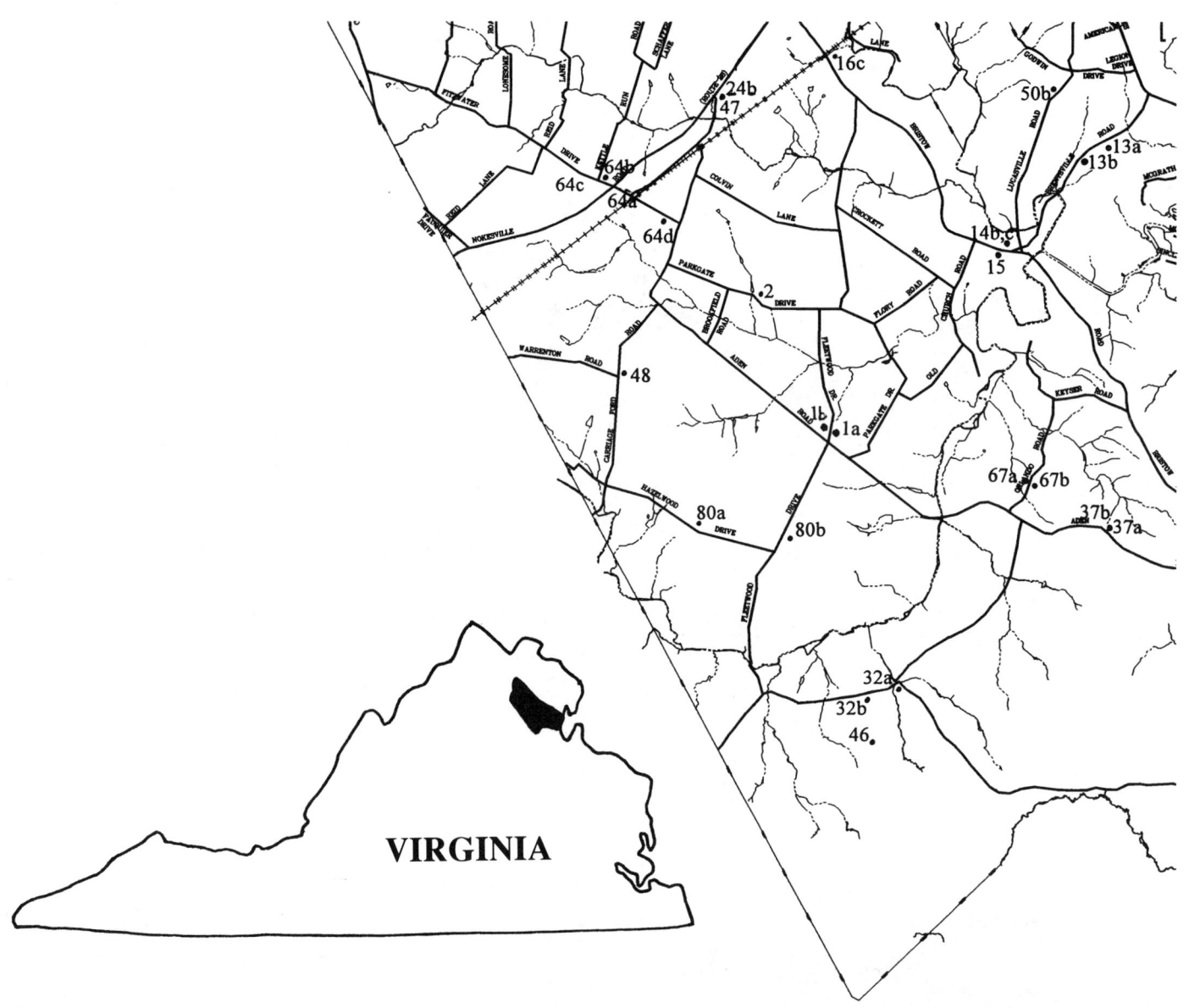

Prepared by Stephen Phinney and the Prince William County Office of Mapping and Information Resources.

PRINCE WILLIAM COUNTY

—**SOUTHERN SECTION**

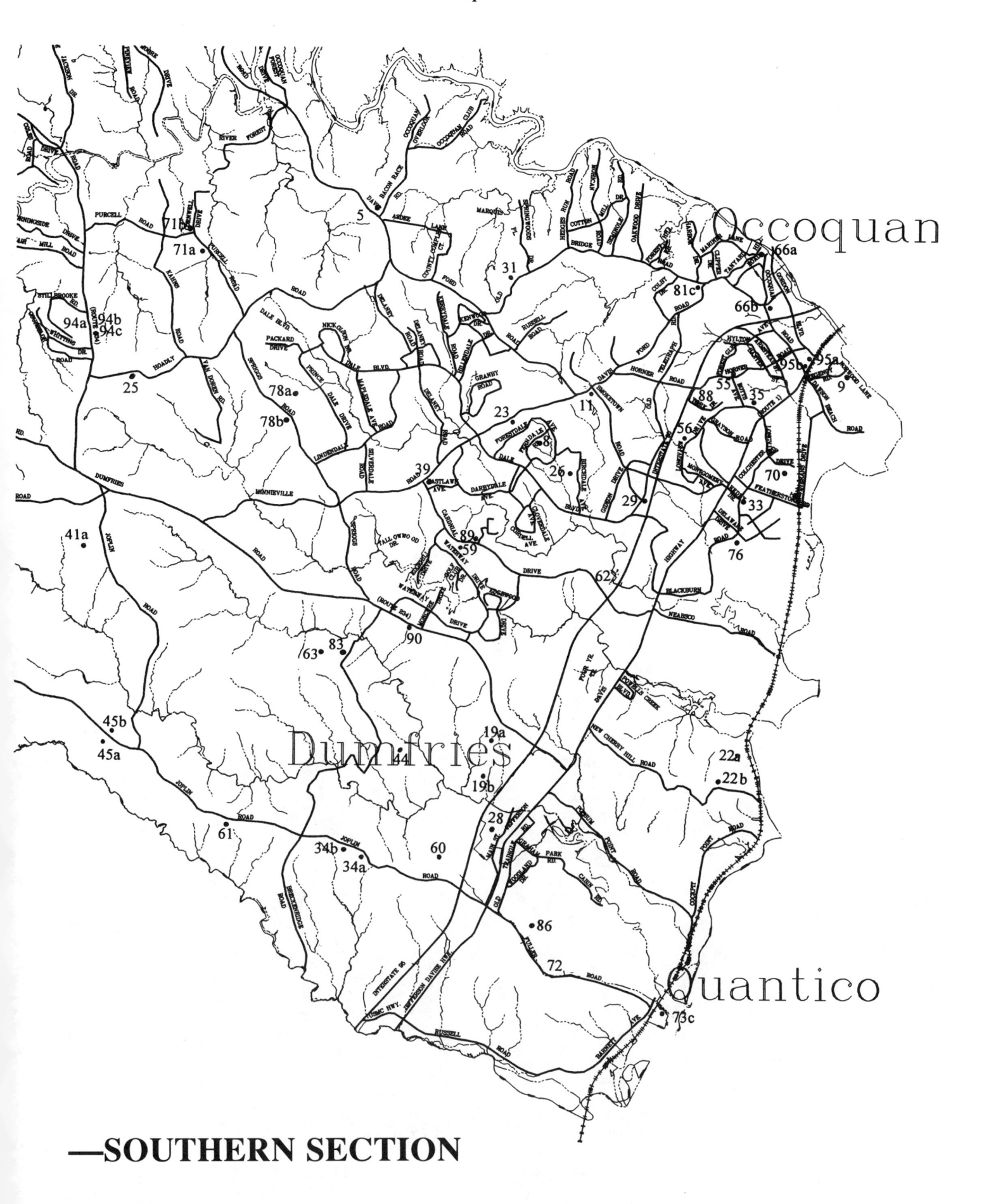

KNOWN LOCATIONS OF SCHOOLS

Schools with several names and buildings over their lifetimes are listed by a,b,c,d below.

*Indicates school building which is standing in 1993.

ADEN SCHOOL
   a. Lodge Building (1897-1909, 1916-1921) NE corner Aden Road/Fleetwood Drive, across from Aden School*.
   b. Aden (1909-1915,1921-1946) NW corner Aden Road and Fleetwood Drive, 500' North on Fleetwood*.

ALLENDALE SCHOOL
   (1884-1908) Parkgate Road, adjacent to Allen home.

ANTIOCH (MURRAY)/ANTIOCH/ANTIOCH-NORTH FORK
   a. Antioch (Murray) (1871?-1880) 0.6 miles S of intersection of Waterfall Road and Jackson Hollow Road in village of Waterfall.
   b. Antioch (first Waterfall Schoolhouse) (1880-1904) Mountain Rd, behind Olive Branch Baptist Church, now a parking lot.
   c. Antioch-North Fork (1904-1953) Jackson Hollow Road near the old town of Bridgetown.

ANTIOCH-MACRAE SCHOOL
   (1953-1982) 0.3 miles south of Marshall Hwy (Rt 55) on Thoroughfare Road*.

BACON RACE SCHOOL
   (1890-1928) NE corner of intersection of Davis Ford Road (Prince William Pkwy.) and Bacon Race Road.

BAILEYSBURG SCHOOL
   (1882-1884) West side of corner of Old Burwell Road and Edward's Road (Owl's Nest Road).

BALDWIN ELEMENTARY
   (1965-present) East side of Main St., Manassas, near Osbourn High School*.

BEL AIR ELEMENTARY
   (1969-present) 14151 Ferndale Road Dale City*.

BELMONT ELEMENTARY
   (1968-present) 751 Norwood Lane, Woodbridge*.

BENNETT SCHOOL
   a. (1909-1977) Lee Ave., Manassas, near County Courthouse*.
   b. (Old Osbourn building)(1926-1953) next door to Bennett School.
   c. (1977-present) about 500' north on east side of Stonewall Road from Center Street, Manassas*.

BETHEL SCHOOL
   a. (1914-1927) SW corner of intersection of Davis Ford Road and Smoketown Road.
   b. (1927-1966) on site of the first schoolhouse.

BETHLEHEM SCHOOL
   (1870-1930?) on south side of Wellington Road 0.2 miles E of Bethlehem Road, in Manassas.

BRADLEY SCHOOL
   a. (1871) E of Brentsville Road near Piney Branch, north of intersection of Brentsville and Winchester Roads.
   b. (1872-1930) SE corner of Bradley Forest Road and Brentsville Road*.

BRENTSVILLE SCHOOL
   a. (1870-1912) Brentsville Village Schoolhouse, location unknown.
   b. (1912-1927) Brentsville Courthouse on Bristow Road*.
   c. (1928-1944) On Bristow Road west of Courthouse*.

BRENTSVILLE COLORED SCHOOL
  a.(1909-1914) in house owned by Rev. Richard Jackson, location unknown.
  b.(1914-1918) near "old colored church" in Brentsville.
BRISTOE SCHOOL
  a.(1877-1879) assumed to be in a temporary room in an unknown location in community of Bristoe.
  b.(1879-1893) location unknown, building moved once.
  c.(1893-1907) near Chapel Springs, intersection of Vint Hill Road, Bristow Road, Linton Hall Road, and Nokesville Road.
  d.(1907-1936) in Bristoe, N side of Bristow Road between Post Office and Methodist Church.
BROWN SCHOOL
  a.(1870-1926) E side of Liberty Street near Prince William Street on current Manassas Museum land; then building moved across Liberty Street*.
  b.(1927-1947) S side of Prince William Street west of Grant Avenue.
BUCKLAND SCHOOL
  (1841-1924) wooded hillside behind Trone House on Buckland Mills Road, near Lee Hwy.
CABIN BRANCH(OLD)/CLARKSON/CABIN BRANCH SCHOOL
  a.Old Cabin Branch/Clarkson (1889-1924) E side of Mine Road in Batestown, 2 miles, NW of Dumfries (now in Prince William Forest Park).
  b.Cabin Branch (1924-1950) W side of Mine Road, less than one-half mile south of the old school, about 0.9 miles north of the intersection of Mine Road and Old Mine Road.
CANNON BRANCH SCHOOL
  (1889-1927) part of Harley's Farm, W side of Cannon Branch, SE side of present Nokesville Road near Godwin Drive in Manassas.
CATHARPIN SCHOOL
  a.(1874-1898) NE corner of intersection of Sudley Road and Sander's Lane*.
  b.(1898-1936) Same location as first school*.
CHERRY HILL SCHOOL (DUMFRIES DISTRICT)
  a.(1900s-1918) (early location) near bluff overlooking Powell's Creek, (second location) on Cherry Hill Road near Apple Lane.
  b.(1919-1936) on knoll, about 1 mile from Cherry Hill (old village) on Cherry Hill Road*.
CHERRY HILL (OCCOQUAN DISTRICT)
  (1880s-1916) S side of Minnieville Road, just west of Dale City Post Office*.
CHINN (MARSTELLAR)/(KETTLE RUN)
  a.(1874-1888) location unknown, Nokesville.
  b.Chinn(Marstellar)/(Kettle Run)(1888-1896) Marstellar Road, just north of Kettle Run, near junction of Aden and Nokesville Road.
COLES ELEMENTARY
  (1955-present) 7405 Hoadly Road, about 0.6 miles east of Dumfries Road*.
DALE CITY ELEMENTARY
  (1967-present) 14450 Brook Drive, Dale City*.
DEAN (JENNIE DEAN)
  (1960-present) 9601 Prince William Street*.
DUMFRIES SCHOOL
  a.(1881-1916) in Village of Dumfries, location unknown.
  b.(1917-1939) 300 S. Cameron Street, Dumfries.
  c.(1939-present) same as second schoolhouse*.
EMORY CHAPEL SCHOOL
  (1895?-1923) Southern end of Old Telegraph Road between I-95 and Potomac Mills Road in Dale City.
ENGLISH CHAPEL SCHOOL
  (1886-1901) One and one-half miles East of Greenwich on Vint Hill Road, N side, opposite Prince William Golf Course*.

FAIRVIEW SCHOOL
   (1877-1924?) N side Old Bridge Road, across from Hedges Cemetery, west of Old Woodbridge Airport (now Festival Shopping Center in Lake Ridge).
FAYMAN SCHOOL
   a.(190?-1913) S side of Elk Run Road, just east of Fayman, near intersection of Old Concrete Road (presently near the entrance to Camp Upshur on MCB 8 in the Quantico Marine Base).
   b.(1913-1931) N side of Elk Run Road, W of Fayman, about one-half mile west of first schoolhouse.
FEATHERSTONE ELEMENTARY
   (1964-present) 14805 Blackburn Road, at intersection of Reddy Road in Woodbridge*.
FOREST HILL/JOPLIN SCHOOL
   a. (1885?-1912) S side of Forest (Joplin) Road in community of Forest Hills (near Dumfries).
   b. (1912-1938) near first school, next door to Liming's Store, E of Forest Hills Church.
FRED LYNN ELEMENTARY
   (1963-present) 2451 Longview Drive between Rt. 1 and Botts Avenue*.
GAINESVILLE ELEMENTARY
   a. (1875?-unknown) near present Gainesville School, exact location unknown.
   b. (1906?-1909?) rented room in Purcell Building, later a general store and post office.
   c. (1909?-1929) former Gaines property, W of Gainesville on Lee Highway.
   d. (1935-present) 14550 John Marshall Highway, N side of highway, just east of Haymarket*.
GOLD RIDGE SCHOOL
   a. (1874-1903) N side of Aden Road about two miles west of Independent Hill, one mile east of Aden.
   b. (1903-1932) N side of Aden Road, west of first school.
GREENWICH SCHOOL
   a. (1901-1912) W side of Greenwich Road just south of Vint Hill Road across from the Greenwich Church.
   b. (1912-1944) W side of Greenwich Road just south of earlier building.
GREENWOOD SCHOOL
   (1883-1899) estimated location-S side of Hoadly Road east of Minnieville Road, between present Presbyterian Church and Greenwood Baptist Church.
GROVETON(BROWNSVILLE)
   a. (1870-1917) W side of Groveton Road just south of Lee Highway on the edge of Manassas Battlefield.
   b. (1917-1924) same location*.
HAYFIELD SCHOOL
   a. (1881-1914) W side of Hayfield Road, about one mile south of Independent Hill in present Quantico Marine Base.
   b. (1914-1935) on unimproved road three miles from Rt. 234; exact location unknown.
HAYMARKET SCHOOL
   a. (1883-1900, 1935) in Town Hall, S side of John Marshall Highway, in center of town*.
   b. (1900-1941) on Fayette Street, NW part of town where apartment building now stands.
HICKORY GROVE (OAK GROVE) SCHOOL
   (1877-1935) S side of Logmill Road, Haymarket, 0.4 miles east of intersection with Rt. 15*.
HICKORY RIDGE
   (1933-1943?) In Hickory Ridge Odd Fellows Hall, W side of Gallows Hill Road just north of intersection with Orenda Road near Mary Bird Branch of Quantico Creek in present Prince William Forest.
HOLMES/BELLE HAVEN SCHOOL
   a. (1895?-unknown) W side of Elk Run Road, 0.4 miles north of intersection with Joplin Road, currently inside Quantico Marine Base.
   b. (?-1927) across road from first school (foundations visible).
HORTON SCHOOL
   (late 1800s-1906?) N side of old Horton Road midway between John's Branch of Cedar Run and Fayman-Stafford Springs Road (now in Quantico Marine Base).

KETTLE RUN SCHOOL
   (1888-1938) SE side of Aden Road between Nokesville Road and bridge over Kettle Run, in Nokesville.
KING'S CROSSROADS (HERRING) SCHOOL
   a. (1895-1919) on Carriage Ford Road in Nokesville near intersection with Warrenton Road.
   b. (1919-1926) NE corner of Carriage Ford Road and Warrenton Road.
LOCH LOMOND ELEMENTARY
   (1961-present) 7900 Augusta Road, Manassas*.
LUCASVILLE SCHOOL
   a. (1883-1886?) near community of Lucasville, located at intersection of Lucasville Road and Godwin Drive, Manassas.
   b. (1886?-1926) W side of Lucasville Road just south of Godwin Drive.
MACRAE SCHOOL
   a. (187?-1888) two to three miles W of Gainesville on Lee Highway (Rt. 29).
   b. (1888-1907?) center of Gainesville on Lee Highway.
   c. (1907-1914) used Mt. Pleasant Baptist Church, N side of Lee Highway west of Gainesville.
   d. (1914-1953) E side of Gainesville Post Office on Lee Highway.
MANASSAS PARK ELEMENTARY
   (1958-present) Colburn Drive, Manassas Park*.
MANASSAS VILLAGE/RUFFNER SCHOOL
   a. Manassas Village School (1869-1872) room in Asbury Methodist Church, center of Church Street opposite present Post Office in Old Town Manassas.
   b. (1872-1926) N side of West Center Street near Peabody Street.
MANLEY SCHOOL
   a. (1871-1926) on hill at intersection of Balls Ford and Bethlehem Roads, seven miles from Manassas.
   b. (1926-1936) on same site as the first schoolhouse.
MARUMSCO/KILBY ELEMENTARY
   (1959-present) 1800 Horner Road, Woodbridge*.
MARUMSCO HILLS ELEMENTARY
   (1966-present) 14100 Page Street, Woodbridge*.
McGREGOR'S (ROY'S) SCHOOL
   (1891-1920?) E of Bethlehem Road about one mile south of Wellington Road.
MILL PARK SCHOOL
   (1882-1924) NW corner of Milark Road and Rt. 15, across from James Long Park, north of Haymarket.
MINNIEVILLE SCHOOL
   a. (1886-before 1915) school site is location of second house on south side of Dyer Drive on edge of Montclair.
   b. (before 1915-1931) same site as first schoolhouse.
MT. PLEASANT SCHOOL
   (late 19th-early 20th century) E side of Old King's Highway, one mile north of Forestburg and two miles south of Dumfries.
MT. ZION SCHOOL
   (1925-1928) in the Mt. Zion Church, one and a half miles west of the old Post Office on Joplin Road in present Prince William Forest Park.
NEABSCO SCHOOL
   a. (1901?-unknown) rented house on Cardinal Drive near settlement of Neabsco, one mile south of Minnieville; exact location not known.
   b. (?-1939) E side of Cardinal Drive in Neabsco, near Dyer Drive.
NELSON SCHOOL
   (c.1900) about one mile W of Thornton School on old Ridge Road, now in Prince William Forest Park.

NOKESVILLE SCHOOL
- a. (1870-1883) at Wilkins Corner (intersection of Nokesville Road and Fitzwater Drive); moved once nearer to Nokesville.
- b. (1883-1908) NE corner of intersection of Kettle Run Road and Fitzwater Drive.
- c. (1908-1929) S side of Fitzwater Drive less than one-quarter of a mile from second schoolhouse.
- d. (1929-present) 12625 Fitzwater Drive*.

OAK HILL/BUCKHALL SCHOOL
(1870-1936) W side of Moore Drive at Old Davis Ford Road.

OCCOQUAN SCHOOL
- a. (1905?-1929) 310 A/B Commerce Street*.
- b. (1929-present) 12915 Occoquan Road, N side of Occoquan Road, E of Davis Ford Road*.

ORLANDO SCHOOL
- a. (1872-1920s) W side of Orlando Drive, midway between Aden and Bristow Roads*.
- b. (1920s-1932) across Orlando Drive from the first schoolhouse, between Barbee's Store and Post Office and the Methodist Church.

PARKSIDE ELEMENTARY
(1962-present) 8602 Mathis Avenue, Manassas*.

PITTSYLVANIA SCHOOL
(1871?) on Pittsylvania Plantation, NE section of the Manassas Battlefield Park.

POTOMAC VIEW ELEMENTARY
(1963-present) 14601 Lamar Road, Woodbridge*.

PURCELL SCHOOL
- a. (188?-1906) SW side of Purcell Road between Cornwell Drive and Hunter's Grove Road*.
- b. (1906-1933) NW corner of Purcell Road and Cornwell Drive.

QUANTICO COLORED SCHOOL
- a. (1910?-1932) met in church in Quantico, location not known.
- b. (1932-1939) on low swampy area outside of the town on present Fuller Heights Road.

QUANTICO WHITE SCHOOL
- a. (1910?-1923) in or near Quantico, location unknown.
- b. (1923-?) near center of present day town of Quantico.
- c. (?-1956) 224 Third Avenue, Quantico*.

RED HILL/PINEY BRANCH SCHOOL
- a. Red Hill (1870s-1886) N side of Wellington Road near intersection of Piney Branch Road.
- b. (1886-1920s) NE corner of intersection of Piney Branch Road and Linton Hall Road.

RED SHOALS SCHOOL
- a. (1870-1872) old mill (?) near Greenwich, location not known.
- b. (1872-1886) Vint Hill Road east of Greenwich.

RIPPON ELEMENTARY
(1966-present) 15101 Blackburn Road, Woodbridge*.

SINCLAIR ELEMENTARY
(1968-present) 7801 Garner Drive, Manassas*.

SMITHFIELD SCHOOL
- a. (189?-1916) E side of Spriggs Road behind present Hylton High School.
- b. (1916-1930) across Spriggs Road about one-quarter mile south of the first school.

STONE HOUSE
(1916-1917) Stone House on the Manassas Battlefield, corner of Rt.29 (Lee Highway) and Sudley Road*.

SULPHUR SPRINGS/VANCLUSE/HAZELWOOD SCHOOL
- a. Sulphur Springs/VanCluse (1871-1877) N side of Hazelwood Drive east of (old) Law's Ford.
- b. Hazelwood (1877-1908) NE corner of Fleetwood Drive and Deepwood Lane.

SUMMITT SCHOOL
   a. (1882-1919) Town of Occoquan, location unknown.
   b. (1919-1947) N side of Davis Ford Road, just west of Old Bridge Road.

THORNTON/CATHARPIN COLORED SCHOOL
   (1877-1938) N side of Thornton Drive near junction with Pageland Lane, north of Gainesville.

THORNTON (FLORENCE) SCHOOL
   a. (1890-1923) At the NW corner of intersection of Mawavi and Taylor Farms Fire Roads, now in Prince William Forest Park.
   b. (1923-1930) E side of Ridge Road, near location of the first schoolhouse.

THOROUGHFARE WHITE SCHOOL
   a. (1880-1890?) S side of John Marshall Highway just east of Thoroughfare Road.
   b. (1890?-1920s) E side of Thoroughfare Road near John Marshall Highway, northwest of first schoolhouse site.

THOROUGHFARE COLORED/NORTH FORK SCHOOL
   (1884-1936) on knoll S side of John Marshall Highway, 400' feet west of (old) railroad station.

TRIANGLE ELEMENTARY
   (1959-present) 3615 Lionsfield Road, Triangle*.

TYLER ELEMENTARY
   (1968-present) 14550 John Marshall Highway, Gainesville*.

VAUGHAN ELEMENTARY
   (1965-present) 2200 York Drive, Woodbridge*.

WAKEFIELD SCHOOL
   (1870s) site near (old) Minnieville School on Cardinal Drive.

WASHINGTON-REID ELEMENTARY
   (1950-present) W side of Dumfries Road across from Pattie Elementary School in Montclair*.

WATERFALL SCHOOL
   a. (1871?-1887) Mountain Road, behind Olive Branch Church in community of Waterfall at the base of Bull Run Mountain.
   b. (1887-1927) in Waterfall, N side of Waterfall Road, just west of Jackson Hollow Road*.

WELLINGTON SCHOOL
   (1906-1932) NW side of Wellington Road, just N of Cushing Drive.

WESTGATE ELEMENTARY
   (1964-present) 8031 Urbanna Road, Manassas*.

WOODBINE SCHOOL
   a. (pre-1901-1916) W side of Dumfries Road across from site of present school.
   b. (1916-1953) E side of Dumfries Road next to site of present school.
   c. (1953-present) 13225 Dumfries Road, Independent Hill*.

WOODBRIDGE SCHOOL
   a. (1892?-1919) NW corner of Rt. 1 and Occoquan Road in Woodbridge.
   b. (1919-1927) near corner of Gordon Blvd. and Rt. 1.

WOODLAWN SCHOOL
   (1899-1935) N side of Vint Hill Road, three-quarters of a mile west of junction of Vint Hill and Kettle Run Roads.

YORKSHIRE ELEMENTARY
   (1952-present) 7610 Old Centreville Road, Manassas*.

INDIVIDUAL SCHOOLS

Each of the individual schools tells its own interesting story. A few of the stories have been written in the past (Gainesville's, Featherstone's, Haymarket's and Cannon Branch's for example), but most have not been told before. The vast majority had to be pieced together from many sources—old School Board minutes and records, reminiscences of former pupils and teachers, maps and lists, photographs, newspaper accounts, unpublished manuscripts and papers, bits and scraps of notes—because the information has never before been put together. There are still missing pieces but, in researching a topic, that is often the case. As new data is uncovered, history gets revised, refined, and rewritten. That is what makes it fun.

The schools which opened in Prince William County during the century between 1869 and 1969 are arranged here in alphabetical order. The first name which was given to a school is listed first and so they are alphabetized that way. When a new name was given to a school, usually because a new building was erected to replace an older existing building, that name is listed second, with a "/" separating the two (or more) names. If a school was commonly called by its colloquial or informal name, that is given with parentheses. For example:

RED HILL/PINEY BRANCH (RED HILL #2) SCHOOL

The first schoolhouse was called the Red Hill School but when a new building was erected for that school population in a different location, it was given a new name—Piney Branch School. To local residents, the new school was often known as the Red Hill #2 School, its colloquial name. Because the two schoolhouses served the same population and that population moved en masse into the new building, both schoolhouses are treated as one "school". They are, however, counted as two one-room school buildings because, in fact, two separate buildings were used.

With each school is a notation of either its School District, if it was opened during the years when School Districts administered the schools within their District (1869-1923), or Magisterial (the word School does not appear) District, if the school opened after 1923 when all schools were governed by the Prince William County School Board alone. This is included partly because long-time county residents and school historians still think of the schools as being part of a particular District and partly because it makes geographic placement of the schools easier for everyone. When the boundaries of a Magisterial District were redrawn putting a school into a new district or city, that is indicated by a "/" with the original district listed first.

A greater weight is placed on the schools which opened prior to World War II than those which are of the more modern era. In the first place, there were simply more of them. Secondly, the schools which opened during the forties, fifties and sixties were much more like each other and like the schools of today than were the small, individual, mostly rural schools which preceded them. In other words, the older stories are the more interesting stories. Thirdly, the reader can relatively easily gather his or her own information about the newer schools, most of which are still in existence and still educational facilities. It is not necessary to dig back into the dark reaches of history to tell the tale of the post-war schools. A century is a long time and the ninety-seven schools opened during that century are a big story all by themselves.

THE ADEN SCHOOL

Brentsville School District
White
1897-1946

A 1935 listing of Prince William County schools by the man who was Superintendent of Schools at that time (Richard C. Haydon) includes an Aden School beginning in 1897. A reference to the Lodge Building in the village of Aden having been used for several years as a temporary schoolhouse prior to 1908[1] is the only other report found of a school in Aden earlier than 1908. School Board minutes do not mention such a school nor is it found on the 1901 map by Brown of Prince William County. That one existed is probably true, but its size, location and history are unknown.

Aware of what they called the "proliferation of schools" in their District, the Brentsville District School Board, around the turn of the century, began to look at the consolidation of small schools into center schools. In July 1908, the Board voted to consolidate the Hazelwood and Allendale schools into a larger school located in the center of the village of Aden. They agreed to purchase two acres "adjoining the store property" from Mrs. J. P. Smith for $95 but she changed her mind and withdrew the offer.[2] Not quite three weeks later, the Board voted to buy two acres from Mrs. Smith "on the Harrison Ford road as near the cross roads as there is a suitable location".[3] Something went wrong with this arrangement too because before the month was over, the Board rescinded the motion and voted instead to rent the Lodge building at Aden to temporarily accommodate the students from Hazelwood and Allendale schools.[4]

The Board then contracted to have a two-room schoolhouse built on Fleetwood Drive less than a quarter of a mile from the intersection with Aden Road. On February 17, 1909 the building was inspected by the School Board and accepted into the system. It was called the Aden Sub-center School and served the community's needs for seven years.

The Aden School, c. 1930
(Courtesy PWC Schools)

At the end of June, 1916, the School Board heard a report that ninety-five to one-hundred students were expected to enroll in the Aden School in the fall of 1916. The two-room schoolhouse could not hold such a large number of children so the Board agreed to rent "the hall at Aden" (probably the Lodge Building which had been used several years earlier as a temporary schoolhouse) for seven months at $5.00 per month.[5] This would serve as a third classroom.

For five years, this rather awkward arrangement continued. Finally in July of 1921 the School Board agreed to build two more classrooms across the rear of the school house using $208 raised by patrons (parents) who also agreed to pay $15.00 per month toward a third teacher's salary.[6] Several months later, in October, the Board also agreed to add a small (6'x10') back porch with a cement floor onto the building.

From that fall of 1921 until the end of the 1924-25 school year, one of the teachers at the Aden School was Miss Cora E. Beahm whose father was principal teacher at the Woodlawn School. From the Aden School, Miss Beahm went to the Nokesville School for one year and then took over as the primary grade teacher at the Woodlawn School where her father had recently taught. At the Aden School, Miss Beahm taught with W. Davis Nolley and his wife, Pearle S. Nolley. The three divided up the six grades which were taught there during those years[7]. During the

---

[1]Brentsville District School Board minutes of June 30, 1908.

[2]Brentsville District School Board minutes of July 9, 1908.

[3]Brentsville District School Board Minutes, July 27, 1908.

[4]Brentsville District School Board minutes of July 31, 1908.

[5]Brentsville District School Board minutes of June 30, 1916.

[6]Brentsville District School Board minutes of July 26, 1921.

[7]Seventh grade students, and, later, high school students were bused to the Brentsville District High School in Nokesville.

week, Cora Beahm boarded with a widow who lived nearby the school and travelled by buggy to her family's home in Nokesville for the weekends.[8] When Miss Beahm left the Aden School in 1925, her place was taken by Miss Elizabeth Vaughan who went on to a long and distinguished career in education. She taught at Haymarket in the early 1930s before becoming principal at the Occoquan District School in 1934. An elementary school in Woodbridge is named for her.

From the 1934 and 1935 reports by the Superintendent of Schools, Richard Haydon, as well as from memories of students who attended Aden during its final years, a clear picture of the four-room schoolhouse is formed. Set on a concrete slab measuring 50'x61', the building was made of wood painted yellow. Each of the four rooms had a seating capacity of forty-two students although by 1935 only two rooms were being used. Pupils in the first grade used tables and chairs. Primary grades used double adjoining desks while students in the upper grades had single desks. The floor was made of tongue and groove pine and the ceiling was also wood. The inside was painted and there were screens for the twenty-eight windows. A cupola and four chimneys graced the roof line. Wood stoves were the source of heat and janitorial service was provided. There was a water pump on the school grounds but toilet facilities in 1935 were labelled inadequate. The playground space had no equipment and was called "very undesirable" in the superintendent's report.

Enrollment in first through sixth grades in November 1934 was seventy-four students. The average daily attendance that year was sixty-five students, a percentage of 87.8. That enrollment was up from sixty-three the previous year. Of those sixty-three, fifty-four were promoted at year's end, eight failed and one dropped out of school. The two teachers in 1934 were both college graduates with Normal Professional certificates. The Primary teacher had six years' experience; the upper grade teacher had been teaching for eight years.[9]

When the first addition of rooms was put on the Brentsville District High School in Nokesville in 1946, the Aden School consolidated with it and the yellow schoolhouse was put up for sale. It eventually was converted into an apartment house and it continues to be used as such today. It is still yellow with a tin roof and looks much as it did in its heyday as a schoolhouse.

Students of the four-room Aden School, 1921
(Courtesy of Mr. Robert Beahm)

---

[8] Robert Beahm.

[9] Richard C. Haydon. "An Administrative Survey of the Public School System in Prince William County, Virginia", A Thesis for Master of Science at the University of Virginia, 1935.

THE ALLENDALE SCHOOL

Brentsville District School #8, #7 and,
    after 1900, #3
White
1884-1908

The Brentsville District School Board minutes first mention the Allendale School in their minutes of October 16, 1884. At that time, they accepted the school into the District system. It was built by W. T. Allen and opened on October 28. The first teacher was W. A. Bryant, followed by J. C. Weedon and Miss Lizzie W. Nelson. The year Miss Lizzie took over the school, 1887, its number was changed to School #7. The old School #7, Baileysburg, was sold out of the system that year, which created a number vacancy which needed filling. Allendale remained #7 until the general District renumbering of 1900 assigned it to be #3.

The schoolhouse was located near the community of Aden on Parkgate Road. It was adjacent to Parkgate, home of the Allen family from whom the school probably got its name. Various School Board references to the buying of supplies for the school over the next few years are proof that it continued to provide education for the children of the surrounding farm community.

On January 14, 1895 the District Board ordered a new stove for the Allendale School to replace the old one which was found to be unsafe. The Board bought one for $6.75 including freight from Manassas to Bristow. When the stove made it to Bristow, the Clerk of the Brentsville Board hauled it to the Allendale School taking the old stove to his home to await the Board's instructions.[1]

In the summer of 1908, the School Board rescinded an earlier order to build a new Allendale school and instead ordered the consolidation of Allendale and Hazelwood Schools at Aden.[2] Records show that a group of parents from both the Allendale and Hazelwood school petitioned the School Board to keep the Allendale school open but it did not happen.

The Board decided to rent the Lodge Building at Aden for the consolidated school's use during the 1908-09 school year. In October of 1910, ten of Allendale's desks were given to the Brentsville Colored school; the rest of the desks, the maps and charts were given to the primary department of the Aden consolidated school. The Allendale Schoolhouse stood empty.

In July of 1911, sixteen citizens presented the School Board with a petition to re-open the Allendale School. The matter was tabled and one year later the school property was sold to W.F. Hale for $105.[3] By 1917 the old schoolhouse had been moved beside the barn on the nearby Beahm property where it was used as a granary for several years before it was torn down.

---

[1]Brentsville District School Board minutes of January 14, 1895, p.176.

[2]Brentsville District School Board minutes of July 31. 1908.

[3]Brentsville District School Board minutes of July 13, 1912

THE ANTIOCH (MURRAY)/ ANTIOCH/ANTIOCH-NORTH FORK SCHOOL

Gainesville School District #3
Colored
1871?-1953

The Antioch School was one of the northern group of four colored schools which also included Macrae, North Fork or Thoroughfare Colored, and Thornton Schools. During the course of its history, it has been located on three different sites, all in the foothills of Bull Run Mountain.

The first Antioch Schoolhouse was located about 0.6 miles south of the intersection of Jackson Hollow and Waterfall Roads.[1] No records remain which pinpoint the exact date of its opening but it was probably during the very early 1870's. Antioch was the third schoolhouse to be established by the Gainesville District School Board. It was a one-room

The Antioch-North Fork School as it looked in 1980
(Courtesy of PWC Historical Commission)

schoolhouse up on a hill on land owned by the Murray family and was referred to, in the early years, as the Murray School. In 1879, Mr. Joshua Murray was appointed to teach the school for a salary of $20 a month.[2] He may have been the teacher prior to that, but no records corroborate this. The Murray School served the black community around Waterfall for nearly ten years. When increased enrollment made a move to larger quarters necessary, the Antioch

---

[1]Private correspondence from Elizabeth Nickens to the author, 1992. Ms. Nickens' mother began her teaching career at the Antioch School in 1906.

[2]Gainesville District School Board Minutes Book of 1879.

(Murray) School was abandoned and sold several years later to Mr. Mack Helm for a total of $15.00.[3]

Very early District School Board records state that in 1880, the Antioch schoolhouse for white children was given over to the education of the black children of the community. A new school for white students was built in Waterfall in 1880 so the old building would have been surplus. This second Antioch School building was located on Mountain Road behind the Olive Branch Baptist Church where the parking lot now stands.[4] This was also the location of a Waterfall Schoolhouse, according to the 1901 map of county drawn by Mr. William H. Brown.

District School Board minutes in 1883 show that the teacher, Mr. Robinson, requested from the School Board either an assistant or more compensation because of the large number of pupils. His request was denied at the time, but at the end of the school year he was given an additional month's salary of $25.00. According to those same 1883 School Board minutes, a request by local citizens to use the schoolhouse for entertainment was also denied by the Board. The second Antioch Schoolhouse served the black children of the Waterfall area until 1904.

For the third and final Antioch School building, the District School Board and Superintendent of Schools Clarkson chose a site on Jackson Hollow Road near the area known as Bridgetown (also called Bridgett Town on the historic map of the county drawn in 1992 by Eugene Scheel). A sum of $2000 was set aside for the erection of a two-room school. In 1896 the Board purchased half an acre of land from Mrs. George Smith for $15[5] and gave the contract for the building of the schoolhouse to Mr. E.C. Walter. That half an acre was barely large enough to hold the schoolhouse, the well and the privies. This was often the case when schools for the black children were built; it was the white schools, generally, which sat on parcels of land big enough for a nice playground. Mr. Walter's work was so good that he was given an additional $5 bonus as well as a contract to build two outhouses for $20. It must have been a good job, because that Antioch School remained in service for nearly fifty years, until it combined with the Macrae School in 1953. The Board also paid Mr. H. Howdershell, the District Board chairman, $1.50 to move the desks, stove, etc. from the old to the new building.

That third schoolhouse was a one story, two room frame building with a peaked metal roof. The walls and ceiling were of wood and each room was heated by a wood-burning stove.[6] It was a design commonly used by the county for school construction of the time. Two teachers were employed. The teachers and pupils all shared in the care of the school. Sometime around 1920, a group of school friends and parents organized the Armstrong School League for the purpose of buying a playground for the school. They purchased one acre of land along the north side of the school site from W. N. Darnell[7]. The one and a half acre site continued to be slowly improved and, eventually, electricity was added. The toilets were pits but they did meet state standards of acceptability.

In 1906, Mrs. Susie Nickens began her long teaching career in Prince William County when the School Board hired her to teach the primary students at Antioch. Two years later, the School Board directed the Clerk of the School District to notify the Commonwealth's Attorney that a distillery was located "very near" the schoolhouse. The Board asked that it be abolished if it was found to be closer to the school than the law allowed.[8]

In 1926-27, the teacher of grades 4-7 was Miss C.T. Dunkins who was only twenty-three years old but already had six years experience in teaching. She was a high school graduate, unusual for black teachers in that time, but was still paid the usual $60 a month or $420 for the seven month term. She paid $15 monthly for her room and board in the community. The teacher for grades 1-3 was Pearl Fletcher.[9] There were twenty-six children enrolled that year, nine in the first four grades and seventeen in grades 5-7. Of that number, eight failed and two dropped

---

[3]Gainesville District School Board minutes, March 28, 1896.

[4]Elizabeth Nickens' correspondence.

[5]County Deed Book #44, p.274.

[6]Engineering Report prepared for the Prince William County School Board by Viola D. Proffitt Insurance Agency of Manassas, Va., October 1953.

[7]County Deed Book 76, p.96. This information was supplied by the present owner of the land, Mr. Carl Palmer of McLean, VA.

[8]Gainesville District School Board minutes, March 7, 1908, p.268.

[9]Virginia Daily Attendance Register and Record of Class Grades for the Antioch School, 1927.

out. There were no books in the school library and no school official made a visit to the school that year.

The following year, Mrs. Fletcher had been replaced by Dorothy W. Brice, but Miss Dunkins stayed on. By the 1929-30 school year, both of these teachers were gone and their places were taken over by Ella Lee Morgan who taught the fourth through seventh grades and Miss Louise Gertrude Knight who taught the primary classes. It must have been difficult to teach in such an isolated and poorly equipped school. In 1934, when Superintendant Haydon wrote his report on all county schools, water still had to be carried from a distance though a well was in the future plans. In that same year, the desks were rated "fair", bookcases were needed although there were only a few books other than texts and those came from the teachers, and no maps or globes.[10]

During the 1933-34 school year, the enrollment was fifty-four with an average daily attendance of thirty-five. That year there were thirty-eight promotions, seven failures and nine students who dropped out of school. The following year, the enrollment stood at forty-seven with an average daily attendance of forty-one, or a much-improved eighty-seven percent. A large number of the children lived way up in the mountains and had to walk four to five miles to school when the weather permitted. The head teacher at that time was a principal who was there on a temporary assignment until a permanent teacher could be hired. She was a Manassas Industrial School graduate with a provincial elementary certificate and four years of teaching experience. The assistant teacher had the same credentials but with seventeen years of experience.

On December 4, 1935, a joint delegation headed by Mrs. Mary Fields from the Thoroughfare Colored School and Mrs. Hattie Gaskins of the Antioch Colored School went before the Gainesville District School Board. Their purpose was to express approval of the Board's plan to close the school at Thoroughfare beginning with the 1936-37 school year. An additional room at Antioch was to be built to provide room for the Thoroughfare children as well as all the black children along Bull Run Mountain back of Hickory Grove.[11] The School Board decided that the Thoroughfare Community League should contribute the $400 they had already raised for a new school in their village toward the new room at Antioch. The Board agreed to provide the additional money needed for the room and also to operate a bus to transport the children from Thoroughfare and the mountain to Antioch beginning in September of 1936. The addition was built and the combined schoolhouse became known as the Antioch-Northfork Elementary School, North Fork being the earlier name for the Thoroughfare School.

During the years of the second World War, the black children who lived closer to the Gainesville School than the Antioch School walked to Gainesville because gasoline was difficult to come by.[12] When the war was over and gas rationing stopped, the children returned to Antioch. In 1953, the Antioch-Northfork School was combined with the Macrae School in a new building called the Antioch-Macrae. The first principal was Louise Allen who had previously taught at both the Antioch and Thoroughfare Schools. The Antioch-Macrae School served the black children of the northern county area until 1966 when it was annexed to the Gainesville Elementary School. It served as the integrated kindergarten and first grade section of that school until 1982 when it was no longer needed.

In October of 1954, about a year after the Antioch School closed, the property was sold to Mr. James R. Gossom. Six years later, Mr. Elton Stewart bought it[13] for use as a residence. Following his death, the old schoolhouse remained unoccupied and burned down in early 1992. The property which the Armstrong League had purchased for use as a playground remained in the possession of the inactive League until 1960 when it was bought by Mr. Carl Palmer. In 1969, he also acquired the schoolhouse lot and both are still in his possession.[14]

Humble beginnings, increased enrollment, a new and larger building which lasted for fifty years, consolidation, integration and finally extinction tell the tale of the Antioch School. It is the tale of so many of the early schoolhouses across the county, the state and the nation.

---

[10]Richard C. Haydon. *Survey of the Public School System in Prince William County.* Master's Thesis, University of Virginia, 1936, p.91.

[11]Prince William County School Board minutes of December 4, 1935.

[12]Oral history done by the author with Mrs. Mary Fields, 1991.

[13]County Deed Book 262, p.697.

[14]Interview with Mr. Carl Palmer by the author, March, 1993.

ANTIOCH-MACRAE ELEMENTARY SCHOOL

Gainesville School District
Colored, then desegregated in 1965
1953-1982

The Antioch-Macrae Elementary School, abandoned in 1982.
(Photo by the author)

The Antioch-Macrae School opened in 1953 when several of the small colored schools in the Gainesville District were combined. Two of those small schools gave their names to the new consolidated building which, like its counterparts built during the early fifties, was built of cinder block covered with brick. The kitchen, cafeteria, office, five classrooms and two bathrooms had acoustical ceiling tiles and asphalt floor tiling.

Mr. Russell Fincham was named head teacher and unofficial principal of Antioch-Macrae when it opened in 1953. He wasn't officially named principal until 1959 despite the fact that, after spending a whole day teaching classes, he worked into the late afternoons doing administrative work. Throughout those years, he had neither a secretary nor even a telephone to make his task easier. At one time, Mr. Fincham even borrowed a county truck to drive, on his own free time, to Manhattan where a friend had arranged for him to pick up textbooks which were more up-to-date than those which the county supplied to his school.[1] He stayed at Antioch-Macrae until 1966 when he was hired to be the assistant principal of Jennie Dean Middle School. He was named principal there in 1977 and remained until his retirement in 1981.

Antioch-Macrae continued as a colored schoolhouse until "freedom of choice" became the desegregation policy of the Prince William County schools in 1965. In 1966, Antioch-Macrae was annexed to Gainesville Elementary School to house the kindergarten and first grades, thereby easing the overcrowded conditions which resulted from desegregation. The arrangement worked well and the two schools operated in that manner until 1982. At that time, the population of school age children in that area of the Gainesville District had declined and Tyler Elementary had opened, so the Antioch-Macrae Schoolhouse was no longer needed. Today children attend Tyler for kindergarten and first grade before moving down the road to Gainesville Elementary for grades 2-5. The Antioch-Macrae School sits abandoned and boarded up on the Antioch Road between Gainesville and Thoroughfare.

[1] Alexandra B. Stoddard. "Four teachers were in the vanguard of change in schools", *Potomac News*, February 11, 1993, p.3.

BACON RACE SCHOOL

Occoquan School District
White
1890?-1923

No records exist to document the year the Bacon Race one room school opened. The small frame building was located at the intersection of Davis Ford Roads and Bacon Race Roads (then called Telephone Road) across from the Bacon Race Church and served the children from the Hoadly area. Hoadly was a loosely organized community in the Hoadly-Bacon Race-Davis Ford Road area of the county where the McCoart Administrative Center is now located. The people of Hoadly were mostly small farmers who also earned some money from timbering and making moonshine.[1]

When no teacher could be found for the 1923-24 school year, the Bacon Race school was closed. Consolidation of the small schools at larger center schools was a major objective of the School Board at that time, too, so the closing was permanent. Beginning in September of 1923, the children from

[1] Prince William County Historical Commission. *Home Place*. Prince William, Virginia, 1990, p.65.

Hoadly were bused to the Bethel Elementary school further down Davis Ford Road.

In the fall of 1927, Mrs. Davis who lived in Hoadly, asked the School Board about buying the Bacon Race School. The clerk notified her that the property was not for sale at that time.[2] However in May of 1928, the Board decided to advertise the school and the land on which it stood for sale.

---

[2]Minutes of the Prince William County School Board of October 5, 1927.

THE BAILEYSBURG SCHOOL

Brentsville District School #7
Colored
1882-1884

In September of 1882, responding to a petition from community parents, the Brentsville District School Board agreed to establish "a Negro School in the neighborhood of Greenwich"[1]. It was located in a rented house on land which was part of a 1000 acre plantation owned in the early 19th century by Mr. Carr Bailey.[2] The site was at the corner of old Burwell and Edwards Roads (now Owl's Nest Rd.) about a mile south of the village of Greenwich. It was called the Baileysburg School and given the District designation as the #7 school.

Apparently, the Baileysburg School lasted less than two years. At the January 12, 1884 meeting of the District Board, it was ordered that "the school at Greenwich" be closed because the house had been condemned by the County. Since the Greenwich white school did not meet in a house, this reference has to be to the colored school. In September of 1887, the Board ordered that the condemned schoolhouse be sold for $53.63 in mid-October.

Those January minutes of 1884 also speak of the opening of two new schoolhouses: one at Nokesville and the other at Greenwich. While it's possible that this latter was the Chinn School for black children, later entries in the minutes make it appear doubtful.[3] Perhaps the Baileysburg School found another location; perhaps the talk of a new school opening was just talk as sometimes happened. It does seem quite clear that only one school for black children existed in the Brentsville School District by 1885-86.

---

[1]This is the only instance where the term "Negro" is used. The more usual designation of the times was "Colored". The term "Black" is much more recent.

[2]Eugene Scheel map information, 1992.

[3]See section on The Chinn School.

BALDWIN ELEMENTARY SCHOOL

Manassas District/City of Manassas
1965 to present

In 1965, the Baldwin Elementary School was built on Main Street in Manassas. The Baldwin family, prominent citizens of Manassas in the late nineteenth century whose home eventually became a succession of educational buildings, was honored with the naming of the school. When the City of Manassas became an entity independent of Prince William County in 1977, it purchased the Baldwin School which lay within its boundaries. It continues to operate as a City of Manassas public school today.

BEL AIR ELEMENTARY SCHOOL

Neabsco District
1969-present

One hundred years after the opening of the first public school in Prince William County in a room in the Asbury Methodist Church in Manassas, the Bel Air Elementary School opened in 1969. It was the second school built in the Dale City subdivision of Woodbridge, on Ferndale Road in the Forestdale section of that community. Its name came from the nearby Bel Air Plantation which dates back to the early eighteenth century.

BELMONT ELEMENTARY SCHOOL

Occoquan/Woodbridge District
1968-present

The Belmont Elementary School, built in 1968, was the seventh elementary school to be erected in the then Occoquan District during the decade of the sixties. Prince William County was hard pressed to keep up with the rapidly growing demands for education in the Woodbridge area. Belmont, located on Norwood Lane, was named for Belmont Bay on the Potomac River which forms the northern boundary of the school property. In 1976, the school became part of the newly created Woodbridge District.

THE BENNETT SCHOOL

Manassas District School
1909-present
White

The Bennett School building, now standing on Lee Avenue in Manassas across from the new courthouse, was built in 1909 to house the first agricultural high school in Virginia. In 1908 the General Assembly provided for an agricultural school for each of the ten congressional districts into which the state was divided. Manassas was chosen as the site for the school for the eighth district and its school, Bennett, was the first to be completed in the state. However, because of a very large elementary school age population, Bennett was never used as a high school, opening instead as an elementary school which it remains (though in a newer building) to this day. The Ruffner School was enlarged to accommodate the agricultural and secondary students; in 1913 it was enlarged again. Teacher training courses were taught in the Bennett School along with the elementary grades.

The Bennett School was an impressive building when it was built in 1909.
(Courtesy of Manassas Museum)

The Bennett School was built on two acres of land donated by Dr. Maitland C. Bennett, father-in-law of School Trustee George C. Round who had been a driving force behind the agricultural high school. During excavation for the building, graves of unknown Civil War soldiers were discovered. It was decided by Mr. Round, a Union veteran, and Superintendent of Schools George Tyler, a Confederate veteran, to leave the graves undisturbed and build the schoolhouse over them.[1]

The new two-story schoolhouse cost $16,000. It was built of brick with a peaked slate shingled roof and contained nine rooms, eight with a seating capacity of forty-five each and one only large enough for twenty-five. There was an auditorium and a gymnasium, as well as a principal's office. All the floors were of double wood board; the interior walls and ceilings were lath and plaster. It was centrally heated by three coal fired boilers, fully electrified, and had running water for toilets and drinking fountains. Children within a nine mile radius attended grades 1-8 there.

A big playground was built alongside the Bennett School. It was hoped that this would become a center of community life for the children of Manassas. It was kept open during the summer to "draw the children away from the railroad and other places of danger."[2] Mrs. Moffett goes on to quote Governor William Hodges Mann of Virginia who said, on a visit to the school in 1911,

> Of course, everyone knows the Bennett Building is the most beautiful building of its kind in the state. This splendid building is being equipped with reproductions of the old masterpieces, new furniture, kindergarten tables and chairs, a lavatory and a sanitary drinking fountain in each basement, a rest room and reading room; all making it a fine educational institution for the development of character and of social efficiency.[3]

In 1921, the Manassas Good Housekeeper's Club set up a plan to furnish hot soup to the school children beginning at the end of January.[4]

In 1926, the white citizens of Manassas passed a bond issue to provide funds for a new high school. Their children were educated in a seemingly confusing fashion in the old Ruffner School, the Manassas Institute and the Bennett School for both elementary and secondary grades. All were overcrowded and Ruffner, at least, was in danger of losing its State accreditation. So a thirteen-room brick high school with an auditorium was built on land next door to the Bennett School and called the Osbourn Building. It served as the high school for the students from western Prince William County until 1953 (when the "new" Osbourn High School was built). At that point the old building became an annex to Bennett Elementary and it served in that capacity until the new Bennett School was built on Stonewall Road (where it still functions) and both the old Bennett and old Osbourn were closed. The old Osbourn building was torn down in 1986 but the old Bennett School still stands sentinel on its site as it has since 1909.

Miss Grace Metz's (center back) class at Bennett School, 1923.
(Courtesy of The Manassas Museum)

In the early 1930s, Bennett continued to be overcrowded and had to spill over into parts of the Osbourn Building. One section of the first grade was housed in the agricultural building of the Osbourn High School; one section of grade four was held in the library; a section of the sixth grade and all of the seventh met in high school classrooms.

In 1928, the Patrons League (PTA) of the Bennett and Osbourn schools advanced the necessary funds to build a sidewalk connecting the two schoolhouses with the neighboring county courthouse. The monies for half of the first block and all of the second were to be paid back to the League from the 1929 tax levies.[5]

---

[1] Catherine T. Simmons. *Manassas, Virginia 1873-1973. One Hundred Years of a Virginia Town.* Manassas City Museum, 1986, p.38.

[2] Mrs. Mary Moffett, supervisor of the Manassas graded schools wrote this in the *Manassas Journal* in 1911. It is quoted in *Now and Then*, p.92.

[3] *Now and Then*, p.93.

[4] *The Manassas Journal.* January 28, 1921, p.6.

---

[5] Simmons, p.75.

A small kitchen was built in the early 1930s in the basement of Bennett so that hot lunches for "undernourished children" could be provided.[6] According to Superintendent Haydon's 1934 report on the county schools, the student population of Bennett for the 1933-34 school year was 545. Of that number, 474 were promoted at year's end, fifty-two failed and nineteen students dropped out. The average daily attendance was 522 (in a school with a seating capacity of 385!), most of whom were bused.[7]

The furnishings of the classrooms varied. First and second graders used tables and chairs; the third grade children had single desks and the fourth grade used chair desks. By the fifth grade, students went back to single desks. Sixth grade classrooms had both single and chair desks; seventh graders were back to single desks. Every teacher had a desk and chair. Each classroom was equipped with a victrola, a globe, maps and books. In addition, the school library was available. Beautification of the school grounds and equipment for the playground were provided by the Patron League.

The teachers during the mid-thirties varied in teaching experience from one to twenty years. Nine of the faculty graduated from a teachers' college; two came from liberal arts colleges; one was a university graduate. The new curriculum provided by the State Department of Education was used in every classroom.[8]

The new Bennett School opened its doors in 1969. In 1977, Manassas gained city status and established its own school system, independent of the Prince William County. As a result, 750 students living in the city of Manassas were withdrawn from the (county) Bennett School now located within city boundaries. Today, students at Bennett are bused to the schoolhouse from their homes in the county nearby. The old Bennett School, a landmark in Old Town Manassas, is today being used by the Prince William County Police Department for storage.

---

[6]Richard C. Haydon. "An Administrative Survey of the Public School System in Prince William County, Virginia." A Thesis for Master of Science at the University of Virginia, 1935, p.70.

[7]Ibid., p.70.

[8]Ibid., p.71.

THE BETHEL SCHOOL

Occoquan School District
White
1914-1966

The first Bethel School was a four-room, gray frame building located at the intersection of Davis Ford and Smoketown Roads, in the long-gone village of Agnewville. It was built on land donated to the School Board by Mr. E.S. Davis with the playground donated by Mr. C.N. Snapp. It was dedicated on September 3, 1914 and housed grades 1-9 in two rooms upstairs and two down.[1] The first, second and third grades met in one of the lower rooms; fourth and fifth grades met in the other. Upstairs, grades six and seven met in one room and all upper grades met in the other. That was the first high school in

The second Bethel Schoolhouse.
(Courtesy of the PWC Schools)

the Occoquan District and the first principal was Mr. Richard C. Haydon who later became Superintendent of Schools for Prince William County. He was at Bethel only one year as principal teacher. He then went to the University of Virginia for his B.S. and M.S. degrees so evidently he had only a high school education when he was at Bethel.[2]

---

[1]Thomas Nelson. <u>Woody. An Interview With James Woodrow Taylor.</u> An oral history for the Prince William County Historical Commission, January 1982, Second interview, p.7.

[2]Thomas Nelson. "Transcript of Interview with Historic Occoquan, Inc." Prince William County Historical Commission Oral History Project, September 24, 1985, p.4.

The Bethel School served the communities of Agnewville, Hoadly, Woodbridge, Occoquan, Minnieville and Dumfries because of the high school classes offered there. Former students remember walking, bicycling or being driven by horse and buggy to get to the school. Children who had to come from the more distant areas often stayed with local families during the school week until roads were improved and bus travel was initiated in the early 1920s.

The students carried their lunches to school in half gallon syrup buckets or whatever else was available. Baseball, a favorite recess activity for the boys, was also a favorite sport with the community as a whole. The Bethel Schoolhouse was the center of community life as was the case with the other schools in the County. Various entertainments, Community School League and farm meetings, suppers and fairs were held there.

After 1923, children from Hoadly were bused to Bethel following the close of the Bacon Race school. The bus was driven by Walter Davis whose wife Ida ran the Hoadly General Store from 1913-1954. Mr. Davis drove an old Reo truck made over into a school bus. That truck was followed by a Model T Ford and then by a Model A. Mud often stopped travel since no roads were paved until World War II. The worst place on the school bus route was the little hill on Davis Ford Road going up to Sullins' Store (at the present corner of Davis Ford and Minnieville Roads). The children would have to get off and push the bus to the top!

On Sunday, June 12, 1927 the school was struck by lightning during a severe thunderstorm and was destroyed. The last principal of the Bethel High School was Mr. Warren Coleman. Since the Occoquan High School had opened its doors the year before, grades seven and up attended there although the Bethel community was not happy with the location so far away from the area. The younger grades from Bethel attended school for a few months in the old Bethel Church across the road until a new Bethel schoolhouse could be built.

The new two-room brick building, erected to house the Bethel School students was completed at the end of 1927 at a cost of $5500, all but $300 of which came from a fire insurance policy on the old schoolhouse. Since grades seven through twelve now attended the new Occoquan High School, a smaller Bethel school than the first one was built. In this new Bethel school, one teacher taught grades one through three while the second teacher had fourth through sixth grades. Each teacher earned $50 a month salary out of which came room and board often with a neighborhood family.

According to the 1934 year-end report of Superintendent of Schools Richard C. Haydon, enrollment that year at Bethel was seventy-three with an average daily attendance of sixty-eight or almost ninety-four percent. The previous year, enrollment had been eight-two. The primary grades had an average attendance of thirty-three and the upper grades averaged twenty-six a day. At the end of the 1933-34 school year, fifty-six students were promoted, fifteen failed and eleven dropped out. The primary teacher that year had a Normal Professional diploma and four years' experience. The teacher of the upper grades had a Collegiate Professional diploma from a liberal arts college and no teaching experience.

The school, built of brick, was in good condition for most of its life. A beautiful pressed tin ceiling remained in excellent shape until demolished by a wrecking crew. In the 1930s, there was a piano in the building and students used attached desk and chair combinations. A coal stove provided heat and a janitor was part of the staff. Water came from a pump in the school yard and the outdoor toilets were "adequate". While the playground was large enough for that size student body, the equipment was almost nonexistent (as was the case in most of the schools in that era) so pupils had to bring their own from home. Very little beautification had been done to the school grounds at that time because of the poor soil.[3]

Because the schoolhouse was divided into two rooms by a moveable wooden wall, the space could be opened up to accommodate large groups of people and the Bethel School was indeed a focal point for the farming community it served. Socials, dances, bees, and programs reflecting a simple, rural lifestyle- were often held there.

Bethel, the last of the county's two-room public schoolhouses, continued to serve the area until 1966 when the building was turned over to the

---

[3]Richard C. Haydon. "An Administrative Survey of the Public School System of Prince William County, Virginia", A Thesis for Master of Science at the University of Virginia, 1935, p.79.

Prince William County Mental Health Organization. During the summer of 1967, the structure was readied for its new role as the first educational institution in eastern Prince William County for handicapped persons. It opened as the Muriel Humphries School for the Mentally Retarded in September of 1967 and was dedicated on March 31, 1968. It was used in that capacity until October 24, 1986 when road construction prevailed and the Bethel schoolhouse, with its tin ceiling and beautiful pink dogwood trees, was demolished.

THE BETHLEHEM SCHOOL

Manassas School District #7
White
1871-1930?

There is no record of when the Bethlehem School opened, but available information makes it possible to determine the year, if not the exact date. It was Schoolhouse #7 in the Manassas District which means that it opened after #6 (the Bradley School) and before #8 (the Manley School) both of which were built in 1871. Therefore, the Bethlehem School was also built in 1871 since the schools were numbered in the order in which they were established.

Bethlehem was a one-room school on the Wellington Road where it crossed the road leading to Milford Mill. It had a checkered pattern of openings and closings due to fluctuations in enrollment. In 1873, among the students at Bethlehem were Dave and Katie Harrover (see Groveton School for more about these two); Ashby Lewis of Rosemont and his brother Charles and sister Molly; the three Lewis brothers, Robert, Warner and Charles of Portici; and the four Lee brothers-Matthew, Mark, Luke and John. It was a long walk to school to school (Rosemont was two miles from Portici) for this group but they did it daily with the big ones watching out for the little ones along the way.[1]

District School Board minutes show that in 1893-94, the Bethlehem School, with an average daily attendance of only sixteen students, was, at a per pupil cost of $11 a year, the most costly of the white schools to run. The School Board obviously could not keep it open regularly with expenses at such a high level.

Indeed it did close sometime in the next few years, because in January of 1905, the School Board records note that the Board voted to re-open the school for the remaining five months of the school year. It stayed open for a year and a half until August 23, 1906 when the Board voted to close the school and consolidate the students at the Wellington School.[2]

In 1907 however, after parents objected to having to transport their children from their communities to the Wellington School, that school was closed and the Bethlehem School was opened again. On Sept. 16 of that year, the teacher appeared before the School Board to plead for footbridges over Dawkins Branch and an adjacent creek to make the students' walk to school safer.[3] The Board promised to pursue the matter but its outcome is unrecorded.

In a 1920s listing of Manassas District Schools, the Bethlehem School is included but no later mention of it has been found. Presumably it was closed sometime in the twenties when consolidation began to take hold in Prince William County. No trace of the building remains.

---

[1] Elizabeth Harrover Johnson. *Sea-Change*, Princeton, NJ: Pennywitt Press, 1977, p.7-8.

[2] Manassas District School Board minutes of August 23, 1906.

[3] Manassas District School Board minutes of September 16, 1907.

THE BRADLEY SCHOOL

Manassas School District #6
White
1871-1930

When the Manassas School Board called upon local citizens to donate land and/or buildings for use as public schools, Thomas and Martha Jones, who owned land east of the Brentsville Road along a small creek called Piney Branch, gave one acre of land with, apparently, a small building on it, to the Trustees of the School Board for a free public school for white children of the area. The small building was evidently a log cabin, which had served the community for many years as a private school.[1] During the Civil War, the Union troops used the log cabin schoolhouse as a barracks and damaged it enough that the Manassas School Board declared it to be unusable for a public school. Board minutes from December 1871 show that group agreed that the schoolhouse, built by subscriptions from the community and occupied by the Federal Army "during the late war", was unfit and therefore they agreed to seek help from U.S. Congressmen from Virginia in collecting compensation for damages.[2]

After a year, a new schoolhouse was built on the land donated by the Joneses.[3] It was located on the Brentsville Road at the juncture of the proposed road to Sinclair's Mill. The small, frame, one story, one-room building of weatherboard on a stone and brick foundation with a metal covered gable roof and a one story, shed-roofed open porch across the front was heated by a wood burning pot-bellied stove.

The Manassas Public School records of March 4, 1872 show that the School Board "voted to employ Miss Sarah E[lizabeth] Johnson to teach Bradley School for two and one half months at twenty-five dollars per month to commence April 15, 1872."[4] This is the first mention of a teacher for the school but whether she was actually the first teacher or was finishing the unexpired term of someone else is unknown. Until the Bradley School expanded its school

The Bradley School, pictured here in 1981, is one of the oldest schoolhouses in the County.
(Courtesy of PWC Schools)

term from five months to seven and then eight months, she alternated her teaching there with teaching at both the Bristoe and Cherry Hill Schools. Miss

Miss Sarah E. Johnson who taught at the Bradley School from 1872-1913.
(Courtesy of Mrs. Alice Johnson)

---

[1] Prince William County Deed Book #30, p.60.

[2] Manassas District School Board minutes of December 18, 1871.

[3] Manassas District School Board minutes of October 10, 1871.

[4] Manassas Public School records, Vol. 3, p.71.

The Bradley School, its students, its teacher (Sarah Johnson) and the teacher's horse, Dolly.
(Courtesy of Mrs. Alice Johnson)

Johnson continued to teach at the Bradley School until January 12, 1913, a career of more than forty years! She was then sixty-eight years old and lived another four years in "retirement".

Miss Johnson, whose home was Clover Hill Farm in Manassas, travelled to school in a spring wagon pulled by her horse, "Dolly". She is remembered by her pupils as one who "ran a tight ship" and expected a lot from her students. Every morning she would stand at the top of the school steps and as each student entered the building, he or she was expected to say "Good morning, Miss Sally." If they failed to do so, they had to go back down the steps and try again. Her diction was remembered as being perfect.[5] A photograph taken in front of the schoolhouse during those early years shows Miss Johnson standing in the doorway with thirty-five students ranging in age from probably five years old to big teenagers. No wonder she had to "run a tight ship". Mr. George C. Round, a Trustee of the School District, had this to say about the Bradley School under Miss Johnson:

> In contest with other schools of the county her pupils were splendidly grounded in fundamentals of common English, penmanship, reading, spelling, arithmetic, grammar and geography. Her school room was a model of exactness and order. In use of charts, library books and school building she excelled.[6]

Miss Sally obviously cared about her students and they, in turn, looked back on those schooldays with fond memories. In 1910, Mr. Hugh H. Weedon of Weedon Fick Publishing Co. of Pittsburg sent a donation of books for her school's library. Included in this wonderful gift was a thirty-two volume set of the writings of Dumas, a set of Dickens's works, a set of Shakespeare's works and a set of Historical Memories of Europe. During the years 1898 to 1909, at least three members of the Green family—Raymond, Lucille and Mary Allie—attended the Bradley School. In the Green family there survives a souvenir booklet filled with poems and drawings, a gift from Miss Johnson at the end of the 1909 school year, "with best wishes from your teacher". The list of students in that booklet of 1909 shows that there were forty-two students that year, twenty-four girls and eighteen boys.

Miss Sarah Johnson was a pillar of her community. She not only was the schoolma'am for forty years, she was active in the United Daughters of the Confederacy as well as the Bethlehem Church. In addition, Sally[7], as she was often called, helped her mother, sister and brother run the family farm, Clover Hill, often taking in sick relatives or neighbors and nursing them back to health. She "still managed to find time to write letters to relatives, make gifts using 'the needle or shuttle' and to do for others....She was known far and near and loved by young and old."[8]

Like most early schoolhouses, the Bradley School served several purposes in its community. In 1885, for example, it is known that Reverend Abraham Conner of the German Baptist Brethren Church preached there before he settled in the Cannon Branch area of Manassas.

By 1906, the little schoolhouse was at least forty-five years old and in need of both repair and

---

[5] Johnson, p.1.

[6] Quoted in *The Manassas Journal*, January 14, 1916.

[7] According to her nephew's wife, Alice Johnson, Sarah was also known as "Doshes" and the background of this is as follows:

When her niece Emily James Johnson (1884-1966) was very small she would stand at the window and watch for Sally to return home from teaching at Bradley driving the horse named Dolly [hitched] to the spring wagon. Upon seeing her she would excitingly [sic] exclaim "Da she is!", thus the nickname "Doshes".

[8] Alice W. Johnson. "Sarah Elizabeth Johnson", unpublished correspondence with the author, 1992, p.2.

enlarging. On August 23, 1906, the School Board authorized Trustee Payne to see that it was done.

In the early 1920s, enrollment began to decline. The teacher during the 1925-26 school year was Mrs. Ruth Ormonde Butler, age twenty-one and a recent high school graduate. She had only twenty-five students enrolled with eighteen attending on a daily average. Of those twenty-five, seventeen were in grades 1-4 but at year's end, two of them had dropped out and eight had failed. Eight students were in grades 5-7 but one dropped out during the year and one failed at the end of the term. Mrs. Butler was paid $65 a month for the eight month term and paid $20 monthly for room and board. It must have been hard at such a young age to live away from home during the school year. The year end report also said that there were 225 books in the library at the little school, a drop from the 300 which made up the library during Miss Johnson's years.[9]

The following year, the teacher was another young woman, Miss Virginia Estelle Polen. She was only eighteen years old and this was her first teaching experience. She was in charge of twenty-two children, the majority of whom were enrolled in the first four grades. The average attendance on a day was only fourteen however, below the accepted level of a minimum of sixteen. Miss Polen's salary was the same as Mrs. Butler's had been the previous year.[10]

The next year, 1927-28, enrollment was up a little, with twenty-eight students. Twenty-two were in grades 1-4; six were in grades 5-7. That was the last year for the Bradley School and the last teacher was Miss Mary Harley who was also the last teacher of the Cannon Branch School.

On July 2, 1930, the Board recommended that the school be closed and the children be given a choice of taking a bus to Manassas or attending the Brentsville School. The little schoolhouse was rented as a residence to Archie Muddiman. Unfortunately, Mr. Muddiman, in November 1935, was in jail and the Board received a report that the building and grounds were being "misused". Mr. Muddiman was ordered to vacate the property within thirty days.

On Sept. 15, 1936, the school house was sold at auction to Mrs. Hannah O'Calloghan for $200 ,which was deposited to the credit of the Manassas District School Fund. The building was willed to her grandchildren, Patrick Bradley and Patricia Holland who rented it to the Bradley Forest Bible Church. It was then sold in 1986 to the Calvary Gospel Church which met there until the pastor moved on in 1992 when the building was again sold. It was purchased by Doreen McIntosh whose parents live next door. It is now rented to a church who uses it for storage purposes. Its owner is committed to its preservation as one of the oldest standing schoolhouses in the county.

---

[9]"Virginia Daily Attendance Register and Record of Class Grades" for the Bradley School filed at the end of the 1925-26 school year.

[10]"Virginia Daily Attendance Register and Record of Class Grades" for the Bradley School filed at the end of the 1926-27 school year.

THE BRENTSVILLE SCHOOL

Brentsville District School #1
1871-1944
White

The Brentsville District School Board held its first meeting on December 12, 1870. Superintendent of Schools Thornton explained the duties of the Board which immediately moved to pay Mr. John Sinclair $20 to take a census of all the District's children between the ages of five and twenty-one. At that first meeting, the Board also contracted with Mr. P.G. Slaughter to take over the Brentsville Village

The Brentsville Schoolhouse looks the same in this 1992 photograph as it did when it was built.
(Photo by the author)

Schoolhouse for the then princely sum of $50 a month. That change of a private school into a public school marks the first venture of the District into public education. It became known as District School #1, a designation which remained unchanged throughout the school's existence. It must have been the largest of the early Brentsville District schools because it was insured in 1877 for $300, twice the amount for the other schoolhouses.

By 1878, enrollment at the Brentsville Village School warranted the hiring of an assistant teacher. The records of August 1880 show that Mr. R. H. Stewart was hired to teach at Brentsville but no assistant was taken on. Mr. Stewart had taught the last two months of the previous school year at the Bristoe School.

By 1886, when W. T. Woodyard was the teacher at Brentsville, the school was badly in need of repair.[1] Whether or not the repairs were made is not recorded, but we do know that Miss Ida Nicol replaced W.T. Woodyard as teacher the following year. Miss Nicol remained at Brentsville for several years.

In 1908 an assistant teacher was hired to relieve the overworked Miss Ella Garth. Miss Garth was paid a salary of $30 a month; the assistant received $25. At that time, the School Board also urged the teachers to find a suitable two-room school building while maintaining the legal daily average attendance which would warrant a larger schoolhouse and the second teacher.

When Manassas became the center of the government for the county in 1893, the Brentsville Courthouse was no longer needed as a courthouse. It became the Prince William Academy, a private school, until 1905. In September of 1907, it was offered to the Brentsville District School Board for use as a public school. The sale price was $800 but the matter was tabled and no further action was taken for two years. Then in 1910, the Board re-opened negotiations to purchase the old Courthouse and two acres of surrounding land. An agreement was reached with Dr. W. J. Bell to buy the building, the land and all slates, desks and other equipment for $900. The plan was to remodel it into a two-room school.

When the remodelling plans were submitted to the State Board of Education, however, they were rejected because the first floor ceiling in the old Courthouse was too low.[2] Plans were redrawn and on July 13, 1912, the Board agreed to architect I.A. Cannon's plan to remodel the Courthouse by removing the upper floor and putting in a false ceiling, higher than the original one but eliminating the second floor. The lower floor would then be divided into the two rooms the School Board felt were necessary. The Board agreed to pay $900 for both the old Courthouse and the two acres. The remodelling work was done by citizens of the community who had subscribed to provide labor. All was under the supervision of the architect. In August of that summer, the Board agreed also to erect a solid board fence between the Courthouse, now the schoolhouse, and the old jail building.[3]

After the remodeling was complete and the building accepted into the District school system, the old Courthouse continued life as the Brentsville School for another fifteen years.[4] On June 30, 1916 the School Board agreed to rent the pasture at the school lot to Mrs. Bowen "to pasture one cow at $1.50 per month."[5] They also agreed to allow the Presbyterian Church to erect a tent for a meeting during August in the pasture "provided satisfactory arrangements can be made with the renter of the pasture."[6] In 1919, the Board agreed to appropriate $150 for a metal ceiling and to recruit citizens to do the work.[7]

Two teachers continued to handle grades 1-7 at the Brentsville School. In 1921 a group of citizens petitioned the School Board for a high school and the Board did hire a third teacher to provide high school subjects for students who desired them. In 1923-25, Mr. George W. Beahm, a well known educator who had most recently taught at the Woodlawn School, was principal teacher at Brentsville. Mr. Beahm's son, Robert, remembers his father's years there as follows:

---

[1] Brentsville District School Board minutes of May 3, 1886, p.117.

[2] The Brentsville Courthouse at that time was a two story building.

[3] The Bennett School of 1993 faces a similar problem of proximity to the county jail. History does indeed repeat itself.

[4] The first white schoolhouse at Brentsville was moved in 1914, for a cost of $15, to the newly acquired site for the Brentsville Colored School. It served the black children of the community for another four years.

[5] Brentsville District School Board minutes, June 30, 1916.

[6] Ibid.

[7] Brentsville District School Board minutes, September 16, 1919.

My father made the six miles trek [from his home in Nokesville] by either buggy or horseback, and on occasion was marooned in Brentsville by high water. Several times as a three year old I accompanied him and had to tolerate the older girl students who wanted to "mother" me.[8]

The rest of the faculty during that time consisted of Miss Shields and Miss Naomi C. Pearson. Miss Pearson stayed on at Brentsville after Mr. Beahm left and filed the 1925-26 year end report. She was at that time, a young-twenty years old-high school graduate ending her second year of teaching the primary grades at Brentsville. Only eighteen children were enrolled but the daily attendance averaged seventeen. Two pupils failed that year. Miss Pearson was paid $80 a month, the highest salary known to be paid any teacher that year in the county, for the eight months' school year. She had to pay room and board of $28 monthly, which was also the highest in the County.[9]

Then, in 1926, Anne Ross Keys came from Greenwich to teach reading, writing, arithmetic and geography to the lower grades. She was twenty-two years old, a high school graduate in her first year of teaching. Twenty-one children were enrolled in first, second, third and fourth grades but only fourteen attended on an average day. Miss Keys was paid $65 a month for the eight month term. The school library had 125 volumes that year although the previous year Miss Pearson reported that there were only forty books. Perhaps she counted only those suitable for her primary children and the larger figure represents what was available to the school as a whole. It is unlikely that any school would have had the resources to purchase sixty-five books over one summer!

In 1928, the District Board agreed to build a new schoolhouse to serve the white children of Brentsville. The Courthouse, by that time, was over one hundred years old and in need of replacement. The new high school in Nokesville had been built and the older Brentsville students were bused there. A smaller building would suffice.

---

[8] From an interview with the author in 1992.

[9] "Virginia Daily Attendance Register and Record of Class Grades" for the Brentsville School filed at the end of the 1925-26 school year.

The new building was a one-room school with a white weatherboard exterior and five large sash windows, as well as a door across the front to let in light. The floors were narrow tongue-and-groove maple and the ceiling was made of pressed tin. Hanging lamps provided light on dark days and blackboards lined two walls. Coats, lunch pails and the wash bucket were kept in the cloakroom by the front door. The gable roof was metal covered. The teacher in the new schoolhouse was Lucy Mae Motley.

From Superintendent of Schools Richard Haydon's report at the end of the 1933-34 school year, we know that the enrollment at the Brentsville School stood at thirty-nine with an average daily attendance of ten less than that. There were twenty-three promotions that year, eight failures and eight dropouts. The next fall, thirty pupils were enrolled and an average of nearly twenty-nine attended on a daily basis. At that time, first through fifth grades were housed at Brentsville. The sixth graders were bused to the Woodlawn School, the seventh grade students went to Greenwich and the high school students went to Nokesville. The seating capacity of the schoolhouse was forty-five, but attendance during its lifetime generally ranged from twenty to thirty pupils.

Until 1941, first through fifth grades were taught at the Brentsville School. That year, only grades 1-4 were housed there. The teacher was Miss Mary Senseney, who had attended Cannon Branch, Bennett Elementary and Manassas High School in the Manassas District before going off to college to earn her teaching degree. She returned to Prince William County to begin a long career as a teacher, and Brentsville was her first assignment. She was paid $80 per month that first year and $85 the second year. From that salary, Mary paid Mr. and Mrs. Seymour $25 a month for room and board during the week. She went home to Manassas on weekends. The Seymours also boarded two children in their house and the teacher and pupils walked a mile each way to school. On really bad days, Mrs. Seymour drove them.

Mary's description of those first two years of teaching tell so well what it must have like for most beginning teachers in the early years of public education. She says,

> Student teaching had not been in a one-room school, and I was poorly prepared for such

an assignment. It was very hard not to have anyone to turn to for advice.... I tried to rely on my memories of the one room school that I attended as a child.

> The school had a coal and wood stove in the middle of the room. There was a desk for each child with larger ones for the big children. There was an old piano which served no purpose except to hold the two coal oil lamps for night meetings. We had a little wind-up record player and a few records. There was no "recitation bench" as I had in my former school [Cannon Branch]. I didn't think I could do without one, but I put the first grade desks together and the same way for each grade. I went from one group to the other. I had ten first graders and they were my favorites because I could see that they actually did learn to read and count. The children in the other grades had no idea of phonics [which made teaching them more difficult].[10]

Mary's description of outside play at recess time brings back those days of fifty years ago as if they were yesterday. There was a fifteen minute recess in the morning, another in the afternoon and an hour long lunch break. Most of the students brought their lunch to school, although a few walked home to eat. Mostly the bigger boys, and an occasional girl, played baseball. The previous teacher had often joined in those games but Mary preferred the circle games and jump rope twirling with the little children. Mary goes on:

> The former teacher had bought two pairs of boxing gloves [for the school]. The biggest boys kept begging me to let them put on the gloves and box...although I didn't approve of boxing. At last one day I let them have the gloves and almost precipitated a family feud. The boys got very angry and fought madly. That was the end of the boxing as long as I was there.
>
> Also I did not know that I should stay on the playground at recess. In my school experience the teachers had always stayed inside at recess to plan or help an individual pupil. I found that I had to stay outside to try to settle fights. Later "supervised play" became mandatory.

By the 1940s, people had become more aware of the importance of sanitation. Each child in Mary's classroom had his or her own cup for drinking just as each had his own clean basin of water in which to wash hands before lunch. Water came from the school's own well via a pump in the front yard. Mary had to sweep the schoolroom floor herself but Mr. James (Cookie) Wolfe made the fire in the coal stove every morning in the winter.

As the term went on, Mary again sets the scene. She says,

> The first year [I taught] I tried to have a very ambitious Christmas program with a play and lots of carol singing. I had no accompaniment and I wasn't a good singer. The actors in the play got a little rowdy, but we muddled through. One parent, Mr. Spicer Keys, told me how much he enjoyed the singing.
>
> Things became a little easier for me [about Christmas time] and I became engaged to be married in June. The mothers of the children got together and made me a quilt (Dresden Plate). Each lady pieced a square and embroidered her name on it, then they quilted it. I still treasure this keepsake. They also gave us sheets and pillowcases for a wedding gift.

After her marriage, Mary, now Mrs. Kline, lived in Manassas and drove to Brentsville to teach each day. As is the case with most teachers, she found the second year easier.

> I approached my second year with much more confidence. I felt that I knew how to help the children. There was only one fifth grader that year so he was allowed to go to Nokesville. Also there was only one first grader, but she was very bright and received help at home so she got along fine.
>
> I remember most of the parents with fondness and found them helpful and understanding.

The next year, Mary went to teach at Nokesville Elementary School and later moved to Baldwin

---

[10] All the recollections of Mrs. Mary Senseney Kline are from written correspondence with the author, 1991-92.

Elementary in Manassas for a teaching career which covered more than twenty-five years.

The Brentsville School remained open for two more years under the tutelage of Mrs. Wilma Tomlinson and then, at the end of the 1943-44 school year, the school closed and the children were bused to Nokesville or Manassas. It was the last of the one-room schoolhouses to close and it marked the end of an era. In the 1953 Prince William County School inventory, the building is listed as a dwelling with heat being supplied by a stove. Later, it became a storage and then a working area for the county Parks and Recreation Department. It is now part of the Brentsville Historic Recreation area located in the village along the Bristow Road.

The Brentsville Village schoolhouse is today one of the best preserved of the old county schools in its original state. The blackboards are still on the wall inside and the pressed tin ceiling is in fine condition. The fixtures for the old hanging lamps are even in place though now florescent lights are used. The narrow tongue-and-groove maple floors are covered with serviceable linoleum. The old cloakroom is now a storage area and a 1960s addition along the back of the building houses a small kitchen and office as well as a rest room.

THE BRENTSVILLE COLORED SCHOOL

Brentsville School District
Colored
1909-1918

As early as 1892, the black citizens of Brentsville petitioned their School Board to open a school for their children in Brentsville. However, funding was short and interest on the part of the Board lagged. White schools took precedent.

Finally, in October of 1907, the Board agreed to establish a colored school at Brentsville for a five months' term. The Board would pay the teacher of salary of $20 a month if the legal daily average attendance figure could be attained. "The patrons [were] to furnish building and furniture, wood, and [etc.].[1] This came at the same meeting where the Board agreed to buy five new desks for the Woodlawn School for white children. Other than the Brentsville Colored School, no formal name seems to have been used for the schoolhouse. During the 1909-10 school year, the school apparently was held in a house owned by the Reverend Richard Jackson because at the end of the year the School Board agreed to pay Rev. Jackson $10 for the use of his house that year.[2] At the same time, the Board also agreed to move six of the best desks from the Allendale schoolhouse, as well as the old blackboard from the Bristoe schoolhouse, to the Brentsville Colored School. The arrangement with Reverend Jackson continued for another three or four years until 1914 when he agreed to sell for $25 the one acre lot on which the old colored church at Brentsville was located.[3] Mr. Smith Moore then agreed to move, at a cost of $15, the old white Brentsville schoolhouse onto the lot to be used for a colored school. Thus, for the sum of $40, the black children of Brentsville got a "real" schoolhouse. In August of 1917, Miss Cordelia Jennings was appointed as the teacher for what seems to have been the final year in the life of the Brentsville Colored School.

In August of 1918, due to low enrollment, the School Board agreed to close the school and transport the children to the Kettle Run school if they were willing and it cost no more than $2 a day to do so.[4] Vandalism at the school added to its problems. No further mention of the Brentsville Colored School is made in District School Board minutes, so apparently the arrangement with Kettle Run came into being. School Board member Mr. J.R. Cooke was authorized in 1925 to apply to the Court for permission to sell the Brentsville Colored School property. However, it wasn't until eight years later that Mr. John Petty bought the old school, but not the land on which it stood, for $15 with the proviso that he remove the building from the property as soon as possible.[5] What

---

[1] Brentsville District School Board minutes of October 4, 1907, p.274.

[2] Brentsville District School Board minutes of June 21, 1910.

[3] Brentsville District School Board minutes of January 16, 1914.

[4] Brentsville District School Board minutes of August 13, 1918.

[5] Prince William County School Board minutes of September 10, 1933.

Mr. Petty did with the building or its materials is not known but that is not quite the end of the story. In May of 1935, Mr. F. H. May requested permission from the District School Board to "take in" the old Colored School lot by straightening the fence line.[6] He agreed to pay a "reasonable price" for this. The School Board was agreeable, but since no proper title to the property could be found, Mr. May was advised to petition the Court.[7] This, as far as we know, is the end of the story. No pictures have been found of the old school and even its exact location has never been pinpointed.

[6]Prince William County School Board minutes of May 8, 1935.

[7]Ibid.

THE BRISTOE SCHOOL[1]

Brentsville District School #6
   (#2 after 1900 renumbering)
White
1877-1936

The Brentsville District School Board minutes of August 13, 1877 contain the first mention of a schoolhouse at Bristoe. "The people of Bristoe Station and vicinity having given the Board of District School Trustees sufficient evidences of their ability to sustain a school with a legal average, it is ordered that a school be established at or near this point." Because no mention is made at that time of building a schoolhouse, it is assumed that a room was temporarily rented for use as a school.

Less than one year later, on June 10, 1878, the School Board advertised in *The Manassas Gazette* that it would be accepting bids for the erection of schoolhouses at Bristoe Station and Towles Gate. Specifications were clearly spelled out and from them we know what both those schoolhouses were like. The building measured 16'x24' with a ten foot ceiling. There were three windows on each side of the school, each with twelve 8"x10" panes as well as one window fronting the door at one end. The outside was of undressed weather boarding; cypress or drawn oak shingles were used for roofing. The flooring was of random width pine. The interior walls up to a height of four and a half feet were covered with wainscoting. Above that the walls were plastered and covered with white wash. The Board even prescribed the exact measurements of all boards which would be used in the construction and called for locks on the door.[2]

The Bristow Schoolhouse next to the Post Office, c. 1930.
(Courtesy of PWC Schools)

The Board accepted the bid of Mr. W. Raymond Free to build both schoolhouses for a total fee of $219.50. Half the money would be paid when the contractor put the building materials on the school site and the rest would be paid upon completion of the job. On May 19, 1879 the Bristoe School opened for one month. Miss Sally Johnson, teacher at the Bradley School which had closed for the term, was hired for a salary of $25 per month.

The Brentsville District School Board, in the 1880s, began moving their schoolhouses from one location to another apparently to accommodate changing demographics. In August of 1887, the Board ordered "that the Bristoe School be moved out on the County Road joining Church lot"[3] and placed on stone pillars. The Allen Brothers agreed to move the schoolhouse on the Bristow Road to sit on nine stone pillars. Their fee was $49 and the work was to be finished by October 1, 1887 so that school could be opened for the term. Miss Nettie F. Weedon was the teacher during this period.

[1]The spelling of the village's name was changed from "Bristoe" to "Bristow" on August 1, 1884.

[2]Brentsville District School Board minutes of June 10, 1878.

[3]Brentsville District School Board minutes of August 15, 1887, p.119.

On May 4, 1891, the School Board decided not to move the Bristoe schoolhouse again but ordered that the building be abandoned and a new one built near Chapel Springs, the community located at the junction of the Bristoe Road, Vint Hill Road, Linton Hall Road and the Nokesville Rd. (Rt. 28). No records of this school have been found, however, and it seems likely that the plan was not carried out. Instead, in June of 1893, the Board ordered that a new schoolhouse be built at Bristow. It was to measure 26'x30' with three windows on each side, tongue and groove walls, pine flooring and a brick flue. On the outside, the building was covered with weatherboarding with a tin roof with "all work to be done in workman like manner."[4] The contract was awarded to Davis and Snook who submitted the low bid of $378. Work proceeded quickly and the new school was accepted into the system on September 2, 1893, in good time for the term to open.

In an Engineering Report prepared for the County Schools in 1953 by a Manassas Insurance Agency, it is reported that the last Bristow school house was built in 1907 at a cost of $1200. It was located in the village of Bristow on the dirt Bristow Road between the Post Office which was along the railroad tracks and the Methodist Church. The frame building had two rooms but only one was used as a classroom. Electricity was provided. A few years later, on January 20, 1912, the School Board agreed to spend $30 to purchase a library for the school; $15 was to be raised by the community and the other $15 was appropriated from the Board's budget. By 1927 there were twenty volumes in the library.

In the School Board minutes of October 21, 1912, it noted that the Bristow school was closed for two weeks because of smallpox in the neighborhood. The building was fumigated and disinfected before re-opening with the approval of the County Board of Health.

In 1925, only one room was still being used as a classroom and it remained that way until the school closed. During the 1925-26 school term, the teacher, Mrs. R. M. Weir, reported that the average daily attendance was eighteen although thirty-two children were officially enrolled in the first through seventh grades. There were nine dropouts and five failures at the end of the year, mostly in the upper grades. Mrs. Weir was paid a monthly salary of $65 ($520 for the term of eight months). The following year, Miss Elizabeth V. Hovey, who at the age of twenty-three years had one year of teaching experience and a high school diploma, took over the teaching duties at Bristow. Enrollment figures that year show thirty-five students on the books but only twenty-four attended on a daily average. The salary was raised that year to $70 a month out of which Miss Hovey paid $20 every month for room and board in the community.[5] Enrollment numbers remained fairly steady over the next decade. Figures for 1933 show twenty-nine children on the rolls with an average daily attendance of twenty-six. At the end of the year, there were nineteen promotions, five failures and five who dropped out. The following year the enrollment was twenty-five with an average attendance of twenty-two or almost ninety percent.[6]

The school room provided tables and chairs for the first graders, double desks for the older children. Heat was furnished from a wood stove and there was a piano. No janitor was hired. Both water and toilet facilities called for changes. Water had to be brought from a patron's well and the privies were not built to state regulations. Additionally, the playground was too small and lacked equipment. Students brought their own equipment from home.[7]

On October 7, 1936 the School Board approved the closing of the Bristow school due to low enrollment. Children were transported to Nokesville and their teacher was also assigned there to fill a vacant position. On March 8, 1939, the Board agreed to sell the school building to Mr. John A. Mowry for $495. It is no longer standing.

---

[4]Brentsville District School Board minutes of June 5, 1893, p.165.

[5]"Virginia Daily Attendance Register and Record of Class Grades" for the Bristoe School filed at the end of the 1925-26 school year.

[6]Richard C. Haydon. "An Administrative Survey of the Public School System in Prince William County, Virginia", A Thesis for Master of Science at University of Virginia, 1935, p.56.

[7]Ibid.

THE BROWN SCHOOL

Manassas District School #2
Colored
1870-1954

The second public school established in the county was in the Manassas School District, as was the first one. Like that one, this second school probably evolved from a private school. In this case, however, the school was for black children who previously had been educated privately using funds from white benefactors as well as the black community.[1] The original building was a two-room frame structure located, on a map from 1869, near the intersection of Liberty and Prince William Streets in the village of Manassas.[2] Not long after it opened, the school building was moved to a nearby lot on Liberty Street where it still stands today, covered in yellow siding and used as a residence.

The new location was an open lot on a muddy street. The building had no porch and no fence but a large stone at its entrance. The "Friends Society for the Aid and Education of the Freedman", a Philadelphia Quaker group, had been sending funds for the education of black children for several years. When the school system became public in 1870, the newly formed Manassas District School Board asked the Friends to transfer their funding to the public schools. That benevolent group agreed to continue to pay $25 toward the salary of what was then called the Manassas Village Colored School.[3]

That arrangement continued during the next school year also. In July of 1871, the Manassas District Board agreed to pay the "Colored School teacher" $35 a month for a five month term. $25 of that salary would continue to come from the Friends Society of Philadelphia; the remainder would be paid by the School Board.[4] That group, a year later, invited the Friends to name the #2 school of the Dis-

The second Brown School building, c. 1940.
(Courtesy of PWC Schools)

trict since their funds were that school's main support. The name Brown School was chosen, honoring Mary D. Brown of Philadelphia, a member of the Friends Society.[5]

For many years, the Brown School was the only educational facility for young black children in Manassas and it served as the feeder school for the Manassas Industrial School. It also served as the center of the black community in a large area of the county for eighty-three years.

The early history of the Brown School is a checkered one. In 1893, the Manassas School Board elected Leonera Joice as principal teacher at a salary of $25 a month. Mary V. Lucas was appointed as assistant at $20 monthly. (In contrast, the principal at the white Ruffner School was paid $40; his assistant, $25). From 1897 to 1904, the principal of Brown was Mr. George Harris who left the school system for the higher salary offered by a career in government service.[6] His place was taken by Mr. Powell W. Gibson who served as principal of the Brown School until 1912. During the early years of his tenure, Mr. Gibson was assisted by Miss Georgia Hannah Bailey who left to marry and then resumed her teaching career at the Manley School. Professor W.C. Taylor took her place to finish the school term. He was a retired Industrial School principal, a veteran educator who nevertheless left Brown in disgust at the condition of the building, the poor equipment it offered and the parents who came into the school to whip teachers who disciplined their children.[7]

Miss Bailey's (now Mrs. Berry) vacancy was finally filled by Mrs. Bessie Loving White at the request of Mr. George C. Round who, in his capacity as trustee of the Manassas Industrial School, was

---

[1] Commodore Nathaniel Bennett. *View From the Mountain: Jennie Dean of Virginia*. Unpublished monograph, Manassas, Virginia, 1986, p.70.

[2] R. Jackson Ratcliffe. *This Was Manassas*, privately published in Manassas, VA., 1973, p.40.

[3] Manassas District School Board minutes of their second meeting, December 17, 1870.

[4] Manassas District School Board minutes of July 21, 1871.

[5] Manassas District School Board meeting of August 17, 1872.

[6] Bennett, p.70.

[7] Bennett, p.71.

familiar with her ten year record of teaching at that school. Mrs. White was appointed by Superintendent of Schools Clarkson and given a first grade teaching certificate based on that "splendid" record.[8] Then, in 1912, Mr. Gibson left the Brown School to become a public school principal in Winchester where he later retired. Personnel problems were not the only troubles endured by the Brown School. In January of 1907 the District School Board received a report that the Brown schoolhouse had been "seriously damaged" by fire.[9] School was suspended until repairs could be made.

Finally, in 1924, Mrs. White became principal and thus a new era, with a woman in charge of "a tough spot like the Brown School", began for the troubled school.[10] That year, history records that parents began to cooperate with the school. Mrs. White, along with the students and other faculty, raised money from the school patrons[11] to fence the school lot, move the big rock from the entrance, put up a porch on the front of the old building, and hire "local carpenters of color" to do it all. This cooperation soon led to the formation of the School League, a necessary ingredient for the success of any of the early schoolhouses. When a law was passed requiring running water and sewers, the School Board said that funds just were not available for those things and the school was threatened with closure. One parent of several students at Brown offered to lend money to the School Board so that the necessary improvements could be made. This offer was accepted and the school stayed open for the rest of the 1924-25 school year.[12]

Then, in 1926, with funds raised by patrons of the Brown School, a lot was purchased for a new school building on Prince William Street just west of South Grant Avenue in Manassas. The property was then deeded by the Brown Colored School League to the Prince William County School Board along with $1000 in cash raised by the community and a promise of all the unskilled labor necessary to build the new building. Additional funds of $6500 came from Rosenwald money. In January of 1926 bids were opened for construction of a four-room schoolhouse.[13] The low bidder was the Appomattox Construction Company of Appomattox, Va. whose bid came in at $6631.53. Using some of the $1000 raised by the community, Dr. John Williams, an alumnus of the Brown School and a prominent black physician in Manassas who was also deeply involved in the education of black children, drove into Washington, D.C. and bought radiators which he and several young men installed in the new school building. In the 90 degree heat of a Manassas summer, they also laid a water line to the school from the town center to provide water for the drinking fountains and for steam heat.[14] Prince William Street was opened to the site, the old schoolhouse was abandoned (and sold in 1928) and the new Brown School opened.

The new school was a very definite improvement over the old building. The Rosenwald frame structure, with its peaked metal roof, had six rooms, four classrooms and two industrial skills rooms. There was a cafeteria in the basement, a school office and two bathrooms. Cloakrooms were also part of the layout. The walls and ceilings were of lath and plaster; the interior floors were of wood which was oiled once a month. There were shades on all the windows, a furnace to provide steam heat and a janitor to operate the system. The pupils took great pride in their school and, under the supervision of the teachers, took good care of it.[15] The library contained 150 volumes. Students from the Lucasville School and the Manley School as well as those children from Nokesville who lived near enough were consolidated at the Brown School despite opposition from some long time residents who felt that the heritage of the Brown School as the center of the black community of Manassas would be lost.[16] As was the case with most other schools, the Brown School served as a center of community social activities.

---

[8] Bennett, p.71.

[9] Manassas District School Board minutes of January 26, 1907.

[10] Bennett, p.72.

[11] Supporters of the school, usually parents, friends and neighbors. The patrons and later the League were the forerunners of the PTA groups which came into being in the twentieth century.

[12] Bennett, p.72.

[13] Prince William County School Board minutes of January 4, 1926.

[14] Robin Tunnicliff. "No task too tall for devoted doctor," *Potomac News*, September 27, 1990. The article gives the opening date of the Brown School as 1923 but no corroborative evidence has been found.

[15] Richard Haydon. "An Administrative Study of the Public School System of Prince William County, Virginia", A Thesis for Master of Science at the University of Virginia, 1935, p.97.

[16] Bennett, p.76.

Plays, spelling bees, suppers, May Day celebrations and Christmas pageants were all held there.

In the 1929-30 school year, there were thirty-seven children in the first grade and thirty-one in the second, all under the tutelage of Lutie Irene Lewis, a twenty-two year old high school graduate with only one year of teaching experience. Imagine a classroom of sixty-eight students today. For that she was paid $55 a month, less than almost all other county teachers that year though her class was certainly the largest. She also had to pay $20 for room and board in the community. Of her students, forty-four were promoted, eight failed and sixteen dropped out. Miss Lewis noted in her year end report that in her classroom were two sisters, Kate aged thirteen and eight year old Mary Washington who had to walk four miles to school. They were able to attend for only forty days although the school year lasted from September to May.[17]

That same year, Miss Lucille V. Ford, who was also a twenty-two years old high school graduate but with two years experience, taught seventeen pupils in the second grade, thirteen in the third and nine in grade four. The average daily attendance was thirty-three and at the end of the year only two dropped out and no one failed. Like Miss Lewis, Miss Ford was paid only $55 a month for a yearly (nine months) salary of $495. Her room and board was $20 a month.

Louise Smith Brown, as both a student and later a teacher at the Brown School, remembers a curriculum using readers, spellers, math and geography books and handwriting exercises. A school day began at 9 AM and went until 3:30 in the afternoon with two breaks as well as lunch. Baseball was a favorite outdoor sport with balls being brought from home. Another favorite recess game during good weather was tag.[18]

By 1933-34, according to the report of Superintendent Haydon, the total enrollment of the Brown School was 158 with an average daily attendance of 110. By year's end, 114 students were promoted,

The first Brown School on Liberty Street
(Courtesy of Manassas Museum)

seventeen failed and twenty-seven dropped out. The following year, total enrollment had fallen to 136 with an average daily attendance of 122 or 90%. Only three of the classrooms were used during those years. One of the teachers was a college graduate with a Normal Professional certificate and five years of teaching experience. The other two teachers held Elementary Teaching certificates and took summer courses and extension work at Hampton Institute and Virginia State College. They were both experienced teachers having taught for twenty-six and nine years. All three had musical ability and two were skilled seamstresses. The two lower grades were trying the newly revised curriculum encouraged by the administration.[19]

In 1934, pit style outhouses were still in use. They were "fly-proof" and in fair condition. All the students had desks or tables and chairs depending on their grade level. The school had a piano and more than two hundred books in the library. The younger children had a sand table in their classroom. Maps, charts and globes were available in every room but there was no playground equipment and no electricity.

From 1936 to 1943, Mr. Oswald Robinson taught at the Brown School. He had been a teacher in several of the small schools for black children since

---

[17] "Virginia Daily Attendance Register and Record of Class Grades" for the Brown School filed at the end of the 1929-30 school year.

[18] From an interview with the author in 1992.

[19] Haydon, p.97.

1928. Toward the end of his tenure at Brown, in order to support his family, he also worked from 11 PM to 7 AM in Washington, DC before putting in a full day of teaching. Equal pay for equal work did not apply to blacks and whites in those days.

In 1947, modernization and additional rooms for the Brown School cost the County School Board a total of $23,990. Seven years later, following the "Brown vs the Board of Education" Supreme Court decision, which declared school segregation unconstitutional, the Regional High School[20], which occupied the facilities of the old Manassas Industrial School, was closed because each county was responsible for the education of its own black young people. The students of the Brown Elementary School were moved over to the old Regional High School building in 1954 and the Brown School building was abandoned. In 1960, the Jennie Dean High School, for grades 1-12 was built on the site. In 1966 the Jennie Dean High School became the Jennie Dean Middle School and in 1991, it became the Jennie Dean Elementary School. Although the first Brown School building is still standing, no trace of the second Brown schoolhouse remains and only fragments of the old Industrial School have been uncovered.

[20] The Regional High School was a joint venture between Prince William, Fauquier, Fairfax and Warren counties for the education of their black youth.

THE BUCKLAND SCHOOL

Gainesville District School #1
White
1841-192?

Opened in 1841 as a private school for grades 1-7, the Buckland School was a one-room building on a wooded hillside behind the Trone House in the town of Buckland. The school building was heated by a pot-bellied stove in the center of the room with wood carried by the boys. The teacher called students to classes with a handbell, as was common in many of the little schools across the country. Water came from a spring at the bottom of the hill and there were two privies in back which were called "Garden Houses".[1]

Pupils at this early school included the five sons of Circuit Court Judge John W. Tyler, who lived at Woodlawn Plantation located in present day Fauquier County less than a mile west of the community of Buckland in Prince William County. The teacher, when the school opened, was Eppa Hunton who, in turn, was instructed in the law by Judge Tyler.[2]

Twenty years later, Colonel Eppa Hunton organized the Eighth Virginia Infantry and rose to the rank of General. At the end of the Civil War, General Hunton returned to the field of education where he actively promoted adequate schooling, both public and private, for all the county children. Another teacher was Mr. Clyde Glascock, who later became a professor at Yale University.

When public education came to Prince William County in 1870, the Buckland School became part of the system and was given the #1 designation for the Gainesville District. No mention of a new building is found in School Board records so presumably the old one sufficed though it would have been thirty years old by then if it had been new when it opened.

Continuing the tradition of hiring distinguished teachers, in the fall of 1912, Mr. Richard C. Haydon became the teacher for the Buckland School, beginning a long and distinguished career as an educator. He remained at Buckland for only two years when he became principal of the Bethel School. In 1925, he became Superintendent of Schools for Prince William County, a position he held until 1946 when he left the county to become Assistant Superintendent of Public Instruction for the Commonwealth of Virginia.

In the spring of 1924 the School Board decided that the Buckland school was no longer needed so they authorized Mr. C.B. Allen to apply to the court to sell the building and its grounds.[3] Apparently there were

[1] Martha Leitch. "Buckland, Prince William County, Virginia", *Echoes of History*, Pioneer America Society, Inc., Vol. III, No. 6, November, 1973, p.86.

[2] Eppa Hunton. *Autobiography*. Richmond: William Byrd Press, Inc., 1933, Foreword.

[3] Prince William County School Board minutes of April 10, 1924.

no buyers and the decision was rescinded three years later by the Board when it was decided to wait until the State road in that area was completed.[4] Finally, on November 7, 1927 the Board authorized the sale,

but it wasn't until a public auction in front of Partlow's Store in Gainesville on March 28, 1929 that W. H. and Sara F. Butler bought the schoolhouse and lot for $70.00. The old building is no longer standing.

---

[4]Prince William County School Board minutes of August 3, 1927.

THE CABIN BRANCH (OLD)/ CLARKSON/CABIN BRANCH SCHOOL

Dumfries School District
Colored
1889-1950

When the Cabin Branch Mine opened in 1889 to produce high grade pyrite ore, a community of support services grew up in the area near where the North and South branches of Quantico Creek met. As miners and their families began to create a community, a school house was established to serve the black children who lived around the mine. The community became known as Batestown and the school was called the Cabin Branch or, later and more formally, the Clarkson School. The Superintendent of Schools beginning in 1891 was W. M. Clarkson and very likely the schoolhouse was named in his honor. It was located on the east side of Mine Road about two miles northwest of the village of Dumfries in what is now Prince William Forest Park.[1]

The Prince William County school inventory reports that a new one-room frame Cabin Branch schoolhouse was built in 1916 on the west side of Mine Road less than half a mile south of the site of the old school. The total cost was $1400. Located next to the Little Union Baptist Church, the new school continued to serve the children of Batestown until 1950.

Reference is made in the April 10, 1924 School Board minutes to the decision of the Board to sell an abandoned school and lot in the Cabin Branch area. This was the Clarkson or Old Cabin Branch School. Apparently no sale occurred because four years later records show that the school site was again offered

The Cabin Branch School
(Courtesy of PWC Schools)

for sale by the Board.[2] It was finally sold to Mr. J. H. McInteer at a public auction in front of Ratcliffe's Store in Dumfries on Friday, March 29, 1929. The winning bid was $10.[3]

The end of the year report for 1926-27 was filed by teacher Mrs. Florence Simes and gives an idea of how the Cabin Branch School was faring ten years after it was built. Mrs. Simes had only two years' teaching experience at that time, but she was thirty-four years old and the holder of a Normal Professional Certificate. She was paid $60 a month, or $448.31 for the eight-month term and had to pay $20 every month for room and board. She had a school with thirty-seven children enrolled although the daily average attendance was twenty-eight. Of the twenty-nine students on the rolls in grades 1-4 and the eight in grades 5-7, fifteen dropped out and eleven failed by year's end. At that time, there were only twenty books in the school library, not even enough for each child to have one.[4] That unfortunately was not unusual in the small colored schools during that time.

---

[1]William Brown. 1901 map of Prince William County.

[2]Prince William County School Board minutes of June 6, 1928.

[3]Prince William County School Board minutes of April 3, 1929.

[4]"Virginia Daily Attendance Register and Record of Class Grades" for the Cabin Branch School for the 1926-27 school year.

The school did, however, come into praise in Superintendent Haydon's 1933-34 year end report. He called it "a school building remarkable in construction as well as in condition" with a teacher's desk "of a splendid type". The one large room had "proper window arrangement" and a cloakroom.[5] It was heated by a wood stove and maintenance was done by the children under the direction of the teacher. The schoolhouse sat on two acres of land part of which was cleared and in use as a playground. Beautification of the grounds was planned for the spring of 1934. Also planned was the installation of a water pump so it would no longer have to be carried from nearby homes. All these improvements would come from the school's patrons. The outdoor toilets came in for the Superintendent's disapproval; they were in "very poor" condition, unsanitary and located too close to the building.[6]

The students' desks were deemed "suitable"; chairs and kindergarten tables were provided for the smallest children. In the classroom there was also a reading table but with very few books other than textbooks. There were no maps, no charts and no globes. The teacher did have a hectograph which was used to prepare materials for the students. The teacher had four years' training at the Minor Teachers College in Washington, D.C. and held a Collegiate Professional Certificate. 1934 was her first year of teaching; the Superintendent characterized her as "eager".[7]

The enrollment for November of 1934 was fifty-four with an average daily attendance of forty-one or almost 80%, quite a handful for a first year teacher!

At year's end, thirty-six students were promoted, ten failed and eight dropped out of school.

On June 6, 1937, Adeline Penn and Ernestine Grayson presented a letter to the School Board from the General Welfare and Educational League of Prince William County recommending that the three colored schools in the lower end of the county (Cabin Branch, Hickory Ridge and Quantico Colored) be consolidated at Cabin Branch. This apparently was not acted upon for awhile because it wasn't until January of 1939 that the Superintendent presented a plan to the School Board to dismantle the abandoned Gold Ridge and Minnieville schoolhouses and use the materials to add two rooms to the Cabin Branch school in order to carry out the consolidation plan for colored schools in the Dumfries District. The estimated cost of this addition was $1200-$1500 plus the salvaged materials. The Board gave its tentative approval and authorized the Superintendent to prepare the construction plans.[8]

By 1941, when Mrs. Mary Porter began her thirty-one-year long teaching career in Prince William County, Cabin Branch was a three-room school. Mrs. Porter taught first and second grades. She later taught at both Washington-Reid and Dumfries Elementary Schools[9] before retiring.

The Cabin Branch School continued to provide an education to the children of Batestown until 1950 when the larger and brand new Washington-Reid Elementary School opened for black students on the Dumfries Road. The Cabin Branch School was sold in 1952 by the School Board.

---

[5] Richard C. Haydon. "An Administrative Survey of the Public School System of Prince William County, Virginia", A Thesis for Master of Science at the University of Virginia, 1935, p.103.

[6] Ibid., p.104.

[7] Ibid., p.104.

[8] Prince William County School Board minutes of January 4, 1939.

[9] Mrs. Porter was one of the four black teachers assigned to previously all white schools in 1965 as part of the county's program to integrate its schools. She was assigned to Dumfries Elementary at that time.

THE CANNON BRANCH SCHOOL

Manassas District School #9
White
1889-1927

In July of 1888, the Manassas School Board ordered a ninth schoolhouse to be built in their district. Though located only two miles from Bennett in Manassas, the center school of the District, poor

The Cannon Branch School as sketched by Mr. Carroll Conner.
(Courtesy of Mrs. Mary Senseney Kline)

transportation meant a need for a neighborhood school. In this case a school was needed to serve the families along Cannon Branch, named for a family named Cannon who had a farm in the area. The Board paid $1.00 for the deed to a piece of land on Isaac Harley's farm near the point "where Cannon's Branch crosses the Manassas and Milford Mills public road"[1], across from where Godwin Drive intersects present day Nokesville Road (Rt. 28). Funds for the school were to come from the tax levies of 1888 and 1889.

The Cannon Branch school was unique because it was built to serve children of the German Baptist Brethren, whose "plain garb, Pennsylvania Dutch language, and tendency to stay to themselves caused trouble at times with the non-Brethren. Their northern identity in this war-torn southern land did not help."[2] They were often looked upon as "peculiar" by others, and their efforts to have a school built in their community at first met with resistance. George C. Round, the long time and influential champion of public education in the County, came to their aid, however, and helped them get the school they needed.

The schoolhouse had one room for about thirty students in grades 1-7. It was not uncommon for children to walk two or three miles across fields to get there. The first teacher was Samuel Hinegardner who taught for only one year; the second was Mr. J.D. "Deb" Wheeler who remained two years. The third teacher, Reverend Jerome E. Blough, stayed for eight years. He was a well educated man, called "Professor" by the students, who taught high school subjects to the more advanced pupils.[3] In the middle of his tenure as the Cannon Branch teacher, the average daily attendance was thirty-four. The highest number attending was forty-nine. That year (1893-94) the total cost of the school was $280 for an average cost per pupil of $8.24. It was the least costly of all the white schools. Despite that fact, when Professor Blough petitioned the School Board for an assistant, they turned him down giving him instead a five dollar a month raise in salary bringing his pay to $30 monthly. He continued to earn that salary for the rest of his stay at the school as the enrollment continued to be high. A school term in the early days of the Cannon Branch school was only six months long since the children were needed to help on their family farms during the spring and autumn. Later the year was extended to seven months and finally to eight, closing on the first of May.

As the enrollment grew, a shed room was added onto the back of the little schoolhouse and an open porch was built on the front. Some years, two teachers were needed. During the 1920-21 school year a brother and sister team served the children. Lola Kline taught primary grades in the back (shed) room while Wilmer Kline taught the upper grades in the main room. In 1922, to meet new State standards for accreditation, the School Board decided that one-room schools should only teach grades 1-6. Older children were bussed to Manassas. By 1925, the Cannon Branch School taught only grades 1-4 so only one room was used and this was the pattern for the remaining two years of the school. The shed room with only blackboards and "a very old desk", was then used for a place to study or as an exit when plays were put on at the school.

Recollections from former students at the Cannon Branch school give a good picture of what the little building used to look like. On the walls between the windows were a United States flag, a picture of George Washington and a large picture called "The Lone Wolf". It showed a wolf on a snowy hill looking at a distant farmhouse and as a little girl, Mary Senseney (Kline) thought it was a very sad picture.

Under "The Lone Wolf" was a small bookcase with a glass front containing a few books including a new orange copy of *Pinocchio*. Each grade had only one or two reading texts (many schools had none at all) which book lovers could borrow and take home to read, risking boredom later in the school year when the class read them together. New books were very rare. Textbooks were purchased from older children for a few cents so every book had eight to ten names of owners listed inside the front cover.

In front of the room was the blackboard and in front of that was the teacher's desk and a Recitation Bench where the class being taught at the time would

---

[1] Manassas District School Board minutes of July 1888.

[2] Mary Senseney Kline. *Cannon Branch School, 1889-1927*, privately published, 1988, p.3.

[3] While facts and figures generally come from Manassas District School Board records, nearly all of the personal and human interest information about the early days of the Cannon Branch School comes from Mrs. Kline's delightful writings which she generously gave to this author. As Mrs. Kline says at the beginning of her booklet, "This history is drawn from my memory as well as others who attended this little school, second only to our church and homes, as the most important influence in our young lives." Rather than create cumbersome footnotes throughout, the reader should realize that material not otherwise cited is from Mrs. Kline.

sit. Younger children often learned from the lessons being taught to the older children on the Bench; sometimes the older children were assigned to help the younger ones with their lessons. It was also the task of the oldest pupils to chose the daily Bible reading and prayer.

A great deal of pride in the little school was felt by its students. They established an Improvement Club with fees of one cent a week per member. Those fees, along with money raised by Koffee Klatches, provided funds to repaint the school room, buy a water cooler and some pictures for the walls and fence the schoolyard. In addition, a Community League did what they could to provide funds for the school. Girls would fix lunches in decorated boxes and the boys would buy them, eating with the girl whose box he had purchased. The money went into the Community League fund where it was used for school improvements.

To heat the school, a stove stood in the middle of the room next to the post supporting the ceiling. Two long rows of double desks lined both sides of the room and a shorter row filled the middle of the room from the teacher's desk to the stove. By 1923 coal had replaced wood as the fuel for the stove; Everett Kline, a student, was paid $1 a month to go early to make a fire to warm the building. It was a favorite job of the boys to fill the coal bucket from the supply in the shed behind the schoolhouse. Near the coal shed were two privies, one for boys and the other for girls.

As was the case in most of the early schoolhouses, there was no electricity. Light for night meetings or programs came from two coal burning lamps which stood on the unused piano in a front corner of the classroom. Nor was there running water; indeed there was not even a pump or well on the school property. Twice a day, two boys had to cross a pasture to Alfred Breeden's farm to get buckets full of water which they would then pour into a white earthenware water cooler kept on a bench at the rear of the classroom. Each pupil kept his or her own cup in their desk. On warm days, students remember that the water was often lukewarm since there was no ice available.

Recess time has been the same since children began going to school and Cannon Branch is no exception. While the teacher stayed indoors and caught up on paperwork, the pupils went out onto the playground where they played favorite games such as "Dodge Ball" or "Drop the Handkerchief", "Go In and Out the Windows", "Prisoner's Base" or "Jack and Jill Come Over the Hill", and tag in Uncle Sam Harley's field next to the schoolhouse. The big boys liked to jump hurdles or play softball with equipment brought from home; occasionally even some of the girls played with them! Little girls usually preferred Hopscotch or playing House or jumping rope. Mary Senseney remembers too a game called "High Over" where a ball was thrown by one team over the schoolhouse to another team who was supposed to catch it. If they were successful, they took a member of the opposing team and this went on until all the children were on one team.

When bad weather kept the pupils indoors, there was no rest for the teacher! The students still needed a break from their studies but their favorite activities must have been noisy. They liked to put on plays or act out stories; play "I Spy"; hold spelling bees; make cocoa on the stove in the center of the room or occasionally vegetable soup if the older girls had brought the ingredients. One can imagine that the teacher hoped for good weather as much as the students did!

Memories of students who attended the Cannon Branch School give the modern reader a good picture of how children used to dress. The little girls wore print dresses, black ribbed stockings and ankle high laced boots which often split down the back because in their haste to get them off, the girls didn't unlace them far enough! The boys wore overalls and the same kind of shoe. One pair of shoes had to last for the whole year so sometimes students went barefoot on warm days. They then ran the risk of having oily feet from the oil used to keep the dust from the dirt floor under control.

Schools in the Manassas School District sometimes had reading, spelling and story telling contests with each other. These were held at the Bennett School and students remember how proud the whole school felt when one of their own took a first prize.

Lots of memories have preserved the feeling of those long ago school days at Cannon Branch. Sometimes on winter mornings when it was too dark to see the blackboard, the teacher would read a book to the children. A particularly exciting favorite was *Uncle Tom, Andy and Bill*. One day the stove fell down, crushing Mary Senseney's drinking cup. It was aluminum and soft enough to bend back into shape, however, and no one was hurt but school was dismissed early that day. At butchering time in the fall, one of the boys always brought a pig's tail to school and tried to pin it on the back of a girl's dress. When Mabel Harley was a pupil she remembers that a man came to the school one day leading a big black bear. He said that for ten cents he would make the bear dance. The teacher, Miss Mary Rosenberger, and the children could only raise nine cents among them, but the man made the bear dance anyway.

Superintendent of Schools for the county, Mr. Richard Haydon, occasionally paid a visit to the Cannon Branch School and the students recall how he would stand in the front of the room with his hands clasped behind his back and rock back and forth when he talked to the class. By the time Mr. Haydon wrote his report on the county schools in 1934, the Cannon Branch Schoolhouse was already closed so we do not have the benefit of his expertise in evaluating the school.

Mary Senseney (Kline) remembers Christmas as a "time of enchantment". The children were given a piece to memorize for the Program and time was taken from classes to practice for the singing. The older boys went out into the woods to gather running pine and cedar and holly to decorate the classroom, including the pictures of George Washington and The Lone Wolf as well as the blackboard. A tree was brought in and all the children decorated it with paper ornaments and paper chains. Even a stage was brought in and put up in the front of the room. A wire was strung up in front of the stage and curtains made from bed sheets were hung from it with safety pins. When the big event was over, someone brought a freezer of Beachley's Ice Cream Parlor ice cream for the parents and children to share. Then everyone would ride home in their milk wagons under piles of quilts to keep warm.

In front of the Cannon Branch schoolhouse ran Rt. 28 which was a gravel road. After a heavy rain, the bridge over Cannon Branch was usually under water making passage impossible. To correct the problem, in 1927 a new Rt. 28 was built behind the school. The grading work was done by a team of horses pulling a scoop on wheels that would scrape the dirt from the high places and dump it in low places at the ends of the bridge. The horses and some of the workmen stayed in a camp near the Rose Hill Cemetery. Needless to say, all this going on just outside the schoolhouse windows was distracting for the children but their teacher, Miss Mary, smeared Bon Ami on the lower windows so they couldn't see out!

With the rebuilding of Rt. 28, travel to Manassas became easier and one by one the School Board closed the little schoolhouses and consolidated the students at the Bennett School. In 1927, the Cannon Branch school closed and the children walked to Rt. 28 to catch the bus into Manassas. The bus to Bennett was a dark green open truck with benches along each side and one down the middle and the ride was a rough one.

According to the original 1888 deed for the Cannon Branch School, "...when the land...shall cease to be used for public school purposes, the same shall revert to the tract of land to which it originally belonged."[4] Isaac Harley's son Sam then sold the schoolhouse and lot, now cut off from his farm by Rt. 28, to Albert Breeden whose son Oden made it into a house. The shed room and porch were removed and the building turned so that the long side faced the new road. A new porch was built on the front and the inside was divided into four rooms. Twin daughters were born in that house before Mr. Harley sold it to Walter Breeden whose five daughters were born there. Walter was killed by a train at the Rt. 28 crossing but his widow and family continued to live in the converted schoolhouse till the children were grown. By then, the addition of more rooms and a porch gave it a more residential appearance. A son of Walter Breeden and his family continued living there. In 1988 the widening of Rt. 28 meant tearing down the old schoolhouse, the last remnant of the German Baptist Brethren community.[5]

---

[4] A copy of the deed is found in Mary Kline's booklet, *Cannon Branch School, 1889-1927*, p.10.

[5] Kline, p.7.

THE CATHARPIN SCHOOL

Gainesville School District #2
White
1874-1936

The first Catharpin schoolhouse was built in 1874 on one acre of land given to the School Board by the Buckley family on the north side of Sudley Road in the northeast quadrant of the intersection of a private lane leading to Putman's Ford on Bull Run at the Loudoun county line (now Sanders Land and part of State Route 705). This land was part of the old Chapman farm, which was a large plantation owned, but not operated, by the Chapman family, which owned and operated Chapman's Mill now known as Beverley's Mill, on Bull Run at Thoroughfare Gap. Before the Catharpin school was built, the children of families living on Chapman lands went to a private school operated in St. John's Episcopal Church, one mile west of Catharpin.[1]

That first school was a small, one-room building. One of the first teachers was Mr. Hugh Powell, who read law while his students worked on their lessons. He was admitted to the bar, moved to Texas and was elected mayor of Ft. Worth! He boarded with the postmaster, George Sanders, and his family at their Mount Pleasant farm.[2]

By the late 1890s the one school was not big enough so, in May of 1897[3], the Gainesville School Board decided to build a new schoolhouse. The old building was sold to Mr. Frederick Sanders who had been serving as postmaster since his father's death and continued to do so until his own death in 1932. He paid $30 for the building which he moved on rollers pulled by a horse named Dandy to a location north of his store and post office now known as Alvey's Store. The old schoolhouse was used as a chicken coop and later as a dwelling. Finally, it was again moved and used as a warehouse for Sander's grist mill.[4] In 1940, both the mill and the old school building were torn down.

The Catharpin School. The right side of the building was the original schoolhouse. The bell tower was added in 1898 and the addition (left) was built in 1913.
(Courtesy of PWC Historical Commission)

On July 17, 1897 the Board accepted the low bid of Mr. E.C. Taylor for $448.80 to build a two-story schoolhouse. However, ten days later, on July 27, Mr. Taylor said that he had forgotten to include the cost of the roof, which would add $40 to his proposal, so the Board had to call for bids again.[5] In the interest of time, it was decided to build a one-story schoolhouse and, again, Mr. Taylor was the low bidder at $335. The carpenter who worked on the schoolhouse was Mr. Nalls from Greenwich. The one-room building with frame walls a metal covered gable roof was painted yellow and was ready to open for the 1898-99 school year. It, like most other county schools of the day, had two privies out in back, one for boys and the other for girls. Katie Bell was the first teacher in that new building; long time residents remember other teachers: Etta Lynn, Ben Sanders, Mattie Matthews, Eleanor Wilkins.[6]

In 1913, there were so many pupils that the teacher needed an assistant to handle them all. In the summer of that year, an addition was put up at the west end of the existing building at a cost of $1800. The carpenter was Mr. I. I. Anderson who had recently worked on the nearby Sanders house. Eight grades were taught in the enlarged school building. One of the two first teachers of the school was the same Eleanor Wilkins who had been teaching at the older school but now she was married and known as Eleanor Brower. Other teachers included Neville Dogan, Miss Annie Troth, Frances Dorsey Ristedt and Alice Metz Lynn. The school bell, installed in

---

[1] E. R. Conner, III. "Catharpin, Virginia, A Trading Center of Western Prince William County", *Echoes of History*, November, 1975, pp. 66-67.

[2] Ibid., p.68.

[3] Gainesville District School Board minutes of May 22, 1897.

[4] Conner, p.68.

[5] Gainesville District School Board minutes of July 27, 1897.

[6] Conner, p.68.

the bell tower, was bought in Baltimore by Mr. Sanders who was in that city buying a line of spring dry goods for his store. It was purchased with funds provided by the Catharpin Community League and it was said that it could be heard for three miles around.[7] The school was painted white; it never was the red or yellow it has been in recent years.

A typical school day began with a Bible reading and a song. Then came lessons, followed by a short recess, more classes and then an hour for lunch. Students either carried their lunches in pails or walked home for lunch before returning for afternoon lessons, recess and more classwork. The daily routine rarely varied and indeed was much the same in every school of the time. A portrait of George Washington looked down on every classroom, a memory shared by students as almost all county schools.

In the 1929-30 school year, the two teachers were Margaret Pattie, who had started her teaching career two years earlier at the Wellington School, and Barbara R. McGrath. Miss Pattie evidently got married during the school year, because her end of the year report is signed Mrs. Margaret P. Adams.[8] That must have been exciting for her students. She was only twenty-one years old, in her second of three years of teaching at the Catharpin School. She taught twenty children, eight in the first through fourth grades and twelve in grades 5-7. She remembers that she made soup for the pupils' lunch on the pot-bellied stove in her classroom. Water was brought from her parents' home across the road.[9] In the upper grades that year, there were no dropouts although seven students failed. Mrs. Adams was paid $70 a month for a nine months' school year. She reported that the library contained 139 books. No report from Mrs. McGrath was found, so it is not known what she taught. Evidently, the two teachers did not divide their duties along grade levels as was the more normal custom in schoolhouses of more than one room.

The Catharpin Schoolhouse held many entertainments in which the children participated. Katherine Conner remembers that one teacher, Miss Alice Metz who later became Mrs. Luther Lynn, was quite talented in this field.[10]

By 1933, only grades 1-5 were taught at the Catharpin School. Children in the sixth grade and above were bused to Haymarket. Only one teacher remained at Catharpin and only one room was used. There was a piano though and that was fairly unique. During the 1933-34 school year, the enrollment was thirty-three and the average attendance was twenty-six. At year's end, there were twenty-five promotions, six failures and two students who dropped out. The next November, enrollment stood at twenty-eight with an average daily attendance of twenty-five.[11]

The schoolhouse was heated by wood stoves; a janitor made the fires by the mid-1930s. The students, under the teacher's supervision, kept the building clean. Water came from the well of a family across the street and was kept in a cooler in the classrooms; outdoor toilets existed but in 1934 they failed to meet state standards. The Superintendent of Schools called for changes in both the water and toilet facilities "in the near future". There was no playground apparatus but the area was a good one and the Junior League in 1935 planned a beautification project. The teacher for the 1934-35 school year had no experience other than being a substitute teacher.[12]

At the close of the 1935-36 school year, the School Board decided to close the white school at Catharpin due to low enrollment figures and the desire of area parents to have their children attend a larger, better equipped school.[13] All children would be transported to the elementary school at Haymarket beginning with the next school year.

On September 1, 1937 the Board agreed to sell the two-room building and approximately two acres of land to Luther Lynn for $495. About twenty-five years later, Mr. Lynn sold it to Mrs. Jack Alvey who repaired and repainted it for use as an antique shop. In 1976 its new owner[14] moved the schoolhouse several yards back from Sudley Road, painted it red and

---

[7]Ibid.

[8]"Virginia Daily Attendance Register and Record of Class Grades" for the Catharpin White School filed at the end of the 1929-30 school year.

[9]Recollections of Mrs. Margaret Adams given to the author, 1993.

[10]Recollections of Mrs. Katherine Conner given to the author in 1992.

[11]Richard C. Haydon. "An Administrative Survey of the Public School System in Prince William County, Virginia." A Thesis for Master of Science, University of Virginia, 1935, p.62.

[12]Haydon, p.62.

[13]Prince William County School Board minutes of April 8, 1926.

[14]Mr. John Norman of Haymarket.

converted it to a garden center called "Little Red Schoolhouse", operated by the former gardener for Mr. and Mrs. Paul Mellon. In 1992, after a very brief career as a community marketplace called "School-House Consignments", the building was given a fresh coat of light yellow paint and became the home of The White Oak Nursery, displaced when the Manassas Battlefield Park was enlarged. It is located at 4641 Sudley Road, Catharpin, one of the best preserved old schoolhouses in Prince William County.

THE CHERRY HILL (DUMFRIES DISTRICT) SCHOOL

Dumfries School District
White
1900s-1939

In the late 17th and early 18th centuries, the Cherry Hill Plantation stood in a grove of wild cherry trees on a bluff overlooking the spot where Powell's Creek empties into the Potomac River. This was probably the location of the earliest known public schoolhouse on the Cherry Hill peninsula. What appears to be the second schoolhouse was built by a Mr. Stone near the junction of Cherry Hill Road and Apple Lane. No record of the date of either school's opening has been found. Cherry Hill residents remember that, following many unsuccessful attempts to obtain supplies and get the building repaired, teacher Minnie Keyes set fire to the schoolhouse probably around 1918. It was probably this building which the School Board, in September of 1923, listed as abandoned and "of no use".[2] On October 28, 1927 the school property was offered for sale. It went to the highest bidder, Mr. Robert Waite of Cherry Hill, for $75.[3]

In 1919, a one-room schoolhouse was built for $1400. It was "located on a knoll near a forest on a graded unsurfaced road about a mile from the village [of Cherry Hill] proper and five miles from Dumfries."[4] The building was sturdily made of wood with a metal roof. A wood burning stove stood in the center of the large room and a wood bin was lo-

The Cherry Hill School in the Dumfries District is a residence now as pictured in 1993.
(Photo by the author)

cated just in front of it. Parents cut the wood from the nearby forest and the boys kept the bin full. The school was kept clean by the pupils under the supervision of the teacher. Water for drinking came from a spring in the forest near the school and the boys carried it up a hill for school use. Everyone shared a dipper for drinking. The privies were nearby but did not meet state standards even as late as 1934. The playground area had a tire swing but mostly children brought equipment from home. Ed Dent, who with his brothers and sisters was a student at the Cherry Hill School, remembers that marbles and fighting were two favorite pastimes.

According to Superintendent Haydon's report for the year 1933-34, the building was in good condition. There was a teacher's desk and chair; moveable, single student desks; a bookcase with a few books; maps, globes, scissors, etc. The teacher during the 1933-34 school year had a Normal Professional certificate from a teachers' college and two years' experience in teaching. The total enrollment that year was forty-eight but with an average daily attendance of thirty-four. At year's end there were twenty-nine promotions, twelve failures and only one dropout. The school at that time housed children in grades 1-4. Grades 5-7 were bused to Dumfries Elementary school and high school students commuted to Occoquan.

---

[1]Prince William County Historical Commission. *Home Place.* Prince William County, VA, 1986, p.37.

[2]Prince William County School Board minutes of September 10, 1923.

[3]Prince William County School Board minutes of November 2, 1927.

[4]Richard C. Haydon. "An Administrative Survey of the Public School System in Prince William County, Virginia", A Thesis for Master of Science at the University of Virginia, 1935, p.75.

The people of the Cherry Hill community were mostly workers on the railroad or in the Washington D.C. incinerator and wax factory at the end of Cherry Hill Road. A few were fishermen as they still are today.

Ed Dent and his brother Junior who also attended Cherry Hill school, remember a parrot named Polly which their father won from a Greek man named Jimmy. Polly spoke two languages, English and Greek, and flew at will in the neighborhood. She often would follow the boys to school, perch on the windowsill and mimic the teacher until finally being sent home with one of the children.[5]

The Dent brothers both remember that during its last year of the school when Miss Wodehouse was the teacher, there were no more than fifteen students in the classroom. It was perhaps for that reason that the school was closed at the end of the 1938-39 school year. Enrollment had to average twenty students in order for the School Board to be able to justify keeping a school open in those days of consolidation. From 1939 on, all children were bused to the Dumfries Elementary School. The Cherry Hill schoolhouse was sold to Mrs. Nora Tuell for the high bid of $260.[6] It was later purchased by Ed Dent who converted it into a home where he still lives with his family. Few people can claim to live in the schoolhouse where they were educated.

[5] Oral history with the Dents done by the author on Cherry Hill on April 7, 1991.

[6] Prince William County School Board minutes of June 7, 1939.

THE CHERRY HILL (OCCOQUAN DISTRICT) SCHOOL

Occoquan School District
White
188?-1916[1]

Both the Occoquan and Dumfries School Districts had one-room schoolhouses called Cherry Hill and, oddly enough, both are still standing at this writing (1993). The one in the Occoquan District, however, stands boarded up and ready for demolition along Minnieville Road next to the Dale City Post Office.

The little schoolhouse was built during the late 19th century across the dirt road (now Minnieville) from the Chancellor Plantation. In the late nineteenth century, the Dewey family bought part of the Chancellor land and built Cherry Hill Farm from which the school took its name. Cherry Hill was a one-room school housing first through seventh grades. It served the children of the Dewey, Taylor and other families which made up the local community. One of the first teachers was Lucy Davis. Edna Merrill was the teacher in 1911 when Winfield Dewey of Cherry Hill Farm won a certificate for "the highest average for the entire session in scholarship, attendance and deportment".[2]

Occoquan District's Cherry Hill School sits abandoned on Minnieville Road.
(Photo by the author)

When the larger Bethel School was built in 1916 just down the road, the Cherry Hill School closed. When the aforementioned 1929 public auction apparently was unsuccessful, the School Board may have decided to rent the small building to generate some income. Whatever the case, it was, for many years, used by the secret Patriotic Sons of America[3].

In 1942, the building was purchased by Hobart Hereford who was born and raised on a farm nearby[4]. He converted into a home for his new wife, Ruth, and they lived in it for many years. When Mrs. Hereford moved away after her husband's death, she rented out the dwelling until the late 1980s when it was purchased by a developer. It sits vacant and boarded up.

[1] The dates are those given in Thomas Nelson's "Transcript of Interview with Historic Occoquan, Inc." Prince William County Historical Commission Oral History Project, September 24, 1985, p.9-10

[2] Ibid., p.8.

[3] Ibid., p.10.

[4] Ibid., p.10.

THE CHINN (MARSTELLAR)/ (KETTLE RUN) SCHOOL

Brentsville District School #4(#7 after 1900)
Colored
1874-1896

The District School Board minutes of June 1874 report that a Colored School House #2 was built in the Brentsville District. This apparently was the Chinn School, which seems to have been the second school for black children in the District although no more than a few words from the first Brentsville District School Board meeting are given to a "colored school near Fleetwood".[1] District funds were used to build the schoolhouse though this was not always the case where the colored schools were concerned. The Chinn School officially opened in time for the 1875 school year and was given the designation of District School #4.

Although no official record remains, it is probable that the Chinn School was named after William Chinn, a former slave of the popular lawyer John Gibson who had inherited the house called Fleetwood. Fleetwood, located just outside the village of Aden, was extensively damaged during the Civil War and Gibson's widow, Frances, was left destitute, "supported by the labors" of William Chinn.[2] Mrs. Gibson died in 1873 and assuredly Mr. Chinn was well known in the community and deemed worthy of honor.

In 1876, Mr. Charles German (Jerman) was appointed teacher of the Chinn School and his name comes up year after year on the year end reports filed with the County. He seems to have taken a break at the beginning of the 1887-88 school year because in February of 1888 the Board ordered the Chinn School trustees to rehire Charles German to fill the unexpired term of the originally hired teacher. His salary was to be $28 per month. The last mention of his name comes at the end of the 1890 school term, but he may have continued his career in another school which did not keep all its records.

In 1885, the Board reports that it bought seven school record books for its schools: #1 Brentsville; #2 Nokesville; #3 Red Shoals; #4 Chinn; #5 Vancluse; #6 Bristoe; #8 Allendale. The Chinn School is the only colored school on the list, lending support to the theory that the Baileysburg School #7 was been closed by that time. Presumably, the children from that school now were attending Chinn.

For two years things seemed to have gone along smoothly at the Chinn School, still under the tutelage of Mr. Charles German. Then in September of 1887, the Board ordered that the school be moved to a location near Kettle Run on the Millford Road leading from "the colored settlement at Millford" to Nokesville.[3] At the same time, the building was to be enlarged, keeping the width the same but lengthening it to thirty feet. As always, requests for bids to do the work were published in *The Manassas Gazette*. Less than a week later, the Board had a change of heart and ordered the Chinn School be left where it was for the coming school year.[4]

The next summer, the District School Board ordered that a Colored School House be erected "at or near Kettle Run Railroad Bridge. The size of the House to be as follows 30' x 22' with ten foot ceiling."[5] The site was on the land of L. A. Marstellar and was sometimes called Marstellar's School. The one-room yellow school house was located on Marstellar Road just north of Kettle Run near the juncture of Aden and Nokesville Roads. The school officially retained the name of Chinn until 1896 when it became known, at least in District Record books, as the Kettle Run School. Mr. Charles German was still the teacher.

On February 5, 1893 the District Board decreed that a school term should last seven months and requested that all teachers be notified of this change. An exception was made for School #4, Chinn, "because so many patrons complained about the teacher".[6] This was probably not Mr. German who

---

[1]Brentsville District School Board minutes of December 3, 1870. No name was attached to this early school which probably was located in a temporary building donated to the School Board. The properly constructed Chinn School may have supplanted that first schoolhouse after three or four years.

[2]Writers Program, WPA. *Prince William. The Story of Its People and Its Places*. Richmond, VA: Whitlett and Shepperson, 1941, p.154.

[3]Brentsville District School Board minutes of September 5, 1887.

[4]Brentsville District School Board minutes of September 13, 1887.

[5]Brentsville District School Board minutes of August 25, 1888.

[6]Brentsville District School Board minutes of February 5, 1893.

had served his school for at least fifteen years. In any case, the Chinn School was closed that year after a term of only five months.

In 1900, as part of the renumbering of all Brentsville District Schools, Kettle Run became known as School #7. The rest of its story is told in the section on the Kettle Run School.

COLES ELEMENTARY SCHOOL

Coles District
1955-present

The Woodbine School on the Dumfries Road (Route 234) served the children of the Coles District until 1953. As population figures grew, the need for more classrooms also grew and it was decided to build a new school. A site on Hoadly Road was chosen and in 1955 the new Coles Elementary School opened its doors. The children had been bused for one and a half years, during the school's construction, to the Washington-Reid Elementary School which was located about nine miles west on Route 234. Coles Elementary School, while overcrowded, continues to serve the community to this day.

DALE CITY ELEMENTARY SCHOOL

Neabsco District
1967-present

The Dale City Elementary School was the first school built in the Dale City subdivision of Woodbridge. It opened its doors for the 1967-68 school year in the Neabsco District, which had been created largely out of the Dumfries District but also out of the Coles and Occoquan Districts, in February of 1967. The schoolhouse is located on Brook Drive in the Birchdale section of Dale City.

THE DEAN (JENNIE DEAN) SCHOOL

Manassas District/City of Manassas
1960-present

In 1960, the Jennie Dean High School was built on the site of the Manassas Industrial School for Colored Youth and was named for the founder of that school. When the Industrial School became financially disabled in mid-thirties, the school trustees asked that the school be taken into the Prince William Public School system. At the end of the 1937-38 school year, the Boards of Supervisors of nearby Fauquier and Fairfax counties agreed to join Prince William County in the purchase of the Industrial

School and to administer it as an experimental public Regional High School for black youth.[1]

When school segregation was declared unconstitutional in 1954 and integrated high schools started to open in neighboring counties, students withdrew from the Regional High School in Manassas because they could attend school closer to home. To fill the empty classrooms, children from the Brown School were sent to the Regional High School building and the Brown School was closed. That arrangement lasted for six years, until the Jennie Dean High School for grades one through twelve was built.[2]

Integration of Prince William County's schools was slow in coming, despite the 1954 Supreme Court decision. It was not until 1966 that full compliance with the Civil Rights Act was achieved. Students were assigned to their schools instead of being given a choice of schools. It was at this time that Jennie Dean High School became Jennie Dean Middle School.

For a period of twenty-five years, Dean remained a Middle School. During that time, in 1977, the City of Manassas withdrew from the county and set up its own school system, purchasing the Jennie Dean Middle School which was within the new city's boundaries. In 1991, with the construction of Grace Metz Middle School in Manassas, Dean reverted to what it had been, at least partially, in the beginning—an elementary school.

---

[1] Catherine T. Simmons. *Manassas, Virginia 1873-1973*, Manassas City Museum, 1986, p.45.

[2] Ibid., p.96.

THE DUMFRIES SCHOOL

Dumfries District
White
1873?-present

There has been a school on the site of the present day Dumfries Elementary School on Cameron Street in Dumfries as long ago as the late 1790s. The property once belonged to Thomas Lee, father of Lighthorse Harry Lee, who sold all the lots but one to the Merchant family in 1795. That one lot went to Mrs. Simpson who established Mrs. Simpson's Boarding School for the Womanly Arts there.[1]

In 1873, the Dumfries District School Board acquired half an acre of land at the corner of Duke and First Streets in the town of Dumfries.[2] The purpose for the property was to provide a site for a public school. Whether or not a schoolhouse was actually built there is unknown; no mention of it has been found in school records. Property in Dumfries was also purchased by the School Board in October of 1881 but its purpose is not mentioned.[3] The date fits

The Dumfries frame schoolhouse, built in 1917 and used until 1939.

(Courtesy of PWC Schools)

into the picture of a public schoolhouse being opened in the village toward the end of the nineteenth century, but again no record has been found.

A public school was certainly in existence at the turn of the century because long-time Dumfries residents Eula Waters and Cecil Garrison remember going there. The schoolhouse was a two-room wooden building located next to the site of the present school building. Grades one through three were held in the small room; fourth through seventh grades met in the big room. Most of the local children attended school although it was not compulsory at that time. A school year lasted from September to April. Heat came from wood stoves; water was fetched by the children from a well on the Weems-Botts house property, half a mile away. "Mrs. Nettie Speake was the teacher of the younger children", remembers Mrs. Waters. "She never sat down. She walked around

---

[1] Alice Digilio. "Dumfries Elementary's Lessons in History," *Washington Post*, May 18, 1989, p.V1.

[2] Prince William County Deed Book #29 entry dated November 3, 1873.

[3] Prince William County Deed Book #35 entry for October 27, 1881.

all day working with us."[4] Mr. Garrison remembers that the boys had a playground and the girls had a different one and the children were not allowed to cross the barrier.

In 1917, a larger frame schoolhouse with a metal roof was built by the Dumfries District School Board at a cost of $6500. It was located behind the present school's auditorium. The one story building also had a partial basement floored with concrete. Interior floors were of wood as were the walls and ceilings. There were five classrooms as well as an auditorium with a piano and a reading table with chairs.

As several of the smaller white schools in the Dumfries District were closed in the county's efforts toward consolidation, the Dumfries School became an elementary center school for the District. Enrollment for the 1933-34 school year was 150 children although the average daily attendance was only 116. Of the 150 students, 103 were promoted at year's end, thirty failed and seventeen dropped out. The following year, about the same number of children enrolled (156) but the average attendance improved dramatically to 148 or 95%. Only four of the classrooms were in use at this time, each with a capacity of forty-two students. All four teachers were college graduates with teaching experience ranging from three to eight years.[5]

The younger children sat at tables and chairs while the upper grades used chair desks. Wood stoves were used for heat and janitorial service was provided, as was the case in all of the larger white county schools. Water came from a pump in the school yard and was stored in newly installed water coolers in the building. Since there was no running water, there were no indoor toilets. Playground space was ample and furnished with equipment bought in the summer of 1933. In the fall of that year, teachers and students planted shrubbery around the schoolhouse and the following year, the walkways were laid.[6]

By 1939, the twenty-two year old schoolhouse had become outdated. The Prince William County School Board decided to build a new one story brick building on land available in front of the old school.

---

[4]Digilio, p.V7.

[5]Richard C. Haydon. "An Administrative Survey of the Public School System in Prince William County, Virginia," A Thesis for Master of Science at the University of Virginia, 1935, p.53.

[6]Haydon, p.53.

This new schoolhouse with its part slate, part metal roof cost $40,000 to build. The floors were double wood board and the walls and ceilings were lath and plaster. Steam heat from an outside source kept the building comfortable and electricity provided light. The five classrooms, office, auditorium and two bathrooms called the Dumfries Graded School continued to serve as the elementary center school for the Dumfries District.

PTA groups, once known as patrons, were very important to the life of the Dumfries Graded School. They paid the gas bill, bought milk at four cents a bottle for the children and lobbied the School Board for less crowded school buses.[7] Then, as now, one of the biggest jobs for the PTA was to raise funds for the school. In the 1940s, one of the most popular fund raisers at Dumfries was the "Womanless Wedding" where all the participants were fathers.[8]

In 1956, to handle the increasing school population, a large one story addition was put on the Dumfries School at a cost of $305,049. As was the case with every school built by the county during the fifties, the cinder block walls were covered with brick and the roof was flat. Concrete floors with asphalt tile and ceilings of acoustical tile were used throughout the addition which contained six classrooms, two lavatories, a kitchen and a cafeteria.

The Dumfries School has undergone further remodelling and enlarging during recent years. It is known today as the Dumfries Model School and it remains a very active, vital part of the community it serves.

---

[7]When the PTA learned that one bus was carrying ninety-three students, it successfully got the number reduced to seventy-five.

[8]Digilio, p.V7.

The "new" Dumfries School. the center section was built in 1939.

(Photo by the author)

THE EMORY CHAPEL SCHOOL

Occoquan School District
White
1895?-1923

The Emory Chapel School, sometimes referred to as just the Emory School, appears on the 1901 Brown map of the county at the southernmost end of Old Telegraph Road between Rt. 95 and what is now called Potomac Mills Road. No records have been found which tell anything about this schoolhouse during its lifetime. Its name suggests that it was held in a church building, a fairly common occurrence during that time period. Only its closing is known.

As part of the first consolidation effort by the school system, the children from Emory Chapel and Bacon Race schools were bused to the Bethel School beginning with the 1923-24 school year.

In August of 1938 the Occoquan School Board authorized the sale of the schoolhouse for $40.[1] Up until its end it remains a mystery.

---

[1] Prince William County School Board minutes of August 3, 1938.

THE ENGLISH CHURCH (SUNNYSIDE, RED SCHOOL) SCHOOL

Brentsville District School #3
White
1886-1901

The Red Shoals School had served the community of Greenwich from two different buildings since 1870. When the Brentsville District School Board sold the second schoolhouse, it used the money gained to purchase the English Church near Greenwich for use as a school. That building already had an interesting history. In 1874, a building for an English Episcopal Church was erected by trustees Thomas E. Homer, William Adamson and Arthur A. Marson. It was located on Rt. 215 (Vint Hill Road), one and a half miles east of the village of Greenwich. By 1886, the trustees were either dead or had returned to England and the church, known as Sunnyside Church, was for sale. Mr. Homer, living in Britton, England, deeded the building to the Brentsville District School Board.[1] From that point until the building of a new school in the village of Greenwich in 1901, the school was referred to vari-

The English Church School, under restoration in 1993. (Photo by the author)

ously as English Church School, the Red School[2], Sunnyside or, sometimes, simply the Greenwich School.

The English Church Schoolhouse served the community for fifteen years, until 1901. It was a building with one large room open to the peaked roof. One end of the room forms half of a decagon. It was in this five-sided section, which is raised six inches above the floor of the rest of the building, that the preacher stood to deliver his sermon and presumably this would also have been where the teacher's desk

---

[1] R. Jackson Ratcliffe. *This Was Prince William*, Leesburg, VA: Potomac Press, 1978, p.25.

[2] D'Anne Evans. *Prince William County. A Pictorial History*, Leesburg, VA: Donning Publishing Company, 1989, p.89.

was placed. Six foot wide windows, two on each side, let in light. The flooring was of six inch wide pine boards and a stove in the middle of the lower section of the room provided heat. The first teacher was Mr. Wallace Wood who remained for several years.

When the Board sold the building it was converted to a dwelling where several families have lived over the ensuing years. Today, its owner, who enjoys the company of three ghosts who share the house with him, is dedicated to returning the old building to the way it was when it was built 120 years ago. The vertical board siding, the random stone foundation, the metal roof, the two chimneys, the interior flooring and panelling as well as the thick wooden beams which criss-cross to support the roof are being carefully restored so that the history of this interesting building comes alive. It can be found on Vint Hill Road across from the Prince William Golf Course.

In 1901, the Brentsville District built a new schoolhouse in the village of Greenwich. It was called the Greenwich School and given the designation of #9 because it was the ninth building erected as a schoolhouse by the District. The story of that school, and its successor, is told in the section titled "The Greenwich School."

THE FAIRVIEW (HEDGES) SCHOOL

Occoquan School District
White
1877-1924?

This one-room frame schoolhouse with a metal covered gable roof was located on Old Bridge Road west of the old Woodbridge airport where the new Festival Shopping Center now stands. In 1876, James and Mary K. Davis sold a half an acre of land across the road from the Hedges family cemetery to the school trustees of the Occoquan School District for the building of a school for the children of the nearby farms. The deed stated that, should the school close, the land would revert to the Davises and the schoolhouse would be sold with any profits to be divided among those who had contributed to its building. A well, located on adjoining property, supplied water to the school as early as 1877. Thus the opening year was likely to have been 1877, as soon as the schoolhouse could be built following the donation of the land.

The one-room schoolhouse was panelled with tongue and groove boards. The pine floor was also covered with tongue and groove panelling. Little else is known about this school including the year it closed. It is known that on September 9, 1925 the School Board authorized Mr. E.S. Brockett, Board member, to move the schoolhouse from its location

The Fairview School as it looked, abandoned, in 1980.
(Courtesy PWC Historical Commission)

at that time to Bethel at no cost to the Board.[1] We know that no such move took place because the Fairview school remained in its original location until demolished in the late 1980s when the land was cleared to make way for the shopping center.

Another attempt to move the school came on June 1, 1927 when the Patriotic Order of the Sons of America, through the recording secretary S.T. Cornwell, offered to buy the schoolhouse for $90 if it were removed from its site. This was apparently unacceptable to the School Board because they decided to advertise the sale of the property at Russell's Store, the community center at the intersection of Davis Ford and Minnieville Roads, at 2 o'clock in the afternoon on July 9, 1927.

On August third of that year the sale of the property to Mr. Arthur Hedges was reported. The $127

---
[1] Prince William County School Board minutes of September 9, 1925.

was deposited with the Occoquan School District.[2] Instead of moving the school as was expected, Mr. Hedges added a small room to each side of the building and lived in the structure for many years. In the colloquial, it was known as Hedges School.[3] In 1975, the School Board took the matter to court where it was ruled that Mr. Hedges did not own the land on which the school/home was located but only owned the building itself and he should have moved that back in 1927, forty-eight years before. Ownership reverted to the School Board and Mr. Hedges entered a nursing home to live out the rest of his life. As for the old schoolhouse-turned-home, in 1986 the building had been abandoned and was in poor condition. Vandals added to the problems until demolition ended the life of the little schoolhouse.

---

[2] Prince William County School Board minutes of August 3, 1927.

[3] Thomas Nelson. "Transcript of Interview with Historic Occoquan, Inc.", Prince William County Historical Commission Oral History Project, September 24, 1985, p.13.

THE FAYMAN SCHOOL

Coles School District
White
190?-1931

Because no records survive from the early years of the Coles District, there is no way of knowing the exact date for the opening of the Fayman School. It served the old community of Fayman, located near the present entrance to Camp Upshur on the Quantico Marine Base. The one-room schoolhouse was located just east of the old town at the junction of Elk Run Road and the Concrete Road.[1] Its location, about a mile north of the old Horton School, makes it seem likely that the Fayman School was opened after the Horton School had been outgrown or become too old to serve. Having two white schools so close together, when no natural boundaries such as mountains or creeks existed to make it difficult to get to one or the other, would have been an unusual expense for a school district to underwrite. The Horton School is shown on the 1901 Brown map of Prince William County while Fayman is not. Therefore, one can assume that Fayman opened sometime after 1901.

That first Fayman schoolhouse served until 1913 when early Deed Books[2] show that on June 25, 1913, the Coles District School Board purchased from DeWitt and Viola Herndon, for $30 cash, "[on the] North side of road west of Fayman...one acre, more or less".[3] The property was located on the Elk Run Road about half a mile west of the site of the earlier Fayman school. A one-room schoolhouse was built on the lot and it remained open for nearly twenty years.

Low enrollment figures posed a problem for the Fayman School in 1930. At the end of that school year, the District School Board decided that when the school opened again in September, it would be only for an eight month, rather than a nine month, year.[4] When attendance failed to improve during the 1930-31 school year, the School Board discussed transporting the students to Aden School,[5] the nearest center school to Fayman. Further consideration by the Board during the summer cemented the decision and the Fayman School was closed.

In September of that year, parents petitioned the School Board protesting the decision to close the school because they feared that the frequent high water at Harrison's Ford across Cedar Run would cause loss of some school days for those students who would have to cross it to reach Aden.[6] The School Board, however, refused to change its position saying that only a few days at most might be lost and the longer school year (by one month) at Aden would more than compensate. Thus, starting

---

[1] Eugene Scheel. *Historic Map of Prince William County*. Historic Prince William, 1992.

[2] Deed Book #64, p.10.

[3] It would have been very unusual for a school district to build a new schoolhouse when the one it would replace was less than fifteen years old. Money for school construction was not plentiful, then as now. Thus, the assumption can probably be made that the first Fayman School was held in a building rented by the District School Board for educational purposes.

[4] Prince William County School Board minutes of June 4, 1930.

[5] Prince William County School Board minutes of May 6, 1931.

[6] Prince William County School Board minutes of September 2, 1931.

with the 1931-32 school year, all seven grades from Fayman began attending the Aden School.

On March 8, 1933 the School Board received a bid for the Fayman schoolhouse for $100 but they decided to advertise for sealed bids for cash. Shortly thereafter, on April 5, the Superintendent presented a petition from a large group of community residents asking that the schoolhouse be donated to the community for use as a church. The School Board denied the request when the community representatives failed to guarantee that upkeep and insurance on the building would be maintained. Finally, the Board decided to accept the original bid of $100 cash from Mr. D.H.Herndon and on May 3, the money was deposited to the credit of the Coles District School Fund.

On June 7, 1939 Mr. Van R. Herndon offered to buy the water pump at the school for $5 but the School Board decided to leave it for the use of the community or passersby.

Beginning in 1937, the Board began consideration of the sale of the Fayman School lot. Although several offers were made[7], none were accepted until April 1939 when Mr. Van Herndon paid $25 cash for the Fayman school lot. He also had to bear the cost of drawing up the deed of the sale. There is no trace of the schoolhouse today.

---

[7]Prince William County School Board minutes of March 3, 1937; May 4, 1938; and April 5, 1939.

FEATHERSTONE ELEMENTARY SCHOOL

Occoquan/Woodbridge District
1964-present

Named after a legendary Indian princess named "Featherstone", who also gave her name to the area of Woodbridge lying between Rt. 1 on the west, the Potomac River to the east, Marumsco Acres to the north and Marumsco Woods to the south, the Featherstone Elementary School serves the children within those boundaries. It was built in 1964 in the Occoquan District, but today is in the Woodbridge District which was formed in 1976.

THE FOREST HILL/JOPLIN SCHOOL

Dumfries School District
White
1885?-1938

The beginnings of the Forest Hill School are lost to history. No records have been found which talk about the school's opening or indeed about any of its early years. From the 1901 map of Prince William County drawn by William Brown, it is known that the school was located in the community of Forest Hill along Forest Road, now called Joplin Road. Since the village was established before the Civil War, it is probably safe to say that a schoolhouse

The Joplin Schoolhouse, c. 1930.
(Courtesy of PWC Schools)

opened around that time to serve the children in the area.

For some reason, usually the age of the building or the need for more space, a new schoolhouse was built in 1912 at or near the same location.[1] It was a one-room, frame structure housing grades 1-7 which cost the District Board $1400.[2] Next door was Liming's Store and the Forest Hill Church was just a short distance further west along the road.

The name Joplin was not used until the early twentieth century when named William Crow moved to the area from Joplin, Missouri and opened a store with a post office window. He named the Post Office after his home town and officially the name Joplin replaced Forest Hill. The schoolhouse continued to be called Forest Hill, however, and it was that name which the young teacher, nineteen year old Mary R. Bell, used in 1926 when she filed her year end report. She taught twenty-six children at Forest Hill School for a term of nine months. Her salary was $75 a month or $675 for the term. She paid one third of her salary, $25 a month, for room and board in the Joplin area.[3]

The community was home to workers in the nearby Pyrite mine, mill workers and some farmers. As the mine and mills began to close, several members of the community went to work at the laundry at Quantico; a few continued to farm.[4]

During the 1929-30 school year, the school was taught by Mollie E. Miles. Like the teachers before her, she cooked a kettle of soup on the classroom stove to give the children a good, hot lunch. How wonderful that little schoolhouse must have smelled!

In 1933-34 the enrollment reached thirty-eight. At the end of the year, twenty-five were promoted, ten failed and three dropped out. The average daily attendance that year was thirty-three. The following year there were thirty-nine children on the rolls and the school housed only grades 1-4. Average attendance was thirty-four.[5]

According to Superintendent of Schools Richard C. Haydon's report of 1933-34, the schoolhouse was in good condition on an improved road. It had a seating capacity of forty-five at single desks. Heat (as well as soup) came from the wood stove supplied by the students who also, with the teacher, kept the building clean. Water came from a nearby parent's well, a situation deemed "inadequate" by the Superintendent. This must have been only a temporary arrangement, however, because the School Board minutes of December 5, 1934 note that the Board approved the "cleaning out, deepening and putting in order" of the school's well. The outdoor toilets were not satisfactory either and improvements were urged. There was, however, "ample" playground space but not enough equipment. No effort had been made for beautification although the Junior League was planning on doing some. That year, the teacher had a certificate from a teachers' college but no previous teaching experience.[6]

Despite the high enrollment figures, the School Board, as part of its consolidation effort for white schools in the Dumfries District, decided to close the Joplin school at the end of the 1937-38 year and transport the children to Quantico and Dumfries schools.[7] In October the schoolhouse and lot were sold to Otto Liming, the owner of the store next door, for $400.

---

[1] Prince William County Deed Book #62, p.466.

[2] Prince William County School Inventory of 1935.

[3] Virginia Daily Attendance Register and Record of Class Grades for the Forest Hill School filed at the end of the 1925-26 school year.

[4] Richard C. Haydon. "Administrative Survey of the Public School System in Prince William County, Virginia", A Thesis for Master of Science at the University of Virginia, 1935, p.77.

[5] Haydon, p.77.

[6] Ibid., p.77.

[7] Prince William County School Board minutes of April 7, 1938.

FRED LYNN ELEMENTARY SCHOOL

Occoquan/Woodbridge District
1963-present

The Fred M. Lynn Elementary School, on Longview Drive in Woodbridge, was named after the late Mr. Fred M. Lynn, county educator and longtime member of the Prince William County School Board. Built in 1963, it served the school population in the Longview area of Woodbridge. It is still serving today, but as a middle school.

GAINESVILLE ELEMENTARY SCHOOL

Gainesville District School #6
White
1875?-present

Though Gainesville Elementary School appears on school lists from 1877 on, very little is known about this earliest building including its exact opening date. It was situated near the location of the present Gainesville School and probably closed before the turn of the century, most likely due to low enrollment.

Maintaining adequate enrollment apparently was a long standing problem at Gainesville in its early years. The School Board even agreed to offer premiums of $5.00 to white teachers who achieved the highest enrollment for the 1893-94 school year. In addition, the teacher who showed the highest average daily attendance figures for that term would earn a $10.00 premium, nearly half a month's salary.[1] These incentive awards represented a significant expenditure of District funds at that time. If, on the other hand, enrollment fell below the required average of twenty, the teacher would not be paid at all and would be obligated to notify the Board to have the school closed. As added incentive to keep enrollment figures up, the School Board agreed to pay for textbooks needed by indigent students who might otherwise not attend. Monies for these programs came from State, County and District funds raised by a tax levy of 7 1/2 cents on every $100 worth of property and by the dog tax.

It was probably low enrollment figures which were responsible for the closing of the Gainesville School. In 1904, District Board minutes recorded the sale of the schoolhouse to Mr. C. F. Sinclair for $150.00 with payments spread over three years. The school furniture was moved to the Haymarket School where it was used in the upper room which had just been put into use.[2] Mr. Sinclair converted the building into a residence for his family.

On February 3, 1906 the School Board received a petition from citizens asking for a new school to be opened in their community. The Board agreed to rent a room for $3 per month to be used as a school and they hired Mrs. Mary Entwisle as the teacher at a salary of $25 per month. By September of 1907 the school was still operating out of rented rooms in the Purcell Building, later used as a general store and post office[3]. The school year ended early that spring because of an epidemic of diphtheria. The next school term (1907-08) the school was unable to rent rooms for some reason so apparently no school was held at all.

The Gainesville School in the 1950s after several additions had been made to the original building (center).
(Courtesy PWC schools)

The following August, 1908, the School Board agreed to buy a lot from Miss Somerville Gaines just below Gainesville on the Warrenton Pike. They paid $100 for the two acre site and agreed to use plans and specifications from the State Board of Education as obtained by the Superintendent. In December 1908 the Board accepted a bid of $850 from Mr. A.D. Rider to build the new schoolhouse.[4] He must have been a fast worker, because the new Gainesville School opened the first Monday of January, 1909 with Miss B.M. Hayden of Richmond as the teacher.

Twenty years later, the School Board decided to close the Gainesville School, probably under pressure to consolidate due to low enrollment. Although no records show where the children of Gainesville were educated after 1927, it is likely that they were transported to the school in Haymarket. At the Board meeting of November 7, 1928 it was decided to offer the schoolhouse and lot for sale. It was sold at a public auction in front of Partlow's Store in Gainesville on March 28, 1929 to Mrs. R.M. Merideth for $880.[5]

---

[1] Gainesville District School Board minutes of July 22, 1893.

[2] Gainesville District School Board minutes of January 22, 1904.

[3] Hattie Mae Partlow and Pauline Smith. *Now and Then With P.W.E.A.*, Prince William Education Association, 1963, p.78.

[4] Gainesville District School Board minutes of December 19, 1908.

[5] Prince William County School Board minutes of April 3, 1929.

When the Haymarket School opened in 1920 it housed both elementary and high school students. The high school served not only Haymarket, but also Catharpin, Hickory Grove, Gainesville, Buckland and Groveton and the inevitable result was overcrowding.[6] As early as December 1933, citizens of Haymarket presented the School Board with a petition asking for a new high school building and on February 7, 1934 the Board resolved that a new school be built. A site for the new high school was chosen and land on the northeast side of the John Marshall Highway was purchased from Mr. W.M. Jordan. Although strong opposition developed over paying increased taxes to pay for the school during this Depression Era, the School Board went ahead with its plans to build a two story, seven classroom plus auditorium-gymnasium schoolhouse. Bids were solicited but all came in at least $5000 over the projected costs. It became necessary to contract for a smaller building and on May 29, 1935 a bid by J.H. Bennett Co. of Richmond for $38,888 was accepted. "Local labor was hired to speed the construction of the school over the warm summer of 1935. Working at such low depression wages as 10 cents an hour, there are local residents today that can point with pride to the end product of their labor."[7] Furthermore, it was decided that due to the growing number of elementary school age children in the area, the new school ought to be an elementary school rather than the originally planned for high school.

The new Gainesville Elementary School opened on December 16, 1935 with four classrooms and a combination auditorium-gymnasium. Elementary children in the first through fourth grades attended the new school. Fifth, sixth and seventh grade students stayed in the old Haymarket High School along with the High School students. The same principal served both buildings though a head teacher was in charge of daily activities at the new Gainesville building. The auditorium-gymnasium was used by both schools for assemblies, sports events and graduation. Like most schools, Gainesville also was a focal point of community life where dances were held and programs put on by local groups. That arrangement continued until 1941 when Haymarket High School closed and the high school students bused to Osbourn High School in Manassas.[8]

By 1946, increases in population made an addition to the school necessary. The winning bid was that of the J.L. Vogel Construction Co. of Cumberland, Virginia for the extension of the two hallways on either side of the stage and the addition of a clinic/office, a library and four more classrooms. An open courtyard was built behind the stage. It was full of flowers and birds, visible from halls and classrooms alike. Also, at that time, a small cafeteria and kitchen were added. Students, who had either brought lunches from home or ate "soup-kitchen style lunch" made in the hallway beside the stage could now eat a hot lunch from the cafeteria. Food for the high school was also prepared in the Gainesville cafeteria and transported.[9]

In 1954, the need for expansion again was felt. A contract was awarded to Ballou and Justin Architects for the addition of four more classrooms and a vestibule on the school's west wing. In 1963 the last five classrooms were added and near the end of the decade, the courtyard was enclosed to enlarge the cafeteria.

In 1965, all students in the county's schools were given "freedom of choice" in attending local schools in compliance with the Civil Rights Act of 1964. In 1966 complete desegregation of the schools occurred. To ease the difficulties of integration as well as the problems of overcrowding, the School Board decided to annex the Antioch-Macrae school to Gainesville and house all Gainesville District kindergarten and first grades there. This Gainesville-Antioch-Macrae Elementary school continue to exist for sixteen years. During that time, the George Tyler Elementary School was built just down the road from the Gainesville School and took in the sixth grade students to ease the crowded conditions. When, in 1973, the sixth grade was made part of the middle schools, the original plan to use Tyler as a middle school was no longer viable. A growing population in the western end of Prince William County showed the School Board that Tyler was needed as a second elementary school. "Because the area was now served by two large elementary schools, the County School Board, in an effort to economize, decided to close the Antioch-McCrae School Annex in 1982."[10] The

---

[6]Carolyn Wyrsch. "Gainesville District Elementary School 50th Anniversary, October 5, 1985", privately published, 1985, p.1.

[7]Ibid., p.7.

[8]Ibid., p.3.

[9]Ibid., p.4.

[10]Ibid., p.6

students who would have gone there now go to Tyler until the second grade when they transfer to Gainesville for grades 3-5.

The Gainesville Elementary School is now almost fifty-eight years old. Residents of western Prince William County would like a new school for their children but, in the meantime, the old school continues to serve well.

THE GOLD RIDGE SCHOOL

Coles District School
White
1874-1932

The Gold Ridge School #2. Note the belfrey, an object of community pride.
(Courtesy of PWC Schools)

According to county Deed Books, on March 2, 1874, the School Trustees of the Coles District purchased, for their first school, "one acre of land to build a public schoolhouse...lying immediately on the Dumfries and Warrenton road and on the north side of said road", now the Aden Road. That one acre was bought from John and Elizabeth Brill for $1.00.[1] Probably the School Board, to comply with the State Law of 1870 mandating public education for all white children, asked the citizens of the community to donate land for the erection of a school building and a dollar was a token payment. This first schoolhouse, located about two miles west of Independent Hill and one mile east of the old village of Orlando, derived its name from the nearby gold mine. The Brill family lived across the road but owned property on both sides. This little schoolhouse appears on the 1901 map of the county but no other information about it has been found though it existed for more than twenty-five years. On May 22, 1924 the School Board accepted a bid of $50 from T.E.H. Dickens for the old schoolhouse. Mr. Dickens was given until September to move the building from the grounds.[2] The lot remained the property of the School Board.

In November of 1902, William and Eliza Breeden and Albert and Lydia Breeden sold to the School Board of Coles District, for $10, approximately two and a half acres of land "being situate near Orlando" beginning at the center of the county road at the corner where Breeden and Kincheloe land met (present Rt.646 or Aden Road).[3] This land was for the building of a new schoolhouse which, while not far from the site of the old school, was probably nearer to the center of the small community of Orlando. On the deed, the Breedens reserved the right to "all tie and saw timber" which was cut before January 1, 1904. No timber was to be cut after that date.

This second Goldridge (as it is sometimes written) School served the community for thirty years. It was a one-room schoolhouse probably of frame construction with a metal roof like the other schools built in the county during the first part of the twentieth century. The teacher during the 1929-30 school year was Miss Helen Berg, a young nineteen year high school graduate teaching for the first time. She taught a total of twenty-one children, twelve in the first four grades (two failed and no one dropped out at year's end) and nine in grades 5-7, of whom two dropped out but none failed. For the nine months' term, she was paid $630 or $70 a month. From that she paid $18 monthly for room and board in the community. Miss Berg's year end report states that the library held 250 books, very large for a small schoolhouse.[4]

---

[1] Prince William County Deed Book #30, p.392.

[2] Prince William County School Board minutes of May 22, 1924.

[3] Prince William County Deed Book #51, p.121.

[4] "Virginia Daily Attendance Register and Record of Class Grades" for the Gold Ridge School at the end of the 1929-30 school year.

In 1932, the Gold Ridge School was consolidated with the Aden School as part of the county's move to fewer, larger schoolhouses. Three years later it was reported that the schoolhouse was "more or less" in the hands of the Committee on the Nokesville Agricultural Building.[5] What this meant is not explained but at the same School Board meeting, the Superintendent was authorized to offer the Gold Ridge school for sale at public auction. Mr. Walter Ellicott apparently had submitted a bid of $325 but because of uncertainties about the building's future, the bid was withdrawn.[6] In January of 1938 the Board approved the rental of the schoolhouse to Mr. D.W. Wright for $5 a month with rent to be paid in advance.

In June 1939 the School Board accepted a bid of $40 from W.Y. Ellicott for the "new" Gold Ridge school lot and a bid of $10 from Claude Ellicott for the "old" Gold Ridge school lot.[7] This followed a decision of the Board in January to dismantle the second Gold Ridge School building. The materials salvaged were used to add two rooms onto the Cabin Branch school in order to carry out the consolidation plan for the colored schools in the Dumfries District.[8] No trace of either building remains.

---

[5] Prince William County School Board minutes of August 7, 1935.

[6] Ibid.

[7] Prince William County School Board minutes of June 7, 1939.

[8] Prince William County School Board minutes of January 4, 1939.

THE GREENWICH SCHOOL

Brentsville District School #9
White
1901-1944

The Greenwich School, built in 1901, was the successor to the English Church School which no longer was adequate for the growth of the community. With a limited school budget, the Brentsville District School Board found it necessary to arrange some rather creative funding in order to be able to afford to build a new two-room graded schoolhouse.

The Trustees of the District, always accompanied with Superintendent of Schools Clarkson, met with the Trustees of the Centre School District of neighboring Fauquier County to work out an agreement which would share the expenses of the school as well as its facilities once it was built. The Fauquier Board agreed to pay half of the cost of building the schoolhouse as well as half of the teachers' salaries. In addition, they offered to contribute the furniture from a schoolhouse which would be surplus once Greenwich was open as well as to pay half of the cost of whatever other furnishings were needed. In the end, Fauquier County ended up paying $300 of the $700 it cost to build the new schoolhouse.

Then the District Board approached Mr. M.B. Washington who agreed to sell half an acre of his land to the Board for $20. The only drawback to that

The Greenwich School c. 1930
(Courtesy PWC Schools)

piece of property was that it could only be reached by cutting across land owned by the Greenwich Presbyterian Church. After much discussion, the School Board and the Church signed an agreement allowing the students as well as various school officials to use eight acres of Church land as a right of way to the schoolhouse. The Church did not agree to let the school built a playground on those acres, however.[1]

Once all the details had been worked out, specifications for the new Greenwich School and requests for bids were published in *The Manassas Gazette*. It was to be a building of two rooms, one up and one down, each measuring 24' x 40' with an eight foot

---

[1] The early negotiations for the Greenwich School are detailed in several sets of minutes of the Brentsville District School Board for 1901.

square vestibule. There were to be four windows on each side of both floors, blinds on the windows, a tin roof and two privies out in back. Photographs of that early building also show a cupola on the roof above the front door. On November 7, 1901 the District Board met at the Greenwich Graded School to inspect it and accept it into the system. At the same time, Mrs. Lucy D. Washington was appointed as principal teacher for the school which opened on the eleventh of November. Later an assistant teacher was also appointed for the school whose enrollment continued to grow.

It was not all smooth sailing at the Greenwich School, however. On September 1, 1908, the District Board received a complaint from some parents that the teacher "fails to keep order and fails to hear pupils' lessons". The Clerk of the Board was ordered to investigate and to "request her [the teacher] to be more streneous[sic]."[2] The result of this directive is not known but no further mention is made of the problem. Three years later, the School Board agreed to appropriate $15 for the purchase of books for the school library and directed the Clerk of the Board to make the purchase.[3]

Increased enrollment and overcrowded conditions made the Greenwich School too small only ten years after it was built. On May 1, 1911 the District School Board decided to ask $800 for the Greenwich school building so that the money could be used to build a new schoolhouse. On September 15, 1911 the Board agreed to sell the schoolhouse and the land on which it stood for $750. It was purchased by "The Order of Fraternal Americans" and used as their Lodge home. In the late 1920s or early 1930s, the building was moved beside the present Mayhugh Store in Greenwich, where it continued being used as a Lodge and also a community center for oyster suppers and strawberry festivals. In the late fifties, Mr. Gordon Mayhugh purchased the building and turned it into two apartments. It was later torn down.

The District School Board purchased two acres of land near the old building from Mr. M.B. Washington for $175 and in April of 1912 awarded the contract for a new four-room schoolhouse to Mr. B.B. Walls whose winning bid was for $3150.[4] On August 2, the Board agreed to add a belfry to the school

---

[2]District School Board minutes of September 1, 1908.
[3]Brentsville District School Board minutes of May 1, 1911.
[4]Brentsville District School Board minutes of April 30, 1912.

In the foreground is the second Greenwich School building. The older schoolhouse, seen in the background, was later moved across the street and turned into apartments. The photo dates from around 1920.
(Courtesy of Mr. James Cooke)

which delayed its completion by about three months. Finally on December 21, 1912, the Board inspected and accepted the new school building. The final cost was $3500.

The four-room graded school housed grades 1-7 in three classrooms. The fourth room was used as an assembly room. Actually, folding walls separated the rooms. These walls could be pushed aside thus creating two large rooms, one of either side of the hallway which divided the building in half. There was a cloakroom on either side of the front door. The first room on the left was used for grades four and five. Further down the hallway was the classroom for the first, second and third grades. On the right, the first room was for the sixth and seventh grades. Beyond that was the assembly room with a stage and a piano along the far end. Two privies, one for boys and one for girls, stood behind the school. A pump in the school yard supplied drinking water for the teachers and children. There was a playground where sports such as baseball and basketball were popular.

Inside the classrooms, the first grade used tables and chairs; the older students had desks with attached chairs. There were good maps remembers Mr. James Cooke, who was a student at the Greenwich School from 1919-1926. The teachers during those years were Helen Cooke, Edward House and C.O. Bittle. Wood stoves in each room kept the building warm while the pupils studied penmanship, geography, Virginia history and mathematics. The school day was six hours long with a fifteen minute recess both morning and afternoon and a one hour long lunch hour. The short recesses were used mostly to use the privy and get drinking water from the pump. Students brought lunch from home and supplied their own books. They also were responsible for keeping the schoolhouse clean.[5]

According to the 1934 report by County Superintendent of Schools Richard C. Haydon,[6] the enrollment of the Greenwich School that year was fifty-nine with an average daily attendance of an amazing fifty-eight or 98.4%, the county's highest. The previous year, fifty-four students were enrolled. Of that number, forty-eight were promoted, one failed and five dropped out for various reasons. The average attendance for grades 1-4 was only twenty pupils while in grades 5-7, the average attendance was twenty-seven. By this time, only two rooms were used as classrooms. The auditorium and a small library occupied the rest of the space. The principal, who also taught the upper grades, was a university graduate with a Collegiate Professional certificate and seven years of teaching experience. The primary teacher was a graduate of a teachers' college also with a Collegiate Professional certificate but no previous experience. Both teachers were using the new course of study adopted by the State.

The school remained open until 1945 when the county began busing the remaining students from Greenwich to Nokesville Elementary School. In 1947 the School Board sold the building and it no longer stands.

---

[5]The author is indebted to Mr. James Cooke of Greenwich for these recollections, shared over a period of two years, of his school days at the Greenwich School.

[6]Richard C. Haydon. "An Administrative Survey of the Public School System in Prince William County, Virginia", A Thesis for Master of Science at the University of Virginia, 1935, p.68.

THE GREENWOOD SCHOOL

Dumfries School District
White
1883-1899?

According to School Board records of October 4, 1883, the Greenwood School was "now open". It is never mentioned again in any report. County residents remember a "school on what is now known as Minnieville Road at the Hidden Place. It was a big farm that now adjoins the Presbyterian Church up there and Greenwood Baptist Church. We know that a person who was born in 1876 attended that school."[1]

There is no Greenwood School on the 1901 map of Prince William County done by William Brown so it had been closed prior to that date. Since the Minnieville School was located not far from the site of the Greenwood School, it seems safe to assume that any students needing schooling in that area attended Minnieville after Greenwood closed its doors.

---

[1]Thomas Nelson. "Transcript of Interview with Historic Occoquan, Inc.", Prince William County Historical Commission Oral History Project, September 24, 1985, p.16.

THE GROVETON (BROWNSVILLE) SCHOOL

Manassas District School #3
White
1870-1924

The Groveton School actually began before the Civil War. It was a field school for white boys north of Groveton near Featherbed Lane but was destroyed during the Second Battle of Manassas. After that, school was held in a one-room log building, west of the original school and very near the railroad. One of the pupils at that school, which was taught by Miss Sue Monroe, was May Leachman whose name became synonymous with education in the Groveton area in later years. That log building was later moved and used as a kitchen. A cedar post with an oak tree growing around it marks its final resting place near the site of the final Groveton School.[1]

When public education began in Prince William County in 1870, it was the custom of the local School Board to ask the people of the community to donate land for a schoolhouse. In the Groveton community, northwest of Manassas on the edge of the Battlefield, May's father Mr. Thomas Leachman who lived at Brownsville[2] agreed to give a piece of his large property to be used as a schoolhouse site. On that site was built a one-room school on Featherbed Lane south of its intersection with Rt. 29. This may have been locally known as the Brownsville School, a name, which appears from time to time in informal reports but never on official School District records.

This school was the third one established in the Manassas District and also the third schoolhouse built by the District School Board. At its third meeting on January 7, 1871 the Board hired Mr. Alexander H. Compton as the teacher at a salary of $40 a month, $15 being paid by the school patrons and $25 coming from Public Funds when they were available.[3] Nine days later, on January 16, the school began. It served the white community within roughly a two mile radius of the Groveton area, which was northwest of what was then called Manassas Junction, on the southwestern edge of the Manassas Battlefield.

The Groveton School as it looks today, 1993.
(Photo by the author)

In 1873, Miss May Leachman, daughter of the man who donated the land for the school, became the teacher at the little school. She was sixteen years old and had been trained at the Millers Normal School in Millersville, PA. She lived with her family at Brownsville, also known as "Folly's Castle", and walked the half mile to and from Groveton. Miss May continued to teach at Groveton for seventeen years until 1890 when she left to get married. She was succeeded by Mr. James Davenport (Deb) Wheeler whose career in Prince William County included stints teaching in several of the one and two room schools. He was at Groveton for at least ten years and was succeeded by Miss Lily Evans. Later, Miss May, now Mrs. Frank Dogan, returned to teach at the Groveton School. Since she now lived at Paradise Farm on Sudley Road, she often rode a gray horse to school.[4] She taught at Groveton for a total of thirty years where she was a well loved and respected member of the community.

Two of her first students in 1873 were young James David Harrover and his older sister Katie who, when their mother died, went to live with the Steers family of the Groveton community. They walked to school with their friends Charlie and Molly Lewis who lived at their home called Rosemont.

---

[1] From an oral history with Bladen Oswald Robinson done by the author in 1992.

[2] Brownsville was also known as "Folly's Castle". It burned down in 1899 after a long history dating back to the Carter land patent. A new house was built on the foundation using the original chimney and it can be seen from Rt. 66 near the intersection of Pageland Lane and Groveton Rd.

[3] Manassas District School Board minutes of January 7, 1871.

[4] Elizabeth Harrover Johnson, E. R. Conner, III, Mary Harrover Ferguson. *History in a Horseshoe Curve*, Princeton, NJ: Pennywitt Press, 1982, p.xiv.

Charlie and Molly Lewis left Rosemont and came by the Steers and picked up Katie and Dave....The four of them moved north across the fields past the Wheeler farm, Willow Green, and met up with the Portici Lewises who had traveled from the east. From that point it was a short haul up a ridge toward the twin brick chimneys of Hazel Plain or the Chinn House as it was often called after the family who had lived there at the time of the Battle of Manassas. Once on the ridge, they set a more westerly course along a narrow wagon road that pushed up and down wooded hills to the Wellington Road.

The school stood west of the road, well shaded by a big oak tree.[5]

For many years, enrollment stayed at about thirty students in the seven grades taught at Groveton. When more than thirty children were enrolled, as was the case in 1884, an assistant teacher was hired until the student numbers decreased.[6] Two privies were located outside the schoolhouse; drinking water had to be fetched from a nearby spring. A wood stove heated the single room. On a small rise behind the school there was a shed where the students who rode horses to school could tie them up for the day. A school year lasted from September to June but the older boys often attended only from November to April because they had to help with the fall and spring crop work.

Geography, reading, grammar, spelling and Virginia history were taught from books purchased or borrowed by the students. Some of the children had slates and there were blackboards for class work. A single bookshelf held the school's library. A favorite game of the boys was a form of hockey using homemade sticks of dogwood or ash (known as "shinny sticks") and whatever was available for a puck—mock oranges, walnuts, tin cans, or the occasional hard rubber ball. Kick-the-Can, Red Light, Fox and Hounds, Prisoner's Base and various circle games were other favorite games at recess.[7]

Ellsworth, May, Freddie, and Harvey Senseney, as well as Hulda and Minnie Swart, are among these students posing on the steps at Groveton School with their teacher, Deb Wheeler, 1900.
(Courtesy of Mrs. Mary Harrover Smith)

Big excitement must have come to the Groveton community in the early winter of 1896 because on Dec. 7 the School Board paid Mr. Leach $4 for removing and rebuilding a closet of #3 school (Groveton), which had been blown down by a cyclone![8] Ten years later, on August 23, 1906, the Board voted to close the school and consolidate the students at the Wellington School, which would then become School #3. That apparently lasted one school year; in 1907 the Board reopened the Groveton School and hired Mrs. May Dogan to teach a seven month school year at a salary of $50 a month.

Transportation to the Groveton School evidently was a matter of concern. On August 12, 1907, the School Board voted to ask the County Supervisors to "erect suitable footbridges' across Youngs Branch and Dogans Branch for children to use on their way to school. In September, Mr. George C. Round, the Clerk of the School Board, was authorized to see to the building of stables for the horses used by students living more than two miles from the schoolhouse. Mr. William M. Wheeler was paid $19.38 to build them.[9]

---

[5]Elizabeth Harrover Johnson. *Sea Change*, Princeton, NJ: Pennywitt Press, 1977, p.9.

[6]Manassas District School Board minutes of December 3, 1884.

[7]Recollections of Mary Harrover Ferguson Smith who was a student at the Groveton School in 1917. From an unpublished report in the author's possession.

---

[8]Manassas District School Board minutes of December 7, 1896.

[9]Manassas District School Board minutes of September 16, 1907.

Children at the Groveton School advertising milk for a forthcoming Dairy Festival c. 1920.
(Courtesy of the Full Staff Communicator)

In 1914, Miss Grace Metz began, at the Groveton School, her long and distinguished teaching career. She taught sixty-five pupils, without an assistant, in the seven grades and remained at Groveton for three years. In 1917 Miss Metz went to Manassas to teach seventh and eighth grades until she retired in 1962.

With so many students in one room, it became clear that something needed to be done. At a meeting of the Manassas School Board held at Groveton School in June of 1915, the decision of the Board at their meeting a month earlier to build a new schoolhouse was vehemently discussed. There was much controversy between those parents who wanted a new building near the site of the old and those parents who wanted it located at the Stone House, on the Manassas Battlefield.[10] Strangely, no decision appears to have been made at that time, because it was not until a year later, in the early spring of 1916, that bids were sent out for the building of the new schoolhouse. On May 6, 1916, the Board accepted the bid of Mr. O.H. Evans for $1772 to build a one story, two-room schoolhouse with a cloakroom at Groveton although many parents continued their objections.

Despite those objections, the Groveton School opened in its new building in 1917 and the old schoolhouse was torn down. The new school, which contained grades 1-6, was built in front of the old building. The two privies remained behind the schoolhouse and all maintenance was done by the teachers and parents who volunteered to help.

Each day started with a prayer and Bible reading followed by the Pledge of Allegiance and a song. The teachers taught grade by grade using a course of study followed by all county schools. The curriculum included reading from McGuffey's Readers, spelling, Virginia history, geography, penmanship using the Palmer method, arithmetic, and writing. All books were supplied by the parents. Pull down maps were hung at the front of the classroom and blackboards lined one wall. Pictures of George Washington, Robert E. Lee and Stonewall Jackson hung above the blackboard along with a portrait of the English Baby Stuart by Hans Holbein! There were windows along the opposite wall and more windows in the rear of the rooms. The school library was kept in bookcases under the rear windows.[11]

As in most of the schools, the parents group, called the Community League, was very active. Night meetings were held to solve problems as they arose. Mothers provided hot soup on cold winter mornings: bean, potato, onion or chicken, watered down by the teachers to provide enough for everyone and held raffles to raise funds. A Christmas pageant was held every year and spelling bees with both students and parents participating were popular events.

An interesting account of the last two years of the Groveton School comes from Elizabeth Harrover Johnson in her account, "Memories of Groveton School". Libbie was the youngest in a family of four and was lonesome when everyone went off to school, so at the age of three and a half, she began school too. "On good days we walked the mile from our farm on Featherbed Lane to the school, toting our lunches in empty molasses pails. On bad days we rode double on a bareback pony and horse, then when we reached the school, slipped off the bridles, slapped our steeds on the rump, and sent them galloping back along Featherbed Lane to the farm. They always made it. On very bad days our Uncle Ellsworth Senseney hitched up the buggy and drove us to school."[12] Libbie goes on to describe her school day:

> I sat on the front row of desks all by myself. The other pupils were seated in desks behind me. The first thing I had to learn was to print my name, "LIBBIE". You see, there was a slate

---

[10] The Stone House did serve as a schoolhouse during the 1916-17 school year.

[11] Elizabeth Harrover Johnson. "Memories of Groveton School", unpublished correspondence to author, 1992.

[12] pg.1

placed on a desk in the back row. Printing one's name on this slate was necessary for being excused to go to the outhouse.

As the school day progressed the teacher moved back and forth along the blackboard wall, covering each class and each subject. She chalked up arithmetic problems for first one class and then the other. She heard the times tables chanted in unison....

My favorite time was when students had to read aloud from their reading assignment. Singsong or halting though some of the recitations were, they were pleasant stories to listen to. And all the while I was listening I was doing my sole assignment for each and every day — writing from one to ten, then from ten back to one. When I couldn't stand this regimen any longer, I left my desk and sat in the back row with Roy Sowers. He would always welcome me with a hug.

Gamey, wintertime odors were strong at Groveton School—and memorable. Many of the older boys set traps for possum and skunk, then skinned and stretched the pelts on boards. They earned ever-welcome cash this way. They tended their traps before school and the scent of their quarry clung not only to their clothes, but to the shoes which they had probably bought at Emmet N. Pattie's store in Catharpin and treated with neatsfoot oil. When they walked through the door of the Groveton Schoolhouse, the scent wafted throughout the stove-heated rooms. Every student knew when they had trapped a polecat!

The new Groveton School remained open for only eight years when, as part of its move toward consolidation of the smaller schools, the Board closed it in 1924. Two buses took the children to the Haymarket School. Four years later the School Board decided to sell the two-room schoolhouse at a public auction on March 28, 1929.[13] It was sold to Frank Gue, Jr. who paid $730 for both the schoolhouse and the lot. The last payment was made in October 1931 and the Board turned the deed over to Mrs. Gue.

When the school was converted into a dwelling, it was covered with a stone veneer and asphalt shingles were added to the gabled roof. It is located at 6706 Groveton Road, Manassas and is owned by Mr. B. Oswald Robinson who has deeded it to the Manassas Battlefield upon his death. It is still standing.

---

[13] Prince William County School Board minutes of November 7, 1928.

THE HAYFIELD SCHOOL

Coles School District
White
1881-1935

On January 10, 1880, Mr. George Taylor and Mr. James Barbie, "public free school trustees [School Board members] of Coles District", purchased one acre of land marked by two white oaks on the left [west] side of Hayfield Road from Luther Wright and Mr. Cornwell.[1] They paid $10 for the land which Mr. Wright had owned for just one year. Like other citizens of the county, Mr. Wright and Mr. Cornwell probably responded to a call from their District School Board to make land available for a schoolhouse as mandated by the 1870 Virginia Law calling for free public education. At the price of $10,

The Hayfield School as it looked in the late 1940s.
(Courtesy of PWC Schools)

the land probably did not have a building on it, so it is likely that the District erected a small schoolhouse soon after the purchase. No records exist which corroborate this or give any information about this first Hayfield School, however. The site is on what is now Quantico Marine Base, about a mile south of what is

---

[1] Prince William County Deed Book #32, p.235.

now the Independent Hill School Administration complex.

By 1914, the schoolhouse was more than thirty years old and probably overcrowded. A second schoolhouse was built that year by the District School Board at a cost of $1350.[2] It was a one-room, frame building for grades 1-7, located on an unimproved highway, three miles from Rt. 234, the Dumfries Road. Apparently, there was no shortage of space around the schoolhouse because on October 21, 1925, Mr. Woolfenden bought an acre of land at the school for $100.[3]

The school had a seating capacity of forty and was still in good condition after twenty years of service, according to Superintendent Richard Haydon. The first grade children used tables and chairs but the upper grades had double moveable desks. A wood stove heated the room but since there was no janitorial service, the children took care of the fires and the cleaning. A pump in the school yard provided adequate water and the toilet was up to state standards. The playground, however, was inadequate with no equipment except for whatever the children brought from home.[4]

The enrollment at the Hayfield School for the year 1934-35 was only twenty-three with an average daily attendance of 91% or twenty-one children in all seven grades. The previous year, enrollment had been up to thirty-two students; twenty-five were promoted, seven failed and none dropped out. One teacher, a graduate of a teachers' college with a certificate and twenty-nine years of experience, taught a traditional curriculum.[5] Low enrollment continued to be a problem for Hayfield so on May 8, 1935 the School Board voted to close the school and bus the children to Woodbine School. Four years later, the Board asked for sealed bids for the purchase of the schoolhouse.[6] No bids were made. In 1942, the Marine Corps purchased 51,000 acres of land west of U.S. Route 1 to expand the training area for Quantico Marine Base. It was the largest acquisition of land in the history of Quantico[7] and the Hayfield School was part it.

---

[2]Prince William County School Inventory of 1935.

[3]Prince William County School Board minutes of October 21, 1925.

[4]Richard C. Haydon. "An Administrative Survey of the Public School System in Prince William County, Virginia", A Thesis for Master of Science at University of Virginia, 1935, p.58.

[5]Ibid.

[6]Prince William County School Board minutes of May 3, 1939.

[7]Fleming, Charles A. et al. *Quantico: Crossroads of the Marine Corps*, Washington, DC: History and Museum Division Headquarters, U.S. Marine Corps, 1978, p.75.

THE HAYMARKET SCHOOL

Gainesville District School #11
White
1883-1941

In 1883, Haymarket's need for a school became critical and a group of citizens petitioned the School Board for one. On September 1, the Board agreed that a schoolhouse should be built providing the Town build it and pay half of the teacher's salary "until this Board should feel justified in assuming the paying of the whole salary."[1] In addition, the School Board agreed to furnish up to $150 worth of furni-

The second school in Haymarket, known as Haymarket High School, housed grades 1-12.
(Courtesy of PWC Schools)

ture for the school. A commission was appointed to raise the funds needed for the schoolhouse and by

---

[1]Minutes of the Gainesville District School Board, September 1, 1883.

October, $411 had been raised by subscription among the townspeople and another $150 had been raised at an oyster supper.[2] With that, a combination Town Hall/Schoolhouse was built and the school rented the rooms it needed.

In 1900, a separate schoolhouse, on Fayette Street near the center of the town, was built for $2500. It was a frame building, originally of two rooms, one up and one down. In the beginning, only the lower room was used for a classroom and one teacher taught grades 1-7. However, at their January 22, 1904 meeting, the School Board noted that forty-five students were enrolled in the school with an average daily attendance of thirty and more were expected. The teacher requested an assistant and the Board granted one for the remaining two months of the school term. The upper room was given to the assistant teacher and furniture was moved from the Gainesville schoolhouse at a cost to the Board of $3.50. A large enrollment for the 1905-06 school year caused the assistant to be hired again and soon, two more classrooms were added onto the building.

In 1905[3], citizens applied to the School Board for a janitor for the schoolhouse. The Board agreed and a janitor was hired to build the fires in the wood stove, cut the wood every Saturday, sweep the floors daily and keep the desks dusted. Two years later[4] Superintendent of Schools Dr. H. M. Clarkson suggested that coal replace wood to heat the school and the Board agreed. Funds for the purchase of two coal stoves were approved as well as funds for the building of coal bins for storage.

In 1920, in order to offer high school classes for students in the Gainesville-Haymarket area, four more rooms were added to the schoolhouse. In that eight-room school, which became known as Haymarket High School, both elementary and secondary classes were taught. It became the educational center of the Gainesville District as high school students from Catharpin, Hickory Grove, Gainesville, Buckland and Groveton were all bused to it.

---

[2]Robert L. Crewdson. *Crossroads of the Past: A History of Haymarket, Virginia*. Prince William County Historical Commission, undated, p.20.

[3]Minutes of the Gainesville District School Board, February 4, 1905.

[4]Gainesville District School Board minutes of November 2, 1907.

The first school in Haymarket was also the Town Hall building, which it remains today.
(Photo by the author)

The exterior of the building was wood siding with a metal roof and a cupola. A large front porch supported by three columns sheltered the front entrance. Inside, the floors were pine, the ceilings were metal and a single staircase gave access to the second floor. Wainscoting covered the lower walls which were painted above it. In addition to the eight classrooms, there was a basement laboratory room, but no auditorium and no gymnasium. A small room on the second floor served as the principal's office and library. Electricity supplied lighting, but wood-burning potbellied stoves heated the classrooms and privies were located behind the building. Water coolers were supplied from a pump in the school yard. The moveable desks were a matter of pride to the school. The first principal was Mr. H. M. Pearson.

A typical school day at Haymarket was much the same as in most of the other county elementary schools. The morning began with a prayer followed by the Pledge of Allegiance. After work from books purchased by the students or at the slate blackboards, the children ate lunch brought from home and played handball in the school yard. There were no clubs but plays were sometimes put on for the community.

Most of the students rode a bus to school by the late twenties.[5]

From the beginning, overcrowding was a problem but a bond issue to build a new high school failed to pass in 1928. The crowded conditions continued for six more years. One of the teachers during those difficult years was Miss Elizabeth Vaughan who had previously taught at the Aden School and later became principal at Occoquan. In 1965 she was honored for her long career in education when the Elizabeth M. Vaughan Elementary School in Woodbridge was dedicated. By 1934, the combination elementary and high school was termed "inadequate" by the Superintendent of Schools, lacking modern equipment and "architectural beauty".[6] The enrollment for the 1933-34 school year was 193 with an average daily attendance of 145. That year 131 students were promoted; thirty-seven failed and twenty-seven dropped out[7], a large percentage.

Briefly, in 1935, the Town Hall was again used for classrooms in order to handle the overflow of elementary students. That year a new school with four classrooms and a combination gymnasium-auditorium was built on the John Marshall Highway and in December of 1935, first through fourth grades were transferred there.[8] Grades 5-7 stayed with the high school in Haymarket and one principal presided over both buildings.

At the close of the 1941 school year, despite great opposition from some citizens, Haymarket High School closed for good. High school students were then bused to Osbourn High School in Manassas and the elementary grades attended the Gainesville school built in 1935. On the first of November 1947, the School Board sold the building at a public auction in front of the county courthouse in Manassas. It was converted into apartments but was later destroyed by fire and is no longer standing. The Town Hall, however, home of the first school in Haymarket, is very much a part of the village.

---

[5]From the recollections of Mrs. Sarah Turner of Haymarket, who attended grades 1-3 and 9-12 at the Haymarket School.

[6]Richard C. Haydon. "Survey of the Public School System in Prince William County, Virginia", A Thesis for Master of Science at University of Virginia, 1936, p.59.

[7]Ibid., p.59.

[8]This new school, the Gainesville Elementary School, is fully discussed in its own section.

THE HICKORY GROVE (OAK GROVE) SCHOOL

Gainesville District School #7
White
1877-1935

Located about six and a half miles north of Haymarket along present day Rt. 15 at its intersection with Logmill Road, the small rural Hickory Grove settlement grew up near the old Hickory Grove plantation, built about 1830 and later known as "Hundred Oaks".[1] In 1877, the Gainesville District School Board secured the deed to a small building on the farm of T.E. Callehers, hired Mr. R.D. Gilliam as the teacher and opened what was at first called the Oak Grove School, probably named for the Hundred Oaks plantation nearby. However, the school soon took

The Hickory Grove School as it appeared in 1980.
It is a residence today.
(Courtesy of PWC Historical Commission)

on the name of the larger community and was thereafter known as the Hickory Grove School.[2]

---

[1]Writers Program, WPA. *Prince William. The Story of Its People and Its Places*. Richmond, VA: Whitlett and Shepperson, 1941, pp. 191-192.

[2]The last reference to the Oak Grove School was found in the Gainesville District School Board minutes during the 1886-87 school year, ten years after the name Hickory Grove School came into common usage.

Mr. Gilliam taught for two years at the Hickory Grove School and then the Board hired Mr. E.H. Bartenstein for the 1878-79 school year. The little school continued to be held in the old farm building for ten years until space apparently became a problem. In October of 1887 the Board decided to have a new room added onto the old schoolhouse.[3] They awarded the contract on December 14 to Mr. E.C. Taylor who at the same time was building the Waterfall School in Thoroughfare Gap. The work was done by the time school reopened in the fall of 1888.

An interesting use of the Hickory Grove School occurred during the summer of 1892. The District School Board[4] agreed to let Miss Ollie Hunt use the building as a private school for a short summer term.

By October 26, 1895 the Board had concluded that the old building, which was attached to the new addition had become a hazard and they ordered it either sold or torn down and the end closed over with weatherboard. On January 4, 1896 School Board minutes show that the old building was sold for $12.50; presumably the new owner moved it to another location. The addition, which remained, then became the "new" Hickory Grove School.

In 1914, the town of Hickory Grove consisted of a post office, a country store and, just down Logmill Road, the one-room brown wooden schoolhouse with a metal roof. George Gossom, a former resident, remembers the outdoor privies and also the walk to his father's store to get drinking water. Two boys would be assigned that task but would usually spill two-thirds of the water on the way back to school.[5]

On March 12, 1921 a meeting of all the teachers of the Gainesville District was held at the school. Then Superintendent McDonald also attended this special Saturday meeting. It was considered an honor to host such a meeting and one can easily imagine how busy the children and teacher were in the days just before March 12, getting their little schoolhouse ready!

In 1925, according to a report by the teacher, Mrs. Selina T. Wilson, the enrollment was twenty-eight with pupils ranging in age from six to fourteen years and evenly divided between boys and girls.

Some, like the Gossom children, lived only a quarter of a mile from the school. Others, like ten year old Francis Watson, lived two and a half miles away on the Bull Run Mountain Road. Eighty-five percent of the students attended on a daily basis. There were fourteen children in first through fourth grades, twelve students in grades 5-7, and only two in grades eight and nine. That year, Mrs. Wilson's salary was $70 per month, $560 a year. There were ninety books in the school library.[6]

Twenty years later, Superintendent of Schools Richard Haydon wrote that the Hickory Grove School was located on the dirt Logmill Road six-tenths of a mile from the "good" soil and gravel James Madison Highway (Rt. 15) and nearly seven miles from the Haymarket High School which was built in 1920. By 1934, the schoolhouse was one of the oldest in the county and its lighting was inadequate. Heat was produced by a wood stove and it was the teacher's job to build a fire every cold morning. The children were responsible for keeping the wood box filled and the building clean. The elementary grades sat at tables and chairs; the intermediate students used double desks. In the late teens or early twenties, a water pump was installed in the school yard thus eliminating the boys' walk from the village but there never was running water. The State Health Department regularly checked the water as well as the privies which were kept sanitary with lime and a weekly cleaning.[7]

At the time of Superintendent Haydon's report, the enrollment stood at thirty-two in grades 1-7. The average daily attendance was twenty-five or nearly 85%. The previous school year of 1933-34 the enrollment figure was high, with forty-two on the roster but only twenty-six came on an average daily basis. Of those forty-two children, at year's end twenty-nine were promoted, five failed and eight others had dropped out of school. The building's capacity was forty-five, a figure commonly used for most of the little one-room schoolhouses. In addition to the inadequate lighting, the playground was "too rocky".[8] An adjoining piece of land was used for games

---

[3]Gainesville District School Board minutes of October 16, 1887.

[4]Gainesville District School Board minutes of April 23, 1892.

[5]Prince William County Historical Commission, *Home Place*, Prince William, Virginia: Historical Commission, 1990, p.61.

[6]"Virginia Daily Attendance Register and Record of Class Grades" for the Hickory Grove School filed at the end of the 1924-25 school year.

[7]Richard C. Haydon. "An Administrative Survey of the Public School System in Prince William County, Virginia", a Thesis for Master of Science at the University of Virginia, 1935, p.61.

[8]Haydon, p.62.

by the children. The Junior League was an active group with plans for shrubbery to beautify their school yard in 1934.

That year, 1934, there were eighty-five volumes in the school's library (they had lost ground since 1925) including two sets of encyclopedias. The one teacher for all grades had been teaching for thirty-four years. She had a special interest in "the cultural side of the curriculum", and arranged for her sister to visit the school every other week to help with this instruction.[9]

On May 8, 1935 the School Board voted to close Hickory Grove School beginning with the 1935-36 school year. The big, new elementary school in Gainesville was open for the first time and many of the small schools, including Hickory Grove, were consolidated there. On August 4, 1937 the schoolhouse was sold at public auction for $300 to Todd Rhodes who converted it into a private residence. It has changed hands three times since then but the stone veneer covered home still stands at 2620 Logmill Road.

[9] Haydon, p.62.

THE HICKORY RIDGE SCHOOL

Dumfries School District
Colored
1933-1943?

Hickory Ridge school is unique among the county schools because it opened in 1933 in a rented hall and apparently never occupied a building of its own.[1] Black children who lived in the little settlement of Hickory Ridge, along the present day North Orenda and Pyrite Mine roads in what is now Prince William Forest Park, were only about one and a half or two miles from the Cabin Branch School but the ridge and two broad streams which had no bridges separated them. According to the Superintendent of Schools, Richard Haydon, there was "an urgent need" in the community of Hickory Ridge for a schoolhouse. When a group of citizens appealed to the School Board for a school, their "petition [was] graciously granted"[2] provided that a building could be found and regular attendance promised.

The Hickory Ridge Odd Fellows Hall, which also served as a church building, was pressed into service as a schoolhouse too. It was located along Gallows Hill Road near the Mary Bird Branch of Quantico Creek about a mile west of the Cabin Branch pyrite mine. The twenty or so homes in the community provided enough pupils to keep the school open five months a year for about ten years.

When the Hickory Ridge School opened, twenty-nine children enrolled and attended regularly. As Superintendent Haydon reported, "Appreciation of this opportunity for learning is shown by their regular attendance."[3] The rented hall was large enough to accommodate all the students but it was not really a satisfactory facility. Eventually, new window panes were furnished to replace broken ones but there were open spaces in the floor which needed attention. The room was heated by a large stove which was the responsibility of the teacher and pupils as was general maintenance. The school grounds were only a quarter of an acre and water came from a nearby well.

The teacher's desk was a table; the students had desks and these were arranged so that the room looked as much like a school room as possible. Some charts and a few maps which came from advertisements decorated the walls and there was "a fairly good supply of books for the children's pleasure."[4]

For the first six weeks that the school was in session, the teacher was a substitute who had taught on a regular basis in the county the previous year. A teacher from another school was transferred in after those first few weeks. She was a graduate of the St. Paul Normal and Industrial School in Lawrenceville with a Normal Professional certificate and six years of teaching experience.

From the beginning, the need for a new schoolhouse and proper school site was recognized. There

[1] The Wellington School in the Manassas District is the only other school in the county which never had its own building but existed in a rented room or hall.

[2] Richard C. Haydon. "An Administrative Survey of the Public School System of Prince William County, Virginia", A Thesis for Master of Science at the University of Virginia, 1935, p.107.

[3] Ibid., p.107.

[4] Ibid.

was also a great need for more equipment, water facilities on the school grounds, sanitary toilets and a wood shed. As early as 1935 the Superintendent of Schools was considering having the children transported to another school rather than trying to build a new building but local residents recall the Hickory Ridge School as being in existence for about ten years.[5]

---

[5] Patricia L. Parker. *The Hinterland: An Overview of the Prehistory and History of Prince William Forest Park, Virginia.* Occasional report #1, Regional Archeology Program, National Capital Region, National Park Service, October 1985, p.107.

THE HOLMES/BELLE HAVEN SCHOOL

Dumfries School District
White
1895?-1927

This one-room schoolhouse was located just inside the present eastern boundary of the Quantico Marine Base on the old Elk Run Road about a quarter mile west of Joplin (then Forest) Road. It was near the Holmes Store and the Holmes house, adjacent to the Belle Haven Baptist Church, in the old village of Voy, or Kopp as it was once known. Because it was common practice in those days to name the local school for its location in the community, it was called the Holmes School.[1]

The school served the white children of the area and the names of Holmes, Lynn and Woolfenden were found on the school records year after year. At some point, a new schoolhouse was built across the road and renamed the Belle Haven School. It was not, however, affiliated with the nearby Belle Haven Church.

Low enrollment and the push toward consolidation of the small schools led to the closing of the Belle Haven School at the end of the 1926-27 school year. The children in the lower grades were transported to the Joplin school, the upper grades to the Dumfries school.

An offer to buy the school for $100 was received by the School Board as early as 1931[2] but the Board was not ready to sell. In 1933, the School Board received another offer of $100 to buy the school but again rejected it because it was felt that the value was at least $300. If no one offered that amount, the Board would use the materials from the school to build the three teacher school at Woodbine[3]. Since no further records of offers either tendered or accepted have been found, apparently the Board did just that. In any case, the building was torn down because in July of 1933 permission was given to the Board of Deacons of the Belle Haven Baptist Church to use "the abandoned school lot" for parking as long as the church agreed to "protect the property at all times".[4]

The foundations of the schoolhouse can still be clearly seen in the woods across from the Belle Haven Cemetery beside which the church used to stand.

---

[1] The 1901 map of Prince William County by William Brown refers to the school as the Holmes School. How long it kept that name is unknown.

[2] Prince William County School Board minutes of October 7, 1931.

[3] Ibid., February 1, 1933.

[4] Ibid., July 5, 1933.

THE HORTON SCHOOL

Coles School District
White
late 19th century-1906?

There is almost no information available about the Horton School. It appears on the 1901 William Brown County map along the old Horton School Road midway between John's Branch of Cedar Run and the old Fayman-Stafford Springs Road in what is now part of Quantico Marine Base. Less than half a mile from Horton's Store and Post Office, the little school served a small community in what was then a rural area of the County.

When, in 1891, population shifts caused the Horton Post Office to be moved to the village of Fayman about a mile north, it is likely that the future of the Horton School, too, was in jeopardy. Fayman became the center of the community and sometime after 1901 a new schoolhouse opened just up the road. Since two schools serving the same population would not have been needed, it is apparent that when Fayman opened, Horton closed.[1]

[1]The Horton School is shown on the map drawn for the school system by William Brown in 1901 but the Fayman School does not appear. It probably opened shortly thereafter.

THE KETTLE RUN SCHOOL

Brentsville School District
Colored
1888-1938

According to an undated Prince William County inventory of school properties, the small frame one-room Kettle Run Schoolhouse was built in 1892, but during the summer of 1888 the Brentsville District School Board ordered that a colored schoolhouse be built "at or near Kettle Run Railroad Bridge".[1] The one-room yellow building was built on land owned by Mr. L. A. Marstellar just north of Kettle Run where it crosses Aden Road between Nokesville and Bristow. Occasionally called Marstellar's School, it was formally named Kettle Run for its geographic location. It supplanted the old Chinn School which had been outgrown. In the new building at Kettle Run, about twenty-five black children who lived in the rural Nokesville and Bristow areas south of Manassas were educated.

In 1911, the School Board resolved for safety reasons to move the schoolhouse back from the road and place it on a concrete foundation. It probably had a dirt floor, not uncommon in the early buildings.[2] No record shows that any action was taken; indeed, sixteen years later, patrons of the school petitioned the Board to show that there was an urgent need for a "Go Slow" sign on the road on both sides of the school as it was very dangerous for the children, so the problem of safety still existed.

In July of 1920 the School Board appointed Mrs. L.E. Crouse as the teacher of the Kettle Run School at a salary of $55 a month. Five years later, the teacher was Mrs. Julia A. Holbert who, at age fifty-eight was one of the oldest County teachers of the day. She had been teaching for thirty-seven years following high school graduation but earned the same salary as did beginning teachers with no experience, $60 monthly. From that, she paid $16 for room and board because her home was in distant Front Royal, Virginia. Thirty-two children, nineteen boys and thirteen girls, were enrolled in Mrs. Holbert's classroom of grades 1-6 but daily attendance averaged twenty.[3]

The Kettle Run Schoolhouse as sketched by a former student whose parents taught at the school.
(Courtesy of Elizabeth Nickens)

The teacher following Mrs. Holbert was Mrs. Nettie V. Williams who taught at Kettle Run at least during the 1926-27 school year. She had been the teacher at the Thornton Colored School the previous year and had twenty-two years of teaching experience. She was forty-five years old and earned the usual $60 a month for a seven months' term. There were thirty-five children enrolled that year, but only eighteen attended on an average day.[4] Mrs. Williams noted on her year end report that not only was there a need for a "Go Slow" sign near her schoolhouse, but, after forty years, the roof needed fixing "as soon as possible".

The teacher for the 1929-30 year was Mrs. Susie B. Nickens. She and her family lived in Gainesville, about fifteen miles from the Kettle Run School.

[1]Brentsville District School Board minutes of August 25, 1888.
[2]Brentsville District School Board minutes of May 1, 1911.
[3]"Virginia Daily Attendance Records and Report of Class Grades" filed for the Kettle Run School at the end of the 1925-26 school year.
[4]"Virginia Daily Attendance Records and Report of Class Grades" for the Kettle Run School filed at the end of the 1926-27 school year.

During the week, she and her young daughter Elizabeth boarded with a local family and walked to school. On the weekends, Susie drove her Model A Ford back home to Gainesville and the rest of her family.[5] Mrs. Nickens had previously taught, along with her husband, at the Macrae School. Indeed, she had been a teacher for twenty-one years. She earned a yearly salary at Kettle Run of $480. She wrote that the library had forty books in it, thirty-five less than had previously reported.[6]

By 1933, the condition of the building was "not very good".[7] The roof still needed repair and weatherboarding was missing in several places. The steps and underpinning of the vestibule were in need of work. The condition of the interior also was not good. The floors and blackboards were in poor condition and the walls needed paint. Windows on both sides of the small room let in more light than was considered good but shades were provided to help solve that problem. A large stove "barely heats the room" and needed work. The students' desks were poor and equipment was "scarce". There was one map, one reading chart and only a few books on shelves built into a corner.

The grounds, too, needed improvement. Water came from a pump on the school grounds, which was not unusual, but the toilets were pits and needed to be made more sanitary.

Despite such drawbacks, enrollment for the 1933-34 school year was thirty-five with an average daily attendance of twenty-three. At the end of the year, there were twenty-four promotions, seven failures and four dropouts. The teacher was a Normal School graduate of Virginia State College with some "college work" there also and the holder of a Normal Professional Certificate with one year of teaching experience.[8]

A year later, when Superintendent of Schools Haydon made his annual report, nothing had changed. Kettle Run was in the worst condition of any school in the County. Haydon listed eight immediate improvements needed:

1. Repairs on the exterior.
2. Interior painting.
3. More and better blackboard space.
4. Better desks for teacher and pupils.
5. Equipment (books, maps, charts, globes).
6. Woodshed on grounds.
7. Toilets made more sanitary.
8. Improvement of grounds.[9]

Four years later, the school was still in operation with no record showing any improvements at all. Finally, at the end of the 1937-38 school year, the Board decided to close the school and transport the children to the Brown School in Manassas.[10] Shortly after this decision, the little school house burned down. Luckily the fire came at the end of the afternoon after the children had gone home, but the teacher was still there working and longtime residents of Nokesville remember her standing by and crying as it burned. By May 4, the Superintendent had received a $600 check from the Royal Insurance Company as full payment for the damage. The money was put into the County School Fund to be used for improvements to all buildings. On October 5, 1938, the Board sold the lot to T. L. Blackwell for the high bid of $131.

---

[5] From an interview with Elizabeth Nickens with the author, 1992.

[6] "Virginia Daily Attendance Reports and Record of Class Grades" for Kettle Run School filed at the end of the 1929-30 school year.

[7] Richard C. Haydon. "An Administrative Survey of the Public School System of Prince William County, Virginia", A Thesis for Master of Science at the University of Virginia, 1935, p.98.

[8] Haydon, p.98.

[9] Haydon, p.101.

[10] Prince William County School Board minutes of April 9, 1938.

THE KING'S CROSSROADS (HERRING) SCHOOL

Brentsville District School #5
White
1895-1926

In March of 1895, the Brentsville District School Board, in response to a petition from residents of the King's Crossroads area of the county, ordered that a schoolhouse be built in the community. King's Crossroads, more frequently referred to as King's Xroads, got its name from the Al King family who lived nearby.[1] Mr. H. W. Herring agreed to donate one acre of land, chosen by the Board and Superintendent of Schools H. M. Clarkson, on Carriage Ford Road near the point where it crossed the Warrenton Road. Thus it was that during its first couple of years the school was sometimes known as the Herring School, because of its location on Mr. Herring's land.

In May of 1895, having secured the land on which to build, the District Board met to decide on the specifications for the schoolhouse in order to advertise for bids. It was to have one room measuring 26'x22' with a twelve foot ceiling and six windows, three on each side. The frame building with its tin roof was to be set on a stone foundation. This was very much like several of the other schoolhouses in the District, and in the County in general. The winning bid of $270 went to Mr. P. J. Stephens[2] who completed his work in time for the start of the 1895-96 school term.

After the little red schoolhouse in the field was built, Mr. Herring asked permission from the School Board to preach and have Sunday school at the King's Crossroads School. His request was refused.

As early as 1908, attempts were made to consolidate the King's Xroads School, the Allendale School and the Hazelwood School at a central school in the village of Aden. While Allendale and Hazelwood did close and consolidate at Aden, King's Crossroads School stayed open despite shaky enrollment figures.

Enrollment apparently remained low because during the summer of 1910, the School Board agreed

Students at the King's Crossroads School, c. 1920.
(Courtesy of Marie Caton)

to open the school only if the community could secure a teacher and guarantee an average daily attendance of twenty pupils.[3] This done, the little schoolhouse opened its doors for the 1910-11 school year on schedule. Things continued to improve and in January of 1912 the Board ordered a fence put around the school yard. Later that year, on July 13, the Board voted to require the Cedar Run District School Board of Fauquier County to pay a share of the teacher's salary at the King's Xroads School as long as students from that District continued to attend there.

The next ten years brought great changes. Whereas in 1908 the school was in danger of being closed because there were not enough students, in May of 1919 the School Board was ready to build a large, two story schoolhouse at King's Crossroads. The Board agreed to contract to build a new 46'x30' building if the citizens paid $500 of the $860 needed to have a public hall built above the two rooms on the ground floor, donated two acres of land and hauled the materials needed. A belfry was to be added for $25 more. The contract was won by J. W. Cooke who agreed to complete the building by September 15, 1919.[4] In 1921 the old school building was sold at auction to Mr. Herring, on whose land it was located, for $80. It is no longer standing.

---

[1] Robert Beahm

[2] Brentsville District School Board minutes of May 27, 1895.

[3] Brentsville District School Board minutes of August 24, 1910.

[4] Brentsville District School Board minutes of May 28, 1919.

A "Tom Thumb Wedding" was held at King's Crossroads School to raise funds. The "bride" is Violet Herring Lomax.
(Courtesy of Marie Caton)

According to Robert Beahm, a Nokesville resident and historian whose father taught at both the old one-room King's Crossroads School and the new one, "the Nokesville Church of the Brethren had a part in providing this structure and it was used for some years by that church for worship services."[5] It was the center of the community and also served as a site for oyster suppers, box socials and even a Tom Thumb wedding![6]

The Horse Show Grounds with a grandstand were located behind the school house. Even people from Washington came down for the events held there. Notables such as Melvin C. Hazen, owner of Pilgrims' Rest and Commissioner of Washington, DC, was a frequent visitor and often rode in the horse shows. Other local people such as the Kerlins, the Hales and the Herrings also rode in the horse shows.[7]

Local residents remember that female single teachers at King's Xroads School stayed with Mrs. Herring who lived nearby but they rarely stayed very long. Men were always looking for a good wife and they married the new school teachers! Agriculture was taught at King's Xroads School. Crops were planted by the students and so were irises, which bloomed for many years on the site, long after the school house was gone. One of the male teachers even took students on a field trip into Washington, a big trip in the early days of transportation.

Consolidation of the small rural schools of Prince William County finally meant the end of the King's Crossroads School only six years after the new building was erected. Beginning with the 1926-27 school year, the children from the lower grades (1-6) went to the central school at Aden. Seventh graders and high school students went to the Brentsville District High School in Nokesville.

The big two story schoolhouse continued to be used for several years for various area functions. In March of 1929, the school and land were sold at a public auction in front of the Nokesville Bank in Nokesville to H.W. Herring who paid $500.25 to the School Board on April 3.[8] On July 24, a citizens' committee requested that one-sixth of the sale price be returned to the Community League, which had put up one-sixth of the original cost of the school building. The School Board agreed. In the 1930s it became a house for laying hens and eventually burned to the ground.[9]

---

[5] From an unpublished account of the King's Crossroads Schools prepared by Mr. Beahm for this author in 1992.

[6] From an interview with Marie Caton by the author, 1992.

[7] Interview with Marie Caton, 1992.

[8] Prince William County School Board minutes of April 3, 1929.

[9] Robert Beahm.

LOCH LOMOND ELEMENTARY

Manassas/Gainesville District
1961-present

The Loch Lomond Elementary School, named for the lake in Scotland called Loch Lomond, was built on land donated to the school system by developer C.D. Hylton. It was located on the old Ben Lomond tract on Augusta Road in Manassas. When it opened in 1961, the building was surrounded by pasture land. The student body came from split shifts at the Manassas Park School and numbered 586. The principal when Loch Lomond school opened was Mr. Robert E. Link. The school continues to serve Prince William County children in the Ben Lomond area of Manassas.

THE LUCASVILLE SCHOOL

Manassas District School
Colored
1883-1926

In November of 1883, the Manassas District School Board authorized the opening of a school to serve the black children who lived near the community of Lucasville. The schoolhouse (which occasionally but inconsistently was given the #5 designation for the Manassas District) and the fuel to heat it were to be provided by the patrons. Mr. George H. Harris was appointed teacher at a salary of $25 a month.[1] Imagine the disappointment of the parents when the resolution providing for the opening of the school was revoked the following March by the Board which said that the parties were not authorized to agree to it. The short-lived school was closed and everyone was to be compensated for the furniture, fuel and building which had been donated.[2]

The problems were somehow ironed out and the school re-opened for the 1884-85 school year. At a School Board meeting held in October 1884, patrons petitioned for a new schoolhouse to be built on the road to Brentsville on land of Edward Francis.[3] The Board approved the plan and decreed that a schoolhouse could be built on the site using blueprints earlier used for the District's Bradley School. A bid by H.W. Lloyd to do the work for $267.13 was accepted on November 8, 1884. Two years later, District School Board minutes reported the final payment on Mr. Francis' land. The new school building was located at the intersection of Lucasville Road and Godwin Drive less than one mile from the present-day Prince William County Fairgrounds.

In February, 1888 District School Board minutes show that the Lucasville School was again threatened by closure, this time due to low enrollment figures. However, "by reason of a factious spirit upon the part of the patrons", the Board decided that, out of fairness to the teacher and the "good students", the school would be kept open as long as ten students came each day.

Low enrollment continued to plague the school over the ensuing years. In February of 1893 the Board ordered the school closed for the rest of the year. The following school year, 1893-94, figures show that the Lucasville School was the most costly of the colored elementary schools to operate, at an average of $10 per student. Nevertheless, in July of 1894, the Board ordered the school to be open for seven months because it had maintained an average daily attendance of twenty-one students the previous year.

In the autumn of 1901, the Manassas District School Board decided to put the school and one acre of land up for sale to the highest bidder and consolidate the students with the Brown School in Manassas. Apparently no sale occurred, because on August 23, 1906, the School Board voted to postpone the re-opening of the school as petitioned for by the patrons. The next year, the school opened and Mr. William A. Taylor was hired to teach for five months at a salary of $25 a month. It was still open in 1912 when Alice A. Taylor was hired at a salary of $30 a month for a seven months' school year. The higher salary and longer school year indicate success in the Lucasville School.

In 1926, the school closed for good and this time the students really were bused to the Brown School in Manassas, which had just opened in its new building.[4] On December 7, 1927, Prince William County School Board member Mr. D.J. Arrington was authorized to sell the school building and its lot and no further mention is made of the Lucasville School.

---

[1] Manassas District School Board minutes of November 14, 1883.

[2] Manassas District School Board minutes of March 31, 1884.

[3] Manassas District School Board minutes of October 18, 1884.

[4] Commodore Nathaniel Bennett. *View From the Mountain: Jennie Dean of Virginia.* Unpublished monograph, Manassas, Virginia, 1986, p.76.

THE MACRAE (McCRAE) SCHOOL

Gainesville District #5
Colored
187?-1953

The first Macrae[1] schoolhouse opened in the 1870s on land owned, and probably donated to the School Board, by the Macrae family in Gainesville. According to the 1901 Prince William County map, the Macrae property was located two or three miles from the center of the village which would have made a long walk to school necessary for most students. Nonetheless, that school served the black community of Gainesville until 1888.

On the day before Christmas 1887, the County Superintendent recommended that the school be moved "to some more suitable place toward Gainesville"[2] and the site offered for sale. On July 28, 1888, a Mr. Taylor was awarded the contract to remove the Macrae schoolhouse to a location nearer to the center of Gainesville. However, shortly thereafter, the School Board decided to build a new schoolhouse instead of moving the old one since the cost was determined to be about the same.[3]

Mr. Taylor was again awarded the contract, this time to build the new schoolhouse, to measure 20' x 25', for $275 on a lot to be selected by the School Board.[4] One hopes that Mr. Taylor didn't depend on the School Board contracts to make his living, because on September 22, 1888 the Board purchased half an acre and an existing building from Mr. Haywood Triplett for $200. This building was located right in the center of the village on the Warrenton and Alexandria Turnpike. The contract with poor Mr. Taylor was again canceled since a new building was not needed now. The first Macrae schoolhouse and lot were sold for $35 to George W. Smith on

The Macrae School, c. 1930s.
(Courtesy of PWC Schools)

March 22, 1890. The second building served until shortly after the turn of the century.

Personnel matters seem to play a major role in what records remain from the old Macrae School. District School Board minutes from March of 1884 relate that the Board had dismissed the teacher for drunkenness and "behavior unbecomeing [sic] to a teacher of a public school". The Board also found that the teacher had been leaving the schoolhouse with only an assistant in charge, although the teacher claimed he had been present "at all times". Appearing before the Board in April, the teacher asked to be reinstated, but the Board denied his request.

Five years later, in the new building, another scandal surfaced. Early in the 1889-90 school year, the teacher suspended a girl because "she had at some previous time become a mother." At their November 1889 meeting, the School Board voted not to uphold the suspension but to allow the girl to return to school. The Board gave as its reason its belief that "the object of education is to improve morals as well as mind."[5] Pretty radical thinking for a Victorian era School Board!

Almost exactly five years later the teacher at Macrae, Emma Harris, "went off and left her school."[6] Since the school had not met the required average of twenty students anyway, the Board declined to keep the school open after the flight of the teacher despite petitions from the patrons (parents). However, soon after Christmas, having been assured by the community that the enrollment requirement would be met, the School Board decided to

---

[1]The two spellings, Macrae and McCrae, are interchangeable and are so used throughout the book. Neither seems preferred over the other in county records or residents' memories.

[2]Gainesville District School Board minutes of December 24, 1887.

[3]Gainesville District School Board minutes of August 25, 1888.

[4]Ibid.

---

[5]Gainesville District School Board minutes of November 23, 1889.

[6]Gainesville District School Board minutes of November 24, 1894.

open the school for four months with a new teacher.[7]

Troubles continued to plague the school, however. In the autumn of 1896, the School Board decided to close the school after two months because the teacher, Mr. Fontain Botts, was not "able to enforce proper order and discipline in his school."[8] How long it remained closed after that is unknown but the next notation found was made on October 12, 1907. On that date, the Reverend Moses Strother, teacher and minister of the Mt. Pleasant Baptist Church of Gainesville petitioned the School Board to move the school from the building then in use to a hall "situated by the Colored Church on the Warrenton Pike and belonging to the same." Most of the students had to cross the North Fork Run (of Broad Run) and high water often kept them away. He pointed out that the building was old, uncomfortable and too small. The School Board agreed with Rev. Strother's plan and arranged to pay rent to the church of $20 per session for use of their facility. The old schoolhouse (the second one) was sold on August 29, 1908 for $100 to Mr. Haywood F. Triplett from whom it had been bought twenty years earlier.

The school held in the hall does not sound like much of an improvement. It was a frame building of rough, unpainted boards. The floors were also rough and unpainted but there were curtains at the windows. Although it was located on Lee Highway near the Gainesville community which it served, it was still a long walk for some of the children. Mrs. Nellie G. Butler lives in Haymarket, five miles away, as she did when she attended the Macrae school in the first decade of the twentieth century. She remembers that there were about twenty-five children under one teacher, Mrs. Georgetta Hughes. The students took care of the school maintenance by sweeping the floor, bringing in the wood for the stove and carrying water in a bucket from a well across the road.

The school day, which began with cleaning the classroom, singing "Good Morning" to the teacher and a prayer, lasted the usual six hours; a school year was six months long. The main subjects taught were arithmetic, history and spelling using books bought by the parents. In the classroom was a map of the United States and a blackboard; there was no library. At Christmas, a play was presented and another was put on at the end of each school year. Lunch was carried to school by the children either in a paper bag or a tin bucket. It usually consisted of sliced bread or a biscuit with jelly or preserves, an apple and a cookie or piece of cake. During recess, the girls played "Ring Around the Roses" while the boys played ball.[9]

Apparently the arrangement with the church lasted seven years until the new schoolhouse was built in 1914, for a cost of $2100. This was a two-room, two-teacher school located on land adjoining the east side of the Gainesville Post Office on Route 29. It was a one story, frame building with a peaked metal roof, wood floors and wall board walls and ceilings. The school population generally numbered about fifty.

At the end of the 1926-27 school year, the teacher, Mrs. Susie B. Nickens, filed her report. Mrs. Nickens was then forty-one years old and a high school graduate with eighteen years of teaching experience in the county. She had begun her long teaching career at the Antioch School in 1908. In 1926, she was paid $60 a month for an eight month term teaching twenty-nine children in grades 1-3.

Mrs. Nickens' husband, James M. Nickens,[10] was also a school teacher who began teaching at the Macrae School around 1925. During the 1926-27 school year, he taught the twenty-four students enrolled in grades 4-7 at Macrae and was paid a salary of $65 monthly, or $455 for the school year. Mr. Nickens, age forty-six, was also a high school graduate with eighteen years of teaching experience. For ten years prior to his move to Macrae he taught at the Thornton School for black children in Catharpin. The Nickens family lived in Gainesville about four miles from the Macrae School. The older daughters, Eunice who was eleven during that 1926-27 school year, and Susie who was nine, were in their father's

---

[7]Gainesville District School Board minutes of January 2, 1895.

[8]Gainesville District School Board minutes of October 24, 1896.

[9]All these reminiscences came from Mrs. Nellie Butler in an unpublished history interview with the author in April of 1993.

[10]The Nickens family have been prominent "Free People of Color" in the history of Prince William County since the Revolutionary War. Education has always been important to the family. Elizabeth Nickens, who still occupies the family home in the western end of the county, remembers that her great-grandmother, Sallie Nickens, in 1865, allowed freed slaves to use a small building on her property as a schoolhouse to learn reading and "figuring". Elizabeth's aunt, Louise Allen, taught at both the Antioch and Thoroughfare Schools and served as the first principal of Antioch-Macrae School when the two schools combined in 1953. As the main text reports, both Elizabeth's parents taught school in Prince William County for many years.

classroom; the younger two, Helen, aged eight and Elizabeth who was only five, were in their mother's. When the roads were passable, the family drove to school; when cars could not make the trip, the Nickens either walked or rode horseback.[11]

Toward the end of that 1926-27 school term, the schoolyard lost ten feet of its frontage when the School Board agreed to allow the State Highway Commission to widen its "right-away[sic]" by ten feet on the school property. A fee of $25 was to be paid to the School Board and all fences were to be put back in satisfactory condition.[12]

From 1931-1936, Mr. Oswald Robinson taught at the Macrae School. Part of that time, he worked with Mrs. Susie Nickens and the rest of the time with her sister-in-law, Mrs. Louise Allen.

The school day lasted six hours. The children studied reading, arithmetic, writing, history, geography, spelling, punctuation, music and drama. The only textbooks were readers, which were supplied by the students. There were no books in the school library. Elizabeth Nickens remembers that while some groups were working at the blackboard, the rest of the class was assigned seat work. The work was generally of a subjective nature and the answers had to be written in prose. Lack of copying machines made short answer questions sheets time consuming for the teacher to produce and workbooks were not available. The children brought lunches from home. On good days they ate lunch and played outdoors; during inclement weather, lunch and studies were combined indoors.

When the weather allowed, the children had recess outdoors. Singing ring games, skipping rope, baseball and feeding and watering the horses were favorite activities as they were in most of the schoolhouses of the day.

The Macrae Schoolhouse served the black community of Gainesville in many ways. Spelling bees, Christmas pageants, special programs at the year's end were attended by students and their families. Sports, however, were not part of the school extra-curricular activities. Churches and families provided the outlet for those things.

Superintendent of Schools Richard C. Haydon, in his 1934 report on the schools of Prince William County, said that the building was one of the area's best with two "bright and cheerful" large rooms.[13] It was heated by wood stoves. Having windows on both sides of the room was considered at that time to be a disadvantage due to eyestrain, but shades were provided to cut down on the glare. The teachers and pupils did the janitorial work. The school was located on two acres enclosed with wire fencing. Water came from a pump where it was tested safe. The outdoor toilets were built to meet state requirements except for the ventilation pipe. Beautification of the grounds was being planned during 1934. Superintendent Haydon went on to say that "few schools in the county have the equipment that is found at Macrae." The desks were "all right"; there was a "splendid" set of maps (not available during the years when the Nickens taught there); a piano (another later addition); several free product exhibits assembled by the teachers; charts made by the teachers and pupils and a few supplementary books.[14]

Superintendent Haydon goes on to report that the two teachers, Mr. Robinson and Mrs. Allen, were "active and wide-awake". They attended summer school at Virginia State College to be able to change their Provisional Certification to a Normal Professional Certificate. The "young man" who served as principal was an "organizer" and community worker. The assistant, Mrs. Allen, was trained in piano and industrial arts.[15]

Enrollment, no longer a problem, stood at forty-seven for the 1933-34 school year with an average daily attendance of thirty-eight. There were thirty-nine promotions, two failures and six dropouts. The following autumn, enrollment increased to fifty with an average attendance of 48.8 or 91.6%.[16]

In 1953 when several of the county's schools for black children were consolidated, the Macrae School was combined with the Antioch School. At

---

[11]From interviews with Elizabeth Nickens during 1992.

[12]Prince William County School Board minutes of March 2, 1927.

[13]Prince William County School Board minutes of August 2, 1933 report that Mr. John Lane was paid $30 to put two coats of paint on the Macrae Schoolhouse that summer. In addition, the Board paid Henderson Brooks $8 to glaze all the windows, repair the roof and make "other minor repairs" as needed. School Board member, Mrs. Piercy, purchased the necessary supplies for the jobs.

[14]Richard C. Haydon. "An Administrative Survey of the Public School System in Prince William County, Virginia." A Thesis for Master of Science at the University of Virginia, 1936, p.93.

[15]Ibid. p.93.

[16]Ibid., p.93.

that time, Macrae closed its doors as a separate school after serving the community for almost eighty years. The consolidated Antioch-Macrae School remained open until 1962 and the building still stands on Thoroughfare Road less than half a mile south of the John Marshall Highway (Rt.55).

MANASSAS PARK ELEMENTARY SCHOOL

Manassas School District
1958-present

The Manassas District built an elementary school for the children of Manassas Park subdivision in 1958. An addition was put on in 1960 to accommodate the increasing enrollment. When Manassas Park became a city in 1976, it took over the schools within its boundaries, buying the Manassas Park Elementary School from Prince William County. From that time to the present, it has been part of the Manassas Park City school system.

THE MANASSAS VILLAGE/ RUFFNER SCHOOL

Manassas School District #1
White
1869-1926

The citizens of Manassas, realizing that the new 1869 Virginia State Constitution would require every county to set up a public school system for all its children, decided to be in the forefront of education and establish the first school in Prince William County even before the new constitution went into effect. In October of 1869, the Prince William County Court had divided the County into six school districts, one of which was Manassas.[1] The newly chosen Prince William County School Board, under the leadership of George C. Round, immediately set about opening the Manassas Village School for the white children of the community. Because the state school system was still being put into place, no public funds had yet been collected to help the either Prince William County or the Manassas School District establish any schools. The School Board, therefore, had to rely on private donations to acquire the money it needed to hire a teacher, rent a room, pay for fuel to heat the room, and purchase furniture, books and other necessary supplies for its new school.

The Ruffner School, in a postcard view, c.1905.
(Courtesy of the author)

Money came from several sources. Dr. Barnas Sears, the first agent for the Peabody Fund[2], contributed $300, as he did again in 1870. The rest of the $694.24 required came from subscriptions by the citizens and from donations given by people living north of the Mason-Dixon Line (the recent "enemy" of the Civil War). A room in the rear of the Asbury Methodist Church in Manassas was rented to use as a school room and secondhand furniture was purchased from the Washington, DC school system. Some books

---

[1] The other five were Brentsville, Coles, Dumfries, Gainesville and Occoquan.

[2] The Peabody Fund was started in 1867 by philanthropist George Peabody to help with the education of children in the South.

were donated by their New York publishers. Miss Estelle Greene (later Mrs. Estelle Cross) was appointed teacher for the five and a half months' term.[3] In December of 1869, the first true public school in Prince William County opened its doors.[4]

For the second year of the school, the entire church building was rented during the week. Two teachers were appointed, Mr. George Bennett who was to act as principal or head teacher and Miss Greene as assistant teacher. Mr. Bennett taught in the main room and Miss Greene used the classroom.

In November 1870, the school was officially turned over by the Prince William County School Board to the newly chosen Manassas District School Board's three Trustees, John T. Leachman, John H. Butler and George C. Round. The first meeting of the District Board to be convened under the new law was held on December 12, 1870.[5] The Board invited citizens to sell or give land for schoolhouses in order to enact the new law. A petition was also circulated asking for funds to run the schools.

By the beginning of 1871, the Manassas Village White School, as it was then known, had raised enough money to consider building a schoolhouse of its own. Mr. George Round, one of the Trustees of the District Board, recommended that it be a graded[6] school of two rooms with two teachers and this was approved.[7]

In an election held in the spring of 1871, the school trustees submitted a proposition to the voters for a district tax of forty cents on $100 assessed value to build schoolhouses. Despite strong opposition, the measure passed and the District Board began to build its first schoolhouses. However, the Manassas Village White School continued to meet in the church building for another year. With the support of the patrons (parents and friends) of the school, George Bennett was again hired as the principal teacher at a salary of $50 per month, very high for the time. To raise the money to pay him, the Board used $25 from the Public Funds and $25 from subscriptions by the patrons. Miss Estelle Greene was also rehired as the assistant teacher.[8]

The Ruffner School in 1890.
(Courtesy of The Manassas Museum)

In the spring of 1872, the District School trustees contracted with a newcomer in the building business, John A. Cannon, to raise and partially finish a "real" schoolhouse to replace the temporary church facilities. The building, a two story structure in the Second Empire style, was designed by George C. Round who also supervised its construction, which was completed on July 20, 1872. It was located on West Center Street at Peabody Street which was so named for the first benefactor of the school. To honor the first State Superintendent of Schools in Virginia, Dr. William H. Ruffner, it was called the Ruffner School Number One.[9] The first teacher was Miss Elizabeth A. Chamberlain (later Bennett) who also was the only teacher to teach at Ruffner without an assistant. This was because the Peabody Fund no longer offered assistance and there were not enough students to warrant two classes.

The following year, Prof. William R. Will assumed the position of principal and Estelle Greene returned as assistant. At this time, the school was divided into upper and lower grades. These two teachers remained with the school until the end of the

---

[3]Catherine T. Simmons. *Manassas, Virginia 1873-1973*. Manassas City Museum, 1986, p.32.

[4]The earlier public schools in the county were only available for indigent children, both black and white. The new law provided for a free education for all students without regard for income or race or sex.

[5]Manassas District School Board minutes, December 12, 1870.

[6]Unlike a one-room school where all grades met in the same classroom, a graded school divided students into grade levels and housed them in more than one room. In a two-room school, the children in grades one through three would meet in one room while those in fourth through seventh would meet in the other. It was a radical departure from the little schools where students progressed at their own speed in different subjects.

[7]Manassas District School Board minutes of January 7, 1871.

[8]Manassas District School Board minutes of July 13, 1871.

[9]Simmons, p.33.

1875-76 school year. Mr. Will, originally from Louisiana, was apparently an excellent teacher who soon left Prince William County for a better opportunity in Maryland where he taught at a college in Baltimore.

After the departure of Mr. Will and Miss Greene, Mr. Charles S. Scott (principal) and Maggie Foley were appointed for the 1876-77 school year. Miss Foley remained until the end of the 1882 year but the principalship was taken over by Mr. J.B.T. Thornton for four years, until 1881. That year B.B. Thornton worked with Maggie Foley for one school year. (Mr. J.B.T. Thornton later became superintendent of schools for the county). At the beginning of the 1882 school year, Austin O. Weedon became the principal teacher and Mary D. Weir was hired as the assistant. She remained at Ruffner till the end of the 1886 school year, but Mr. Weedon stayed only one year. He was succeeded by Isaac P. Markel for a year and then R.E. Thornton was hired until the end of the 1888 school year. Midway through his tenure, Ida M. Lickle became his assistant and she remained until 1891. Mr. Thornton was succeeded by M. Ella Lipscomb for one year after which Mr. Thornton returned for one more year. Then Ida Nichol took over again for just one year.

In 1891, the town of Manassas elected to incorporate and became a separate Manassas City School District. For a period of six years, until 1896, the City School Board hired the teachers for the Ruffner School. In 1892, Mr. J.D. Wheeler was hired as principal teacher at a salary of $35 a month, later raised to $40. Lucy Hixson was given the job of assistant teacher. However, in 1896 the General Assembly abolished the separate district and consolidated the schools back into the Manassas District.

With the new consolidation, Ruffner's two rooms were no longer enough and the old town hall was rented for the third or primary classroom. The three teachers, until the new century began, were Charles E. Ruffner, Roberta Leachman and Maggie G. Maddox. By December of 1899 the school had grown so much that a realignment of the faculty and the hiring of a fourth teacher became necessary. The School Board directed that the principal teach grades seven and eight, the first assistant take grades five and six and a second assistant be in charge of the third and fourth grades. A primary assistant was hired to teach grades one and two.[10]

In 1899, Andrew Carnegie donated money for a library to be located at the Ruffner school. It would also serve as the public library. The teachers of Ruffner agreed to serve as librarians if they were relieved of cleaning and fire tending duties for the school. With $2500 of Carnegie money, a third story was added to the school to house the library, which was dedicated on January 1, 1901.

On January 1, 1900 the School Board directed the principal to "arrange for instructing pupils in the high school or academic branches" beginning immediately.[11] Pupils paid $2.39 a month (payable in advance) and could come from either inside or outside the district, entering at any time. Mr. Ruffner continued his duties as principal teacher but also divided the high school teaching duties with the assistant principal who was also the fifth and sixth grade teacher. Mr. Ruffner was paid a salary of $50 a month; the assistant received $30 monthly.[12] The experiment proved short-lived, however. On June 2, 1902, the School Board decided that funds were inadequate to operate high school level classes at Ruffner. Only the ninth grade was allowed to continue but by June 1905 only four students were enrolled and that didn't justify further funding. The majority of high school students chose to attend the Manassas Institute, a private high school, and the public school system just could not compete. Manassas' trial balloon was unusual; few rural school systems in the state asked permission of the State Board of Education to be allowed to teach the "higher branches".[13]

Finally, in 1908 when the state mandated free public high school education, the Ruffner School again became, in part, an institution of both elementary and secondary grades. The building was enlarged to accommodate the new agricultural and domestic science classes and it became known as the Ruffner School and Manassas High School building until 1926 when a new brick high school (The Osbourn School) was built.

Dorothea Randall (Payne) remembers her days as a student at the Old Ruffner School. She was taught reading, writing, arithmetic, spelling, geography, biology and history during a school year which

---

[10] Manassas District School Board minutes of December 4, 1899.

[11] Manassas District School Board minutes of January 1, 1900.

[12] R. Ward Peters. "Secondary Education in Manassas, Virginia 1890-1935." A Thesis Presented to the Academic Faculty of the University of Virginia in Candidacy for the Degree of Master of Arts, 1939, p.96.

[13] Ibid.

lasted from September until June. The school served the entire countryside plus the town of Manassas.[14] Drinking fountains supplied water and bathrooms were indoors. Every year a Halloween party was held at the school and both children and adults took part in the games and music. There were spelling bees, community suppers and Christmas pageants held too; as in most communities, the schoolhouse was a social center.

By 1925, the Ruffner School-Manassas High School was so overcrowded that it risked losing its state accreditation. The building was also more than fifty years old and no doubt showing its age. The District Board decided to close its first school and educate the children at Bennett, which was not far away.

On September 14, 1927 the School Board advertised the Ruffner School for sale. In October, the Manassas Town Council was given permission by the Board to take as much of the school property as necessary for the widening of Center Street.[15] On May 28, 1928 the Board again advertised the building for sale with the request that it be removed from the site. When no buyers appeared, the old building was razed in 1930 and an elm tree planted on the spot. An historic marker stands to mark the spot today.

---

[14] Mrs. Payne reports that a piece of metal was imbedded in the sidewalk at the corner of Center and Main Streets outside of what is now the First Virginia Bank (then it was the National Bank). The town extended 1/2 mile north, 1/2 mile south, 1/2 mile east and 1/2 mile west of that marker. Children who lived beyond those boundaries, like Alma Rennow who lived on Signal Hill Road, were "country folk".

[15] Prince William County School Board minutes of October 5, 1927.

THE MANLEY SCHOOL

Manassas District School #8
Colored
1871-1936

The Manley, or Manly as it was sometimes spelled, School was one of three colored schools serving the county's central area; the other two were the Brown School in Manassas and the Kettle Run School in the Brentsville District. The first Manley Schoolhouse was located at the juncture of Balls Ford, Compton and Bethlehem Roads about seven miles outside the town of Manassas. We can assume that Manley opened in late 1871 or early 1872 because in December of 1871 the Manassas District School Board hired Mr. Josiah Thomas as the teacher.[1] He had been the teacher at the Pittsylvania School, which had closed the previous June.

In 1906, Miss Georgia Hannah Bailey was appointed as the teacher of the Manley School and she continued to teach there until 1930. During the early years, Miss Bailey married Mr. Berry and they had a daughter who attended the Manley School. Another pupil was Bladen Oswald Robinson who began attending the first grade at Manley in 1917 when he was seven years old. He had to walk three miles each way to school enduring the taunts of the white children who passed him in their bus on their way to their own school. Oswald Robinson finished grades one through seven under Mrs. Berry and then walked six miles to the Manassas Industrial School for Colored Youth from which he graduated in 1928. At that point, Mr. Robinson became the teacher at the Manley School while Mrs. Berry took a year off for health reasons. She returned for one more year of teaching at the Manley School and Mr. Robinson went to teach at the Macrae School. His distinguished career as an educator in both Prince William and Fairfax Counties continued for many years. He also married Mrs. Georgia Bailey Berry's daughter.[2]

In 1926, after fifty-five years of service, the Manley School was replaced by a new building paid

The Manley School built in 1926.
(Courtesy of PWC Schools)

---

[1] Manassas District School Board minutes of December 18, 1871.

[2] From an oral history done with Mr. B. Oswald Robinson by the author in the fall of 1992.

for in part with money from the Rosenwald Fund.[3] The one-room frame structure cost $1500 and was located on a hill at the intersection of Balls Ford and Bethlehem Roads, not far from the site of the first building. A year later, the School Board decided to advertise the old building for sale with the proviso that it be removed from its site.[4]

The move from the old to the new building came during Mrs. Berry's tenure at the Manley School. At the end of the 1926-27 school year, she filed her report. She was then a forty-seven year old lady who had been teaching for twenty-one years. She was a graduate of the Manassas Industrial School for Colored Youth, but had no college diploma. In her classroom, thirty-three children were enrolled, twenty-six in grades 1-4 and seven in grades 5-7, but only twenty attended on a daily basis. Mrs. Berry was paid $60 a month for a seven months' term. She also reported that there were 107 books in the school library, more than were found in most of the colored schools[5] though those books were no longer there when Oswald Robinson took over the teaching duties a year later.

Even eight years later, Manley was being called "about the best rural negro school anywhere".[6] It had one classroom and a cloakroom. The schoolhouse was situated on two acres of cleared land, though stumps remained a problem. A wood shed kept a supply of wood for the classroom stoves dry and ready and the toilet facilities were "sanitary". Because there was no running water on the school grounds, drinking water had to be carried "quite a distance". As was usual for the time, all janitorial work was done by the teacher and students. At the beginning of the school year, the colored schools were given two brooms, a box of blackboard crayons and six erasers. A table served as the teacher's desk and students' seats were "satisfactory". There were several maps and charts as well as sixty books in the bookcase.[7] Pictures of George Washington and Abraham Lincoln faced each other on opposite walls.

Enrollment figures for the 1933-34 year were the same as they had been during the 1926-27 term: total enrollment was thirty-three with an average daily attendance of only twenty, just enough to keep the school open. Of the total, seventeen students were promoted, six failed and ten others dropped out. The next year, the enrollment fell to twenty-six but the average daily attendance rose to twenty-three or 88.4%.[8] The school managed to stay open another two years, finally closing its doors in 1936. No trace of the Manley School can be found today.

---

[3]For an explanation of the Rosenwald Fund and Rosenwald Schools, see p. 41.

[4]Prince William County School Board minutes of June 1, 1927.

[5]"Virginia Daily Attendance Register and Record of Class Grades" for the Manley School filed at the end of the 1926-27 school year.

[6]Richard C. Haydon. "An Administrative Study of the Public School System in Prince William County, Virginia", A Thesis for Master of Science at the University of Virginia, 1935, p.99.

[7]Haydon, p.99.

[8]Haydon, p.99.

MARUMSCO/(R. DEAN) KILBY ELEMENTARY SCHOOL

Woodbridge School District
1959-present

In 1959, the Marumsco Elementary School opened on Horner Road in Woodbridge. The first principal was Mr. R. Dean Kilby. Then, in 1966, the Marumsco Hills Elementary School opened also in Woodbridge. Mail destined for one school often ended up at the other; the public called Marumsco School when they really wanted to talk to someone at Marumsco Hills. The situation became untenable so the PTA decided to do something about it. When Mr. Kilby left the school, they voted to rename the Marumsco School in his honor. In those days, such a move could be accomplished without all the red tape involved in going through the School Board and so the school became known as the R. Dean Kilby School. It still serves the children of Woodbridge today.

MARUMSCO HILLS ELEMENTARY SCHOOL

Occoquan/Woodbridge District
1966-present

With the development of the Marumsco Hills subdivision west of Rt. 1 in Woodbridge came the need for a school for the area's children. In 1966 the County built the Marumsco Hills Elementary School on Page Street. When new Magisterial District boundaries were drawn ten years later, the school became part of the new Woodbridge District.

When Marumsco Hills Elementary was built, there was already a Marumsco School in Woodbridge and confusion ensued with the schools getting the wrong mail, the wrong phone calls and so forth. The problem was solved when the earlier Marumsco School voted to rename itself after R. Dean Kilby, its first principal.

Marumsco Hills School was built using architectural plans for what is known as a Bailey building. It was made up of circular pods surrounding an open atrium. As time went by and the classrooms became too crowded, the atrium areas were covered and used as more classroom space. In its twenty-seven years of existence, Marumsco Hills has only had three principals. It continues to serve the children of Woodbridge today.

THE McGREGOR (ROY'S) SCHOOL

Manassas School District #10
Colored
1891-1920?

While the white children who lived along the Nokesville Road west of Manassas had the Cannon Branch School to attend and the white children who lived along Wellington Road northwest of Manassas could go to the Bethlehem School, the black children who lived in that part of the Manassas School District had no school to attend. In response to petitions from parents, the School Board agreed in 1891 to establish a school for the black children who lived in the area. Certain conditions had to be met however.[1] A suitable room had to be found and rented for no more than $1.50 a month. A suitable teacher had to be hired at a salary not to exceed $15 per month. The schoolhouse was to be equipped with unneeded furniture from the Cannon Branch School which the parents would be responsible for moving.

A building near Joseph Roy's farm along Bethlehem Road was rented, Mrs. J. Ella McKay was appointed as the teacher and the furniture was moved in time for the school, known then as Roy's School because of its location, to open for the 1891-92 school year. All went well apparently, because the next year Mrs. McKay was given a raise in salary to $17.50 a month.[2] Also during this time, the school became more widely known by its formal name, the McGregor School and it is referred to by that name in all future school records. The origin of the McGregor name is unknown.

The teacher for the 1892-93 school year was Lucille Robinson who was hired to teach for the same $17.50 per month salary. Records show that during that 1893-94 school year, the McGregor School was the least costly to run in the Manassas District. The average cost per pupil was only $5.83 a year and most of that was salary.

Although the McGregor School is shown on a 1901 map of Prince William County, it does not appear in any other school records or inventories. It is not included on a county map drawn in 1925 and no trace of it has been found.

---

[1] Manassas District School Board minutes of September 26, 1891.

[2] Manassas District School Board minutes of August 27, 1892.

THE MILL PARK SCHOOL

Gainesville District School #10
White
1882-1924

In September of 1882, the Gainesville District School Board decided to build a one-room schoolhouse "on the Carolina Road at or near Mill-park lane". Mr. C.A. Heineken, owner of Mill Park Plantation, agreed to donate the land, build the schoolhouse for $250 and pay one-third of the teacher's salary.[1] This arrangement lasted for two years until August 1884 when the Board agreed to relieve Mr. Heineken of having to pay the salary of the teacher.[2]

Mill Park was the name of the old plantation owned by the Tyler family who operated a grist mill in the years before the Civil War. The schoolhouse was located at the corner of the Old Carolina Road (now Rt. 15) and the road leading to the mill (now Rt. 679). It served the rural families of the small community of Mill Park which was about two miles south of where routes 15 and 234 (Sudley Road) intersect. From 1899 to 1901, the teacher at Mill Park School was Miss Blanche E. Wilkins who boarded at Snow Hill in the community of Woolsey. Snow Hill was a large home owned by Mr. Henry Lynn, the first president of the National Bank of Manassas. Each day, Miss Wilkins walked the mile to and from the school, sometimes having to climb the banks of the Carolina Road to avoid the large horse drawn wagons which travelled the narrow road on their way to the nearby mill.[3]

Miss Wilkins, who married Emmett N. Pattie, had a daughter named Margaret, who later taught at the Wellington and Catharpin Schools. Margaret Pattie (Adams) writes thus of her mother:

> The "Articles of Agreement" (contracts) which she signed, stated her salary for a period of six months, the lawful school year, provided there was a daily average of fifteen (15) pupils.

The old Mill Park Schoolhouse just before its demolition in 1992.
(Photo by the auhor)

> Her beginning salary was $27 and ended with $30 per month, the school to open at "9 o'clock, 60 minutes at 12 o'clock to be given, and to close the school at 4 o'clock, the day to consist of 7 hours". The Agreements also stated that the fire should be made, the floor swept regularly, with the Board providing the fuel, brooms, etc. They were signed by the Chairman of the Board, H. Howdershell and attested by Wm. H. Brown, Clerk of the Board.[4]

Unfortunately, during the fall of 1901, enrollment could no longer be maintained at an average daily attendance of fifteen so Miss Wilkins submitted her resignation and the School Board closed the little school.[5] Miss Wilkins then married Mr. Pattie and settled with him in Catharpin.

A year later, in December of 1902, a committee of parents appeared before the School Board promising that twenty-six students would attend if the school were re-opened. The Board agreed to open it and hired Miss Anna L.F. Taylor to teach the remainder of that school year.[6] During the 1903-04 and 1904-05 years it was closed because not enough pupils were available to meet minimum enrollment requirements.

Once more, before the start of the 1905-06 school year, the parents of the community petitioned

---

[1] Gainesville District School Board minutes from September, 1882.

[2] Gainesville District School Board minutes from August, 1884.

[3] E. R. Conner, III. *Water Milling on Catharpin Run, Prince William County, Virginia*, privately published, p.14.

[4] Margaret Pattie Adams in her remarks to the author about the Mill Park School, January 1993.

[5] Gainesville District School Board minutes of December 7, 1901.

[6] Gainesville District School Board minutes of December 20, 1902.

the Board to open the school and guaranteed that they would pay the teacher's salary if the enrollment fell below fifteen. The Board agreed and again opened the school and hired a teacher.[7] This time the school remained open until 1924 when it finally closed for

good. Two buses then took the children to Haymarket Elementary school.

The Mill Park School was sold and converted into a residence. The abandoned and dilapidated building stood at the corner of Milark Rd. (Rt.679) and the James Madison Highway (Rt.15) across from today's James Long Park until 1992.

---

[7]Gainesville District School Board minutes of September 30, 1905.

THE MINNIEVILLE SCHOOL

Dumfries School District
White
1886-1931

According to county Deed Books[1], on June 4, 1885 Ellen Henderson sold to the Dumfries School Board for $8.50 cash, half an acre of land "situated near the old Wakefield School House and immediately in the forks of the roads one leading to Dumfries and the other leading to Neabsco Mill." The site was on present day Dyer Drive, about one hundred feet from its junction with Cardinal Drive. It is probably safe to assume that a schoolhouse was erected on the site as soon as possible after the purchase of the land; thus the opening date of 1886. That first Minnieville School was a log building, which served the community for about fifteen years before it was moved down Neabsco Road (now Cardinal Drive) for use as a colored schoolhouse.[2] Drinking water for the school came from a spring on the farm property of Mr. George Thomas whose pasture also became a baseball field for the students. Mr. Thomas' farm was across the road from the Minnieville School but he was a member of the black community and his children were not allowed to attend that school. Instead they had to walk nearly fourteen miles round-trip to the nearest school for black children at Cabin Branch.

When the log schoolhouse was moved, a second Minnieville School was built on the Dyer Drive

The Minnieville School, c. 1930.
(Courtesy of PWC Schools)

site. The year is unknown, but it was in operation in 1915 and probably long before that. It was a one-room frame building, housing first through seventh grades. Raymond Curtis started as a student at Minnieville in 1915. He remembers a teacher named Aussie Green who "just beat the children something awful with switches all the time".[3] The parents were very upset with the situation; Raymond's father wouldn't send his children to school at all during 1917 (this was before the days of compulsory education).

Another teacher at Minnieville School was Mr. William (Willie) Endicott, remembered by county residents as "just a tiny little bitty thing, and he wore great big thick glasses. He was just kind of a standing joke with all of us, but he was just a great guy...".[4]

According to the account in *Now and Then*[5], a health nurse visited the school and told the children to wash their hands before eating lunch. "The students all marched by the outdoor well-pump, washed their hands, and the next day drank the water that had drained back into the well." This was probably

---

[1]Deed Book #35, p.519.

[2]Thomas Nelson. "Transcript of Interview with Historic Occoquan, Inc.", Prince William County Historical Commission Oral History Project, September 24, 1985, p.14. The only colored school in the area to which the log building was moved, was the old Neabsco School, which did begin its life in a small rented building. It could very possibly have been that old log building.

[3]Ibid., p.15.

[4]Ibid., p.15.

[5]Hattie Mae Partlow and Pauline Smith. *Now and Then With P.W.E.A.*, Prince William County Education Association, 1963, p.75

not an unusual situation in the early days of the one-room schoolhouses.

During the 1929-30 school year, the nineteen year old schoolteacher was Miss Lula J. Hammond, in her first year of teaching. She lived in Meredithville, Virginia and paid $27 for room and board in the Minnieville community. She earned $74.25 a month or $675 for the nine month term. There were twenty-seven children enrolled that year, sixteen in grades 1-4 with five failures and no dropouts and eleven in grades 5-7 with no failures but two who dropped out. There were 150 books in the school library according to Miss Hammond's year end report.

The teacher for the next year, which also turned out to be the last year, was Mrs. Gladys Cherry who was one of the two final teachers the previous year at the Thornton school.

On May 6, 1931, due to low enrollment and the fact that a school bus passed by the Minnieville school on its way to Bethel school, the School Board decided to close Minnieville starting with the 1931-32 school year. The children would be transported to either the Bethel or Occoquan schools. Some members of the Minnieville community were not happy with this decision and presented a petition to the Board on September 2, 1931 asking that the school be reopened. At the same meeting, other citizens presented the Board with a counter petition approving the closure of the school and the use of the bus to Bethel and Occoquan. The School Board concluded that more citizens wanted the school to close than wanted it to stay open. They further discovered that of the forty-four children in the Minnieville community, twenty-eight already attended either Bethel or Occoquan by choice. Of the sixteen remaining children, half had parents who preferred that their children be bused instead of attending Minnieville, so the Board stayed with their decision to close the school.

For a while, the schoolhouse was used for Sunday School and other religious purposes by the Minnieville (Greenwood) Church. In 1937 an offer was made to buy the schoolhouse and lot for $100 but the Board said that no offer of less than $300 would be considered. Apparently no one came forward to offer that much because in January of 1939 the Superintendent came forward with a plan to dismantle the school building, along with the Gold Ridge schoolhouse, and use the materials to build an addition to the Cabin Branch school when that building was being prepared to consolidate the colored schools in the Dumfries District.[6] The Board then advertised for bids on the lot and in June accepted the bid of Mr. Raymond Curtis of $25. Mr. Curtis used the foundation of the old schoolhouse and built a house which still stands on the site.

---

[6]Prince William County School Board minutes of January 4, 1939.

MT. PLEASANT SCHOOL

Dumfries School District
Late 19th century-early 20th century

The only reference found for the Mt. Pleasant School is on William Brown's map of Prince William County drawn in 1901. It was located on the east side of what was then called The King's Highway, now Route 1, about two miles south of Dumfries. The site was a mile north of the little settlement of Forestburg, which was at the juncture of The King's Highway and Forest (now Joplin) Road. It must have served the children of that community, but whether it was a white or colored, public or private school is not known. Even the opening and closing dates remain a mystery.

THE MT. ZION SCHOOL

Dumfries School District
Colored
1925-1928

No official mention is ever made of this colored school in the Dumfries District. It does not appear in School Board minutes; no photograph of it has been found. That it did exist is proven by three Virginia Daily Attendance Register and Records filed by the teacher, Mr. John Alexander, for the years 1925-28 as well as a letter from Mr. Alexander to the Superintendent of Schools.[1] That letter, found in the Prince William County School Archives, is quoted in its entirety at the end of this section.

The Mt. Zion School was held in the Mt. Zion Church about one and a half miles west of the old post office on Joplin Road. It was in existence for three years only, 1925-1928, and Mr. Alexander was its only teacher. He began his teaching career in 1901 in King George County, Virginia and from there went to Gastonville and then to Stafford County where he taught in the Mt. Zion Church on Graysontown Road. That school was held in one room of the church in the northern part of the county and, for at least one year, one hundred students attended. In the late teens and early twenties, when the coal fields of Pennsylvania opened, many of the black families of Stafford County migrated north to work in the mines and the enrollment at the Mt. Zion School fell dramatically. The classroom in Stafford closed but Mr. Alexander moved the school to the Mt. Zion Church in southern Prince William County, closer to the new center of the black community. The children still living in Stafford County now had to walk, in some cases, five miles to school but the majority of the students lived in Prince William County.[2] Whether the non-residents paid to attend is not known but that was usually the case in schools whose pupils came from more than one county.

The one-room school had little equipment. There was a globe and only a few books though Mr. Alexander "got hold of every book he could get his hands on" both for himself and his students.[3] From his end of the year report, we know that when the Prince William County Mt. Zion School opened Mr. Alexander was forty-five years old and had taught for twenty-four years. He did not have a high school diploma. During that first year, Superintendent of Schools Richard Haydon visited the little school only once. There were sixteen children enrolled, fourteen in grades 1-4 but only two in grades five, six, and seven. The average daily attendance was thirteen and by year's end, five of the students had failed but none had dropped out. Mr. Alexander was paid $60 a month for a term lasting not quite six months; he earned $354 for the whole term. Two years later, when the school closed, enrollment had risen to twenty-one students but there still were no books in the library other than those lent to it by the teacher.

It is not clear why the Mt. Zion School closed at the end of the 1927-28 school year. Perhaps the enrollment was low or the children from Stafford County were able to get their education closer to home. The Prince William County students were bused to both the Brown School in Manassas and the Cabin Branch School near the pyrite mine in Batestown. Mr. Alexander ended his career as an elementary school teacher but taught adult education classes for many years.[4]

The following letter, written by Mr. Alexander, was found among loose pieces of paper in the Prince William County School Archives. Written on two small pieces of plain white paper at the end of the 1928 year, which was also to be the last year for the school, it gives an idea of the conditions and uncertainties under which he had to work.

Joplin, Va.
March 22, 1928

Supt. R.C. Haydon,
Manassas, Va.

Mr. Haydon,

Dear Sir - I am inclosing [sic] my term reports I have closed my school, after a very successful term. There was an increase in the enrollment. and good attendance. I am glad to be able to get out so that I can attend to my

---

[1] In addition, Mr. Alexander's son John, remembers his father's tenure at the Mt. Zion School and shared those memories in a telephone interview with the author.

[2] From an interview with Mr. John Alexander, May 1993.

[3] Ibid.

[4] Ibid.

farm work. But I was sorry to see the children have to leave school so early.

The patrons wish me to thank you for this term and hope that you can give them a longer term next year.

I also wish to thank you for my part. I thank you for the interest you have taken in me and the school.

> With best wishes
> I am yours. Resp'y
> John Alexander

NEABSCO SCHOOL

Dumfries School District
Colored
1901?-1939

The old Neabsco schoolhouse was built shortly after the turn of the twentieth century for about $1000. An undated, and often inaccurate School Inventory, states that the Neabsco School was built in 1893 but it is not located on the 1901 map of Prince William County done for the School Board by Mr. William H. Brown. The Neabsco School was established to serve the black children who lived in the Minnieville area of the county. The white children attended the old Minnieville School, but the black children were not allowed there. The nearest school for them was the Cabin Branch School, nearly a seven mile walk away. Mrs. Annie Thomas Williams remembers that her father, George Thomas, collected money from the community to hire a teacher and rent a small house for use as a classroom for black students.[1] By this time, Annie, who was born in 1893, and her brother had been attending the Cabin Branch School for awhile although the white Minnieville School was located across the road from their father's farmhouse. Thus it seems apparent that the Neabsco School opened shortly after 1900.

The rented house was soon replaced by a small, one-room, frame building with side windows and a porch across the front. It was located on Cardinal Drive in the black community of Neabsco, about a mile from the community of Minnieville and seven miles from the town of Woodbridge. The Williams children were the only black children who made the long trek to Cabin Branch but now there was a school in the neighborhood available to any child who

The Neabsco School as it looked soon after it closed in 1939.
(Courtesy of PWC Schools)

wanted to attend. It remained part of the community for almost forty years.

Inside the little school, the students had "suitable" desks, the teacher had a desk and there was a bookcase with a few textbooks. Maps and charts were displayed on the walls but, at least according to a school inventory in 1925, there were no books in the school library despite a plea from the teacher that they were needed. Heat was provided by a wood stove but there was no wood shed on the school grounds. The teacher and students cared for the stove and building. Pits, covered by outhouses, were the sanitary facilities and water came from premises off the school grounds.

Official school personnel rarely visited the school; during the 1925-26 term, none came at all.[2] This must have been difficult for the teacher and parents, giving them a feeling of isolation. The teacher that year was Mrs. Edna J. Woodson, a middle aged lady who had by then taught twenty-one years although she herself never graduated from high school. She taught twenty-four children in grades 1-4

---

[1] D'Anne Evans. "Abstract of an Interview with Annie Thomas Williams", July 18, 1988, p.6.

[2] E. J. Woodson. "Virginia Daily Attendance Register and Record of Class Grades" filed at the close of the 1925-26 school year.

and five in grades 5-7, but the average attendance was nineteen. For this Mrs. Woodson earned $60 a month for a seven month school year. At the end of the year, six of the original twenty-nine had dropped out of school and four more failed their level.[3]

Superintendent of Schools Richard C. Haydon did visit the Neabsco School during the 1933-34 school year. According to his year-end report[4], the best feature of the "old style" schoolhouse by that time was the "levelness and smoothness of the land surface".

Enrollment figures kept dropping gradually and during the 1934-35 school year, the enrollment was only fourteen, the smallest in the county system. The average daily attendance was only ten, half the number required by the School Board to keep a school open. The previous year there were nineteen enrolled but only eleven were promoted while five failed and three dropped out. The teacher during these years was a young woman holding a Normal Professional certificate from St. Paul Normal and Industrial School in Lawrenceville, Virginia. She had six years of experience and was "working very successfully with this little group of children".[5] It seems likely that this is the same teacher who transferred to the Hickory Ridge school the next year.

At the beginning of the 1935-1936 school year, the School Board authorized the operation of the Neabsco School on a short term basis and further authorized the Superintendent to hire a "satisfactory emergency teacher".[6] Given the problem of low enrollment, it is surprising that the school was not included in the petition presented to the School Board in June, 1937 asking that three of the colored schools in the district be consolidated at the Cabin Branch School.[7] A year later, the uncertainty continued. In September of 1938 the Board approved operating the little school for seven months with an itinerant, or travelling, teacher if the enrollment could be built up to sixteen regularly attending students. A teacher was hired to build it up and teach for $2.50 a day.

That, apparently, was the last year of operation for the Neabsco School. Enrollment figures just did not justify keeping the old building open any longer although there was not a school nearby to which the few remaining students could transfer easily. No trace remains of this schoolhouse.

---

[3]Richard C. Haydon. "An Administrative Survey of the Public School System in Prince William County, Virginia", A Thesis for Master of Science at the University of Virginia, 1935, p.105.

[4]Haydon, Richard. "An Administrative Survey of the Public School System in Prince William County, Virginia", A Thesis for Master of Science at the University of Virginia, 1935, p.105.

[5]Haydon, p.105.

---

[6]Prince William County School Board minutes of August 7, 1935.

[7]The three schools to be consolidated were the Cabin Branch School, Hickory Ridge School and the Quantico Colored School.

NELSON ELEMENTARY SCHOOL

Dumfries School District

c.1900

The Nelson school appears on the 1901 Brown map of the county, but it is not mentioned anywhere in any school records. Its appearance on that early map is the only place its name is found. Located within the present boundaries of Prince William Forest Park along the old Ridge Road, it was only about a mile west of the Thornton School which also is shown on the 1901 map. It is unlikely that two schools would have existed so close to each other at the same time serving the same population. Since the Thornton School was for white children, does that mean that the Nelson School served the black children of the area? Did it cease to exist soon after the turn of the century? Did the Thornton School, which opened sometime in the 1890s, replace the Nelson School which might have closed during the four years it took to get the map published? Did the white children of the community then transfer to the Thornton School after Nelson closed? The answers are lost in history.

NOKESVILLE/BRENTSVILLE DISTRICT HIGH/NOKESVILLE ELEMENTARY SCHOOL[1]

Brentsville District School #2 (after 1900, #8)
White
1870-present

Nokesville Elementary School as it looks today (1993)
(Photo by Stephen Phinney)

The Nokesville Elementary School, on Fitzwater Drive in the village of Nokesville, has been housed in at least four separate buildings. To confuse matters even more, it has been known by two different names, both of which are still in use for two schools in the Nokesville area. Putting the pieces of the puzzle together when some are missing, some might belong to a different puzzle, and some are broken has been a challenge.

The Nokesville Village School began in 1870 in a log cabin on Wilkins Corner, now the junction of Nokesville Road and Fitzwater Drive. Grades 1-9 were taught in that one-room school. By December of 1871, the search for a new school site had already begun[2] although it is not clear whether any action was taken at that time. In any case, enrollment apparently continued to grow because an assistant teacher was hired for the Nokesville School at the beginning of the 1877-78 school year.[3]

Five years later, the District School Board ordered School Trustee Mr. Dulin to make arrangements to have the Nokesville School moved from its location near the railroad to another place "above and near the village of Nokesville". The location of the old log cabin schoolhouse was about half a mile from the railroad so presumably this was the building considered to be too close to the railroad.

By 1883, a new schoolhouse was in use in Nokesville.[4] Longtime residents of the area remember the one-room schoolhouse located at the northeast corner of Fitzwater Drive at the intersection with Kettle Run Road. It was indeed further from the railroad which was about half a mile to the east, nearly twice the distance away that the old school had been.

Halfway through the first year in the new schoolhouse, the District School Board hired an assistant teacher at a salary of $15 per month. The assistant would only report to work when the school enrollment reached forty and the daily average attendance was thirty.[5] In those days, a teacher was paid $25 a month as long as the average attendance stayed at fifteen students or more per day. If the figure dropped below that, then the teacher's salary dropped to a per capita wage of $1.50 a pupil. It obviously was to the teacher's advantage to keep enrollment figures up.

As was the case in all county schools, routine maintenance of the Nokesville School rooms was the responsibility of the teacher and the pupils. Students swept the floors, cleaned the blackboards, kept the wood stove filled and generally kept the room orderly. Before the start of the 1888-89 school year, the School Board ordered the teachers to have a fire made in the stove by 8:30 every morning in preparation for the 9 o'clock school opening.[6]

That one-room Nokesville School served the community for twenty-five years until it was outgrown in 1908. That year, a new two-room frame schoolhouse was erected on the south side of Fitzwater Drive less than a quarter of a mile from the recently closed one-room school. The old building was dismantled and rebuilt as a garage which still stands in the village.

The new school building had tongue and groove pine flooring which was regularly oiled to prolong its life and keep the dust down. The walls were covered with wainscotting, the windows were large but

---

[1] The Nokesville Elementary School became known as the Brentsville District High School when the new building, housing grades 1-11 was built in 1929. It was known by that name until 1964 when the new High School (the present building) was built for grades 6-12 and the name was transferred to the new school. The older building reverted to the name Nokesville Elementary School and it is still known as that today. It currently houses grades K-5.

[2] Brentsville District School Board minutes of December 18, 1871.

[3] Brentsville District School Board minutes of September 1877.

[4] Brentsville District School Board minutes of January 1, 1884.

[5] Brentsville District School Board minutes of January 12, 1884.

[6] Brentsville District School Board minutes of August 5, 1888.

not weather tight.[7] In February of 1912, $30 for a school library was approved by the School Board.

As early as 1904, while school was still being held in the one-room building, pressure had begun to be put on the Board to provide high school courses for those students who wanted them. Citing lack of funds, the Board deferred the matter until it could no longer be ignored. Finally, less than five years after the new schoolhouse was built, the citizens of Nokesville held two mass meetings to discuss the need for a new and larger building. In the spring of 1914, District School Board members heard the minutes of those two meetings. Mr. J. A. Hooker offered a site of five acres for a graded four-room school. It was also reported that a sum of $315 had already been subscribed for a new building "with the prospect of more".[8] The Board agreed to accept the land offer and look into the matter.

Less than two months later, on May 25, 1914, the Board agreed to accept bids on a six-room brick school building. In June they agreed to sell the old school house and its grounds for a minimum of $1500. For some reason, however, all this came to naught and the two-room schoolhouse continued as before. Finally a year later, the Board accepted Mr. E. S. Hoon's bid of $1525 to build a two-room addition to the 1909 schoolhouse despite continuing pleas by the citizens for a new building.[9] Each room had its own cloakroom and the two classrooms on the east end of the building were separated by folding doors which could be opened to provide a large assembly room. They did not provide much soundproofing, however.[10] Now that the school had four rooms, two years of high school courses were added to the curriculum.

Troubles continued to plague the school. On March 28, 1917, it was reported to the School Board that the principal, Mr. E. S. Napier, "has left the school without notifying the Board". Mr. L.C. Messick, who had been substituting, was made a full time principal with an emergency certificate granted by the Board.

---

[7]Reminiscences of former student and Nokesville resident Robert Beahm as told to the author in 1992. Mr. Beahm's mother and sister attended the old one-room Nokesville School.

[8]Brentsville District School Board minutes of April 3, 1914.

[9]Brentsville District School Board minutes of May 13, 1915.

[10]Robert Beahm's recollections.

Students at the Nokesville School, c. 1899. The teacher, Katie Kewitt, is in the center.
(Courtesy of Mr. Robert Beahm)

One of the last teachers in the two-room Nokesville Elementary School was Martha Via Owens who taught at Nokesville from 1913 to 1918, covering the transition of the building from a two-room school to a four-room school. Several years later, her daughter, Mary Owens, attended the Nokesville School, then called Brentsville District High School, for her entire public education from 1931 to 1942. Teaching with Martha Via was Mrs. Fannie Mae Ellis whose memories today stretch back nearly a century to the earliest days of Prince William County's public education.

Mrs. Ellis herself attended the old Greenwich Elementary School, one mile from her home, in 1900. She then went on to Eastern College, about ten miles from home, for her secondary education before earning a degree from Harrisonburg Normal College in 1915. She returned to her home and began her teaching career with Martha Via at the Nokesville Elementary School. Mrs. Ellis remembers that this building was a two-room school with privies out in back. The teachers were responsible for the maintenance of the building. Heat came from wood stoves; drinking water from wells. The school day lasted from 9 AM until 4:30 PM with two short recesses in the morning and the afternoon as well as a one hour break at lunchtime. The rest of the day was taken up studying reading, arithmetic, grammar and Latin, a subject not taught at most of the county elementary schools. Books were supplied by the students themselves although slates were provided by school. Unusually, both basketballs and baseballs were available at the school. The school year lasted from September until either late March or April. Mrs. Ellis taught the primary levels at the Nokesville school, but she transferred to the Greenwich School where she taught the intermediate grades (4-7).[11]

The four-room Nokesville School was a graded school in which each classroom was set aside for a particular grade or grades. The first and second grades met in one room, grades 3-5 met in another and a third room held sixth and seventh graders. The fourth room was used for the first two years of high school.

About ninety students attended at any one time. Maintenance was done by a couple of the older boys until the last two years of the school's existence when Charles Beahm and Willard Wilkins performed the janitorial duties. Heat was provided by wood burning stoves which the students kept fueled with wood they brought from a woodshed on the school property. Water came from an outside well with a hand pump, a common sight in the early days of county education.

The school day began at 9 o'clock in the morning, when the principal pulled a rope to ring the large bell on top of the building. Students lined up according to grade and marched into their classrooms where the daily routine started with a scripture reading and a prayer. At 10:30 there was "little recess" which provided time to visit one of the two privies located about 250' away and to get a drink from the well. "Big recess", lasting from noon to 1 o'clock, was used to eat lunch and play games such as tag, leap-frog, Fox and Goose, dodge ball and, for the older boys, baseball. The ringing of the bell called students back to class. At 2:15 came the second ten minute "little recess" and at 3:30 the bell signalled the end of the school day.

Robert Beahm, who attended the four-room Nokesville School from 1926-1929, the last years of its existence, remembers it well and his memories bring the old school to life. He studied reading from the classics, Child's World Readers, New Barnes Readers, Story Hour Readers and The Silent Readers by Lewis and Roland; spelling; penmanship; arithmetic; local history and geography. As was the practice throughout the county, students purchased their own books. Maps and blackboards were part of the equipment in each classroom. Some classes even had a limited supply of balls and bats. There was always a Christmas pageant as well as annual reading and story telling contests.

Lunch time was as important to the children of the early schools as it is today. Robert remembers a typical lunch he brought from home: a scrambled egg sandwich, jelly and butter on a biscuit left from breakfast, ginger snap cookies or Fig Newtons and an apple. Drinking water came from the schoolyard pump. One winter parents arranged to bring hot soup into the school and sold it for ten cents a cup.

During the 1925-26 school term, the teacher of the first and second graders was Miss Cora E. Beahm, Robert's older sister. As noted above, Miss Beahm had attended the old one-room Nokesville School. In 1926, she was twenty-six years old, a high school graduate, and had already been teaching for six years. She had twenty-eight children in her class that year, thirteen boys and fifteen girls, but usually only twenty were in class on any given day. She was paid $85 a month for a nine months' term and had to pay $15 per month for room and board in the community. She was fortunate to have use of a 250 volume school library, large for that day.[12]

Miss Olga E. White was the third and fourth grade teacher during the same school term. She was twenty-nine years old and had been a teacher for the eight years following high school graduation. She had thirty-four children enrolled in her classroom ranging from ages seven through thirteen. Miss White's salary was the same as was Miss Beahm's but she had to pay $20 a month for her room and board.[13]

Busing came to Nokesville in the late 1920s. Robert Beahm, who was in the second grade at that time, tells the story:

> Nokesville's first school bus service was provided by one of its teachers. W. Davis Nolley, a farmer-teacher, taught 6th and 7th grades in 1927-28. He owned a farm truck that was considered large by those days' standards. It was an open truck, but he covered the top with canvas and installed canvas curtains on the

---

[11]From recollections made available to the author in 1993 by Mrs. Ellis. For the rest of her story, see the section about the Greenwich School.

[12]"Virginia Daily Attendance Register and Record of Class Grades" for the Nokesville School filed at the end of the 1925-26 school year by Miss Beahm.

[13]"Virginia Daily Attendance Register and Record of Class Grades" filed by Miss White for the Nokesville School at the end of the 1925-26 school year.

sides that could be rolled to the top in pleasant weather. His route began at Aden and ended at Nokesville school. Most of the passengers had completed the six grades at Aden and were getting their "advanced" education at Nokesville. On arrival at Nokesville school, Mr. Nolley parked his bus, shed his work overalls and stepped into the schoolroom in suit and necktie, ready to teach. We second grades felt that education was making great strides when students were bused to school. *We* had to walk!

In September of 1928, the citizens of the Brentsville District passed a bond issue for $30,000 to construct a new school building. Though the four-room Nokesville schoolhouse continued to be used during the 1928-29 school year, the addition of students from the seventh grade at King's Xroads and Aden schools meant that the School Board could no longer ignore the overcrowded conditions. In December of 1928, $100 was paid to Mr. J. A. Hooker for the lot on which to build a new school house. When the deed was delivered to the Board in February of 1929, the $900 balance was paid.[14] The old school and lot were sold at a public auction in front of the Nokesville Bank in Nokesville on Wednesday, March 27, 1929, to M.J. Sheppard for $1203 who paid the full amount to the School Board on April 3. Eventually, the four-room school building was dismantled by Mr. Charles Dove who used the materials to build a house for his family on the same site. The house still stands on Fitzwater Drive in Nokesville.

Once construction began on the new school building, troubles did not end. As Miss Hattie Mae Partlow reports,

> The first scoop of dirt was moved by Maude and Mollie, a pair of baldfaced mares owned by M. J. Shepherd and driven by Lawrence Foster. The work began in the spring of 1929. By May 2, the boiler room had been dug, and the walls were window height with the window frames set when a tornado swept through the community and leveled much of the construction.

It should be noted that this school was built as a result of the keen interest and loyalty of its patrons. Money and labor were contributed as were the huge boxwoods flanking the doorway which were gifts of the late George Snooks from his farm near Bristow. Mr. Snooks also gave and cut all the frame work for the gym, erected in 1931 by volunteer labor. For several years it had only a dirt floor.[15]

The new building was called the Brentsville District High School, a name which better reflected its status as a center school for the District housing grades one to eleven. "The Nokesville Elementary School was such an integral part of BDHS that it hardly had its own identity", according to former student Aliene Nolley Beahm. At the time of the school's opening on September 5, 1929, it had an enrollment of eighty-eight students with eight teachers. The new building contained six classrooms and an auditorium with a room behind the stage which was used as a seventh classroom when needed. Running water came from a well on the school grounds. Drinking fountains replaced the bucket and dippers of old. There was an indoor bathroom for girls and another for the boys. The lights were electric and central heat came from a coal furnace. Keeping that big furnace fired was a big job, done by Mr. Nathan Wells who also drove one of the two school buses. Additionally, Mr. Wells often built special projects for the teachers such as the very large doll house for the first grade. He worked late into the day sweeping the school's floors after returning from his bus route.[16]

The daily school routine changed very little when the children moved into the larger building. Student Mary Owens remembers that the school year went from September first to June first. The school day lasted from 9 AM to 3:30 PM. She remembers being taught reading, writing, arithmetic, geometry, algebra, English, science and Home Economics. Presumably these last few were studies in the high school classes. Books were supplied by the students who often bought them from students who had used them the year before. Mary recalls that baseball, softball, basketball and soccer were the favorite outdoor

---

[14] Prince William County School Board minutes of February 28, 1929.

[15] Hattie Mae Partlow and Pauline Smith. *Now and Then With P.W.E.A.*, Prince William Education Association, 1963, pp.69-70.

[16] These personal memories of the new BDHS are from Aliene Nolley Beahm, Robert Beahm's wife, who attended the school from 1935-1942.

sports of the school which the students played without teacher supervision. Aliene Nolley (Beahm) also remembers roller skating on the sidewalk in front of the school during "big recess" after lunch. There was still a ten minute "little recess" each morning and a structured activity "play period" every afternoon.

Mr. C. O. Bittle, who had earlier been a teacher at the Greenwich School, served as principal of the Brentsville District High School from 1929 until June of 1947. He comes alive again with the following description:

> Short of stature, with piercing eyes and a resounding voice, "Prof." stood for high standards, strict discipline, and conservatism. His office was a huge packing case in the corner of [his] classroom used as a homeroom, laboratory and Latin class. Too short to reach the wall telephone, he kicked a box into place and hopped upon it to ring vigorously for the local operator who knew everyone in the community by first names and the latest happenings - good or bad. Respected, and often feared, Prof. Bittle made the most of every opportunity offered B.D.H.S. from 1929 until he returned to teaching at Osbourn in 1947.[17]

In 1931, the tile gymnasium with its dirt floor and two more classrooms, one of which served as a laboratory, were added to Brentsville in a separate but nearby building. New playground apparatus was put into place in 1932. According to the Superintendent of Schools report of 1934[18], the first, second, third, sixth and seventh grades were housed in the main building while grades four and five met in the gym which was heated by a coal stove. By that time, Mr. Ben Hedrick served as maintenance man for the complex and also drove the school bus. In addition to the main schoolhouse and the gymnasium building, a community cannery was built in 1940 and attached to the gym. Mrs. Martha Irven was hired to prepare meals in the cannery which were served to the students on the sidelines of the gym floor. That practice continued until the high school addition with a proper cafeteria was erected in 1953.

By 1933, four years after the new building opened, enrollment had grown to 149 with an average attendance of 116. At year's end, there were 107 promotions, twenty-one failures and twenty-one dropped out. All four elementary grade teachers that year tested a new course of study from the state. Three of those teachers had graduated from a teachers' college while the fourth was a university graduate.[19]

In 1937, the School Board contracted to buy 1.8 acres of land adjoining the school property from J.A. Hooker for $200. In addition, they contracted with R.B. Grissom of Waterfall to build a Home Economics Cottage at a cost of $3925. This small bungalow contained a kitchen, a living and dining room combination and bedroom which also held several treadle sewing machines on which the girls were taught to sew. This was for the older students but it was still a physical part of the elementary-secondary school of Brentsville which, by then, was made up of four separate buildings.

In 1946, the Aden School and the Brentsville District High School were consolidated and an addition of three rooms was put onto the Brentsville building. In 1946 also, the Greenwich school closed and those children were transported to Brentsville/Nokesville, adding even more to the school's enrollment. The High School wing was added in 1953 but overcrowded conditions still led to temporary classrooms in neighboring buildings and trailers. Finally, when the County schools were integrated in 1964-65, it became necessary to build a new high school separate from the elementary grades. That new building took the name Brentsville District High School and the elementary school reverted to the name of Nokesville. The building is still being used as one of Prince William County's elementary schools.

---

[17]Partlow, p.72.

[18]Richard C. Haydon. "An Administrative Survey of the Public School System in Prince William County, Virginia", A Thesis for Master of Science at the University of Virginia, 1935, p.63.

---

[19]Haydon, p.63.

THE OAK HILL (HAMMETT)/ BUCKHALL SCHOOL

Manassas District School #4
1870-1936
White

The earliest reference to a schoolhouse in Prince William County places it at or near Buckhall "some years prior to 1755".[1] Whether this school was publicly or privately supported is not known. The building which became the Manassas District School #4 was actually erected as a private school at the end of the Civil War in 1865.[2] When the State Law providing for free public education was passed in 1870, the Manassas District School Board asked for donations of buildings and/or land for schoolhouses. At that time, the citizens of Buckhall donated the schoolhouse and its lot to the Board and so the Buckhall School became part of the county's public school system. It was the fourth public school in the District; hence the #4 designation.[3] The schoolhouse was located at the intersection of Old Davis Ford Road and Moore Drive. It can still be seen there today.

Apparently Buckhall was not the original name for this school. The School Board minutes of January 7, 1871 talk about hiring D. T. Arrington to teach at the Oak Hill School in Buckhall for a salary of $40 a month.[4] There were not two schoolhouses in Buckhall so it seems evident that Oak Hill was an earlier name for the school as well as for the nearby church. Occasionally, the name of the Hammett School is also used in some early records for the Oak Hill/Buckhall school. It is likely that a public school was set up in the Buckhall community before a permanent building was available. It would not have been unusual for a room in a private home or business to be used as a temporary classroom and the school thus established to be called by the name of its borrowed quarters. The Oak Hill Church in Buckhall may well have been the site of the Oak Hill School. In similar fashion, Hammett may have been the name of a member of the community who gave space for a classroom until a more suitable space could be found. Because it is not known exactly when the Buckhall Schoolhouse was given to the District Board, one can only guess the whole story. However, before the year 1871 was out, Board minutes talk only of the Buckhall School which, by then had been given its #4 designation; Oak Hill and Hammett do not appear again as school names. As was true in most communities the Buckhall School was the center of community life. In 1885 the Rev. Abraham Conner, of the German Baptist Brethren Church, who had recently moved from Pennsylvania, preached at the Buckhall School, as well as the Bradley School while waiting for his own church to be built at Cannon Branch.[5]

On June 2, 1902, the Manassas District School Board authorized one of its members, Trustee Payne, to put up an addition to the little schoolhouse. He hired the workers and got the needed supplies. The new part of the building, which was added onto the front of the existing structure was two feet higher than the original and three feet longer. One room

The Buckhall Schoolhouse today.
(Photo by the author)

---

[1] R. Worth Peters. "Secondary Education in Manassas, Va. 1890-1935." A Thesis presented to the Academic Faculty of the University of Virginia in Candidacy for the Degree of Master of Arts, 1939, p.17.

[2] Prince William County Historical Commission. *Prince William: A Past to Preserve*, Prince William County, VA., 1982, p.82.

[3] The Ruffner, Brown and Groveton Schools had been established prior to the date that Buckhall became one of the District's schools.

[4] The $40 monthly teacher's salary was to be paid by both the school patrons who were to contribute $15 of that amount, and Public Funds which would supply $25 "when available" according to the Manassas District School Board minutes of January 7, 1871.

[5] Mary Senseney Kline. *Cannon Branch School, 1889-1927*. Privately published, 1988, p.1.

measured 18'x24', the other 22'x21'.[6] A wainscotted cloakroom was walled off at one end of the school. Both classrooms were heated by wood stoves vented through a brick chimney at either end of the building. The floor was made of tongue and groove pine boards. The walls were painted plaster; the roof was metal as it was for most of the County's schoolhouses.

Two rooms were not needed for long apparently, because three years later the Board voted "that the two rooms be thrown into one" and then hired Beatrice Limstrong at a salary of $36 a month for a year of eight or nine months instead of the usual six.[7] Then, by the beginning of the 1916-17 school year, enrollment at the Buckhall School had increased enough to warrant the hiring of a second teacher although it remained a one-room schoolhouse. By 1920, the second teacher was gone leaving one teacher to cope with fifty students in first through eighth grades.

Friday was baking day at the Buckhall School in the early years of the century. Parents furnished the materials which the teacher taught the students to use. They baked breads and cakes, some of which the children ate and some of which made their way home.

At the end of the 1926-27 school year, the teacher, Miss Lula Brydie, filed a report. By then, only grades 1-4 were taught at the Buckhall School. Miss Brydie, a twenty-two year old high school graduate with no previous teaching experience, was in charge of twenty-four students, half of whom dropped out of school by the end of the year. That dismal statistic has never been matched by any other school in the county. Miss Brydie was paid $70 a month for an eight month term and paid $20 monthly for room and board in the community.

The following year, Miss Brydie was again the teacher, this time with twenty-eight students enrolled but an average daily attendance of eighteen. At the end of the year, seven of these had dropped out and five more had failed. Strangely, the 130 volume library reported the previous year, numbered only ninety-eight one year later. Incidentally, the next school year, 1929-30, found Miss Brydie teaching at Occoquan District High School. Perhaps she was better suited to teaching the older students than her record would indicate at Buckhall.

During the 1933-34 school year, enrollment at Buckhall was thirty-two in four grades under the tutelage of one teacher. The daily average attendance was twenty-six. At year's end, twenty-five students were promoted, seven failed and none dropped out. The following school year, enrollment had fallen to twenty-five with an average attendance of twenty-three.[8] Since the capacity of the school was forty-two students, there must have been lots of empty spaces.

The schoolhouse, according to the November 1934 report of Superintendent of Schools Richard Haydon, was in very good condition. It had a piano and double desks for every grade. Heat still came from a wood stove and the children kept the building clean. Adequate water came from a pump on the school grounds but toilet facilities were labelled "inadequate". The playground was all right but with minimal equipment. Students brought their own from home. The teacher that year was a graduate of a teachers' college with a certificate but no experience.

Falling enrollment figures finally caused the School Board, on April 8, 1936, to close the Buckhall School at the end of the school year. The parents from the farm and dairy community were happy to have their children transported to a larger school in Manassas where facilities were better. The schoolhouse was sold at auction soon after its closing. In 1965 it was restored by the Buckhall Civic Association which held meetings there until around 1986. It is still standing at 7601 Old Davis Ford Road in the Buckhall area of Manassas.

---

[6]Engineering Report prepared for the Prince William County School Board by the Viola Proffitt Insurance Agency of Manassas, Va. in October, 1953.

[7]Manassas District School Board minutes of June 3, 1905.

[8]Richard C. Haydon. *Survey of the Public School System in Prince William County*. Master's Thesis, University of Virginia, 1936, p.71.

THE OCCOQUAN/OCCOQUAN DISTRICT HIGH (OCCOQUAN) SCHOOL

Occoquan School District
White
1905?-present

Though there was a school in Occoquan as early as 1867, it was not a public school. It was known as Township Hall and was located on the Janney property along the Occoquan River. Citizens raised the money to pay the teacher's salary and when the money ran out, the school closed for the year. An exception to that occurred when the grandfather of Fred Lynn, a Prince William County educator for whom Fred Lynn Middle School was named, taught one term without pay in order to keep the school open.

The first public school opened sometime between 1901 (it does not appear on the county map of that year) and 1909 when it was painted by Mr. Selecman.[1] The two-room schoolhouse was located at 310 A/B Commerce Street and the building is still standing.

Each of the two classrooms had its separate entrance. There were two cloakrooms for each room, one for boys and one for girls. A heavy sliding door separated the "Big Room" where fifth, sixth and seventh grades were taught and the "Little Room" where the first through fourth grades met.[2] Children were called into school by a big bell rung by the principal using a rope in the "Big Room".

Each classroom had a water cooler that was filled with water from the spring at Rockledge, Mrs.

The first Occoquan School building on Commerce Street as it appeared in 1981.
(Courtesy of PWC Historical Commission)

Giles Carter's home three buildings away. In each room there was a large iron stove with a galvanized shield around it to prevent burns. The windows were covered with diamond mesh heavy wire on the outside; no screens were needed. Map cases were on the wall above the blackboard on which the teacher often stenciled special designs in several colors to celebrate holidays, etc.[3]

In the front of the Big Room was a platform, about eight inches high, which served as a stage for programs and entertainments. A white sheet, strung on a wire, became the stage curtain. When Margaret Selecman was a student she remembers one program in particular where the children sang "Topsey, turvey, here we go; half on head and half on toe...". Half of the pupils had their shoes on their hands and a short curtain was hung in front so that only hands and "feet" were seen.[4] Other entertainments included parents and friends of the school and graduation exercises were held on the platform too.

Since the school was in the middle of town, most of the students were able to go home for lunch. Being in town had another, unusual, advantage. Margaret Selecman remembers that when she was in the Big Room, the pupils were "marched" to the flour mill in Occoquan and each was weighed on the platform scales there!

The playground was a grassy area in back of the schoolhouse. A tall, solid board fence divided the boys' and girls' sides each of which had an outdoor privy. A fence also ran across the back of the play area.

---

[1] Oral history done by Thomas Nelson with Rosemary Selecman, mother of Margaret.

[2] Since there was no high school in the eastern end of Prince William County, students who wanted an education beyond the seventh grade had to go either to Manassas High School or to school in Alexandria. In the case of the latter, pupils caught the train in Woodbridge and took it to school. Some made the trip every day while others boarded in Alexandria during the week. If they chose to go to Manassas, they usually boarded there with a local family, coming home for holidays and an occasional weekend. The roads were really not good enough for daily travel although a few students did make the trip every day. Train travel, tuition fees and boarding fees were not cheap; a high school education was beyond the means of many county residents.

[3] This description of the two room Occoquan School comes from Margaret Selecman Peters whose family was prominent in the town.

[4] Personal memories of Margaret Selecman Peters.

In 1927, as part of the effort toward consolidation, a new and larger school building was built to serve the needs of the white children in the southeastern part of the county. At that time, the District School Board decided to sell the old building and offered it at a public auction at the schoolhouse on March 29, 1929. Mr. Edson M. Lynn bought the building for $1000, put two porches on it and converted it into two apartments. It was further remodelled in 1980, became a French tea room and it is still a restaurant today. The frame schoolhouse with its stone foundation and metal covered gable roof was a thing of the past!

The new school was a two-story, eight-room brick structure on six acres of "well-graded land", according to Superintendent Richard Haydon's 1934 report on the schools. It cost $28,500 to build and it housed first through eleventh grades. There were six classrooms, three for the elementary grades, three for the high school; a laboratory; and an auditorium with a stage. The stage was partitioned, front and back, with the rear part being used as a library. The High School part of Occoquan served a large geographic area: Quantico, Triangle, Dumfries, Woodbridge, Hoadly and Occoquan. The elementary grades served those children living in the more immediate community.

Unlike the old schoolhouse, the new building was not built in the center of the village where little room was available. Instead, it was built on the Old Occoquan Road midway between the towns of Occoquan and Woodbridge and about one mile from the Richmond-Washington Highway (Rt. 1). Many of the parents worked at the Lorton Work House (prison) or in Washington, D.C.. The majority of the students commuted by bus, among the first to do so. One of the first bus drivers was Mr. Easton Keys who lived in Dumfries. George Cooper, a student at the school, also drove a bus from his home in the Minnieville area picking up students on his way. Another early bus driver was Mr. Hal Barnes who also lived in the Minnieville area. The county furnished him with the bus, but the students who rode it had to buy the gas. Whenever he bought five gallons of gas, he had to take up a collection.[5]

The new Occoquan District School had been built with "all modern conveniences".[6] Miss Elizabeth Vaughan, who had previously taught at both Aden and Haymarket, was named the first principal, a position she held for the next thirteen years. As one of six teachers, she also taught algebra and Latin I. Alice Williams and John Kline also taught the high school; Fannie Nunnick was the sixth and seventh grade teacher; grades four and five were taught by Ercelle Savage Weedon; the primary classes, grades 1-3, were under the tutelage of Florence Gossom Wayland who had taught at the Woodbridge Elementary School before its closing.

According to Superintendent of Schools Richard C. Haydon's report of the 1933-34 school year, enrollment was 157 with an average attendance of 117. The teachers' experience ranged from one to nine years; all graduated from a teacher's college. That year there were 105 promotions, twenty-seven failures and twenty-five who dropped out. The village of Occoquan, in 1930, had a population of only 250. Remember, most of the high school students did not live in the town. By 1950, the student body numbered 225. There were twenty-one teachers.

Janitorial service was provided for many years by Mr. George Russell. There were drinking fountains with water supplied by a well on school grounds, water toilets, electric lights and a central heating system. Each classroom had a desk and chair for the teacher, reading tables with chairs, maps, a globe, books and general supplies. The playground was adequate for the elementary children but it lacked equipment.

By 1941, there were fourteen rooms on two floors arranged around a central auditorium. The coal, later oil, furnace was located in the basement heating plant. The floors were made of wood although in the hallways that wood was covered with asphalt tile and there were bathrooms on each floor. The classrooms had plaster walls and ceilings.

Following Miss Vaughan came Mr. Caldwell for one year and then Mr. Ward Peters, who became Superintendent of Schools in 1946, held the job from 1931-34. He taught chemistry, biology, Latin and

---

[5]Thomas Nelson. "Transcript of Interview with Historic Occoquan, Inc." Prince William County Historical Commission Oral History Project, September 24, 1985, p.7.

[6]Richard C. Haydon. "An Administrative Survey of the Public School System in Prince William County, Virginia," A Thesis for Master of Science at the University of Virginia, 1935, p.74.

American History. According to Woody Taylor, a student under Mr. Peters,

> He would come in to teach us chemistry, and he would say, "We're going to have an experiment today on so-and-so." And he'd throw the manual down and never look at it and set up that thing and go through the whole experiment without looking at nothing. And when we had biology class, he'd do likewise. The same way with Latin and the same way with American History. I mean, he never used any book. He talked out of his head, but he was always right.[7]

Elizabeth Vaughan returned as principal from 1934-37. The last principal of the Occoquan District High School was Mr. Herbert Saunders who held the position from 1947-52. That fall, with the opening of the new Gar-Field High School on Route 1 in the Gar-Field Estates area of Woodbridge, Occoquan became just an elementary school once again. Actually, the new high school was not ready for occupancy until December of 1952, so the teachers unpacked their boxes and taught their high school students at Occoquan for a few more months.

Students remember that the Occoquan School during the 1940s had about fifteen to twenty rooms with somewhat more than 220 students and about twenty-one teachers. That ratio of ten students to every teacher is a fine one. The library was good and there was a large assembly room with a gymnasium in a separate building. For the upper grades, there was an excellent commercial department. Many of the teachers who taught at the Occoquan School had long careers in education and their students recall their names with pleasure. Among these are Mr. Herb Saunders, Mrs. Nellie Curtis, Miss Nellie Barnes, Mrs. Mildred Bruckner and more. Students remember their days at Occoquan with fondness.

The 1953 School Board Report talks about the Occoquan New Elementary School, built in 1952. This was a third separate building erected adjacent to the existing schoolhouse. It was a one-story school with a flat roof and a basement of concrete block faced with brick. The basement contained the boiler room, kitchen and cafeteria and home economics room all with open ceilings and walls and asphalt covered concrete floors. The first floor with its acoustic tile ceiling and asphalt tile floors had eight rooms and two lavatories.

The school changed in 1953 when Gar-Field High School was built taking children in grades 8-12 from Occoquan. Three years later, one wing of the school was remodelled to suit the needs of younger children. In the mid-1960s, sixth and seventh grade students also left Occoquan and went to Fred Lynn Middle School. In 1967 the school was remodelled once again. It now houses grades K-5 in three separate buildings which can be seen on Occoquan Road in Woodbridge.

---

[7]Nelson, Thomas. "Woody. An Interview with James Woodrow Taylor". An oral history for the Prince William County Historical Commission, January, 1982, p.9.

THE ORLANDO SCHOOL

Brentsville School District
White
1872-1932

The earliest reference to a school in the Orlando Courthouse area of the county comes in the Brentsville District School Board records in 1872. There it is mentioned that the Board rented a room from Mr. George M. Goodwin who owned property on the west side of Orlando Drive about midway

The first Orlando School as it appears in 1993— still red!
(Photo by the author)

between Aden and Bristoe Roads. This became the first Orlando schoolhouse and it is standing today. It had one room, a dirt floor and was heated by a potbellied stove. Two windows on each side let in light. Above the schoolroom, under the eaves, was an unfinished room reached by a winding staircase. It was also heated with a potbellied stove and that is where the schoolteacher lived. The schoolhouse was painted red, one of the few red ones in the county, and its green shutters can still be found in the attic room. Big trees surrounded the building and a fence enclosed the school yard.[1]

Strangely, the Orlando school is not mentioned again in the minutes of the Brentsville District School Board until the time came for the old schoolhouse to be sold. The school does not appear on the 1901 map of the county either. Is this because, at that time, it was a rented building not belonging to the School District? Did it possibly close for a period of time? No answers have been found.

According to longtime residents, sometime in the 1920s a new Orlando Schoolhouse was built. Perhaps this was to conform to the new state standards set for public schools. After all, the old building was over fifty years old by that time. In 1935, at the direction of Richard Haydon, Superintendent of Prince William County Schools, the first Orlando schoolhouse was sold at public auction. A retired couple purchased it, added a porch, a kitchen and a bedroom, turned the classroom into a living room and used it as a residence. It is still a residence today, appropriately occupied by a current teacher in the Prince William County school system.

The second building was located between Barbee's Store and Post Office and the Methodist Church, directly across Orlando Road from the site of the first school. The new one-room Orlando schoolhouse, like the first one in its later years, was under the tutelage of Mr. William Y. Ellicott, a descendant of one of eastern Prince William County's earliest families. He was the school teacher at Orlando for so long that the little school was often referred to as Mr. Ellicott's school. When he left Orlando, he went to teach at the Woodbine school and then became a truant officer. In all, he served the county schools for forty years.

The Orlando School is not mentioned in the 1933-34 year end report of the county schools by Superintendent Richard Haydon so it can be assumed that it had been closed at least a year by that time. It probably fell victim to the consolidation movement, which closed most of the small schoolhouses of the county in the twenties and thirties. The second building, as well as the church and store which flanked it, no longer exist. Only the cemetery of the church marks that part of the community of Orlando.

---

[1] From an interview done in 1993 by the author with Janet Graham who currently lives in this early schoolhouse.

PARKSIDE ELEMENTARY

Manassas/Brentsville District
1962-present

Parkside Elementary School opened for the 1962-63 school year in a new building located on Mathis Avenue near the town of Manassas Park. It was built on thirty acres of land originally patented to Richard (King) Carter. Part of the land was the roadbed of the historic Orange and Alexandria Railroad.

The student body numbered 1500 in the school's opening year. Six hundred were in grades 1-6; nine hundred were pupils in grades 7-9. Additions were built in 1964 and again in 1972. The organization of the county schools underwent a change in 1966. Previously, there were six elementary grades, three intermediate grades and three grades in high school. After 1966, that was changed to five grades in elementary school, three in intermediate (including sixth grade) and four in the high school program. When kindergarten was added in 1974, the division became 6-3-4 and it remains that way today. In 1975, the elementary part of Parkside became a separate entity although it continues to share a building with Parkside Middle School.[1]

When the town of Manassas Park became a city in 1977, it established its own school system. Parkside Elementary remained a County school, now in the Brentsville Magisterial District, and began to draw students from geographical areas outside the new boundaries of Manassas Park.

---

[1] Prince William County School System. "Self Study of Parkside School", 1980-81.

THE PITTSYLVANIA SCHOOL

Manassas School District
Colored
1871 and earlier

Although there is no existing record, Pittsylvania may have been a privately run school for black children before it became part of the public school system in 1870. Pittsylvania was the name of a large plantation owned by Landon Carter, a descendant of the Robert "King" Carter family, so prominent in the early history of the western part of Prince William County. The house itself was burned shortly after the Second Battle of Manassas in 1862, but the area continued to be known as Pittsylvania. The Stone House, now at the intersection of routes 234 and 29, was built on the Pittsylvania Plantation around 1812 and it is likely that the Pittsylvania School was located somewhere in the vicinity.

At the second meeting of the Manassas School Board in December of 1870, the members voted to hire Mr. Josiah Thomas "to teach the colored school at Pittsylvania" for a salary of $15 a month as requested by Mr. Thomas.[1] Likely, the school was already in existence since the Board did not address the question of opening a school.

While the salary was low, it did not have to cover Mr. Thomas' board since that was provided to him by patrons of the school. The school opened on January 23, 1871 as a public school but it did not last long. At the School Board meeting of April 22, 1871 it was reported that the Pittsylvania School fell below attendance requirements and additionally, the teacher was ready to "close his contract" so the little school was closed immediately. Mr. Thomas was not unemployed for long. School Board minutes later that fall show that he had been employed to teach the Manly (Manley) School, which had recently opened.

Other than a very few references in the old Manassas District School Board minutes of 1870-71, no other mention has ever been found of the Pittsylvania School. Perhaps because it was open for such a short time as a public school, it was never given a number as were other schools in the District. When it closed, the few remaining children probably transferred to the Manley School. It opened in 1871 and would have been a three to four mile walk for the students of the Pittsylvania neighborhood, not an unusual distance for black children to have to travel.

[1] Manassas District School Board minutes of December 17, 1870.

POTOMAC VIEW ELEMENTARY SCHOOL

Occoquan/Woodbridge District
1963-present

The Potomac View Elementary School was built in what was then the Occoquan District in 1963. It was situated on a hill from which one could, at the time it was built, view the Potomac River. When the Woodbridge District was created in 1976, Potomac View Elementary on Lamar Street was within its boundaries.

THE PURCELL SCHOOL

Coles School District
White
188?-1933

The Purcell School was located on Purcell Road in the small community of Purcell, all of which were named for a prominent family of the area. The School Board purchased a piece of property on the south side of Purcell Road about a quarter of a mile from

Purcell, the only metal schoolhouse built in the county, burned down in 1982.
(Photo by Stephen Phinney)

where that road and Spriggs Ford Road used to intersect. The Board then contracted to have a one-room schoolhouse built for the community's children. No deed was recorded by the School Board however, so an exact date for the opening of the school is lost to history. One of the students at that first school was Delley Cornwell who was born in 1881 and so probably began attending school in 1885 or 1886. Mr. Cornwell's wife later taught at the new Purcell School and his children, Zella and James, attended there and still live in the Purcell community.

The small frame building continued to serve the community until 1906 when the School Board decided to build a new schoolhouse for the Purcell community. The old school became the property of Mr. Fair who already owned the land on that side of Purcell Road. Mr. Fair moved the building closer to the road where it served as a community store for many years. After the store had closed, Mr. Fair's house on the other side of the road burned down and he used the old schoolhouse/store as a temporary dwelling while his new house, which still stands today, was being built. Today, the old building stands in ruins, covered in honeysuckle vines, beside the road, a silent reminder of its days as a schoolhouse a hundred years ago.

Called "Public School Building No.2", the new schoolhouse was built across the road from the old one on land purchased from the same John Fair. As recorded in the Prince William County Deed Books, the property was located on the northwest corner of the intersection of Purcell Road and the old Spriggs Ford Road. Bids for construction of the one-room building were called for on July 21, 1906. It must have been completed quickly because it was ready for opening at the beginning of the 1906-07 school year. For the exact specifications of the new Purcell School, see Appendix D. Children from within a two mile radius of the community were educated there for the next twenty-seven years.

The Purcell school looked unlike any other in Prince William County in that its frame walls were covered with brick-simulated metal siding and with a metal covered gable roof. It was entered through a small 5' by 10' vestibule. On the left side of the vestibule was a marble topped water cooler kept filled with drinking water from a nearby spring. On the right were hooks on which the students hung their coats. An inside door led to the one classroom, which measured 18' by 30'. The walls of the classroom were covered with tongue and groove panelling, painted brown on the lower part and tan on the upper.

The school housed twenty-five or thirty students in grades 1-7. Recollections of former students bring the old classroom to life.[1] The pupils sat in two rows of double desks with attached folding seats facing the teacher's desk which was on a raised platform at the front of the room. A large wood burning stove stood in the center of the room with a stove pipe running along the ceiling to a flue at the rear. Since there was no electricity, kerosene lamps, with silver colored reflectors, were hung on the side walls between the windows. Chalkboards lined the walls and an organ was prominently displayed. The only other furnishings were the teacher's chair, a rack for maps and a bookcase with glass doors. By 1925 there were 124 books in the school library. Two outhouses were located behind the schoolhouse.

The first teacher in the new Purcell School was Emma Weber (Carter), a Prince William County resident who, after two years at Purcell, continued to teach in the county for many years. One of her students was Carrie Fair (Cornwell) whose education had begun in the old schoolhouse. Carrie, now aged ninety-seven years, still lives in the Purcell community and still remembers that though she looked forward to summer, she felt sad that she wouldn't be seeing "Miss Emma" every day!

Miss Gertrude Seaton of Fauquier County taught at the Purcell school from 1908-1910, following "Miss Emma". Because Miss Seaton's home was such a distance from the Purcell community, the School Board found a home in which she could board. Unfortunately, it was two miles from the school and after one month of walking every day and with winter coming on, Miss Seaton found a place to board nearer the school. Six years after she began her teaching career at Purcell, the school teacher married a local gentleman, in this case the aforementioned Mr. Delley Cornwell. The couple had two children, James and Zella, whose memories contributed so much to this story.

Gertrude Seaton was followed as teacher by a resident of Buckhall, a minister's daughter named Mrs. Maude Winslow Chandler. Mrs. Chandler commuted the four miles between Buckhall and Purcell by horse and buggy every day. She had to ford the Occoquan River at Spriggs Ford. During the school day, she kept the horse in a shed which was also used to store wood for the school's stove.

---

[1] Zella Cornwell Tiller and her brother James shared their memories generously with the author.

After her marriage, Gertrude Seaton Cornwell again taught at the Purcell School from 1920-22, two years before her daughter Zella began attending there. Zella remembers the school day starting at 9 o'clock in the morning when the teacher rang the hand bell summoning all the pupils to class. They first gathered around the organ and sang songs. Then the roll was called and the teacher inspected the hair, fingernails and dress of each student. Reading was taught to all the grades in the morning for an hour; from 10:15 to 10:30 was recess. Then came writing, arithmetic, history, geography, hygiene and, in the seventh grade, English grammar. Each subject had its own textbook, supplied by the parents. The first grade primer was about Baby Ray, Zella remembers. From noon to 1 o'clock was the lunch and play hour. The children brought lunch from home. Some had milk in a thermos bottle but most just had sandwiches made with biscuits, fruit and cake. The day continued with teaching from 1:00 to 2:15 when another fifteen minute recess came. Then it was back to the books until 4:00 when school was dismissed.

Recess was an important break in the long school day, both for teacher and pupils. Zella Cornwell remembers that on those days when good weather permitted outdoor play, circle games were the most popular activity. "Blind Man's Bluff" and "Drop the Handkerchief", popular even long ago when Carrie Fair was a student, were two favorite games which the students organized. During inclement weather, recess had to be held indoors. In that case, games were played at the chalkboard or at the students's desks.

In later years, the Community League[2] held fund raising activities which provided equipment, supplies and occasional hot lunches to the school. Some years at Christmas, they even gave gifts to the school children. Most parents took an active role in school life. One problem seems to have been keeping a teacher for any length of time. During the 1920s and 1930s, the list of teachers included the above mentioned Gertrude Seaton Cornwell, Nellie Mae or Naomi Pearson, Susan Jeffries, Lily Wise, Louise Atkins, Alice Breeden, Louise Schults, Rilla Holler and, during its last year, Ila Breeden—nine teachers in thirteen years!

One of those teachers was Miss Susan Jeffries who came to the Purcell School in 1925, her first year of teaching after graduating from high school. According to the report Miss Jeffries filed at the end of that school year, the twenty-one year old teacher had a classroom of twenty-eight students, sixteen of them in grades 1-4 and eight in grades 5-7. To teach them, she was paid $65 a month for an eight month term (for a total of $520 for the year). From that she had to pay $20 a month for room and board.[3]

As was the case with all the early schools, Purcell was a center of community activity. Spelling bees, suppers, Christmas pageants, parties and ice cream socials were often held there. One can imagine that if there were twenty-five students in the school, each with two parents, brothers and sisters, aunts and uncles, the little building must have been very crowded at times.

In 1933, the Purcell school was closed, presumably due to low enrollment and the push for consolidation of schools in the county. The remaining students were transferred to Woodbine, the center school of that area. The Purcell school then had a brief life as a church school before being modified into a home. The School Board turned the property over to the county in 1977 and in 1979 it was sold to the same James Cornwell who had been a student there and who now owns the land surrounding the tract. After several years standing vacant and being subject to vandalism, the schoolhouse burned to the ground in 1982. Now the site, at the intersection of Purcell Road and Cornwell Drive, is covered with underbrush. Fortunately, photographs and memories preserve the little schoolhouse.

---

[2]The Community League was a forerunner of today's Parent and Teacher Association.

[3]"Virginia Daily Attendance Register and Record of Class Grades" for the Purcell School filed at the end of the 1925-26 school year.

The Purcell School in 1925. Teacher (#2) is Naomi Pearson.
(Courtesy of Zella Cornwell Tiller)

THE QUANTICO COLORED SCHOOL

Dumfries School District
Colored
1910?-1939

School Board records of 1931 make reference to a school building in Quantico which was taken over by the United States Government when the Quantico Marine Base was established[1] in 1918, but when that school opened or who it served are facts lost to history. It could have been the Quantico White School or the Quantico Colored School since the beginnings of both are unknown. Because the village was a busy one in the late nineteenth and early twentieth centuries as a fishing center, a hub for local tourist and excursion activities[2] and, beginning in 1916, the home of a fledgling boatbuilding industry[3], there certainly would have been a need for schools for both white and black children. At some date, the Quantico Colored School began to meet in a local church. School Board minutes of 1932 refer to a "church located on the Government reservation at Quantico formerly used for a colored school [which] was destroyed by fire during the summer months".[4] Although the year of this schoolhouse's beginning is unrecorded, several mentions of it are found in records of the 1920s.

During the 1925-26 school year, the teacher was Miss N.A. Saxon, a Normal School graduate, thirty-three years old with three years of teaching experience. Her home was in Washington, D.C. so she boarded in Quantico during the week, paying $35 a month for room and board which was expensive by the standards of the day. She was paid $60 a month or $380.40 for a term lasting six months and nine days. Twenty-two children were enrolled in grades 1-6, fifteen boys and seven girls, but the average daily attendance was only nine. This was far below the minimum number required to keep a school open but for some reason the school did not close. There were no books in the school library. At the end of the school year, Miss Saxon wrote, "[I] want to length [sic] term and organized [sic] a community league and garden clubs."[5] She did not return the next year.

The teacher for that 1926-27 school year was Miss Grace L. Evans, age twenty-seven, a graduate of Miner Normal School in her first year of teaching. Like her predecessor, she was from Washington, D.C. and lived in Quantico during the week. However, Miss Evans only had to pay $20 a month for room and board. There were twenty-one children enrolled in the school that year, thirteen in grades 1-4 and eight in grades five and six. No one enrolled in seventh grade that year. The lower grades had only one dropout and one failure that year; no one failed the upper grades and only one dropped out. Miss Evans was paid $55 a month for a school year lasting only six months.[6]

Following the fire in the summer of 1932, the School Board decided to buy one acre of land and "a small bungalow which can be easily converted into a rather desirable one-room school"[7] to use as a replacement schoolhouse for the black children of Quantico and vicinity. Instead of buying the property, however, the Board rented it from Mrs. Emma Johnson of Hyattsville, Maryland on a monthly basis. In October of 1936, Mrs. Johnson increased the monthly rent from $5 to $6 but the Board did not object.[8]

The one acre school lot was in a low swampy area outside the Marine Base "on the highway that leads into town"[9], today's Fuller Heights Road, with

---

[1] Prince William County School Board minutes of May 6, 1931.

[2] During those years Quantico was known as Potomac although it was not chartered under that name. When the Quantico Company was formed to promote the town on Quantico Creek as a summer resort area for residents of both Washington, DC and Richmond, the Quantico became more widely used than the name Potomac.

[3] Charles A. Fleming, Robin Austin and Charles A. Braley. *Quantico: Crossroads of the Marine Corps*, Washington, DC: History and Museum Division Headquarters, U.S. Marine Corps, 1978, pp. 18-19.

[4] Prince William County School Board minutes of September 14, 1932.

[5] "Virginia Daily Attendance Register and Record of Class Grades" for the Quantico Colored School filed at the end of the 1925-26 school year.

[6] "Virginia Daily Attendance Register and Record of Class Grades" for the Quantico Colored School filed at the end of the 1926-27 school year.

[7] Prince William County School Board minutes of September 14, 1932.

[8] Prince William County School Board minutes of October 7, 1936.

[9] Richard C. Haydon. "An Administrative Survey of the Public School System in Prince William County, Virginia." A Thesis for Master of Science at the University of Virginia, 1935, p.106.

a creek flowing close by the front door. In 1934, the little rented schoolhouse was in satisfactory condition according to the Superintendent of Schools. It had been recently painted on the outside and the "unusually small" room was kept warm by a wood stove. The teacher and students kept the crowded[10] classroom clean. The outhouses were sanitary but there was no drinking water on the grounds. A nearby well supplied the needs of the school. Since the parents' main objective had been to get a larger school for their children, they did not plan improvements for the little schoolhouse. The teacher used a table as her desk. The students' desks were "not very comfortable" although the children "cheerfully make the best of it".[11] There were charts and maps for the pupils, but they were very few in number.

In 1933, the teacher was a graduate of Virginia State College with a Normal Professional certificate and one year of teaching experience. She was "active, wide-awake" and had artistic ability, according to the Superintendent's report. She was one of the very few black teachers in the county who used at least part of the new state curriculum adopted by the school system.

In 1934, nearly ten years after Miss Saxon reported that there were no books in the school library, the County School Board helped the little school acquire a new $36 Rosenwald Library of thirty-three books on various topics. A bookcase was built to hold the collection which must have been a major addition to the classroom. This is the only instance found where help was given to the Quantico Colored School by the School Board.

In the summer of 1937, a committee of parents urged the School Board to consolidate the Cabin Branch, Hickory Ridge and Quantico Colored Schools at the Cabin Branch School.[12] It was nearly two years, however, before the Board agreed to enlarge that schoolhouse to accommodate the students from all three schools.[13] No trace of the Quantico Colored School remains.

---

[10]There were thirty-five children enrolled at the school during that year. The average daily attendance was between thirty and thirty-one children, or 87%.

[11]Haydon, p.106.

[12]Prince William County School Board minutes of July 6, 1937.

[13]Prince William County School Board minutes of January 4, 1939 note a plan for consolidation which called for the dismantling of two abandoned schoolhouses so that the salvaged lumber could be used to help defray the expense of adding rooms to the Cabin Branch School.

THE QUANTICO WHITE SCHOOL

Dumfries School District
White
1910?-1956

No school in Quantico is shown on the 1901 Brown map of the county but there was a school in town early in the century. When this school was established and who it served are not known but School Board minutes of May 1931 note that

> ...on the 4th day of November, 1918, by a proclamation of the President of the United States, the United States took possession of one acre of land at the village of Quantico, Dumfries Magisterial District, Prince William County, Virginia, together with a school building and out buildings thereon, which was then in use as a public free school....[1]

---

[1]Prince William County School Board minutes of May 6, 1931.

The Quantico White School, shown here in the 1950s, is the Lillian Carden Community Center today.
(Courtesy of PWC Schools)

The money paid by the U.S. Government for the property was used to build the four-room Dumfries School, a situation which "aroused such ire that citizens of the two communities [Quantico and Dumfries] ceased speaking."[2] For the next five or six years, Quantico presumably found another location for its schoolhouse although no record of this has been found.

Finally, a new schoolhouse was built in Quantico for the white children in 1923. It was erected near the center of the town, on a lot which the School Board purchased from Messrs. Ford and Goolrick for $1400. The three-room Quantico White school was built for $5500[3], contracted by personal loans from the community's citizens since "their" money had been used for the Dumfries School. With its wood frame, masonry foundation, shingle covered gable roof, running water, indoor toilets and electricity, the Quantico White School was certainly one of the most modern of the county's schools of that era. The interior floors were covered with asphalt tile and wood covered both the walls and ceilings of all the rooms. The coal stoves were taken care of by a janitor. Two of the rooms, each with a seating capacity of forty-two, served as classrooms. One housed first through third grades; the other was used by grades four, five, and six. Seventh grade students were transported to the Dumfries School. The third room was a library which served, on occasion, as an auditorium too. By the end of the 1930 school year, there were 225 volumes in that library.[4]

Mrs. Norah B. Keys, age twenty-six and a high school graduate with eight years of education experience, was the teacher during the 1925-26 school year. There were twenty-seven children enrolled, nine in grades 1-4 (two of whom failed and two who dropped out at the end of the school year) and eighteen in grades 5-7 of whom two dropped out and three failed. Mrs. Keys was paid $100 a month or $900 for the whole term, a princely sum in those days and the highest in the county on record.[5] No other year end reports were found and Mrs. Keys did teach all grades, so perhaps she was the only teacher that year. This could account for her unusually high salary. By the 1929-30 school year, there were again two teachers, Moneta Matthews and Helen McDonald.

In the spring of 1931, it was brought to the attention of the County School Board that in regard to property taken by the United States Government for the establishment of the Marine Corps Base at Quantico in 1918, "certain litigation is now pending in the circuit Court .... Its object [is] the recovery [by land owners] of their respective properties, or in lieu thereof, a just compensation therefore, which litigation was instituted by Edmond C. Fletcher, of Washington, D.C. [who also] had agreed to represent the County School Board"[6]. The Board authorized Mr. Fletcher to "take such steps as he may be best advised to recover such additional compensation for [the] school property so taken..."[7] when the Government took possession of one acre of land at the village of Quantico, which contained the school building.

In 1933, at a time when the population of the village of Quantico stood at about three-hundred, the enrollment of the three-room school was eighty-three. The average attendance for the primary grades was twenty-four; for the upper grades, thirty-eight. At year's end fifty-seven children were promoted, fifteen failed and ten dropped out. The following year enrollment figures had dropped by twenty pupils but the daily attendance averaged fifty-nine pupils, or 94% of the total enrollment. Both teachers that year had Normal Professional certificates with two and four years' experience.[8] The students sat at tables and chairs and helped keep the schoolhouse clean. The playground and equipment were deemed inadequate by the Superintendent of Schools but he also reported that the Mothers' Club had ordered seesaws and swings. Also, the teachers and students had planted irises, among other flowers, to beautify their grounds.

In the spring of 1936, the School Board agreed to buy a 25' x 150' lot adjoining the school property for $450 from Mr. Peter Raftelis. A down payment of $50 was made and a note drawn on the rest at six percent interest.[9] A year later, the Board renewed

---

[2]Hattie Mae Partlow and Pauline Smith. *Now and Then With P.W.E.A.*, Prince William County, VA: Prince William Education Association, 1963, p.76.

[3]Undated Prince William County School Inventory presumably done in the 1930's.

[4]"Virginia Daily Attendance Register and Record of Class Grades" for the Quantico White School filed at the end of the 1929-30 school year.

[5]"Virginia Daily Attendance Register and Record of Class Grades" filed for the Quantico White School at the end of the 1925-26 school year.

---

[6]Prince William County School Board minutes of May 6, 1931.

[7]Prince William County School Board minutes of May 6, 1931.

[8]Richard C. Haydon. "An Administrative Survey of the Public School System in Prince William County, Virginia", A Thesis for Master of Science at the University of Virginia, 1935, p.107.

[9]Prince William County School Board minutes of April 20, 1936. the note for the $400 loan. Times were hard during the Depression years.

the note for the $400 loan. Times were hard during the Depression years.

School property was again on the agenda in the fall of 1937 when the Superintendent showed a plat indicating that a portion of John Hicks' house and property encroached three to six feet on the school lot. Mr. Hicks offered to buy a two foot wide strip of land running front to back for the full length of the lot for $25 so that the offending property would be on his property.[10] The Board took the offer under consideration but between that time and the following March, Mr. Hicks apparently underwent a change of heart because he notified the School Board that he'd remove the offending window or move his house before he bought land from the Board. The Board said that was fine with them and agreed to ask for their disputed land without house or window by May 15.[11]

In the mid-fifties, presumably in 1956 when the very large addition was put onto the Dumfries School, the Quantico White School closed its doors. The building was sold in 1958 and soon thereafter was acquired by the town. It was turned into the Lillian Carden Community Center and still stands at 224 Third Avenue in Quantico.

[10]Prince William County School Board minutes of November 3, 1937.

[11]Prince William County School Board minutes of March 9, 1938.

THE RED HILL/PINEY BRANCH SCHOOL (RED HILL SCHOOL #2)

Gainesville District School #13
White
1870s-1920s

Sometime in the 1870s, the Gainesville District School Board opened The Red Hill School. There is no record, in School Board minutes of the time, that a new school building was constructed, so, as was common in the early years, an existing building was probably used. It was located on Wellington Road (known then as the Gainesville-Manassas Road) near its juncture with Piney Branch Lane.[1]

In July of 1886, the Gainesville District School Board agreed to establish a new school for white children closer to the Langyher's Mill area of the county. In September of that year, the District Board opened the school at the corner of Piney Branch Road and Linton Hall Road, less than two miles from the Mill and also from the site of the first Red Hill Schoolhouse.[2] The new building was officially named the Piney Branch School but was also called Red Hill School #2 for awhile. It was jointly run by the Gainesville and Manassas School Districts with each paying half of the expenses.[3] In 1888, records show that a Mr. Darrow resigned his position as teacher at Red Hill School #2 and Mr. Bullock was appointed to fill out the remaining two months of the year.

Things must have gone smoothly until March of 1893 when the Gainesville School Board found itself short of funds and voted to close all the colored schools in the District for the remainder of the term as well as the Piney Branch and Thoroughfare Schools which had relatively low enrollment figures. This closure only shortened the school year by about two weeks, but it's indicative of the importance of steady class numbers. Miss Rebecca Peake, the teacher at Piney Branch, apparently shared the Board's concern about the dwindling number of pupils and actively sought out children to attend her school. That she was successful is proven by the $5.00 award she was given in January of 1894 for increased enrollment.[4] Indeed, by the end of January, Miss Peake reported to the Board that there were now sixty-three pupils on the rolls and she needed help. Included in that number were thirteen students who lived in the Brentsville District and did not financially support the teacher. The School Board turned to the State Superintendent of Education for advice on how to handle the problem. Whatever their answer was, it apparently satisfied Miss Peake. She did not get an assistant teacher, but she continued as

[1]Eugene Scheel Map of Prince William County, 1992.

[2]Gainesville District School Board minutes of September 4, 1886.

[3]Gainesville District School Board minutes of April 25, 1891.

[4]Gainesville District School Board minutes of January 7, 1894.

the teacher of the Piney Branch School until the end of the 1904-05 school year. Her salary was $31 a month.

Difficulties again began with the 1905-06 school year. There were no applicants for the teacher's position. However, there is no record that the school closed so the job must have eventually been filled at least on a short term basis. A similar problem, coupled with low enrollment figures, again put the school in jeopardy the following year. The District School Board responded by urging pupils to attend the newly opened Wellington School in the Manassas District. However, a November petition to the Board from the patrons of Piney Branch to keep their school open resulted in a solution which was both unique and effective.

The Board asked the Manassas School Board if it would again cooperate in the running of the Piney Branch School so that students from both districts could combine to produce a student body large enough to re-open the school. An agreement must have been reached because the Piney Branch School did not close for that 1906-07 school year. The co-operative venture, whereby the Manassas School District would pay the teacher's salary for two of the six months in the school year in compensation for the five (out of nineteen) students from their District who attended Piney Branch, continued the next year. In return, the Gainesville District was responsible not only for the remaining four months' salary but for all the fuel needed to keep the schoolhouse heated.[5] The Piney Branch School remained open for several more years on a cooperative basis appearing on a school inventory as late as the 1920s. The exact date of its closing, as well as its opening, is not recorded and no trace of either the Red Hill School or the Piney Branch School remains.

---

[5] Gainesville District School Board minutes of December 7, 1907.

THE RED SHOALS SCHOOL

Brentsville District School #3
White
1870-1886

The Red Shoals School was very possibly an old mill taken over by the Brentsville District School Board early in 1870 to serve as the schoolhouse for the white community near Greenwich. School Board minutes of November 1871 show a concern for needed repairs to the school so it was in existence at that time, but obviously not a new building. The October of 1872, District School Board minutes record that a new schoolhouse in Greenwich had been built and white washed. It became known as District School #3.

One of the first teachers at the new Red Shoals School was Mr. William S. Blackwell.[1] Ten years later, he was still teaching at the school. That year, 1886, proved to be the last year for the Red Shoals Schoolhouse. On May 3, the Board approved the sale of the fourteen year old building and its benches for a total of $87.00. The money realized from the sale of the school was then used to purchase the English Church near Greenwich for use as a schoolhouse for the community.[2] The Red Shoals school building was turned into a private home which burned down in 1979.

---

[1] Brentsville District School Board minutes of August, 1876.
[2] See the section on the English Church School.

RIPPON ELEMENTARY SCHOOL

Occoquan/Woodbridge District
1966-present

Rippon Elementary School was named for nearby Rippon Lodge, the early 18th century home of Richard Blackburn, one of the founders of Dumfries and the builder of Falls Church. The school was built as Rippon Combined School in 1966. It combined elementary and middle school grades in one building under one principal. In the early 1970's, the two split apart and a new principal was appointed for the middle school so its operation was separate from the elementary school. It continues that way today. Both schools are located on Blackburn Road in Woodbridge and serve the children in the subdivisions of Rippon Landing, Newport and part of Marumsco Woods. When the Magisterial District lines were redrawn in 1976, the Rippon School became part of the newly created Woodbridge District.

SINCLAIR ELEMENTARY

Manassas/Gainesville District
1968-present

Like the Loch Lomond School in Manassas, Sinclair Elementary was built on fifteen acres of the original Ben Lomond estate. Located on Garner Drive in Manassas, it opened in January of 1968. Manassas had reached a population of about 7,000 at that time and schools were bursting at the seams. To relieve the situation, 225 students who had previously attended the overcrowded Westgate Elementary were transferred to grades 1-5 at Sinclair. The first principal was Gary DiVecchia who recalls that the "recently opened building twenty-five years ago was a beautiful, contemporary building with dark brown brick and light tan brick."[1]

The school was named to honor Mr. C. A. Sinclair, Sr., a leading citizen of Manassas who served as the Prince William County treasurer for over twenty-five years as well as the mayor of Manassas and Chairman of the Board of Crestar Bank before retiring in 1964. Mr. Sinclair died in 1974.

[1] Mike Fuchs. "Singing the praises of Sinclair", *Potomac News*, May 21, 1993, p.A12.

THE SMITHFIELD SCHOOL

Coles School District
White
189?-1930

The first Smithfield School was located off Spriggs Road behind the present site of the new Hylton High School. It appears on the 1901 county map so was built sometime prior to that date, but due to the lack of county records, it is not known exactly when.

According to county Deed Books, on June 26, 1916 the Coles District School Board bought from Mr. Richard Barnes ("an unmarried gentleman") for $20 a parcel of land "...being situate on the south side of Sprigg's Ford Road" measuring two acres. This was part of a tract called the Frazer Tract conveyed to Mr. Barnes by Mr. George C. Round, who owned adjacent property.[1] This second Smithfield School was across Spriggs Road and about a quarter of a mile south of the site of the first one.

Grades 1-7 were taught in the two-room, single story, frame schoolhouse, originally by two teachers. Later, as enrollment fell, all the pupils met in one classroom under the tutelage of one teacher. As with most of the older schools, the privies were out in back and drinking water came from a nearby well. A wood stove was the source of heat. The school year varied from eight to nine months depending on the number of students who were able to attend on a regular basis. Howell Barnes, who still lives on Spriggs Road, remembers learning history, geography and math from books purchased by his parents. He sat at a desk with a built-in inkwell and, like all the other students, brought a box lunch from home. When Howell went to Smithfield, there was no library and no school clubs were organized.[2]

Like most of the small county schools, this one was a gathering place for the community it served. Performances by students at League (PTA) Meetings

[1] Prince William County Deed Book 68, p.228.

[2] From an interview with Mr. Howell Barnes by the author in 1993.

were highlights of the year then just as they are today. The program of Saturday evening April 2, 1921 gives a good indication of the cultural preferences of the time. It was printed in the *Manassas Journal* as follows:

*Singing by the school, "Juanita"
*Recitation, "Welcome", Mary Barbee
*Recitation, Andrew Lee Holmes
*Song, "Just Before the Battle, Mother"
*Recitation, "The Way of a Boy", Andrew Sedes
*Recitation, "People's Faults", Hazel Lunsford
*Recitation, "A Problem", Charles Barbee
*Recitation, "Springtime", Hilda Barnes
*Duet, "Just Break the News to Mother", Misses Lucille and Hazel Lunsford
*Recitation, "When I Am Big", Donald Sedes
*Recitation, "A Story in Verse", Elizabeth Posey
*"Flower Quotations", by several girls
*Solo, Miss Ethel Florence
*Recitation, "A Resolution", Howard Kincheloe
*Recitation, "Land of Story Books", Vernice Posey
*Recitation, Charles Lunsford
*Recitation, "Valley Shadows", Anna Sedes
*Reading, Miss Ethel Florence
*Recitation, "While Shepherds Watched Their Flocks", Walter Baltzeele
*Recitation, "No Time", Allen Barbee
*Recitation, "Worth Living For", Mary Maraza
*Song, "Work For the Night Is Coming", by the school
*"God Be With You Till We Meet Again", Lucille and Hazel Lunsford

Imagine sitting through a program like that today! Moreover, it was organized and rehearsed during a period of what must have been some turmoil. A notice appeared in the Smithfield column of the *Manassas Journal* of Friday, January 28, 1921 that "our school has closed until further notice". The newspaper later reported on April 8 that the school had been re-opened with Mr. Gerald H. MacDonald, a local gentleman who owned a farm on Spriggs Road about two miles south of the schoolhouse, as teacher. The ambitious League program was presented on April 2, so obviously Mr. MacDonald took over the teaching duties sometime prior to that.

At the beginning of the 1925-26 school year, the School Board approved the bid by James Russell to furnish firewood for the Smithfield School at a cost of $30 for the year.[3] Because no janitorial service is mentioned, nor did other small schools have it, we can safely assume that the teachers and students at Smithfield bore the responsibility of keeping the building warm during the cold weather.

In May 1926, the School Board approved the purchase of lumber from Brown and Hooff Co. of Manassas for the Smithfield School.[4] The records do not tell what that lumber was used for but apparently the schoolhouse was well cared for. Further evidence of this appears in the School Board minutes of July 24, 1929 which reported that Mr. W.H. Ellicott was awarded the contract to put two coats of paint on the building including the roof, to put in window panes, and to glaze the windows. All this was to be done for forty cents an hour with the School Board supplying the materials.

The teacher during the 1927-28 was Ila V. Breeden, twenty-three years old, a high school graduate in her fourth year of teaching. She was paid $85 a month for a nine months' term out of which she paid $16 monthly for room and board in the community. Twenty-five children were enrolled at Smithfield that year in grades 1-7 but only eighteen attended on a daily basis. The library was a large one for the day, 230 books.

On July 10, 1929 the Board hired Gladys M. Cherry as one of the teachers for $70, less than Miss Breeden had earned two years before. Earlier in the summer, Virginia O'Rouck had also been hired as one of the teachers. The reason for a return to two teachers is unclear; perhaps one of them was unable to serve. In any case, these two teachers were the last at Smithfield. In June of 1930, the Board decided to open the school for an eight months' term the coming year. However, low enrollment made them change their minds and before the term began the Board approved a recommendation that the school not open for the year. Instead they agreed to pay former pupil Howell Barnes $10 a month to drive the bus to take the children to Minnieville and Bethel Schools.[5]

---

[3] Prince William County School Board minutes of September 9, 1925.

[4] Prince William County School Board minutes of May 5, 1926.

[5] Prince William County School Board minutes of October 1, 1930.

THE STONE HOUSE SCHOOL

Manassas School District
1916-1917
White

The Stone House, famous for its role as a hospital during the Battle of First and Second Manassas, apparently served as a school house for the children of the neighboring farms for one year. The building is located at the junction of the Warrenton and Alexandria Turnpike, now the Lee Highway or Rt. 29, and the Dumfries Road in the Manassas Battlefield Park. No references are made to it in any of the literature except for two entries in the minutes of the Manassas District School Board. The first mention was made in the summer of 1916 when the Board agreed to establish a school in the Stone House with the understanding that patrons "furnish the building and put it in condition" to use as a schoolhouse. Miss Eleanor Wilkins was appointed as teacher at a salary of $40 per month.[1] The second entry came in May 1918, when the Board decided that, due to low enrollment, "they would not be justified in continuing a public school at that place..." and urged the patrons to send their children to the Groveton School and thus help to "build up a good two-room graded school at that place".[2]

No other records even mention the Stone House school nor do any local residents even recall hearing of it. It would not have been unusual, however, for a community to use an existing structure for a schoolhouse; indeed, it was frequently done because it was more economical than building a new schoolhouse.

The pump on the school grounds was removed to the Summitt School near Occoquan[6] and on June 7, 1939 the School Board accepted a bid by Wilson Posey to buy the schoolhouse for $26. It no longer stands.

[6]Prince William County School Board minutes of December 5, 1934.

[1]Manassas District School Board minutes of August 10, 1916.
[2]Manassas District School Board minutes of May 15, 1918, p.89.

SULPHUR SPRINGS (TOWLES' GATE)/VANCLUSE/ HAZELWOOD SCHOOL

Brentsville District School #5
White
1871-1908

The first school in the southern part of the Brentsville District was the Sulphur Springs School. It was located about a mile southwest of the village of Aden, on Hazelwood Drive at the intersection with the old Law's Ford Road. It was probably located in a rented building for the first seven years, taking its name from its location near a branch of Sulphur Springs. The Brentsville District School Board, in November of 1877, agreed to contract for a permanent schoolhouse to be built at Towles' Gate, replacing the Sulphur Springs schoolhouse which would continue to function until the new building was finished.[1]

A notice was put in *The Manassas Gazette* asking for bids to erect the new schoolhouse at Towles' Gate on the corner of Fleetwood Drive and Deepford Lane about one mile east of the old school.[2] Specifi-

[1]Brentsville District School Board minutes of November 1878.

[2]The Reverend Towles was, according to Brentsville District School Board minutes of November 1877, pastor of a St. James Church "near Aden at Park Gate Road", but the location of this church cannot be verified. He may have lived nearby and given his name to Towles' Gate, the location of the second schoolhouse.

cations for the building were set forth in School Board minutes and give a good picture of what it must have looked like. It was to measure 16' x 24' with a ten foot pitch to the roof. Three twelve-paned windows with venetian blinds were built into each side wall and there was another window fronting the door at one end. The exterior was covered with undressed weatherboarding; the roof had cypress or drawn oak shingles. Inside, there was wainscoting on the lower four and a half feet of the walls with white washed plaster above that. The floors were of 4" - 6" wide pine boards. The building of the school at Towles' Gate was combined with the building of the new schoolhouse at Bristoe and both were built according to the same plan by the same contractor. Mr. W. Raymond Free's bid of $219.50 was the lowest of seven submitted to the Board which agreed to pay half when the materials were deposited on the school grounds and the other half when the job was completed.[3]

Unfortunately, Mr. Free still had not finished the Towles Gate school by June 1879 and it was badly needed. The District Board, therefore, hired Mr. E. C. Taylor at a rate of $1.50 a day to complete the job. Mr. Free apparently lost half of his pay because he did not meet the schedule agreed upon.

The need must indeed have been great because in its opening weeks, an assistant teacher was added at a salary of $10 a month.[4] The new school was named the Vancluse (or VanCluse) School, although the origin of that name is unknown. Towles' Gate was simply a way to refer to the school under construction by its location in the community. The first teacher in the new building was Miss Mollie Bryant who remained there for several years. In 1886, Mr. H. H. Washington took over the school at a salary of $25 a month. He stayed for several years, too.

In 1890, the name of the schoolhouse was changed from Vancluse to Hazelwood. Why this was done is not known. There is no record of a new building at that time, nor does there seem to have been any kind of petition from the school patrons (parents) requesting a change. Perhaps, with the growing number of schools in the District, the Board decided to make things easier by calling the school houses by their geographic location. The Sulphur Springs and Vancluse Schools were both located on land belonging to the plantation called Hazelwood. Hazelwood itself was built on the site of the old Truro House which was destroyed during the Civil War. Historically, the name Hazelwood meant something to the community and so the name change made sense. When the District renumbered their schools in 1900, Hazelwood became #4 after thirty years of being School #5.[5]

Beginning in 1904, debate began over closing the Hazelwood School and building a centrally located schoolhouse in the village of Aden. Several meetings were held with the public, the District Board and the Superintendent of Schools to discuss whether to move the school and, if so, what size the building should be. All of this was sidelined when the Board became embroiled in the business of providing high school courses at the Nokesville Village School.

Finally, on June 2, 1908, the matter of a new school at Aden came up again. The School Board minutes show that it was ordered that a new school house be built on the site of the old school. However, a month later, the Board voted to consolidate both Hazelwood and Allendale schools in the village of Aden where "a graded school [was to] be established at the most suitable point within one hundred yards from the cross roads at Aden".[6]

While the new center school was under construction, the Board voted to consolidate the Hazelwood and Allendale Schools in the Lodge Building at Aden.[7] Finally in October, the Lodge approved the rental of their building as a school for $5 per month and the temporary schoolhouse opened for the 1908-09 school year. Desks from both Hazelwood and Allendale schools were brought to the Lodge Hall but only got as far as Mr. Allen's farm where the movers were issued an injunction to halt their work. Shortly thereafter, there was a call by parents of students at both the Hazelwood and Allendale schools to re-open the Allendale school. This effort failed and, perhaps to prevent any such movement on the part of Hazelwood parents, the Board ordered the Hazelwood school sold to the highest bidder.

---

[3]Brentsville District School Board minutes of June 10, 1878.

[4]Brentsville District School Board minutes of November 1879.

[5]Brentsville District School Board minutes of August 1900.

[6]Brentsville District School Board minutes of July 9, 1908.

[7]Brentsville District School Board minutes of July 31, 1908.

THE SUMMITT SCHOOL

Occoquan School District
Colored
188?-1947?

The founding of the Summitt Elementary school for the black children of Occoquan is credited to the Reverend Henry Bailey, a former slave who also founded the Ebenezer Baptist Church in Occoquan. Married to Ella Jean Dean, sister of Jennie Dean, he was a moving force in providing both educational and religious leadership for the large black community of more than one hundred families in that area late in the nineteenth century. The exact date for the beginning of the one-room Summitt School is unknown though we do know that it was sometime before the church was founded in 1883.[1] It housed grades one through seven.

In 1919, finding the need for additional space, the community built a two-room schoolhouse on two acres on a beautiful site, two and a half miles from the town of Occoquan. While that building was being erected, another place had to found to hold school. The school rented space in the old Odd Fellows Hall in Occoquan, which stood next to the Ebenezer Baptist Church on what is now a vacant lot.[2]

Summitt Elementary was one of the southern group of schools roughly corresponding to the five black settlement groups in the Occoquan District. (The other four were Cabin Branch, Neabsco, Quantico Colored and Hickory Ridge.) Summitt school stood on two acres on a "beautiful site", two and a half miles from the town of Occoquan. The new school was located on what was then called the Occoquan and Manassas Highway (now Davis Ford Road) near the present day corner of Davis Ford and the road to Tackett's Mill.

The frame schoolhouse was built at a cost of $4000. It had two classrooms but, due to low enrollment, usually only one was used. By unfolding a dividing wall, the two rooms could be made into one

The Summitt School, c. 1930.
(Courtesy PWC Schools)

large one. There was also a cloakroom. The building was heated by two coal stoves, with fire building, like maintenance, the responsibility of the teacher and students. Coal was kept in a shed near the schoolhouse.

The black children from Occoquan had to walk the two and a half miles from the town to the school, much of it up Tanyard Hill Road. Sometimes the children were lucky and were given a ride to school, often crowding eight or ten to a car. When the students had received all the lower grade schooling available at Summitt, they either had to find daily transportation to the Manassas Industrial School or board in Manassas with a local family. A few of the more ambitious pupils even went to Washington, D.C. to board and attend school there and one, Miss Saluka Harris, even went to Pennsylvania for higher learning.[3] Later, the older students who desired a higher education were bused to the Industrial School.

Water was apparently carried to the schoolhouse until sometime after 1934 when the pump from the old Smithfield School in the Coles District was given to the Summitt School. By then, a well had been dug and the pump was installed soon thereafter.

During the 1926-27 school year, the teacher was Ernestine P. Grayson. She was twenty-nine years old with seven years' experience and she was paid a monthly salary of $60 out of which she had to pay $26 for room and board. She had a schoolhouse of thirty children on a daily basis although there were forty enrolled. Of that forty, thirty were in the first through fourth grades and, by the end of the year, twelve failed and four had dropped out. The ten children in grades 5-7 all passed. As was the case in many

---

[1] Glenda McQueen. "Church remains tribute to local black heritage.", *Potomac News*, March 25, 1989, pp. A1, A7.

[2] Thomas Nelson. "Transcript of Interview with Historic Occoquan, Inc." Prince William County Historical Commission Oral History Project, September 24, 1985, p.12.

[3] Ibid., p.13.

of the little colored schools, there were no books in the school library.[4]

In his report on the schools in 1934, Superintendent of Schools Richard C. Haydon reported that the "walls have not been painted as yet, but they have been well taken care of".[5] He also said that more equipment was necessary for the school although the desks were in fair condition and of varying sizes to fit different sized students. Apparently there was little uniformity. Only a few maps, charts and story books were available for the children. Additionally, Mr. Haydon reported that the outhouses were "fairly sanitary" and had good drainage. A coal shed had been built near the schoolhouse.[6]

In 1934, the teacher had a Normal Professional Certificate awarded after two years of Normal School training at Minor Teachers College in Washington, D.C. She was a first year teacher and taught using the traditional methods rather than the new curriculum being tried out by a number of schools both white and colored. The enrollment for that year was forty-two with an average daily attendance of thirty-six. None failed and none dropped out—a remarkable achievement not equalled by any other school in the county.

Mrs. Marian Washington, a concerned parent with children in the Summitt school, used her own money to set up a hot lunch program there. A friend in the town of Occoquan where she lived gave Mrs. Washington bones to make soup and she devoted most of her life to seeing that the students of Summitt school were well fed.[7] When that school closed during the 1940s and the children attended the new Washington-Reid school, Mrs. Washington was honored and her name given to the new school building.

The Summitt schoolhouse apparently stood empty for awhile before being converted into what longtime county residents remember as "a most attractive dwelling". It was later sold to a bank and eventually burned down. The land was sold by the School Board in 1952.

---

[4]"Virginia Daily Attendance Register and Record of Class Grades" for the Summitt School filed at the end of the 1925-26 school year.

[5]Richard C. Haydon. "An Administrative Study of the Public School System in Prince William County, Virginia", A Thesis for Master of Science at University of Virginia, 1935, p.103.

[6]Ibid., p.103.

[7]Prince William County Schools." Self-Study Report of the Washington-Reid School", 1973-74, p.2.

THE THORNTON (ELLIOTT, CATHARPIN COLORED) SCHOOL

Gainesville School District #8
Colored
1877-1938

Earliest School Board records give this school the name Elliott but by the 1877-78 school year, it was called the Thornton School, or sometimes, just the Catharpin Colored School. It was a very remote schoolhouse, located on Thornton Drive near its juncture with Pageland Lane in Catharpin, five miles from Gainesville. The nearest good road, even in 1934,[1] was three miles distant. Thornton was one of a group of four northern colored schools in the Gainesville District (the others were Antioch, Macrae and North Fork or Thoroughfare).

The schoolhouse was a small one-room building near a grove of trees. It had windows on both sides but without shades to regulate the light. The large wood burning stove in the center of the room heated the school, which the students and teacher kept clean as was the custom in all the county small schools. There was no water on the school grounds so the children had to carry water from a nearby well to drink. The toilets, in outhouses, were clean and in good condition.

Enrollment at the school at first was small. In December of 1878, only seven students attended Thornton so the School Board asked the teacher to close the school. A dedication to provide an educa-

---

[1]As recorded in Richard Haydon's "An Administrative Survey of the Public School System in Prince William County, Virginia", a Thesis for Master of Science at the University of Virginia, 1935, p.91.

tion to the black children of this remote part of the county and no doubt a lot of walking and hard work on the part of the teacher and/or interested parents must have resulted in larger enrollment figures because Miss Carrie Lucas was appointed to be the teacher at Thornton in September 1879 at a salary of $20 per month. It is known that she taught at Thornton for several years; there is record of her appointment for the 1882-83 school year.[2]

Mr. James M. Nickens began teaching at the Thornton School around 1915 and stayed there for ten years when he transferred to the Macrae School. There he taught the upper grades while his wife was the primary teacher.

Following Mr. Nickens as teacher of the Thornton School was Nettie V. Williams. From the year end report she filed at the close of the 1925-26 school term, it is known that she was forty-four years old at that time, a high school graduate who had been teaching for twenty-one years. Although twenty-six children were enrolled, only half that number attended on an average day. Mrs. Williams was paid $60 a month or $315 a year to teach for five months, one of the shortest school terms in the county. From that salary, she paid $17 a month for room and board.

Mrs. Williams also reported that, although no State course of study was provided to her, she taught a full educational program: English; arithmetic, both primary and advanced; reading; geography; hygiene, in the fifth grade only; health, meaning oral hygiene; history of Virginia; and spelling. This was an ambitious program by any standard. A Community League of twenty-five members gave what support they could, but apparently the School Boards, both district and County, did not. The Board did not supply a flag and the schoolhouse had no library. Mrs. Williams hoped for a visit from supervisory personnel during the term, but no one came. She also requested a desk and chair for the next school year as well.[3]

Things seem to have improved considerably the next year, but Nettie Williams was not there to enjoy them. Instead, the teacher was Mr. Herbert A. Bates, a twenty-one year old high school graduate just starting his teaching career. Despite this lack of experience, Mr. Bates' salary was the same as Mrs. Williams' and she had taught for twenty-one years, or as long as Mr. Bates had been alive. His entire salary for the year was $291, which means that the year was even shorter than it had been in 1925-26. Mr. Bates paid $10 a month for room and board, a necessity because his home was in Wellington, too far on poor roads to drive on a daily basis. Enrollment had risen to twenty-nine with twenty children appearing on a daily average. The thirteen boys and fifteen girls were evenly distributed among the seven grades.[4]

In 1930, Mr. B. Oswald Robinson, who had previously taught one year at the Manley School, was appointed to teach at Thornton. He remembers that when he got to the old schoolhouse in Catharpin he found the following supplies: two brooms, one box of crayons and six erasers. Two pictures hung on the walls - George Washington and Abraham Lincoln. The children got their drinking water from a common dipper in a bucket of water. Mr. Robinson taught one year at Thornton.[5]

At the start of the 1932-33 school year, the school's future was in jeopardy due to low enrollment figures. The School Board appointed Superintendent of Schools Richard Haydon and Gainesville District Board member Mrs. Piercy to study the matter. Parental support for the school's opening was strong and on November first Mr. Haydon and Mrs. Piercy opened the Thornton School for the year. That it was to remain open is evidenced by the School Board's decision the following summer to have needed repair work done to the schoolhouse. Mrs. Piercy was authorized to purchase all necessary materials and pay Mr. Charles Berry a total of $12 to give the building two coats of paint and glaze all the windows.[6]

The Board's confidence in the continuing need for the school was well placed; enrollment figures went up for the year. At the beginning of the 1933-34 school year, twenty-three children were enrolled at Thornton. The Board hired as teacher Miss Katherine Toomer, a graduate of the Manassas Industrial School who had also completed three summer sessions at

---

[2] Gainesville District School Board minutes from October 1882.

[3] "Virginia Daily Attendance Register and Record of Class Grades" for the Thornton School filed at the end of the 1925-26 school year.

[4] Virginia Daily Attendance Register and Record of Class Grades for the Thornton School filed at the end of the 1926-27 school year.

[5] Oral history with Mr. Oswald Robinson by the author in 1992.

[6] Prince William County School Board minutes of August 2, 1933.

Virginia State College. She remained at the Thornton School for two years. During those years, she boarded with Mr. Oswald Robinson's parents, got a ride to the intersection of Pageland Land and present day Route 29 and then walked the rest of the way to school. The Superintendent of School's report at the end of Miss Toomer's first year states that she "sings well and shows ability in art work".[7] The average daily attendance was only sixteen; of that number, at year's end fourteen pupils were promoted, eight failed and one had dropped out.

Then, at the April 4, 1934 meeting of the County School Board, Mr. Montgomery Peters requested action to close the Thornton School and transport the children to the Macrae School. Mr. Peters may well have been a parent who wanted his children to have the advantages a larger and better equipped school could offer. Once again, Mr. Haydon and Mrs. Piercy were appointed to study the matter and make a recommendation. They decided that the school should remain open though the enrollment was only nineteen, one short of legal limits, and the daily attendance averaged sixteen. The School Board approved and Miss Toomer continued as the teacher for the 1934-35 school year.

At the end of that term, the old debate about whether to close the Thornton school or keep it open resumed. Once more, the School Board authorized Superintendent Haydon to hire a "satisfactory emergency teacher" so that the Thornton School could be operated on a short term basis, probably five months.[8] Superintendent Haydon tried very hard to persuade Oswald Robinson to return to teach but he was not interested.[9] Nonetheless, the school remained open on a limited schedule for another three years.

Finally, in the summer of 1938, a new school bus route was set up to transport the black children from the Catharpin area to the Macrae School beginning with the next school year.[10] This eliminated the need for the Thornton School, which had served the community for sixty years. On May 3, 1939 the School Board requested sealed bids for the Thornton Schoolhouse which was sold on June 7 to Wilson W. Cornwell for $25.00. The building no longer exists.

---

[8]Prince William County School Board minutes of August 7, 1935.

[9]Oral history with Oswald Robinson by the author, 1992.

[10]Prince William County School Board minutes of July 5, 1938.

---

[7]Haydon, p.91.

THE THORNTON (FLORENCE) SCHOOL

Dumfries School District
White
1890s-1930

The fact that there were two Thornton Schools in the early days of Prince William County seems to have confused some of the first chroniclers of the county's education. Even the compilation of School Board minutes done in 1983 for the Supervisor of Real Property for the County schools interchanges the two schoolhouses. Actually, they were quite different. The earlier of the two was established in 1877 for the black children of the Catharpin area in the Gainesville District. Since the Superintendent of Schools at that time was William W. Thornton, it is probably safe to assume that the school's name was chosen to honor him.

The Thornton School in the Dumfries District opened sometime at the end of the nineteenth century to serve the white children in an area which now is part of Prince William Forest Park. The Superintendent of Schools then was Mr. J. B. T. Thornton and it is likely that his name was given to that school. There are no early records for the Thornton School in the Dumfries District but it does appear on the 1901 Brown map of the county on what is now the northwest intersection of the Mawavi Fire Road and the Taylor Farm Fire Road/Burma Road/Spriggs Lane Fire Road. In 1901, that was the intersection of Thornton's Road, the Ridge Road and Gallows Hill Road, an area known as Thornton's Crossroads.

For reasons not known (old age of building or higher enrollment figures were the usual reasons), the School Board decided in October of 1923 to build a new Thornton schoolhouse. J.B. Florence, Mary Florence and Fannie Florence sold to the members of the School Board of Prince William one acre of land for $10. The land is described as "lying on the East side of the Ridge Road and adjoining the lands [of the Florences]". The family also agreed "to give for public travel" a thirty foot wide road lying on land adjoining to the east; all in all, they donated one acre.[1] The land was very near the location of the first schoolhouse and today is also part of Prince William Forest Park. The school's location next to the Florence family farm and near the Florence Store and Florence Mill occasionally caused it to be referred to as the Florence School, but most long time residents do not remember or use that name.

The one-room schoolhouse had an alcove which contained an oil burning stove. Every other Friday, the mothers and students brought ingredients for soup, which they cooked on the stove for a hot lunch. How wonderful that little schoolroom must have smelled on soup Fridays! On the Fridays in between, the pupils prepared hot chocolate on their stove.

Grades 1-7 were taught at the Thornton School. During most of the 1920s between thirty and thirty-five children attended school there. According to the year end report filed by teacher Miss Lucile T. Muse at the close of the 1925-26 school year, average daily attendance was twenty-eight although forty-three children were enrolled. Miss Muse that year was only nineteen years old but she had two years of teaching experience and was a high school graduate. For a term of eight months and three weeks, she was paid $641.25 or $75 a month and paid $20 a month for room and board in Dumfries.[2]

Curriculum materials as well as a flag were provided to the school by the Dumfries School Board. Reading, numbers, spelling, hygiene, geography, history and English were taught on a daily basis as they were in most of the County's schools. The library had sixty-nine volumes in it, fairly large by the standards of the day.[3]

Teachers such as Lucille Muse and Mrs. Florence, who later taught at the Smithfield School, made school a happy memory for students like little Mildred Keys who attended Thornton for grades one and two. Mildred represented her school in the annual Reading Contest held in Manassas every year. She travelled all the way to that city where she was given a book she had never seen before to read before the audience and a panel of judges. What an adventure for a little girl! Mildred Keys later married Harvey Watson who attended the Thornton School for first and second grades, probably sometime around 1928-30, the last years the school was open.

At the beginning of the 1929-30 school year, enrollment figures warranted the hiring of two teachers for the Thornton School. However, by year's end, the numbers had fallen so low that closure of the school became necessary. The School Board transferred Mrs. Emma Carter to the Hayfield School and Mrs. Gladys Cherry was sent to the Minnieville School.[4] The remaining children were bused to the Joplin School for the remainder of their education. In December of 1934, Mr. J. B. Florence told the School Board that he would be willing to pay $15 for the two acres of land in the Thornton School lot but his offer was rejected because the government was expected to take it soon for what became Prince William Forest Park.[5] No trace remains of the schoolhouse.

---

[1] Prince William County Deed Book #80.

[2] "Virginia Daily Attendance Register and Record of Class Grades" for the Thornton White School filed at the end of the 1925-26 school year.

[3] "Virginia Daily Attendance Register and Record of Class Grades" for the Thornton White School filed at the end of the 1925-26 school year.

[4] School Board minutes of July 2, 1930.

[5] Prince William County School Board minutes of December 5, 1934.

THE THOROUGHFARE COLORED/ NORTH FORK SCHOOL

Gainesville District #12
Colored
1884-1936

As early as February 1883, a group of black citizens from the Thoroughfare area of the County near Haymarket petitioned the School Board for a colored school but the Board denied their request at that time. Then, according to District School Board records of October 1884, Mr. Frank Fletcher brought to the Board a list of sixty black children who lived within a mile of the village of Thoroughfare. Twenty-five of them had never had proper school facilities. He requested that the patrons[1] be allowed to rent an available house and furnish it with desks for use as a school. He also asked that the Board pay the teacher's salary. This time the Board agreed, as did the County School Superintendent, and ordered that the school open in November as School #12 of the Gainesville District.

The following April the School Board decided to contract to have a proper schoolhouse built.[2] It was to be one room measuring 18'x28' with a ten foot high ceiling, three windows on each long side and one door. Tongue and groove panelling was to be used for both the floor and ceiling. In June the contract was awarded to Mr. Peyton for $204.73; for an additional $38 he agreed to repair the building, which had been serving as the school. On the fourth of July, 1885, the School Board travelled to Thoroughfare and chose a site on a knoll on the south side of the John Marshall Highway near the center of town about four-hundred feet from the station serving the Washington and Harrisonburg branch of the Southern Railroad.

In October of 1898, Mr. R.A. Jones, the teacher of the Thoroughfare colored school, reported to the School Board that his schoolhouse had been occupied for seventeen days over the summer by part of the 2nd Army Corps stationed at Thoroughfare. He stated that the Army had agreed to pay $2 per day rent plus $15 to repair damage to the schoolhouse and its

The Thoroughfare/North Fork School in the early 20th century.
(Courtesy of Mr. Howard Allen and Mrs. Betty Berry)

furnishings for a total of $49, which the Clerk of the Gainesville District Board was directed to collect.[3]

Over the years, the little schoolhouse had begun to bulge at the seams with an ever growing number of students. The School Board refused to enlarge the building so the black citizens of Thoroughfare decided to add another room themselves. By 1899, they had a second room on top of the first and sheathed the whole in wood with a shingled roof. At first the stairway allowing access to the second floor was located outside the building, but in a few more years, the stairs were moved inside the front door.[4]

The two-room, two-teacher school continued to serve the black children of the community of Thoroughfare for thirty-six more years. At some point, the school became known as the North Fork School because of its location along the North Fork of Broad Run. Presumably it also took care of any confusion between the Thoroughfare White School and the Thoroughfare Colored School.

Large families, with twelve to fifteen children were not unusual in the largely rural area and thus a long and steady stream of pupils was assured. Most lived in or very near the village where their families farmed mostly corn and wheat but some came from as far as four or five miles away. As the roads improved and transportation was available, a school bus

---

[1] Parents and friends of the Thoroughfare School.
[2] Gainesville District School Board minutes of April 4, 1885.
[3] Gainesville District School Board minutes of October 1, 1898.
[4] Oral history with Howard Allen, Betty Berry and Mary Fields by the author in 1991.

brought the children from the farthest away homes. Reverend Peter Berry was the school bus driver for many years. The children began their school day at 9 o'clock and didn't go home until 4 o'clock. The hand bell, which the teacher used to summon students is a treasured possession of the grandchildren of the school's founder, Frank Fletcher; they attended the school during the years from 1910-1918 or so. The students had an hour for lunch and two recesses. Lunches were usually biscuits of some sort carried in syrup or lard buckets. Water was brought by the boys from a well at the house at the bottom of the hill where the teachers usually boarded.[5]

The teacher during the 1927-28 school year was thirty-nine year old Mrs. Louise V. Allen, a high school graduate who had been teaching for sixteen years. That year there were forty-four children enrolled at the North Fork School with one teacher using one classroom. Thirty-seven children were in the first through fourth grades (eight of these failed and eight more dropped out) but there were only seven in grades 5-7. One of them dropped out before the end of the school year, but none failed). The actual average attendance on a daily basis was thirty. Mrs. Allen was paid a salary of $60 a month for a seven month term.[6]

By the mid-thirties, a new road had been built through the village so that the schoolhouse then stood only fifteen feet from the highway. In his report on the county schools in 1934, Superintendent of Schools Richard C. Haydon wrote that "the condition of the building, like its location, is far from being desirable."[7] Enrollment for the 1933-34 school year was twenty-nine with an average daily attendance of only nineteen. The following year those figures had fallen to twenty-three and seventeen (a 74% average). The second floor had not been in use for several years. In the original room, the floor was rough and warped though it was kept clean by the teacher and students. Heat came from a wood stove kept supplied by the pupils. Wood was purchased by the School Board in long lengths, which the parents had to cut into useable sizes (white schools were provided with wood already cut into the right length). The playground was a narrow uphill strip of about half an acre located along the highway. The rest of the playground had been lost to road widening. The outhouses were not the pit type and not fly proof; Haydon labelled them unsanitary and "very much in need of improvement". The table and chair used by the teacher stood on a raised platform at one end of the classroom. Students sat at double desks facing the front. There were few books or maps.

Like most of the small schools, North Fork was ungraded. Students advanced at their own pace into the next reader and progress was measured by which book the student was currently reading. In addition to the reading books, there were geography books and primers. The teacher had a Bible out of which a lesson was read each morning. Then came the singing of "America the Beautiful" and lessons began. Any additional learning materials came from the parents.[8]

The teachers at North Fork boarded down the hill from the school in a home which still stands on the site. They paid $10 a month for room and board. During the last years of the school, the teacher was taking in-service training at summer school at Virginia State College to trade her Provisional Certificate for a Normal Professional diploma. In 1933, she had eight years of teaching experience.

As the school population began to decline and the building became more and more in need of repair, it became evident that some changes had to be made. In the early 1930s, families of the area tried to raise money for a new school, but were unable to get the necessary funds together in those difficult economic times. In December of 1935, a joint delegation from the North Fork and Antioch schools appeared before the County School Board. They stated their approval of the Board's plan to close the North Fork school beginning with the 1936-37 school year and to build an additional room onto Antioch to house the children from Thoroughfare and "along the mountain back of Hickory Grove".[9] The Board agreed that if the League contributed the $400 they had raised to build a new building at North Fork

---

[5]Oral history with Howard Allen, Betty Berry and Mary Fields done by the author in 1991.

[6]"Virginia Daily Attendance Register and Record of Class Grades" for the North Fork School filed at the end of the 1927-28 school term.

[7]Richard C. Haydon. "An Administrative Survey of the Public School System in Prince William County, Virginia", A Thesis for Master of Science at the University of Virginia, 1935, p.89.

[8]Oral history with Howard Allen, Betty Berry and Mary Fields done by the author, 1991.

[9]Prince William County School Board minutes of December 4, 1935.

toward the addition, the Board would fund the remaining cost as well as provide transportation for the children. The money was to be paid as soon as the roof of the addition had been completed.

Disposal of the old schoolhouse proved to be a complicated matter. In December of 1936, Reverend Peter G. Berry, an active community member whose wife still lives in Thoroughfare, presented a letter to the School Board offering to tear down the old schoolhouse and use part of the material to build a garage on the site to house the school bus. The Board replied that Reverend Berry must clean up the old lot, remove all the material and pay $25 "additional over and above the labor of building the garage".[10] The following January, Reverend Berry agreed to offer the School Board $25 for the abandoned school lot. The Board told him that the lot was not for sale but as far as the old schoolhouse was concerned they "were expecting him to carry out his agreement...as per his former letter."[11] The next month, on February 10, Reverend Berry told the Board that he was not interested in purchasing the schoolhouse under the Board's terms unless the Board also agreed to sell him the land so that he would have a location for the proposed school bus garage. The Board decided to drop the whole matter at that point.

In September of 1937, the School Board minutes report the sale of the schoolhouse for $40, apparently not to Reverend Berry. Evidently the school building was torn down, because in May 1939, the Board asked for sealed bids on just the school lot. Mr. Robert Fletcher made an offer of $21, which a committee appointed by the Board decided to accept.[12] Today the lot stands empty but long time residents of the village remember it well and have photographs to bring it back to life.

---

[10] Prince William County School Board minutes of December 2, 1936.

[11] Prince William County School Board minutes of January 6, 1937.

[12] Prince William County School Board minutes of June 7, 1939.

THE THOROUGHFARE WHITE SCHOOL

Gainesville District School #9
White
1880-1920s

The Thoroughfare School for white children opened for the 1880-81 school year on the south side of the John Marshall Highway in the community of the same name. Parents of children in that rural area must have petitioned their District School Board to open a schoolhouse (the most common way to secure one) because the Board agreed to authorize funds for a school if the community also paid part of the costs involved. A contract was awarded to Mr. Charles Butler for $125, a small amount even in those days and probably indicative of the remodelling of an existing building. A teacher was hired and school began.[1]

Prince William County Deed Book #35 shows that on August 1, 1884, Dr. Thomas E. Smith and Cornelia Smith of "Washington City" sold to the Gainesville School District, for one dollar, a piece of property "adjoining the lots of Mimi Grigsby and others ... beginning at Grigsby's corner on the Hay Market and Thoroughfare Pike...for a white Free School." Puzzlingly, the next reference to such a school does not appear until 1890 when the District School Board resolved to build a new schoolhouse on "the old lot at Thoroughfare."[2] Presumably this was the lot which had been purchased from the Smiths nearly six years earlier. If a school had been established on that location back in 1884, no reference to it has been found. The School Board minutes go on to say that "the old building" was to be sold and removed from the site but whether this refers to the old schoolhouse which began in 1880 or another one established in 1884 is unknown. The new school was to have one room measuring 30'x20'

---

[1] Gainesville District School Board minutes from the summer of 1880.

[2] Gainesville District School Board minutes of March 22, 1890.

with a ten foot ceiling and a shingled roof. The long delay between the purchase of the Smith's land and the building of the schoolhouse remains unexplained.

An undated Prince William County School Board inventory from the early 20th century lists a Thoroughfare School for white children which was built in 1900 for $1500. It had two rooms connected by a porch. The wooden building with twin gabled metal roof had three doors opening onto the porch and five windows. This description does not fit either earlier or later references to the Thoroughfare schoolhouse. For instance, in January of 1905 the teacher (singular, not the two one would expect in a new two-room school) reported that there were forty-five children enrolled, a much larger number than could easily be handled by one teacher in one room. She pleaded for an assistant, but the School Board decided there was no room for an additional teacher.[3] This would seem unlikely in a two-room school.

[3]Gainesville District School Board minutes of January 6, 1905.

When the hiring of an assistant was refused, the teacher then asked for additional salary to compensate but the Board declined this also, holding to the original contract of $30 per month. They did agree, however, to pay the teacher the princely sum of $32.50 for the month she taught beyond the six months' contract.

At some point, the Thoroughfare schoolhouse was moved from the south side of the road to the north side, where it remained until its closing. Village residents remember the move although they are unsure about that date as well as the date it closed.[4] There are no references to a white school at Thoroughfare in any records after the early 1920s and no trace remains of it.

[4]Oral history with Howard Allen, Betty Berry and Mary Fields done by the author in 1991.

TRIANGLE ELEMENTARY

Dumfries District
1959-present

Located on Lionsfield Road in the town from which it got its name, the Triangle Elementary School was built in 1958-59. It opened its doors in the spring of 1959 with 358 students from the Quantico Town School and the Dumfries School, where crowded conditions had become a problem. The original building had eleven classrooms but within three years, seven more were added. The school has continued to grow and serve the children from the Quantico, Triangle and Dumfries communities.

TYLER ELEMENTARY SCHOOL

Gainesville District
1968-present

After the 1953 opening of the Antioch-Macrae School for the black children of the Gainesville District, it was fifteen years before the county built another school in the District. When desegregation of Prince William County Schools was complete in 1966, the Gainesville and Antioch-Macrae Schools were used together to house the integrated school population. The youngest children attended Antioch-Macrae for the first two years and then went to Gainesville for the rest of their elementary education. Then, in 1968, the George C. Tyler School was erected on the John Marshall Highway in Haymarket, less than a mile from the Gainesville Elementary School, which had served the children in the towns of Gainesville and Haymarket since 1935. Tyler was originally planned as a middle school for the District, but demographics showed a greater need for a second elementary schoolhouse and so the building opened as the Tyler Elementary School.[1] It housed grades one through six until 1973 when the county moved sixth grade into the middle schools and the ninth grade into the high schools. Shortly afterward, Prince William County agreed to support public kindergarten and, once again, innovative use of existing space, as well as the closing of the Antioch-Macrae School in 1982 (because a decline in area population made three school buildings unnecessary), meant changes in the student bodies of the school buildings. Kindergartners and first graders were sent to Tyler Elementary and the second through fifth grades were housed in Gainesville Elementary. It remains thus today.

[1] Carolyn Wyrsch. "Gainesville District Elementary School 50th Anniversary, October 5, 1985", p.5.

VAUGHAN ELEMENTARY SCHOOL

Occoquan/Woodbridge District
1965-present

Named for a well-known Prince William County teacher and principal, Elizabeth Vaughan, this school opened in 1965 on York Drive in Woodbridge. When new District lines were drawn and the Woodbridge District created in 1976, Vaughan Elementary fell within its boundaries.

THE WAKEFIELD SCHOOL

Dumfries School District
White?
1870s

Almost nothing is known of this school. Indeed, it is not even known if it was a private or public school. The only mention made of the Wakefield School is in a county Deed Book of 1885 which records the purchase of land for the Minnieville School near "the old Wakefield school". Minnieville was located where what is now Cardinal Drive forked to go either to Dumfries or Neabsco Mills and it can be presumed that was also the approximate site of the Wakefield School. Obviously it had disappeared by 1885.

It is included in this study only for the sake of completeness and in the hope that future research may reveal more information.

WASHINGTON-REID ELEMENTARY SCHOOL

Dumfries School District
Colored
1950-present

By 1950, the only elementary school in the Dumfries District serving the black community was the old Cabin Branch School, built in 1916. It was small, overcrowded and forty-four years old. The School Board agreed to build a new schoolhouse for the District's black children on the Dumfries Road near the flourishing black communities along Mine

Road and the Dumfries Road. The Washington-Reid Elementary Schoolhouse was built in 1950 at a cost of $150,150.[1] It was a one-story building with a partial basement which contained the heating system. The cinder block walls were covered in brick, the roof was flat and the floors concrete covered in asphalt tile on the first floor. This was standard construction for schoolhouses of the day. Acoustic ceiling tile was used throughout in one of the first schools where that material was used. Steam heat from an oil furnace kept the six classrooms, cafeteria and kitchen, office and two bathrooms comfortable. An addition was built ten years later, in 1960, for $36,940.

The school was named for two black women, active in the Dumfries community, who had once owned the land on which the school was built. Mrs. Marian Washington, who was born around 1855, used her own money to set up a lunch program for poor children who attended the Summitt School, a colored schoolhouse on Davis Ford Road which served the black population of Occoquan. Mrs. Washington died in 1941 at the age of eighty-six. Mrs. Marjorie Reid is thought to have owned eighteen acres of land adjoining Mrs. Washington's property. To honor these two women, the citizens chose to name their new school after them both.[2]

After school integration, the Washington-Reid school was attended by both black and white children. Ruby Strickland, the first black woman principal in the county following desegregation, was named to head the school in 1975. She remained there for five years before becoming principal at Tyler Elementary in Gainesville and, later, at Henderson Elementary in Montclair.

With the building of the community of Montclair, Washington-Reid was no longer large enough to house the mushrooming school population of the area and so Pattie Elementary School was built across the Dumfries Road. Washington-Reid then became the Pattie Annex housing the youngest school children. It is still standing on Rt. 234 near the entrance to Montclair.

---

[1] This figure comes from an undated inventory of Prince William County School property.

[2] Prince William County School System. "Self Study of Washington-Reid Elementary School", 1973-74.

THE WATERFALL SCHOOL

Gainesville School District #4
White
1871?-1927

Although no specific records survive for a school for white children in the village of Waterfall in the northwestern part of Prince William County before 1880, two pieces of evidence were found which show, in a roundabout way, that one did exist. First, School Board records of 1880 report the decision by the Board to use the white Waterfall School for the black children of the community, replacing the outgrown Antioch (Murray) School. Secondly, the Waterfall School was given the #4 designation by the School Board, meaning that it was the fourth school established in the District. Since both the third (Antioch[Murray]) and fifth (Macrae) schoolhouses were opened in the very early 1870s, it stands to reason that the fourth would have also been opened during the same time frame. Later School Board

The Waterfall School is a residence in 1993.
(Photo by the author)

references to the "old Waterfall School" locate it on land owned by Mrs. E.H. Foley[1] This would be consistent with the location of the second Antioch School behind the Olive Branch Baptist Church.[2]

School Board records indicate that a new schoolhouse was built in the village of Waterfall in

---

[1] William H. Brown. Map of Prince William County, 1901.

[2] Interview with Elizabeth Nickens by the author, 1991.

1880. A contract to build the school for white children was given to Mr. J. P. Smith who submitted the winning $125 bid. Why a new school was necessary, where it was located and why it didn't last more than seven years are all pieces of information lost to history. No records have been found to answer the questions. This apparently was the schoolhouse purchased by Mr. G. W. Shirley in 1891 for $25.00. He paid $12 of the purchase price and in July of 1893 still owed the remaining $13 to the School Board. That group decided[3] that if he failed to pay the $13, the old school would be taken over by the School Board and, like its predecessor, become a "new" Antioch School. By September, 1893 Mr. Shirley had decided that he didn't want the school used for the black children. He then agreed to pay whatever he still owed on the building but he no longer wanted the land on which it stood. The School Board agreed to reduce Mr. Shirley's debt by $5.00 and leave the Antioch School where it was. However, the debt remained unpaid nearly three years later, so the School Board resolved to put the claim into the hands of the constable.[4] In July of that year, Justice of the Peace Wharton paid the $8 to settle Mr. Shirley's account.[5]

In 1887 the Gainesville School Board decided that the schoolhouse should be located nearer to the geographic center of the area it served, so Mr. E.C. Taylor was hired to build a new building on Waterfall Road about two miles from the old school site and less than a mile from the Antioch School. This new schoolhouse was built with a wood frame and "random rubble stone" which today is covered with vinyl siding. The cross gable roof was covered with composition shingles. It was a one-room school with six-over-six sashed windows. The narrow pine floor and pine tongue-and-groove panelling on the walls and ceiling must have created a sense of warmth inside the little schoolhouse. In 1915, a second room was added to accommodate the increased enrollment.

In June of 1890, two young boys damaged the outdoor privies of the new schoolhouse by throwing rocks against the building. The School Board decided not to prosecute the children if their parents made the necessary repairs. On February 4, 1905 the School Board approved the hiring of a janitor to take care of the schoolhouse. This was an fairly unusual step to take during those early years of the century. The little schoolhouse was a center of community life in the Waterfall area. The League (or Parents Group) sponsored ice cream socials, baseball games, plays, etc. as was the case in many of the little rural schoolhouses.

As part of the county's consolidation efforts, the Waterfall School was closed either in 1927 or maybe as early as 1926. The last teacher was Mrs. Selina T. Wilson. The children were transported to the Haymarket School.

In 1928, the School Board decided to sell the two-room schoolhouse and lot at a public auction in front of Partlow's Store in Gainesville on Thursday, March 28, 1929. It was purchased for $600 by Mr. George A. Gossom who owned Gossom's Store in Waterfall.[6] The building was converted into a house in the 1930s and a porch was added. Linoleum now covers the pine flooring and modern panelling covers much of the tongue-and-groove panelling. Later in the 1930s, Mrs. May Baker's family purchased the house and later sold it to Mr. and Mrs. Paul Baker. It is still standing at the crest of the hill on Waterfall Road in Haymarket, a white frame building surrounded by a chain link fence.

---

[3]Gainesville District School Board minutes of July 22, 1893.
[4]Gainesville District School Board minutes of May 26, 1894.
[5]Ibid., July 28, 1894.

[6]Prince William County School Board minutes of April 3, 1929.

THE WELLINGTON SCHOOL

Manassas School District
White
1906-1932

The earliest reference to the Wellington School is found in the minutes of the Manassas School Board for August 1906, when the Board voted to close both the Groveton and Bethlehem Schools and consolidate the students at a school in the village of Wellington. The Wellington School would assume the designation of #3, previously held by the Groveton

The third Woodbine Schoolhouse.
(Courtesy of PWC Schools)

was no janitor. The playground was "ample" but lacked apparatus, which the League, the precursor of today's PTO, had agreed to supply. Teachers and students planted native shrubbery to beautify the grounds.[3]

The primary teacher in 1933 had a Certified Professional diploma from a teachers' college but no teaching experience. The teacher of the upper grades had a similar diploma but also had thirty-three years of experience. The enrollment of the Woodbine School that year eighty-four with an average daily attendance in the primary grades of twenty-six and in the upper grades of thirty-eight. At the end of the school year, sixty-six students were promoted, eight failed and ten had dropped out. The following school year the enrollment fell slightly to seventy-eight but the average attendance was greatly improved to seventy-four or a very respectable 95.6%.[4]

Twenty years later, in 1953, a new and larger school was built adjacent to the old structure which was torn down. The original room had, by that time, served the children of the community for nearly forty years. The new schoolhouse was a one story structure with cinder block walls and a flat roof. Concrete floors were covered with asphalt tile; ceilings were covered with acoustic tile. Electricity supplied light and an oil burning furnace supplied the hot water heat. There were four classrooms, a kitchen, an auditorium and two bathrooms.

As the local population continued to grow, even this new school became inadequate to meet the needs of the community. The larger Coles Elementary School was built in 1955 on Hoadly Road, about a mile and a half from the Woodbine School which later became a center for preschool children needing special education. It still serves in that capacity today.

---

[3]Richard C. Haydon. "An Administrative Survey of the Public School System in Prince William County, Virginia", A Thesis for Master of Science at the University of Virginia, 1935, p.73.

[4]Ibid.

THE WOODBRIDGE SCHOOL

Occoquan School District
White
1895?-1927

On the 1901 Brown map of Prince William County, there is a Woodbridge schoolhouse on the northwest corner of Route 1 and Occoquan Road. Its date of opening, due to lack of records, is unknown. Residents of the County recall a small one-room schoolhouse on Route 1 about a mile south of the Occoquan River bridge on the present site of Cowles Ford.[1] The building, which housed grades 1-8, was made of rough lumber and heated by an old wood stove. The wood for the stove often ran out, students remember. In bad weather, the wood was stacked in a corner of the classroom to keep dry. Drinking water was limited to one bucket a day and came from Powell Davis' store nearby. A common dipper served all the children. Two old privies, called "back houses", were located behind the schoolhouse. In a strong wind, these had an unfortunate tendency to blow over and would need to be propped up again.

A typical school term lasted for five months, from the first Monday in October until the first Monday in March. The teacher was paid $30 per month, half of which went to Powell Davis for room and board. In 1906 the teacher was Maude Metz who lived in Manassas but boarded in Woodbridge during the week to avoid what was, in those days, a dif-

---

[1]Nelson, Thomas. "Transcript of Interview with Historic Occoquan, Inc." Prince William County Historical Commission Oral History Project, September 24, 1985, p.4.

ficult commute. She taught a class of 25-30 students in her one classroom. A student during those early years recalled that "we did not have watches in them days. The teacher had an old alarm clock, and one boy was always playing tricks on her. If he got the chance he would move the clock up half an hour to get out early."[2] A student earned $2.00 a month to sweep the floor, split the wood, etc. Despite the fact that there was no lock on the schoolhouse door, nothing was ever stolen, according to local residents.

In 1919, the Woodbridge School outgrew its small building and a new schoolhouse, with two classrooms, was erected on a nearby site. This second schoolhouse also housed grades 1-8 with about thirty students in each classroom. The two privies continued to stand out in the back yard, one for boys and one for girls. Maintenance was still done by a student (in the twenties, this was the job of Walter Haslip, remember Ethel Lynn and Wallace Dawson who attended the school). A wood stove provided heat; drinking water continued to be brought in buckets from Powell Davis' store across Route 1.

A school term now lasted from September through May. A day went from 9 o'clock to 4 o'clock. Books for the students were supplied by the school but the only other equipment remembered by the Dawsons was a blackboard. There was no library. Spelling bees were popular, as they were throughout the county. Wallace Dawson, in the time honored tradition of little boys, recalls studying two things: general studies and girls! Pupils brought their lunches from home in a molasses bucket.

The Woodbridge School remained open until 1927 when the new Occoquan District High School was built to house grades 1-12. The earlier Occoquan School also closed in 1927 since its students would now attend the new building. The merger of the two schools into a big modern building was a major event in the community. A young student at the Woodbridge school remembers that time:

> When it was at the end of the year...all the kids at Woodbridge marched single file from U.S. Route 1 up to the location of the Occoquan District High School. All the kids down in Occoquan from the elementary school marched single file out to the Occoquan District High School for the laying of the corner stone....It was just a great big day. They took all day doing this....Here were all these people throwing coins in this thing in the corner stone.[3]

A year later, in the fall of 1928, the School Board decided to offer the Woodbridge School for sale at a public auction the following spring. On March 29, 1929, it was sold to T. Powell Davis for $2000, the highest price paid for any of the several school buildings offered at the same time. The roof was raised on the building to create a two-story apartment house called the Warden Apartments, which existed at least into the 1940s.[4] The building is no longer standing.

---

[2]Carl Eike as quoted by Margaret Ann Pishock. *Yes, Virginia, There Is a Carl Eike*, Triangle, VA: Privately published, p.83.

[3]Nelson, p.5.
[4]Nelson, p.6.

THE WOODLAWN SCHOOL

Brentsville District School #9
White
1899-1935

In July of 1899, the Brentsville District School Board agreed to build the District's ninth schoolhouse. They chose a site on the road leading from Bristoe to Greenwich, now called Vint Hill Road. Mr. Julius Mertz donated to the School District one acre of land on which the school was to be built. Located in farm and dairy country, the site was in a field about three-quarters of a mile west of the junc-

(Courtesy of The Manassas Museum)

ture of Vint Hill and Kettle Run Roads and about four miles from the center school at Nokesville and four miles from the village of Greenwich.

As was the usual practice, the Board advertised in *The Manassas Gazette* for bids, specifying a building with measurements of 22'x26' with twelve foot ceilings, a teacher's platform and two privies out in back. Mr. P. J. Stephens, who lived on Vint Hill Road not far from the school site, submitted the winning bid and finished the work in good time. On October 21, the Board met at the Woodlawn School to accept it into the system and appoint Miss Olla R. Hunt as the teacher. The term was to be for five months beginning on October 30, 1899. First through sixth grades were to be taught.

Although the county school inventory says that a two-room frame Woodlawn schoolhouse was built in 1907, no District School Board minutes corroborate this. The inventory, on occasion, has been proven inaccurate and it is not likely that the minutes would have failed to mention the building of a new school especially one supposedly erected only eight years after the first. It seems probable, therefore, that the school to which the District School Board added a vestibule containing cloakrooms at a cost of $15 is the 1899 schoolhouse. At the same time, the building was painted white, the usual color for the county's painted schools.[1] By December of that year, the patrons of the school had raised $15 which was used to purchase a library.

In the summer of 1920, Miss Rushia Kiener was appointed by the School Board as the teacher for the next year at a salary of $65 a month. The Board also agreed to add $400, or as much of that as was needed, to the total amount of money the community could raise over the next year and proceed with the construction of a school addition as soon as plans were approved.[2] The following April, the school's Community League was established. They selected as their motto, "A better school building". By September of 1921, the citizens reported to the School Board that the League had raised $215 in cash, $59 in subscriptions and twenty-six hours of labor to add a room to the one-room school house (another reason to believe that the inventory listing a two-room schoolhouse in 1907 was incorrect). The two-room building opened for the 1921-22 school year with Mr. George W. Beahm as the principal teacher and Nora Harley (Kline) as the second teacher. Mr. Beahm's son, Robert, remembers that his father made the daily trip of two and a half miles from his home by horseback on "Old Charlie".[3]

By the 1925-26 school year, enrollment figures show an interesting spread in the upper grades (4-7). There were twenty-six children enrolled, thirteen boys and thirteen girls. One student made up the entire fourth grade; there were twelve in the fifth grade, including a seventeen year old girl who, incidentally, did not pass; six in the sixth grade; and seven in the seventh grade. The teacher for the upper grades that year was Miss Lillie Holland who was only twenty-two years old but who had already been a teacher for five years. She earned $85 a month or $743.75 for the nine months' term. Like most young single teachers, she paid for room and board (at a cost of $20 a month) in the community.[4]

The teacher of the younger grades that year was Mrs. Nita J. Potter, age twenty-three years with three years of teaching experience and a high school diploma. The average attendance in her classroom was nineteen although twenty-two children were enrolled. Mrs. Potter's salary was $75 a month, $10 less than Miss Holland was paid. She, too, paid $20 monthly for room and board.[5]

In 1927, George Beahm's daughter, Cora E. Beahm, with Olga White as principal, taught at Woodlawn. Both had been teachers at the Nokesville Village School the previous year. Miss Beahm taught the first through third grades and Miss White took the 4th, 5th and 6th graders. Seventh graders were bused to the Greenwich Graded School and any high school students living in the area went to the Brentsville District High School in Nokesville.

In the next few years, enrollment at the Woodlawn School began to fall. Enrollment for the 1933-34 school year was thirty-five with an average daily attendance of twenty-nine. At year's end, twenty students were promoted, eight failed and seven dropped out. The following year, the enroll-

---

[1] Brentsville District School Board minutes of September 15, 1911.

[2] Brentsville District School Board minutes of July 27, 1920.

[3] Interview with Mr. Robert Beahm done by the author in 1992.

[4] "Virginia Daily Attendance Register and Record of Class Grades" filed for the upper grades of the Woodlawn School at the end of the 1925-26 school year.

[5] "Virginia Daily Attendance Register and Record of Class Grades" for the younger children at the Woodlawn School filed at the end of the 1925-26 school year.

ment fell to twenty-three with an average daily attendance of twenty-two or nearly 94%.[6] Two teachers were no longer needed and from that time on only one room was used. The teacher had a piano for her use and the students sat at adjustable double desks. The heat came from a wood stove for which the pupils were responsible just as they were for the cleaning of the building, both under the supervision of the teacher. There was no janitor provided. In 1934, the water was deemed "inadequate" and the toilet facilities did not meet state standards. Water came from a nearby well and was stored in a cooler in the school house for daily use. The playground had only home made swings and students shared their own equipment brought from home. The teacher, in 1934, was a teachers' college graduate in her first year of teaching.[7]

After one more year, on May 8, 1935, the School Board voted to close the Woodlawn School and bus all the students to Greenwich. On October 6, 1939, the school was sold at public auction for $425 to Mrs. Daisy Ritenour. A down payment of $155, followed by three notes amounting to $90 each (with 6% interest) to be paid in six, twelve and eighteen months, was accepted and the deed was held until the final payment had been made. The schoolhouse was converted into a home which was destroyed by fire in the 1940s. Today, only a clump of trees in a field marks the site along Vint Hill Road where the Woodlawn School stood.

---

[6] Richard C. Haydon. "An Administrative Survey of the Public School System in Prince William County, Virginia", A Thesis for Master of Science at the University of Virginia, 1935, p.74.

[7] Haydon, Ibid.

YORKSHIRE ELEMENTARY SCHOOL

Manassas School District
White
1952-present

Located at the corner of Yorkshire Road and Centreville Road, this schoolhouse was built in 1952 to relieve overcrowded conditions at the old Bennett School. It was a one story building of cinder blocks faced with brick. Concrete floors covered with asphalt tile were serviceable. Heat was supplied by hot water heated in an oil burning furnace. When it opened, Yorkshire had only four classrooms for grades 1-4 with a student body of about 120 students. There was not even a principal in those early days. For the first two years, classes were not filled to capacity but the next year, 1954, the first grade was so crowded that it operated on a split shift. By 1955 there was room for only grades one and two at Yorkshire.[1]

In 1957, only five years after it opened, a new cafeteria, a library and ten classrooms were added to Yorkshire. First through seventh grades were housed in the enlarged space but soon that too became overcrowded and split shifts were reinstituted in several grades. Additionally, the seventh grade was transferred to the old Bennett School.

The population of the community served by the Yorkshire School continued to expand and in 1961-62 four more classrooms were added. Three years later, when the county went to the Middle School system, the sixth grade was taken out and soon afterward kindergarten was added. In 1992, a $1.3 million renovation brought Yorkshire into the most modern world and it continues to serve the county well.

---

[1] Prince William County Schools. "Yorkshire Elementary School Self Study Report", 1980-81.

APPENDIX A: SUPERINTENDENTS OF SCHOOLS

1868-1870: George C. Round (appointed by Commissioners)

1870-1871: William Willis Thornton

1871-1872: William A. Bryant

1871-1883: William W. Thornton

1883-1885: Samuel Martyne

1885-1887: A. P. Gray

1887-1891: J.B.T. Thornton

1891-1905: H. M. Clarkson

1905-1915: George C. Tyler

1915-1925: Charles R. McDonald

1925-1946: Richard Challice Haydon

1946-1951: R. Worth Peters

1951-1954: Jacob M. Garber

1954-1972: Stuart M. Beville

1972-1973: Herbert J. Saunders

1973-1977: Milton L. Snyder

1977-1980: William L. Helton

1980-1987: Richard W. Johnson

1987 (Jan.-June[interim]): William J. Bloomer

1987-present: Edward L. Kelly

APPENDIX B: THOSE INTERVIEWED FOR THIS BOOK

Some of these people were interviewed orally in their homes. Several more were interviewed by telephone. Others, the majority, responded to a lengthy questionnaire which I sent to them. Most of those added wonderful extra accounts of their particular memories. Some sent photographs. One sent a souvenir booklet given in 1908. Others lent school record books or gave me materials they had written for the School Board or the State Department of Education or just for their own pleasure. All were enormously helpful; I cannot begin to express my thanks.

Abel, Mrs. Katherine Kerlin (King's Crossroads)
Adams, Mrs. Margaret Pattie (Mill Park, Wellington, Catharpin)
Alexander, Mr. John (Mt. Zion)
Allen, Mr. Howard (North Fork, Thoroughfare)
Allen, Mr. Hunter Maphis (Nokesville, Brentsville)
Allen, Dr. Sylvia (Brentsville District)
Andolsun, Saffon (Orlando #1)
Barg, Mrs. Hilda (Cherry Hill)
Barnes, Mr. Howell (Smithfield)
Beahm, Mrs. Aliene (Nokesville)
Beahm, Mr. Robert (Nokesville, Woodlawn, Brentsville, King's Crossroads)
Berry, Mrs. Betty (North Fork, Thoroughfare)
Brown, Mrs. Louise Smith (Brown)
Butler, Mrs. Nellie G. (Macrae)
Caton, Mrs. Marie Caton (King's Crossroads)
Clark, Mr. William, Jr. (English Church)
Clem, Mr. William (Wellington)
Conner, Mrs. E.R., Jr. (Catharpin)
Cooke, Mr. James (Greenwich)
Curtis, Mr. Don (Occoquan, Minnieville)
Curtis, Mrs. Nellie (Occoquan, Cherry Hill)
Davis, Mr. James, Jr. (Brentsville, Nokesville)
Dawson, Mr. Vernon D. (Occoquan)
Dawson, Mr. and Mrs. Wallace L. (Woodbridge)
Dent, Mr. Edward (Cherry Hill)

Ellis, Mrs. Fannie Mae (Greenwich, Nokesville)
Flory, Mrs. Mary Owens Flory (Nokesville)
Graham, Ms. Janet (Orlando #1)
Johnson, Mrs. Alice (Bradley)
Johnson, Mrs. Elizabeth (Libbie) Harrover (Groveton)
Kline, Mrs. Mary Senseney (Cannon Branch, Brentsville)
MacDonald, Mr. Gerald (Smithfield)
MacIntosh, Mrs. Robert (Bradley)
Nickens, Ms. Elizabeth (Antioch, Macrae, Thornton, Kettle Run)
Partlow, Miss Hattie Mae (Catharpin, general information)
Payne, Mrs. Dorothea Randall (Ruffner, Bennett)
Peters, Mr. Carl (Antioch)
Peters, Mrs. Margaret Selecman (Occoquan #1)
Robinson, Mr. B. Oswald (Groveton, Manley)
Smith, Karen (Bethel School)
Smith, Mrs. Mary Harrover Ferguson (Groveton)
Sylvia, Mrs. Jane G. (Bradley)
Tiller, Mrs. Zella Cornwell (Purcell, Woodbine, Bethel, Coles)
Turner, Mrs. Sarah (Haymarket)
Watson, Mrs. Mildred (Thornton)
Wood, Mr. and Mrs. T. Clay (Allendale)
Woolfenden, Mr. Ray (Joplin)

APPENDIX C: THE SCHOOLS FROM 1970-1993

While not the focus of this book, to bring the story of Prince William County's schools up to date, a list of the schools built in the county from 1970 to the present is included here. They are grouped by Magisterial District to make locating them easier[1], but they are county schools run by the Prince William County School Board today. It is appropriate to note that when the first schools were established in the county, and until 1923, they were grouped by School Districts, which were the same geographically as the Magisterial Districts. Since 1923, there have been no separate School Boards; the County School Board administers all the public schools.

The cities of Manassas and Manassas Park, though independent of the County today, were part of the early Manassas District and so were part of the story too. For the sake of completeness, the schools which are new to those two cities are also included here. So, by Magisterial District[2], the following schools were built during the years 1970-1993:

Coles District -
- **Enterprise Elementary**, Lindendale Road, Dale City
- **Martin Luther King Elementary**, Nickleson Drive, Dale City
- **Christa McAuliffe Elementary**, Princedale Drive, Dale City
- **Springwoods Elementary**, Marquis Place, Lake Ridge

Dumfries District -
- **Alexander Henderson Elementary**, Waterway Drive, Montclair
- **Montclair Elementary**, Tallowood Drive, Montclair
- **John F. Pattie Elementary**, Dumfries Road, Montclair
- **River Oaks Elementary**, McGuffey's Trail, Dumfries

Gainesville District -
- **George Mullen Elementary**, Rodes Drive, Manassas
- **Sudley Elementary**, Copeland Drive, Manassas

Manassas City -
- **Richard Haydon Elementary**, Rosewood Park Avenue, Manassas
- **George C. Round Elementary**, Hastings Drive, Manassas
- **Weems Elementary**, Weems Road, Manassas

---

[1] It must be noted that, over the years, redistricting has changed the boundaries of the Magisterial Districts. Those changes occur after every census as population figures change but they also change when the Board of County Supervisors feels that the people will be more fairly served with the boundary lines redrawn. The Districts here are as they were formed following the 1990 census.

[2] The Brentsville District is not included in the list because no new elementary schools have been built there since 1929.

Manassas Park -   **Conner Elementary,** Manassas Drive, Manassas Park

Neabsco District[3] - **Kerrydale Elementary**, Kerrydale Road, Dale City
                       Minnieville Elementary, Greenwood Drive, Dale City
                       Neabsco Elementary, Cordell Avenue, Dale City

Occoquan District -   **Antietam Elementary**, Antietam Road, Lake Ridge
                       Lake Ridge Elementary, Hedges Run Drive, Lake Ridge
                       Rockledge Elementary, Mariner Lane, Lake Ridge
                       Westridge Elementary, Knightsbridge Drive, Lake Ridge

Woodbridge District - **Ann Ludwig Special Education School**, Opitz Blvd., Woodbridge

---

[3]The Neabsco District was created in 1967 by drawing together parts of the Occoquan, Coles and Dumfries Districts. It was created because, with the building of Dale City, population centers changed dramatically.

APPENDIX D: SPECIFICATIONS OF A 1906 SCHOOLHOUSE

On July 20, 1906, the *Manassas Journal* published the requirements for the new Purcell School to be built over the summer in the Coles District. It was customary to call for bids to build a schoolhouse by printing such specifications in the local newspaper and inviting interested parties to submit sealed proposals. These particular bids were to be delivered to Coles District School Trustee, J.M. Ellicott, on the following day at Independent Hill. From these specifications we are able to get a fine idea of how schoolhouses were built at the turn of the century and what they looked like because many one-room buildings were erected using similar plans. There were ten specifics:

1. Building is to be 18x30, 10 feet pitch between floor and ceiling.

2. All framing, siding and sheathing must be good quality, square edge; lumber such as may be obtained from local sawmill, siding to be undressed.

3. The roof must be framed on ceiling joist (not less that six inches wide) spanning the building 2 feet apart and projecting each side 1 foot to receive box cornice; hangers must be fastened to side of rafter and ceiling joist in center of roof to support ceiling. Cornice boards to be dry lumber, dressed 1 side and put up plain finish. No moulding. Roof is to be galvanized steel, properly put on, with pitch of 5 feet to center of roof. The board of trustees reserves right to supply roofing if they desire.

4. Three windows to each side, size 10x12, 12 light 1/3 thick; double shutters to each window made of 7-8 matched flooring with battens screwed on with 1/2 screws, hung with substantial hinges, and fastened inside with bolt; each window must be fastened with sash lock to secure window from inside. Four of the above windows will be supplied by district.

5. A vestibule is to be built on front of building 4 feet deep, 10 feet wide, 8 feet pitch, supported on stone pillars and framed to main building; roofed in same manner as building, but not ceiled inside. Outside vestibule door in center 3x7 made of matched flooring with 3 battens screwed on and secured with stout hinges and lock. The floor is to be level with main floor and no door sill will be used on inner frame. Inside door must be good 4 panel yellow pine 2-10x6-10, 1 3/8 thick, fastened with rim knob lock, both doors hinged on inside.

6. Flooring must be No. 2, laid on 2x8 joist, 20 inches apart with 2 rows of bridging. A platform in rear end of room, 6x8 feet, 6 inches above floor level.

7. A blackboard will be put across entire room (omitting flue) made of dry, smooth lumber, 12 inches wide, to be fastened to wall before ceiling is put on, beginning 3 feet from floor and being 3 feet wide, finished with 3 coats of black paint.

8. The entire room must be ceiled with No. 2 ceiling, walls perpendicular, ceiling lengthwise and inside casing fitted tight over ceiling. Ceiling must be finished with quarter round top and bottom.

9. A brick flue in rear end of building, well plastered inside; must be built on stout upright frame the size of flue and the whole supported on stone foundation of building. The brick must extend below ceiling 3 feet and above comb of roof 3 feet; a 6 inch thimble must be put in 2 feet below ceiling. The frame of flue must be ceiled up on 3 sides to brickwork and capped.

10. The building must be constructed in a substantial, workmanlike manner, well braced and supported on stone foundation laid in good lime mortar. Wall must be no less than 8 inches from ground at any point and not less than 16 inches in ground. The school board reserves the right to reject any or all bids and the work will be subject to the inspection of the trustees from time to time.

APPENDIX E: SCHOOLHOUSES STILL STANDING

1. Aden - Fleetwood Drive, Nokesville
2. Bennett - Lee Avenue, Manassas
3. Bradley - 9209 Brentsville Rd., Manassas
4. Brentsville White - 1 Bristow Rd., Nokesville
5. Brown #1 - 9508 Liberty Street, Manassas
6. Buckhall - 7601 Old Davis Ford Rd., Manassas
7. Catharpin - 4641 Sudley Rd., Catharpin
8. Cherry Hill - 1810 Cherry Hill Rd., Woodbridge
9. Cherry Hill - Minnieville Rd., Woodbridge
10. Dumfries - Cameron St., Dumfries
11. English Church School - 14620 Vint Hill Rd., Nokesville
12. Gainesville - John Marshall Highway, Gainesville
13. Groveton - 6706 Groveton Rd., Manassas
14. Haymarket - Haymarket Town Hall, Haymarket
15. Hickory Grove - 2620 Logmill Rd., Haymarket
16. Nokesville - Fitzwater Dr., Nokesville
17. Occoquan #1 - Mill St., Occoquan
18. Occoquan - Occoquan Rd., Woodbridge
19. Orlando #1 - Orlando Dr., Nokesville
20. Purcell #1 - Purcell Rd., Manassas
21. Quantico - 224 Third Ave., Quantico
22. Stone House - Routes 234 and 29, Manassas
23. Waterfall - 16220 Waterfall Rd., Haymarket

APPENDIX F: SAMPLE QUESTIONNAIRE

A questionnaire was sent to all those people who, for various reasons, could not be interviewed orally. This proved to be most successful, with a nearly 90% response rate. In some cases, follow up calls were made but generally the information gathered exceeded all expectations. Photographs, maps, drawings and wonderfully full essays were returned with the completed questionnaires. An addressed, stamped envelope and a cover letter were included in each packet mailed.

PRINCE WILLIAM COUNTY SCHOOLS QUESTIONNAIRE

Please answer as many questions as you can. I realize that not all of them are relevant to you nor may you be familiar with all aspects of the schools. This is not a test! I hope you enjoy it.

Your name _____

Your address _____

_____

Your phone number _____

Name of school(s) you attended _____

Name of school(s) where you taught _____

_____

Years involved _____

How far from school did you live? _____

How did you get to school? _____

Specific Questions About Your School(s)

1. When was it built?
2. What year did it close?
3. Is the building still standing?
4. Where was it located? (Sketch a map if possible).
5. What grades were taught there?
6. How many pupils attended?
7. How many teachers were there?
8. Names of teachers?
9. How many rooms were there and how were they used?
10. Were there privies? Where?
11. Who did maintenance?
12. What was the source of heat?
13. What was the source of drinking water?
14. How long was the school day?
15. How long was the school year (term)?
16. What subjects do you remember studying?
17. What books did you use?
18. Who supplied the books?
19. What equipment was available (sports, maps, slates, etc.)?
20. What geographic area (roughly) did the school serve?
21. Do you remember any special events held at the school (Christmas pageants, spelling bees, suppers, etc.)?
22. How did the school get its name?
23. What was the daily routine?
24. Describe your school lunch.
25. Describe recess.
26. Were your parents involved in the school?
27. What did the building look like from the outside? (If you can sketch it, great!) Do you have any photographs?
28. What was the school like inside?
29. Was there a library?
30. Did you belong to any school clubs?
31. Anecdotes? Other memories? Anything else? Use as much paper as you need! And, thanks.

PRIMARY SOURCES

Annual Reports of Prince William County Superintendents of Schools, 1892-93, 1890-91, 1887-88.

Cooke, James L. "Bailyburgh", unpublished paper, May 4, 1989.

Gainesville District School Board Minutes, September 2, 1877-1908.

Haydon, Richard C. "An Administrative Survey of the Public School System in Prince William County, Virginia", A Thesis for Master of Science at the University of Virginia, 1935.

Hoagland, Ann. "Transcript of Interview with Cecil Garrison", Prince William County Historical Commission Oral History Project, February 1988, unpublished.

Johnson, Libbie Harrover. "Memories of Groveton School", unpublished correspondence with author, 1992.

Johnson, Mrs. Alice W. "Sarah Elizabeth Johnson", unpublished correspondence with author, 1992.

Johnson, S.E. "Souvenir Booklet of Bradley School", given to students in 1909 and compiled by the teacher.

Manassas District #8 School Board Records, 1883-1908.

Manassas District School Board Records, 1911-22.

Manassas School District Record Book, 1870-79.

Maps of Prince William County: 1901; 1932; 1934; 1936; 1938; 1940; 1967; 1992

Minutes of the Brentsville District School Board, Volume 1, Dec. 3, 1870-Oct.4, 1907.

Minutes of the Brentsville District School Board, Volume 2, 1908-1922.

Minutes of the Prince William County School Board, 1923-1939.

Nelson, Thomas. "Transcript of Interview with Dewitt Bates", Prince William County Historical Commission Oral History Project, April 1984.

---. "Transcript of Interview with Historic Occoquan, Inc. (Schools)", Prince William County Historical Commission Oral History Project, September 24, 1985.

---. "Transcript of Interview with Rosemary Selecman", Prince William County Historical Commission Oral History Project, November, 1980.

---. "Woody. An Interview with James Woodrow Taylor", Prince William County Historical Commission Oral History Project, January, 1982.

Peters, Margaret Selecman. "Occoquan Elementary School", unpublished correspondence with author, Nov. 16, 1992.

Peters, R. Worth. "Secondary Education in Manassas, Virginia 1890-1935", A Thesis Presented to the Academic Faculty of the University of Virginia, 1939.

Phinney, Lucy W. Oral history with Howard Allen, Betty Berry and Mary Fields, Thoroughfare, VA, 1991.

---. Oral histories with Hilda Barg, Ed Dent and Junior Dent on Cherry Hill, Woodbridge, VA, 1991.

---. Oral history with B. Oswald Robinson, Groveton, Manassas, VA, 1992.

Prince William County Deed Books #s 30, 32, 34, 35, 44, 51, 54, 62, 64, 68, 72, 76, 80, 262, 539, 1188.

Prince William County Public School System. *Self Study Reports.*
   Bennett Elementary School, 1980-81.
   Coles Elementary School, 1971-72.
   Loch Lomond Elementary School, 1980-81.
   Nokesville Elementary School, 1980-81.
   Parkside Elementary School, 1980-81.
   Sinclair Elementary School, 1980-81.
   Sudley Elementary School, 1976-77.
   Triangle Elementary School, 1971-72.
   Washington-Reid Elementary School, 1973-74.
   Yorkshire Elementary School, 1980-81.

Prince William County Public Schools. "Basic Information for FY 1993", Prince William County, Virginia, June 1993.

---. "Cumulative ADA and ADM for the Year", Report No. SBCORD, Prince William County, Virginia, June 23, 1993.

---. "Real Property Inventory", n.d.

Proceedings of the Board of Education of Virginia, Vol. I and Vol. II.

Scheel, Eugene. Historic Map of Prince William County drawn for Historic Prince William, Inc. 1992.

Trustees of Prince William County School Board. Records of meetings, 1872-1921.

Virginia Daily Attendance Register and Record of Class Grades, submitted by the teachers of the county schools, 1925-1930.

Virginia State Board of Education. *State Course of Study for Rural and Elementary Schools of Virginia*, "Bulletin of the State Board of Education", Vol. V, No. 4, April, 1923.

Virginia Historic Landmarks Commission. *Survey Forms*. 1976.
   #76-261: Fairview School
   #76-278: Brentsville Schoolhouse
   #76-308: Bradley School House
   #76-141: Groveton School
   #76-204: Partridge School and Meadow Farm
   #76-129: Waterfall North Fork School
   #233-6:   Haymarket Town Hall
   #76-64:   Buckhall School
   #76-145: Catharpin School
   #76-130: Waterfall School
   #76-97:   Hickory Grove School
   #76-236: Purcell School

BIBLIOGRAPHY

Acuff, Lysbeth and Zetzler, Paula (compilers). *Historic Preservation Guide for Prince William County, Virginia.* Prince William County Planning Office, July 1986.

Allen, Sylvia and McKay, Jean. "The Way We Were", *The Fullstaff Communicator* Vol. 12, No. 5, Prince William County Public Schools, April 1986.

Anderson, James D. *The Education of Blacks in the South, 1860-1935.* Chapel Hill: University of North Carolina Press, 1988.

Baldwin, Letitia. "New school superintendent settling in", *The Bar Harbor Times*, July 30, 1992, p.A5.

Bennett, Commodore N. "Educational Transition in Prince William County." Mini Research for the Office of Federal Relations, Prince William County School Board, Manassas, VA, Vol. 1, April 1970.

Bennett, Commodore Nathaniel. *View From the Mountain: Jennie Dean of Virginia.* Unpublished monograph, Manassas, VA, 1986.

Brown, George. *History of Prince William County, Virginia.* Historic Prince William, Inc.. Forthcoming, 1993.

Butchart, Ronald E. *Local Schools: Exploring Their History.* The Nearby History Series, Vol. 1. Nashville, TN: The American Association for State and Local History, 1986.

"Children Show School Work", *The Manassas Journal*, May 11, 1933, p.1.

Clark, Annye B. and Arrington, Catherine S. *History of Prince William County.* Prince William County, VA: County School Board, 1930.

Conner, E.R., III. "Catharpin, Virginia, A Trading Center of Western Prince William County," *Echoes of History*, November 1975, pp. 66-70.

Conner, E.R. III. *One Hundred Old Cemeteries of Prince William County, Virginia.* Privately printed, 1981, pp. 80-81.

Conner, E. R. III. *Water Milling on Catharpin Run, Prince William County, Virginia.* Privately published, 1975.

Crewdson, Robert L. *Crossroads of the Past: A History of Haymarket, Virginia.* Prince William County Historical Commission, n.d.

Curtis, Donald E. *The Curtis Collection.* Prince William VA: Prince William County Historical Commission, 1988.

Digilio, Alice. "Dumfries Elementary's Lessons in History," *Washington Post*, May 18, 1989.

Ellicott, J.M. "Specifications for Public School Building No. 2," *Manassas Journal*, July 20, 1906.

Evans, D'Anne. Abstract of an Interview with Wilmer and Mary Porter at Their Home in Dumfries, October 6, 1988.

---. Abstract of an Interview with Annie Thomas Williams at Her Home in Dumfries, July 18, 1988.

---. *Prince William County. A Pictorial History.* Leesburg, VA: Donning Publishing Co., 1989.

Fleming, Charles A., Austin, Robin and Braley, Charles A. *Quantico: Crossroads of the Marine Corps*, Washington, DC: History and Museum Division Headquarters, U.S. Marine Corps, 1978.

Fuchs, Mike. "Singing the praises of Sinclair", *Potomac News*, May 21, 1993.

Gulliford, Andrew. *America's Country Schools*. Washington,DC: Preservation Press, 1991.

Haymarket High School. "Reunion booklet", June 8, 1991, unpublished.

Haynes, James. "Cherry Hill Peninsula", an address presented at a meeting of Historic Dumfries, Virginia, Inc. at the Dumfries Town Hall, November 6, 1975.

"Historical Development of Virginia's Public School System, 1870-1970." *News Magazine of the State Department of Education Centennial Issue* Vol. 5, No. 4, Winter 1970.

"History of Nokesville Elementary School", in Nokesville Elementary School handbook published by the school, n.d.

Hunton, Eppa. *Autobiography*. Richmond: William Byrd Press, Inc., 1933, foreword.

Johnson, Elizabeth Harrover. *Sea-Change*. Princeton, NJ: Pennywitt Press, 1977, pp. 5-9, 10-13, 42-44.

Johnson, Elizabeth Harrover, Conner, E.R.III, Ferguson, Mary Harrover. *History in a Horseshoe Curve*. Princeton, NJ: Pennywitt Press, 1982.

Kaestle, Carl F. "The Public Schools and the Public Mood.", *American Heritage*. February 1990, pp. 66-81.

Kalman, Bobbie. *Early Schools*. New York: Crabtree Publishing Co., 1990.

Kendrick, Julia. "Trees are all that's left of lost town," *Potomac News*, February 21, 1991.

King, Clyde Lyndon. "The Kansas School System - Its History and Tendencies," *Kansas Historical Collections Vol. XI*, 1910, pp. 1-32.

Kline, Mary Senseney. *Cannon Branch School, 1889-1927*. Privately published, 1988.

LaSonde, Chris. "Supreme Court ruling sets stage for 1966 change", *Potomac News*, February 10, 1993, pp. D1, 6.

Leitch, Martha. "Buckland, Prince William County, Virginia", *Echoes of History*, Pioneer America Society, Inc. Vol. III, No. 6, November, 1973, pp. 81-87.

Link, William A. *A Hard Country and a Lonely Place. Schooling, Society and Reform in Rural Virginia, 1870-1920*. Chapel Hill: Univ. of North Carolina Press, 1986.

McQueen, Glenda. "Church remains tribute to local black heritage", *Potomac News*, March 25, 1989.

Mernit, Susan. "A Lesson in Longevity", *Americana* Volume 19, No. 2, May/June, 1991, pp. 24-31.

Mills, Charles A. *Echoes of Manassas*. Manassas, VA: Friends of the Manassas Museum, 1988.

O'Connor, Marian, compiler. "Historical Data on Prince William County Schools." Taken from Prince William County School Board minutes. December 12, 1983.

Parker, Patricia L. *The Hinterland: An Overview of the Prehistory and History of Prince William Forest Park, Virginia*. Occasional report #1, Regional Archeology Program, National Capital Region, National Park Service, October 1985.

Partlow, Hattie Mae and Smith, Pauline. *Now and Then With P.W.E.A*. Prince William Education Association, 1963.

Pettus, Pekay. "Old school to house nursery center." *Piedmont Virginian*. Pp. 9 and 20. January 21, 1976.

Pishock, Margaret Ann. *Yes, Virginia, There Is A Carl Eike*. Triangle, VA: privately published, 1980.

Prall, Joan. *Schoolbells and Slates*. Privately published by author, 1990.

Prince William County School Board. *Engineering Report*. Submitted by Viola D. Proffitt Insurance Agency. Manassas, VA: 1953.

Prince William County Historical Commission. *Home Place*. Prince William VA: Prince William County Historical Commission, 1990.

---. *Prince William: A Past to Preserve.* Prince William, VA: Prince William County Historical Commission, 1982.

Rabatin, June, ed. *Count the Ties to Manassas.* Manassas, VA: Manassas Museum, 1984, pp. 18-19.

Ratcliffe, R. Jackson. *This Was Manassas.* Leesburg, VA: Potomac Press, 1973.

---. *This Was Prince William.* Leesburg, VA: Potomac Press, 1978.

Round, George C. "History of Manassas." Published in *The Manassas Journal,* May 21, 1897.

---. "Ruffner School No. 1. A Historical Statement," *Manassas Journal,* December 29, 1899.

Simmons, Catherine T. *Manassas, Virginia 1873-1973. One Hundred Years of a Virginia Town.* Manassas City Museum, 1986.

Special Elementary Social Studies Committee of Prince William County. *Around and About Prince William.* Prince William County Schools, 1970.

Stoddard, Alexandra B. "Four teachers were in the vanguard of change in schools", *The Potomac News*, Feb. 11, 1993, pp. C1, 3, 5.

---. "One family's request began integration", *The Potomac News*, Feb. 10, 1993, pp. D1, 6.

Strickland, Susan Cary. *An Administrative History of Prince William Forest Park.* Department of the Interior, National Park Service History Division, January 1986.

Tannenbaum, Dennyse. "First black principal to retire," *Potomac News,* June 22, 1991.

Tunnicliff, Robin. "No task too tall for devoted doctor," *Potomac News,* September 27, 1990.

Work Projects Administration Writers Program. *Prince William. The Story of Its People and Its Places.* Manassas, VA: The Bethlehem Club, 1988.

Wrenn, Tony P., Peters, Virginia B., and Sprouse, Edith Moore (editors). *The Legato School: A Centennial Souvenir,* Fairfax County (VA) History Commission, 1976.

Wyrsch, Carolyn, compiler. *Gainesville District Elementary School 50th Anniversary*, October 5, 1985 program.

General Index

A

Adams, Margaret Pattie 103, 145, 186
Adamson, William 110
Aden School 25, 51, 72, 73, 112, 113, 118, 127, 134, 155, 159, 201
Aden, village of 23, 25, 29
Alexander, John 148, 149
Alexander, Minnie 29
Allen Brothers 91
Allen, C.B. 96
Allen family 30, 73
Allen, Louise 76, 137, 138, 180
Allen, Dr. Sylvia 20
Allen, W.T. 73
Allendale School 24, 25, 30, 39, 45, 72, 73, 74, 90, 106, 133, 173
Antioch School 1, 21, 22, 29, 36, 74, 75, 76, 137, 138, 175, 180, 184, 185
Antioch-Macrae School 22, 27, 40, 42, 76, 77, 116, 137, 139, 182
Antioch-North Fork School 74, 76
apprentice 7
Armstrong School League 75
Arrington, D.J. 135
Arrington, D.T. 156
Articles of Agreement 145
Asbury Methodist Church 9, 21, 26, 79, 139
Ashford, Maude 186
Assistant Superintendent of Public Instruction 96
Atkins, Louise 164
attendance 8, 24

B

Bacon Race School 27, 29, 35, 77, 78, 110
Bailey, Carr 78
Bailey, Georgia Hannah 93, 142
Bailey, Reverend Henry 174
Baileysburg School 24, 29, 73, 78, 106

Baily, Carr 29
Baker, Paul 185
Baldwin Elementary School 28, 78
Baldwin family 78
Barbie, James 124
Barnes, Hal 159
Barnes, Howell 170, 171
Barnes, Nellie 160
Barnes, Richard 170
Bartenstein, E.H. 128
Bates, Herbert A. 176
Beahm, Aliene Nolley 154
Beahm, Charles 153
Beahm, Cora E. 72, 73, 153, 190
Beahm, George W. 87, 190
Beahm, Robert 88, 134, 153
Bel Air Elementary School 27, 28, 79
Bel Air Plantation 79
Bell, Katie 102
Bell, Mary R. 114
Belle Haven Church 29
Belle Haven School 46, 130
Belmont Elementary School 28, 79
Bennett, Dr. Maitland C. 79
Bennett, George 140
Bennett School 26, 27, 29, 51, 79, 80, 81, 87, 88, 98, 101, 142, 186, 191, 201
Berg, Helen 117
Berry, Charles 176
Berry, Reverend Peter G. 180, 181
Bethel School 27, 32, 51, 81, 82, 83, 96, 105, 110, 147, 171
Bethlehem School 26, 29, 83, 144, 185, 186
Beville, Stuart 42
Bittle, C.O. 120, 155
Blackburn, Richard 169
Blackwell, William S. 169
Blough, Reverend Jerome E. 99
Board of Commissioners 21
Boards of Appeal 16

Botts, Fontain 137
Bradley family 29
Bradley School 26, 27, 83. 84, 85, 86, 91, 135, 135, 156, 201
Breeden, Alice 164
Breeden family 117
Breeden, Ila V. 164, 171
Brentsville (School) District 21, 23, 25, 30, 36, 42, 45
Brentsville Colored School 90, 91
Brentsville Courthouse 87, 88
Brentsville District High School 134, 152, 154, 155, 190
Brentsville District School Board 39, 45
Brentsville School 2, 23, 24, 25, 29, 32, 39, 51, 53, 86, 87, 88, 90, 106
Brice, Dorothy W. 76
Brill, Elizabeth 117
Brill, John 117
Bristoe (Bristow) Schoolhouse 23, 24, 25, 29, 39, 51, 74, 84, 87, 90, 91, 92, 106
Brockett, E.S. 111
Brown Colored School League 94
Brown, Louise Smith 95
Brown, Mary D. 93
Brown School 2, 10, 26, 27, 30, 36, 41, 43, 93, 94, 95, 96, 108, 132, 135, 142, 148, 156
Brown vs Board of Education 42, 96
Brown, William H. 15, 75, 149
Brownsville School 121
Bruckner, Mildred 160
Bryant, Mollie 173
Bryant, William A. 10, 73
Brydie, Lula 157
Buckhall School 26, 27, 29, 51, 156, 157
Buckland School 21, 29, 36, 96
Buckley family 102
busing 27, 35, 37, 153
Butler, Charles 181
Butler, J.H. 10
Butler, John H. 140
Butler, Nellie G. 137
Butler, Ruth O. 86

C

Cabin Branch School 26, 29, 36, 97, 98, 129, 146, 147, 148, 149, 150, 174, 183
Callehers, T.E. 127
"Canning Clubs" 32

Cannon Branch School 26, 29, 71, 86, 88, 98, 99, 100, 101, 144
Cannon, John A. 140
Carnegie, Andrew 141
Carter, Emma 178
Carter family 162
Carter, Landon 162
Catharpin 104
Catharpin Colored School 175
see also Thornton Colored School
Catharpin Community League 103
Catharpin Creek 29
Catharpin School 21, 22, 29, 51, 102, 103
certification 11
Chamberlain, Elizabeth A. 140
Chandler, Maude Winslow 163
Chapel Colored School 23, 46
Chapel Springs 24, 92
Cherry, Gladys M. 147, 171, 178
Cherry Hill (Dumfries) School 26, 29, 51
Cherry Hill (Occoquan) Dist. 27, 36, 84, 105
Cherry Hill Plantation 104
Chinn School 23, 24, 30, 39, 46, 78, 106, 107, 131
Chinn, William 106
Civil Rights Act of 1964 42, 108, 116
Civil War 8, 84, 96, 106, 121, 145, 156
Clarkson, H.M. 30, 41, 43, 126, 133, 186
Clarkson School 30, 97
Clarkson, W.M. 97, 118
Clem, William 187
Code of Conduct 33
Coleman, Warren 82
Coles (School) District 13, 14, 21, 25, 27, 29, 42, 46
Coles Elementary School 25, 27, 30, 107, 188
colonial Virginia 7
Colored School, Fleetwood 23, 45, 106
Colored Supervisor of Rural Schools 41
Commissioners of Education 13
Community School League 40, 94, 100, 123, 164, 176, 190
Compton, Alexander H. 121
Conner, Reverend Abraham 85
consolidation 16, 21, 25, 26, 27, 33, 35, 36, 37, 38, 40, 41, 42, 72, 83, 109, 110, 133, 134, 138, 141, 147, 150, 155, 159, 166, 186, 187
contracts 18
Cooke, Helen 120
Cooke, J.R. 90

Cooke, J.W. 133
Cooke, James 120
"Corn Clubs" 32
Cornwell, Delley 163
Cornwell, Gertrude Seaton 164
Cornwell, James 164
Cornwell, Wilson W. 177
County School Board 14, 15, 16, 17, 18, 21, 42
County Superintendent of Schools 9, 10, 11, 13, 22
County Unit Law 17
Course of Study 11, 50
Cross, Estelle 140
Crouse, Mrs. L.E. 131
Crow, William 114
curriculum 49, 50, 95, 123, 125
Curtis, Nellie 160
Curtis, Raymond 146, 147

D

Dale City Elementary School 27, 28, 107
Darnell, W.N. 75
Davis, E.S. 81
Davis, James 111
Davis, Lucy 105
Davis, Mary K. 111
Davis, Powell 188, 189
Davis, Walter 82
Dawson, Wallace 189
Dean, Ella Jean 174
Dean, Jennie 40, 174
Dent, Ed 104, 105
Dervey, Winfield 1
desegregation 36, 38, 116, 184
    see also integration
Dettingen Parish 7
Dewey family 105
Dickens, T.E.H. 117
District Commissioners 13
District Free School System 8, 21
District School Boards 14, 16, 17, 18, 21, 22, 31, 32
District School Trustees 9, 10, 11, 13, 14, 16, 21, 23
DiVecchia, Gary 170
division superintendents 11
dog tax 14, 22, 115
Dogan, May 121, 122
Dogan, Neville 102
Dove, Charles 154

drinking water 32, 80, 89, 92, 94, 103, 104, 109, 114, 128, 143, 146, 153, 166, 188, 189
Dumfries (School) District 13, 14, 21, 23, 26, 27, 29, 36, 42, 46, 47
Dumfries Model School 109
Dumfries School 26, 29, 42, 51, 98, 104, 105, 108, 109, 114, 130, 167, 168, 182
Dunkins, C.T. 75
Dunn, A.F. 13

E

early rules of behavior 33
elected School Boards 15
Ellicott, W.H. 171
Ellicott, William Y. 161
Elliott School 175
    see also Thornton Colored School
Ellis, Fannie Mae 152
Emory Chapel School 27, 35, 110
Endicott, William (Willie) 146
English Church School 24, 25, 30, 110, 118, 169
enrollment 14, 22, 33, 44
Entwisle, Mary 115
Evans, D'Anne 149
Evans, Grace L. 165
Evans, Lily 121

F

Fair, Carrie 163
Fair, John 163
Fairview School 27, 30, 111
Fauquier County 23, 24, 96, 107, 118, 133, 163
Fayman School 25, 29, 112, 113, 131
Featherstone Elementary School 28, 42, 71, 113
Fields, Mary 76
Fincham, Russell 40, 42, 77
first agricultural high school 79
first Code of Conduct 33
first Course of Study 50
first Prince William County Superintendent of Schools 30
first public school 2, 9, 10, 21, 79
first public schoolhouse 26
first State Superintendent of Public Education 30
first teacher 9
Fleetwood 23
Fletcher, Edmond C. 167
Fletcher, Frank 179, 180

Fletcher, Pearl 75
Fletcher, Robert 181
Florence family 29, 178
Florence, Fannie 178
Florence, J.B. 178
Florence, Mary 178
Florence School 29, 178
Foley, E.H. 184
Foley, Maggie 141
Ford, Lucille V. 95
Forest Hill School 26, 51, 113
    see also Joplin School
Foster, Lawrence 154
Francis, Edward 135
Fred Lynn 28
Fred M. Lynn Elementary School 42, 114, 158, 160
Free School System 13
Free, W. Raymond 173
Friends Society see Quakers
funding 13, 15, 22, 31, 35, 39, 40, 41, 44, 94, 115, 141

G

Gaines, Somerville 115
Gainesville 21, 22, 29, 71, 182
Gainesville (School) District 13, 14, 15, 21, 22, 27, 28, 35, 36, 42
Gainesville District School Board 23, 31
Gainesville School 71, 76, 77, 115, 116, 117, 127, 182, 183
Gainesville-Antioch-Macrae Elementary school 116
Gar-Field High School 160
Garrison, Cecil 108
Garth, Ella 87
Gaskins, Hattie 76
George Tyler Elementary School 116, 182
German, Charles 106
Gibson, John 106
Gibson, Powell W. 93, 94
Gilliam, R.D. 127, 128
Glascock, Clyde 96
Gold Ridge School 25, 29, 51, 98, 117, 118, 147
Goodwin, George M. 23, 160
Gossom, George 128, 185
Grace Metz Middle School 108
Grayson, Ernestine P. 98, 174
Green, Aussie 146
Green family 85
Greene, Estelle 9, 140, 141

Greenwich (Red Shoals) 23
Greenwich Presbyterian Church 118
Greenwich School 24, 25, 29, 39, 51, 78, 88, 110, 111, 118, 120, 152, 153, 155, 190, 191
Greenwood School 26, 30, 46, 47, 120
Grigsby, Mimi 181
Grissom, R.B. 155
Groveton School 26, 27, 29, 35, 36, 83, 121, 122, 123, 124, 156, 172, 185, 186

H

Hammett School 156
Hammond, Lula J. 147
Harley, Mabel 101
Harley, Mary 86
Harley, Nora 190
Harris, Emma 136
Harris, George H. 93, 135
Harris, Saluka 174
Harrover, James David 83, 121
Harrover, Katie 83, 121
Hart, Harris 17
Haslip, Walter 189
Hayden, B.M. 115
Haydon, Richard C. 7, 36, 43, 50, 72, 73, 76, 81, 82, 88, 92, 94, 95, 96, 98, 101, 104, 114, 120, 125, 127, 128, 129, 132, 138, 143, 148, 150, 155, 157, 159, 161, 175, 176, 180, 187
Hayfield School 25, 51, 124, 125, 178
Haymarket School 21, 22, 28, 29, 35, 37, 51, 71, 73, 103, 116, 125, 126, 159, 185
Haymarket Town Hall 3, 127
Hazelwood Plantation 29
Hazelwood School 24, 25, 29, 72, 74, 133, 173
Hazen, Melvin C. 134
heating of schoolhouses 31, 80, 82, 84, 89, 94, 96, 98, 100, 103, 104, 109
Hedges, Arthur 111
Hedges family 111
Hedges School 111
Hedrick, Ben 155
Heineken, C.A. 145
Helm, Mack 75
Henderson Elementary 184
Henderson, Ellen 146
Hereford, Hobart 105
Hereford, Thomas P. 15
Herndon, DeWitt 112
Herndon, Van R. 113

Herndon, Viola 112
Herring, H.W. 133, 134
Herring School 133
Hershey, Reverend Mr. 23, 46
Hershey's Shop 23, 46
Hickory Grove (Oak Grove) School 21, 29, 51, 76, 127, 128, 129
Hickory Grove plantation 127
Hickory Ridge School 2, 26, 29, 36, 98, 129, 130, 150, 166, 174
Hicks, John 168
High School Act 1
Hinegardner, Samuel 99
hiring teachers 17, 20
Hixson, Lucy 141
Holbert, Julia A. 131
holidays 14
Holland, Lillie 190
Holler, Rilla 164
Holmes, F.W. 23, 46
Holmes School 23, 26, 46, 130
Holmes Store 130
Homer, Thomas E. 110
Hooker, J.A. 152, 154
Horton School 25, 29, 46, 112, 130, 131
House, Edward 120
House of Burgesses 7
Hovey, Elizabeth V. 92
Howdershell, H. 75, 145
Howison, Charles G. 13
Hughes, Georgetta 137
Hunt, Olla R. 190
Hunt, Ollie 128
Hunton, Eppa 96
Hylton, C.D. 134

I

illiteracy 8
Improvement Club 100
inspection of schools 11, 25
integration 17, 42, 108
    see also desegregation
Irven, Martha 155

J

J.A. Hooker 152
Jackson, Reverend Richard 90

janitorial service 32, 82, 92, 126, 138, 143, 159, 171
Jefferson, Thomas 7
Jeffries, Susan 164
Jennie Dean School 28, 30, 36, 42, 77, 96, 107, 108
Jennings, Cordelia 90
Johnson, Elizabeth Harrover 123
Johnson, Emma 165
Johnson, Sarah E. (Sally) 84, 85, 91
Joice, Leonera 93
Jones Legacy 7, 13
    see also Jones, Samuel
Jones, Martha 84
Jones, R.A. 179
Jones, Samuel 7
Jones, Thomas 84
Joplin School 29, 113, 130
    see also Forest Hill School
Jordan, W.M. 116
Junior League 40

K

Kettle Run School 24, 25, 29, 32, 36, 90, 106, 107, 131, 132, 142
Kewitt, Katie 152
Keyes, Minnie 104
Keys, Anne Ross 88
Keys, Easton 159
Keys, Mildred 178
Keys, Norah B. 167
Kiener, Rushia 190
Kilby, R. Dean 30, 143, 144
Kilby, R. Dean Elementary School 27, 143
King family 30, 133
King's Crossroads School 1, 24, 30, 36, 134, 154
Kline, Everett 100
Kline, John 159
Kline, Lola 99
Kline, Mary Senseney
    see Senseney, Mary
Kline, Wilmer 99
Knight, Louise Gertrude 76

L

Leachman, John T. 10, 140
Leachman, May see Dogan, May
Leachman, Roberta 141

Leachman, Thomas 121
Lee, John 83
Lee, Luke 83
Lee, Mark 83
Lee, Matthew 83
Lee, Robert E. 7, 9
Lee, Thomas 108
Lewis, Ashby 83
Lewis, Charles 83, 121
Lewis, Lutie Irene 95
Lewis, Molly 83, 121
Lewis, Robert 83
Lewis, Warner 83
Lickle, Ida M. 141
lighting 32, 88, 92, 100, 109, 126
Link, Robert E. 134
Lipscomb, M.Ella 141
Literary Fund 7, 8
Lloyd, H.W. 135
Loch Lomond Elementary School 28, 30, 42, 134
Lomax, Violet Herring 134
Lucas, Carrie 176
Lucas, Mary V. 93
Lucasville School 26, 29, 94, 135
Lynn, Alice Metz 102
Lynn, Edson M. 159
Lynn, Ethel 189
Lynn, Etta 102
Lynn, Fred M. 30, 114, 158
Lynn, Henry 145
Lynn, Mrs.Luther 103

M

MacDonald, Gerald H. 171
Macrae (McCrae) School 21, 22, 29, 36, 74, 76, 132, 136, 137, 138, 139, 142, 175, 176, 177, 184
Macrae family 29, 136
Maddox, Maggie G. 141
Manassas (School) District 13, 14, 21, 26, 27, 28, 35, 42, 47
Manassas District School Board 16
Manassas Regional High School 88, 96, 108, 141, 142, 158
Manassas Industrial School for Colored Youth 30, 40, 76, 80, 93, 96, 107, 141, 142, 143, 174, 176
Manassas Park Elementary School 27, 29, 139
Manassas Teachers Institute 15
Manassas Town District 44

Manassas Village Colored School 93
    see also Brown School
Manassas Village White School 139, 140
see also Ruffner School
Manley School 26, 30, 36, 83, 93, 94, 142, 143, 162, 176
Mann High School Bill 11
Mann, William Hodges 80
Manuel's School 45
Markel, Isaac P. 141
Marson, Arthur A. 110
Marstellar's School 106, 131
Marumsco Elementary School 27, 30, 143
Marumsco Hills Elementary School 28, 29, 143, 144
Matthews, Mattie 102
Matthews, Moneta 167
McDonald, Charles 20
McDonald, Helen 167
McGrath, Barbara R. 103
McGregor (Roys) School 26, 30, 144
McGuffey's Readers 49, 50, 123
McInteer, J.H. 97
McKay, J. Ella 144
Melvin, Fannie 17
Merrill, Edna 105
Mertz, Julius 189
Messick, L.C., 152
Metz, Alice 103
Metz, Grace 80, 123
Metz, Maude 188
Miles, Mollie E. 114
Mill Park Plantation 29
Mill Park School 21, 29, 35, 145, 146
Minnieville School 26, 29, 32, 47, 98, 120, 146, 147, 149, 171, 178, 183
Moffett, Mary 80
Monroe, Sue 121
Moore, Smith 90
Moran, Grace B. 19
Morgan, Ella Lee 76
Mothers' Club 167
Motley, Lucy Mae 88
Mowry, John A. 92
Mrs. Simpson's Boarding School for the Womanly Art 108
Mt. Pleasant School 26, 30, 46, 147
Mt. Zion School 26, 30, 148
Muriel Humphries School 83
Murray family 74

Murray, Joshua 74
Murray School 74
Muse, Lucile T. 178

N

Napier, E.S. 152
Neabsco (School) District 27
Neabsco Creek 29
Neabsco School 29, 36, 40, 149, 150, 174
Nelson, Lizzie W. 73
Nelson School 26, 47, 150
Nichol, Ida 141
Nickens, Elizabeth 74, 138, 184
Nickens, James M. 137, 176
Nickens, Sallie 137
Nickens, Susie B. 75, 131, 132, 137, 138
Nicol, Ida 87
Nokesville School 23, 24, 25, 29, 36, 39, 72, 88, 106, 120, 151, 152, 153, 154, 173, 190
Nolley, Pearle S. 72
Nolley, W. Davis 72, 153
North Fork School 21, 22, 29, 36, 74, 76, 175, 179, 180
Nunnick, Fannie 159

O

Oak Grove School see Hickory Grove School, see also Buckhall School
Oak Hill School 156
Occoquan (School) District 13, 14, 21, 27, 28, 35
Occoquan School 27, 29, 36, 42, 51, 73, 82, 104, 147, 157, 158, 159, 160, 189
Old Cabin Branch School 97
"old field school" 8
Orlando Courthouse 23
Orlando School 1, 23, 25, 160, 161
O'Rouck, Virginia 171
Osbourn High School 80, 127, 141
Owens, H.M. 17
Owens, Martha Via 152
Owens, Mary 152, 154

P

Parkside Elementary School 28, 29, 161
Parkside Middle School 161
Partlow, Hattie Mae 115, 146, 154
Partlow, Wallace 37

patrons 23, 94, 98, 106, 109, 121, 135, 136, 149, 169, 172
Patrons League (PTA) 80
Pattie Annex 184
Pattie Elementary School 184
Pattie, Emmett N. 145
Pattie, Margaret 103, 145, 186
Pattie, Susie E. 17
Peabody Fund 9, 139, 140
Peabody, George 9, 139
Peake, Rebecca 168
Pearson, H.M. 126
Pearson, Naomi C. 88, 164
Pearson, Nellie Mae 164
Penn, Adeline 98
Peters, Margaret Selecman 158
Peters, Montgomery 177
Peters, Ward 159
"Pig Clubs" 32
Piney Branch (Red Hill #2) School 21, 29, 71, 168, 169
Pittsylvania Plantation 162
Pittsylvania School 27, 142, 162
Polen, Virginia Estelle 86
Porter, Mary 98
Posey, Wilson 172
Potomac (School) District 27
Potomac View Elementary School 28, 162
Potter, Nita J. 190
"Poultry Clubs" 32
Powell, Hugh 102
Powell, John S. 13
Prince William Academy 1, 87
Prince William County Educational Association 15
Prince William Forest Park 97, 178
privies 16, 43, 82, 92, 95, 96, 98, 100, 102, 103, 104, 109, 123, 128, 152, 185, 186, 188
Public Education Act 10, 31
Purcell School 25, 29, 31, 51, 162, 163, 164, 187

Q

Quakers 30, 41, 93
Quantico Colored School 26, 36, 98, 150, 165, 166, 174
Quantico Marine Base 112, 124, 125, 130, 165
Quantico White School 1, 26, 29, 51, 114, 165, 166, 167, 168, 182

R

Raftelis, Peter 167
Randall, Dorothea 141
Red Hill School 71, 168, 169
Red School 110
    see also English Church School
Red Shoals School 23, 24, 30, 106, 110, 169
Reid, Marjorie 184
Rippon Elementary School 28, 29, 169, 170
Rippon Lodge 29, 169
Ristedt, Frances Dorsey 102
Ritenour, Daisy 191
Robinson, Andrew 186
Robinson, B. Oswald 95, 124, 138, 142, 143, 176, 177
Robinson, Lucille 144
Rosenberger, Mary 101
Rosenwald Fund 41, 143
Round, George C. 8, 9, 13, 15, 16, 50, 79, 85, 93, 99, 122, 139, 140, 170
Round Top School 47
Roy, Joseph 144
Roy's School 144
see also McGregor's School
Ruffner, Charles E. 141
Ruffner School 2, 26, 30, 43, 79, 80, 93, 139, 140, 141, 142, 156
    see also Manassas Village White School
Ruffner, William H. 9, 10, 12, 15, 140
rules of behavior 33
Russell, George 159
Russell, James 171
Russell, Joyce 42

S

salary 12, 14, 17, 22, 23, 24, 25, 40, 41, 43, 46
Sanders, Ben 102
Saunders, Herbert 160
Saxon, N.A. 165, 166
Scheel, Eugene 75
school based management 3, 10, 17
Schults, Louise 164
Scott, Charles S. 141
Sears, Barnas 139
Seaton, Gertrude 163
segregation 39, 96, 108
Selecman, Margaret 158
Senseney, Mary 88, 99, 100, 101, 156
Sheppard, M.J. 154

Shirley, G.W. 185
Simes, Florence 97
Sinclair, C.A., Sr. 30, 170
Sinclair, C.F. 115
Sinclair Elementary School 28, 30, 170
Sinclair, John L. 23
Sinclair, John S. 13, 86
Slaughter, P.G. 23, 86
Smith, Cornelia 181
Smith, Dr. Thomas E. 181
Smith, George W. 136
Smith, J.P. 185
Smith, Mrs.George 75
Smith, Mrs.J.P. 72
Smith, Pauline 115, 146, 154
Smithfield School 25, 30, 170, 171, 174, 178, 187
Snapp, CN. 81
Snephen Springs School 46
Snooks, George 154
Speake, Nettie 108
State Board of Education 3, 9, 10, 13, 14, 16, 21, 31, 87, 115, 141
State Constitution of 1902 11
State standards 16, 99
State Superintendent of Public Instruction 9, 11, 30
Stephens, P.J. 133, 190
Stewart, R.H. 87
Stone House 123, 162, 172
Stone House School 27, 47, 172
Strickland, Ruby 184
Strode Bill of 1908 11
Strother, Reverend Moses 137
Sulphur Springs School 23, 29, 46, 172, 173
Summitt School 1, 27, 30, 36, 172, 174, 175, 184
Sunnyside 110
Supervisor of Colored Elementary Education 19, 20, 41
Supervisor of Curriculum and Research 20
Supervisor of Elementary Instruction 19

T

Taylor, Alice A. 135
Taylor, Anna L.F. 145
Taylor, E.C. 128, 173, 185
Taylor, Fannie E. 46
Taylor, George 124
Taylor, Professor W.C. 93
Taylor, William A. 135
Taylor, Woody 160

Teachers' Institute 15
textbooks 10, 22, 44, 49, 50, 99
Thomas, George 146, 149
Thomas, Josiah 142, 162
Thornton, B.B. 141
Thornton Colored School 21, 22, 30, 36, 40, 74, 131, 137, 175, 176
Thornton, J.B.T. 30, 141, 177
Thornton, R.E. 141
Thornton White School 21, 26, 30, 147, 150, 177, 178
Thornton, William W. 13, 30, 177
Thoroughfare Colored School 30, 74, 76, 175, 179
Thoroughfare Community League 76
Thoroughfare White School 21, 168, 179, 181, 182
Tiller, James 164
Tom Thumb Wedding 134
"Tomato Clubs" 32
Tomlinson, Wilma 90
Toomer, Katherine 176, 177
Towles' Gate 23, 172, 173
Towles, Reverend 172
Triangle Elementary School 26, 27, 29, 182
Triplett, Haywood F. 136, 137
Troth, Annie 102
Truro House 173
Turner, Sarah 127
Tyler Elementary School 22, 28, 77, 117, 183, 184
Tyler family 145
Tyler, George 79
Tyler, John W. 96

U

Underwood Constitution 9

V

vaccinations 15
Vancluse/Hazelwood School 23, 24, 39, 106, 173
Vaughan Elementary 127, 183
Vaughan, Elizabeth M. 28, 73, 127, 159, 160, 183
Via, Martha 152
Virginia Public Education Act 13
Virginia State Board of Education 50

W

Wakefield School 26, 47, 146, 183
Wakeman, Miss 46
Walter, E.C. 75
Washington, H.H. 173
Washington, Lucy D. 119
Washington, M.B. 118
Washington, Marian 175, 184
Washington-Reid Elementary School 26, 29, 36, 42, 98, 107, 175, 183, 184
Waterfall School 17, 21, 22, 29, 36, 75, 128, 184, 185
Waters, Eula 108
Watson, Harvey 178
Wayland, Florence Gossom 159
Weber, Emma 163
Weedon, Austin O. 141
Weedon, Ercelle Savage 159
Weedon, J.C. 73
Weedon, Nettie F. 91
Weir, Mary D. 141
Weir, Mrs.R.M. 92
Wellington Farmers Hall 186
Wellington School 26, 29, 185, 186
Wells, Nathan 154
Westgate Elementary School 28, 29, 187
Wheeler, J.D. (Deb) 99, 121, 122, 141
Wheeler, William M. 122
White, Bessie Loving 93, 94
White, Olga E. 153, 190
Wilkins, BlancheE. 145
Wilkins, Eleanor (Brower) 102, 172
Wilkins, Willard 153
Will, Prof. William R. 140, 141
Williams, Alice 159
Williams, Annie Thomas 149
Williams, Dr. John 99
Williams, Nettie V. 131, 176
Willis, William Thornton 10
Wilson, Selina T. 128, 185
Wise, Lily 164
Womanless wedding 109
Wood, Wallace 111
Woodbine School 25, 27, 30, 51, 107, 125, 130, 161, 164, 187, 188
Woodbridge (School) District 29
Woodbridge School 27, 36, 159, 188, 189
Woodlawn School 24, 30, 40, 51, 72, 87, 88, 189, 190, 191
Woodson, Edna J. 149, 150
Woodyard, W.T. 87
Worker, Jeanas 19
Wright, Luther 124

Y

Yorkshire Elementary School 27, 191

ABOUT THE AUTHOR

Lucy Walsh Phinney, an historian by birth, inclination and profession, received her degree in history from Tufts University. The daughter of an historian and mother of another, she taught high school history before "retiring" to raise three children. During those years, she developed an interest in the history of women in the American West. Since moving to northern Virginia more than twenty years ago, her interests have grown to include the history of Prince William County, Virginia where she lives with her husband. She has served on the Prince William County Historical Commission for thirteen years and, five years ago, founded Historic Prince William, Inc. in which she later served two terms as president.